Ryan Stephens
Arie D. Jones
Ron Plew

Sams **Teach Yourself**

SQL

in **24**
Hours

SIXTH EDITION

SAMS 800 East 96th Street, Indianapolis, Indiana, 46240 USA

Sams Teach Yourself SQL in 24 Hours, Sixth Edition

ISBN-13: 978-0-672-33759-8
ISBN-10: 0-672-33759-2

Library of Congress Control Number: 2015915011

Printed in the United States of America

Second Printing February 2016

Trademarks

Warning and Disclaimer

Special Sales

For information about buying this title in bulk quantities, or for special sales opportunities (which may include electronic versions; custom cover designs; and content particular to your business, training goals, marketing focus, or branding interests), please contact our corporate sales department at corpsales@pearsoned.com or (800) 382-3419.

For government sales inquiries, please contact governmentsales@pearsoned.com.

For questions about sales outside the U.S., please contact international@pearsoned.com.

Editor-in-Chief
Mark Taub

Executive Editor
Laura Lewin

Development Editor
Michael Thurston

Managing Editor
Kristy Hart

Senior Project Editor
Lori Lyons

Copy Editor
Apostrophe Editing Services

Indexer
Lisa Stumpf

Proofreader
Debbie Williams

Technical Editors
Marshall Pyle

Jacinda Simmerman

Editorial Assistant
Olivia Basegio

Cover Designer
Mark Shirar

Compositor
Nonie Ratcliff

Contents at a Glance

Table of Contents

Part IX: Appendixes

About the Authors

For more than 20 years each, the authors have studied, applied, and documented the SQL standard and its application to critical database systems in this book. The authors are experts in data management, specializing in Oracle, Microsoft, and other leading technologies.

Ryan Stephens is the co-founder and CEO of Perpetual Technologies, Inc. and Indy Data Partners in Indianapolis. Ryan has studied and consulted in the IT field for more than 20 years, specializing in data management, SQL, and Oracle. Ryan authored and taught database and SQL classes for Indiana University-Purdue University in Indianapolis for 5 years, and was a programmer analyst for the Indiana Army National Guard for 12 years. Ryan has written a variety of database and SQL books for Sams Publishing.

Arie D. Jones is the Vice President for Emerging Technologies for Indy Data Partners, Inc. (IDP) in Indianapolis. Arie leads IDP's team of experts in planning, design, development, deployment, and management of database environments and applications to achieve the best combination of tools and services for each client. He is a regular speaker at technical events and has authored several books and articles pertaining to database-related topics.

Ronald Plew is retired as co-founder and vice president of Perpetual Technologies, Inc. Ron studied and consulted in the field of relational database technology for more than 20 years and has co-authored several books for Sams Publishing. Ron taught SQL and database classes for Indiana University-Purdue University in Indianapolis for 5 years. He is a retired programmer analyst from the Indiana Army National Guard.

Dedication

This book is dedicated to my strong and driven wife, Jill, and to my three children by whom I'm equally smitten and amazed—Daniel, Autumn, and Alivia.

—Ryan

I would like to dedicate this book to my wife, Jackie, for being understanding and supportive during the long hours that it took to complete this book.

—Arie

Acknowledgments

Thank you to all who have been supportive and patient during the writing of the six editions of this book. This includes, but is probably not limited to, our family, friends, employees, partners, and random people in public who might sense our preoccupied minds. Thank you especially to Ron Plew, my original co-author of this book and business partner. Neither the first edition of this book, nor our company, would exist without your contributions; and to Arie Jones for spearheading this edition and taking on the bulk of the work, while providing leadership during the day at Indy Data Partners. Thanks also to Marshall Pyle and Jacinda Simmerman for technical edits and your perspectives to improve the quality of this text for our readers. And as always, thanks to the staff at Sams Publishing for your attention to detail and patience. It is always a pleasure working with you.

—Ryan

We Want to Hear from You!

As the reader of this book, *you* are our most important critic and commentator. We value your opinion and want to know what we're doing right, what we could do better, what areas you'd like to see us publish in, and any other words of wisdom you're willing to pass our way.

We welcome your comments. You can email or write to let us know what you did or didn't like about this book—as well as what we can do to make our books better.

Please note that we cannot help you with technical problems related to the topic of this book.

When you write, please be sure to include this book's title and author as well as your name and email address. We will carefully review your comments and share them with the authors and editors who worked on the book.

Email: consumer@samspublishing.com

Mail: Sams Publishing
           ATTN: Reader Feedback
           800 East 96th Street
           Indianapolis, IN 46240 USA

Reader Services

Register your copy of *Sams Teach Yourself SQL in 24 Hours, Sixth Edition,* at informit.com for convenient access to downloads, updates, and corrections as they become available. To start the registration process, go to informit.com/register and log in or create an account*. Enter the product ISBN, 9780672337598, and click Submit. Once the process is complete, you will find any available bonus content under Registered Products.

*Be sure to check the box that you would like to hear from us in order to receive exclusive discounts on future editions of this product.

HOUR 1
Welcome to the World of SQL

What You'll Learn in This Hour:

- ▶ An introduction to and brief history of SQL
- ▶ An introduction to database management systems
- ▶ An overview of some basic terms and concepts
- ▶ An introduction to the database used in the examples and exercises

Welcome to the world of SQL and the vast, growing database technologies of today's businesses all over the world. By reading this book, you have begun accepting the knowledge that will soon be required for survival in today's world of relational databases and data management. Unfortunately, because it is first necessary to provide the background of SQL and cover some preliminary concepts that you need to know, the majority of this hour is an overview before we jump into actual coding. Bear with this hour of the book; this will be exciting, and the "boring stuff" in this hour definitely pays off.

SQL Definition and History

Every modern-day business has data, which requires some organized method or mechanism for maintaining and retrieving the data. When the data is kept within a database, this mechanism is referred to as a *database management system (DBMS)*. Database management systems have been around for years, many of which started out as flat-file systems on a mainframe. With today's technologies, the accepted use of database management systems has begun to flow in other directions, driven by the demands of growing businesses, increased volumes of corporate data, and of course, Internet technologies.

The modern wave of information management is primarily carried out through the use of a *relational database management system (RDBMS)*, derived from the traditional DBMS. Modern databases combined with client/server and web technologies are typical combinations used by current businesses to successfully manage their data and stay competitive in their appropriate markets. The trend for many businesses is to move from a client/server environment to the Web, where location is not a restriction when users need access to important data. The next few sections discuss SQL and the relational database, the most common DBMS implemented today. A good fundamental understanding of the relational database and how to apply SQL to managing data in today's information technology world is important to your understanding of the SQL language.

What Is SQL?

Structured Query Language (SQL) is the standard language used to communicate with a relational database. The prototype was originally developed by IBM using Dr. E.F. Codd's paper ("A Relational Model of Data for Large Shared Data Banks") as a model. In 1979, not long after IBM's prototype was created, the first SQL product, ORACLE, was released by Relational Software, Incorporated (which was later renamed Oracle Corporation). Today, it is one of the distinguished leaders in relational database technologies.

If you travel to a foreign country, you might be required to know that country's language to get around. For example, you might have trouble ordering from a menu via your native tongue if the waiter speaks only his country's language. Look at a database as a foreign land in which you seek information. SQL is the language you use to express your needs to the database. Just as you would order a meal from a menu in another country, you can request specific information from within a database in the form of a query using SQL.

NOTE
_____

Communicating with Databases

Think about when you access your favorite online store to order a book, an article of clothing, or just about any other product. When you point and click to navigate the product catalog, enter search criteria, and place items in your shopping cart, SQL code is often executed behind the scenes to facilitate a database connection, while telling the database what data you want to see and how you want to see it.
_____

What Is ANSI SQL?

The *American National Standards Institute (ANSI)* is an organization that approves certain standards in many different industries. SQL has been deemed the standard language in relational database communication, originally approved in 1986 based on IBM's implementation. In 1987, the ANSI SQL standard was accepted as the international standard by the *International Standards Organization (ISO)*. The standard was revised again in 1992 (SQL-92) and again in 1999 (SQL-99). The newest standard is now called SQL-2011, which was officially adopted in December, 2011.

The Current Standard: SQL-2011

SQL-2011 is the current standard, with SQL-2008 being the previous standard. The current SQL standard has nine interrelated documents, and other documents might be added in the near future as the standard is expanded to encompass newly emerging technology needs. The nine interrelated parts follow:

▶ **Part 1, "SQL/Framework"**—Specifies the general requirements for conformance and defines the fundamental concepts of SQL.

▶ **Part 2, "SQL/Foundation"**—Defines the syntax and operations of SQL.

▶ **Part 3, "SQL/Call-Level Interface"**—Defines the interface for application programming to SQL.

▶ **Part 4, "SQL/Persistent Stored Modules"**—Defines the control structures that then define SQL routines. Part 4 also defines the modules that contain SQL routines.

▶ **Part 9, "Management of External Data (SQL/MED)"**—Defines extensions to SQL to support the management of external data through the use of data wrappers and datalink types.

▶ **Part 10, "Object Language Bindings"**—Defines extensions to the SQL language to support the embedding of SQL statements into programs written in Java.

▶ **Part 11, "Information and Definition Schemas"**—Defines specifications for the Information Schema and Definition Schema, which provide structural and security information related to SQL data.

▶ **Part 13, "Routines and Types Using the Java Programming Language"**—Defines the capability to call Java static routines and classes as SQL-invoked routines.

▶ **Part 14, "XML-Related Specifications"**—Defines ways in which SQL can be used with XML.

One of the main enhancements to the current standard with SQL-2011 is *temporal database support*. Temporal database support is a native feature that a SQL implementation such as Oracle provides that allows data to be queried and changed within the database based on a specific time period within which certain data exists. There are various levels of compliance to temporal databases, as well as other standard features, with which database implementations comply. If you work with a database implementation that does not fully comply with any given standard, there are normally workarounds, which involve business logic that is incorporated into the database design. With any standard comes numerous, obvious advantages, as well as some disadvantages. Foremost, a standard steers vendors in the appropriate industry direction for development. For SQL, a standard provides a basic skeleton of necessary fundamentals, which, as an end result, enables consistency between various implementations and better serves increased portability (not only for database programs, but also databases in general and individuals who manage databases).

Some might argue that a standard is not so good, limiting the flexibility and possible capabilities of a particular implementation. However, most vendors that comply with the standard have added product-specific enhancements to standard SQL to fill in these gaps.

A standard is good, considering the advantages and disadvantages. The expected standard demands features that should be available in any complete SQL implementation and outlines basic concepts that not only force consistency between all competitive SQL implementations, but also increase the value of a SQL programmer.

A *SQL implementation* is a particular vendor's SQL product, or RDBMS. It is important to note, as you will read numerous times in this book, that implementations of SQL vary widely. No one implementation follows the standard completely; although, some are mostly ANSI-compliant. It is also important to note that in recent years the list of functionality within the ANSI standard that must be adhered to in order to be considered compliant has not changed dramatically. Hence, when new versions of RDBMS are released, they will most likely claim ANSI SQL compliance.

What Is a Database?

In simple terms, a *database* is a collection of data. Some like to think of a database as an organized mechanism that has the capability of storing information, through which a user can retrieve stored information in an effective and efficient manner.

People use databases every day without realizing it. A phone book is a database. The data contained consists of individuals' names, addresses, and telephone numbers. The listings are alphabetized or indexed, which enables the user to reference a particular local resident with ease. Ultimately, this data is stored in a database somewhere on a computer. After all, each page of a phone book is not manually typed each year a new edition is released.

The database has to be maintained. As people move to different cities or states, entries might have to be added or removed from the phone book. Likewise, entries have to be modified for people changing names, addresses, telephone numbers, and so on. Figure 1.1 illustrates a simple database.

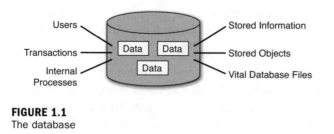

FIGURE 1.1
The database

The Relational Database

A *relational database* is a database divided into logical units called tables, where tables are related to one another within the database. A relational database allows data to be broken down into logical, smaller, manageable units, enabling easier maintenance and providing more optimal database performance according to the level of organization. In Figure 1.2, you can see that tables are related to one another through a common key (data value) in a relational database.

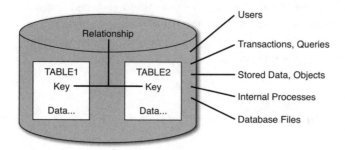

FIGURE 1.2
The relational database

Again, tables are related in a relational database, allowing adequate data to be retrieved in a single query. (Although the desired data may exist in more than one table.) By having common *keys*, or *fields*, among relational database tables, data from multiple tables can be joined to form one large set of data. As you venture deeper into this book, you see more of a relational database's advantages, including overall performance and easy data access.

Client/Server Technology

In the past, the computer industry was predominately ruled by mainframe computers—large, powerful systems capable of high storage capacity and high data processing capabilities. Users communicated with the mainframe through dumb terminals—terminals that did not think on their own but relied solely on the mainframe's CPU, storage, and memory. Each terminal had a data line attached to the mainframe. The mainframe environment definitely served its purpose and does today in many businesses, but a greater technology was soon to be introduced: the client/server model.

In the *client/server system*, the main computer, called the server, is accessible from a network— typically a *local area network (LAN)* or a *wide area network (WAN)*. The server is normally accessed by personal computers (PCs) or by other servers, instead of dumb terminals. Each PC, called a *client*, is provided access to the network, allowing communication between the client and the server, thus explaining the name client/server. The main difference between client/server and mainframe environments is that the user's PC in a client/server environment can think on its own and run its own processes using its own CPU and memory, but is readily accessible to a server computer through a network. In most cases, a client/server system is much more flexible for today's overall business needs and is preferred.

Modern database systems reside on various types of computer systems with various operating systems. The most common types of operating systems are Windows-based systems, Linux, and command-line systems such as UNIX. Databases reside mainly in client/server and web environments. A lack of training and experience is the main reason for failed implementations of database systems. Nevertheless, an understanding of the client/server model and web-based systems, which will be explained in the next section, is imperative with the rising (and sometimes unreasonable) demands placed on today's businesses as well as the development of Internet technologies and network computing. Figure 1.3 illustrates the concept of client/server technology.

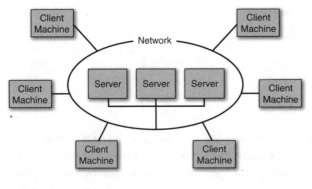

FIGURE 1.3
The client/server model

Web-Based Database Systems

Business information systems have largely moved toward web integration. Databases are now accessible through the Internet, meaning that customers' access to an organization's information is enabled through an Internet browser such as Internet Explorer, Microsoft Edge, or Firefox.

Customers (users of data) can order merchandise, check inventories, check the status of orders, make administrative changes to accounts, transfer money from one account to another, and so forth.

A customer simply invokes an Internet browser, goes to the organization's website, logs in (if required by the organization), and uses an application built in to the organization's web page to access data. Most organizations require users to register with them and issue a login and password to the customer.

Of course, many things occur behind the scenes when a database is accessed via a web browser. SQL, for instance, can be executed by the web application. This executed SQL accesses the organization's database, returns data to the web server, and then returns that data to the customer's Internet browser.

The basic structure of a web-based database system is similar to that of a client/server system from a user's standpoint (refer to Figure 1.3). Each user has a client machine, which has a connection to the Internet and contains a web browser. The network in Figure 1.3 (for a web-based database) just happens to be the Internet, as opposed to a local network. For the most part, a client is still accessing a server for information. It doesn't matter that the server might exist in another state or even another country. The main point of web-based database systems is to expand the potential customer base of a database system that knows no physical location bounds, thus increasing data availability and an organization's customer base.

Popular Database Vendors

Some of the most predominant database vendors include Oracle, Microsoft, Informix, Sybase, and IBM. These vendors distribute various versions of the relational database for a base license fee and are normally referred to as *closed source*. Many other vendors supply an open-source version of a SQL database (relational database). Some of these vendors include MySQL, PostgresSQL, and SAP. Although many more vendors exist than those mentioned, this list includes names that you might have recognized on the bookshelf, in the newspaper, in magazines, on the stock market, or on the World Wide Web.

Each vendor-specific implementation of SQL is unique in both features and nature. A database server is a product—like any other product on the market—manufactured by a widespread number of vendors. It is to the benefit of the vendor to ensure that its implementation is compliant with the current ANSI standard for portability and user convenience. For instance, if a company is migrating from one database server to another, it would be rather discouraging for the database users to have to learn another language to maintain functionality with the new system.

With each vendor's SQL implementation, however, you find that there are enhancements that serve the purpose for each database server. These enhancements, or *extensions*, are additional commands and options that are simply a bonus to the standard SQL package and available with a specific implementation.

SQL Sessions

A *SQL session* is an occurrence of a user interacting with a relational database through the use of SQL commands. When a user initially connects to the database, a session is established. Within the scope of a SQL session, valid SQL commands can be entered to query the database, manipulate data in the database, and define database structures, such as tables. A session may be invoked by either direct connection to the database or through a front-end application. In both cases, sessions are normally established by a user at a terminal or workstation that communicates through a network with the computer that hosts the database.

CONNECT

When a user connects to a database, the SQL session is initialized. The CONNECT command is used to establish a database connection. With the CONNECT command, you can either invoke a connection or change connections to the database. For example, if you connect as USER1, you can use the CONNECT command to connect to the database as USER2. When this happens, the SQL session for USER1 is implicitly disconnected. You would normally use the following:

```
CONNECT user@database
```

When you attempt to connect to a database, you are automatically prompted for a password that is associated with your current username. The username is used to authenticate you to the database, and the password is the key that allows entrance.

DISCONNECT and EXIT

When a user disconnects from a database, the SQL session is terminated. The DISCONNECT command is used to disconnect a user from the database. When you disconnect from the database, the software you use might still appear to communicate with the database, but you have lost your connection. When you use EXIT to leave the database, your SQL session is terminated, and the software that you use to access the database is normally closed.

```
DISCONNECT
```

Types of SQL Commands

The following sections discuss the basic categories of commands used in SQL to perform various functions. These functions include building database objects, manipulating objects, populating database tables with data, updating existing data in tables, deleting data, performing database queries, controlling database access, and overall database administration.

The main categories are

- ▶ Data Definition Language (DDL)
- ▶ Data Manipulation Language (DML)
- ▶ Data Query Language (DQL)
- ▶ Data Control Language (DCL)
- ▶ Data administration commands
- ▶ Transactional control commands

Defining Database Structures

Data Definition Language (DDL) is the part of SQL that enables a database user to create and restructure database objects, such as the creation or the deletion of a table.

Some of the most fundamental DDL commands discussed during the following hours include

- ▶ CREATE TABLE
- ▶ ALTER TABLE
- ▶ DROP TABLE
- ▶ CREATE INDEX
- ▶ ALTER INDEX
- ▶ DROP INDEX
- ▶ CREATE VIEW
- ▶ DROP VIEW

These commands are discussed in detail during Hour 3, "Managing Database Objects," Hour 17, "Improving Database Performance," and Hour 20, "Creating and Using Views and Synonyms."

Manipulating Data

Data Manipulation Language (DML) is the part of SQL used to manipulate data within objects of a relational database.

The three basic DML commands are

- ▶ INSERT

- ▶ UPDATE

- ▶ DELETE

These commands are discussed in detail during Hour 5, "Manipulating Data."

Selecting Data

Though composed of only one command, *Data Query Language (DQL)* is the most concentrated focus of SQL for modern relational database users. The base command is SELECT.

This command, accompanied by many options and clauses, composes queries against a relational database. A *query* is an inquiry to the database for information. A query is usually issued to the database through an application interface or via a command-line prompt. You can easily create queries, from simple to complex, from vague to specific.

The SELECT command is discussed in exhilarating detail during Hours 7 through 16.

Data Control Language

Data control commands in SQL enable you to control access to data within the database. These *Data Control Language (DCL)* commands are normally used to create objects related to user access and also control the distribution of privileges among users. Some data control commands follow:

- ▶ ALTER PASSWORD

- ▶ GRANT

- ▶ REVOKE

- ▶ CREATE SYNONYM

You will find that these commands are often grouped with other commands and might appear in a number of lessons throughout this book.

Data Administration Commands

Data administration commands enable the user to perform audits and perform analyses on operations within the database. They can also be used to help analyze system performance. Two general data administration commands follow:

- ▶ START AUDIT

- ▶ STOP AUDIT

Do not get data administration confused with database administration. *Database administration* is the overall administration of a database, which envelops the use of all levels of commands. *Data administration* is much more specific to each SQL implementation than are those core commands of the SQL language.

Transactional Control Commands

In addition to the previously introduced categories of commands, there are commands that enable the user to manage database transactions:

- `COMMIT`—Saves database transactions
- `ROLLBACK`—Undoes database transactions
- `SAVEPOINT`—Creates points within groups of transactions in which to `ROLLBACK`
- `SET TRANSACTION`—Places a name on a transaction

Transactional commands are discussed extensively during Hour 6, "Managing Database Transactions."

Canary Airlines: The Database Used in This Book

Before continuing with your journey through SQL fundamentals, the next step is introducing the tables and data that you use throughout the course of instruction for the next 23 one-hour lessons. This book uses an example database for a fictitious organization called Canary Airlines. Example data has been generated to create real-world scenarios for examples and exercises in this book. The following sections provide an overview of the specific tables (the database) used, their relationship to one another, their structure, and examples of the data contained.

Figure 1.4 reveals the relationship between the tables that you use for examples, quiz questions, and exercises in this book. Each table is identified by the table name as well as each residing field in the table. Follow the mapping lines to compare the specific tables' relationship through a common field, in most cases referred to as the *primary key* (discussed in Hour 3).

Canary Airlines, like other airlines, is dedicated to getting flights in and out efficiently, and providing passengers (customers and end users) with a safe method of travel to and from their destinations. Following is an overview of some of the basic business rules of Canary Airlines, as well as the relationship between the database tables in Figure 1.4:

- Canary Airlines manages flights for its passengers (customers).
- Canary Airlines has passengers, aircraft, flights, and locations served.

▶ Passengers can select flights.

▶ Flights have various statuses.

▶ Each flight is associated with an itinerary.

▶ Each flight is associated with a specific aircraft.

▶ Flights are associated with routes that involve destinations to which passengers want to travel to or from, in various airports and in various countries.

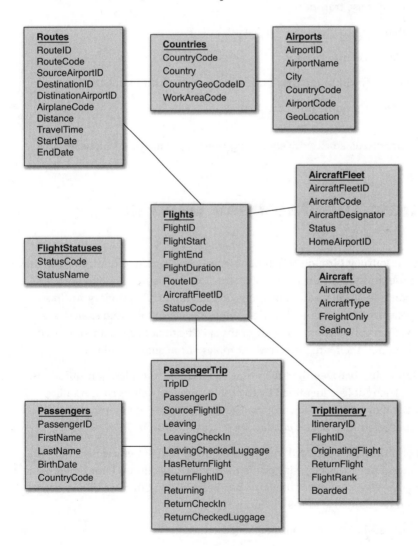

FIGURE 1.4
Table relationships for this book

Table-Naming Standards

Table-naming standards, as well as any standard within a business, are critical to maintaining control. After studying the tables and data in the previous sections, you probably noticed that each table's suffix is _TBL. This is a naming standard selected for use, such as what's been used at various client sites. The _TBL suffix simply tells you that the object is a table; there are many different types of objects in a relational database. For example, in later hours you see that the suffix _INX is used to identify indexes on tables. Naming standards exist almost exclusively for overall organization and assist immensely in the administration of any relational database. Remember, the use of a suffix is not mandatory when naming database objects. A naming convention is merely used to provide some order when creating objects. You may choose to utilize whatever standard you want.

NOTE

Naming Standards

You should not only adhere to the object-naming syntax of any SQL implementation, but also follow local business rules and create names that are descriptive and related to the data groupings for the business. Consistent naming standards make it easier to manage databases with SQL.

A Look at Sample Data

This section offers a sample of the data contained in the Passengers table used in this book. Take a few minutes to think about passengers as you look at the first three records, or rows, from the following Passengers table. Also, try to imagine how passengers might be related to flights and itineraries, and all the variations that might occur within the data.

Passengers

PassengerID	FirstName	LastName	BirthDate	CountryCode
1	Adeline	Wogan	1988-09-24	CA
2	Stephnie	Mastrelli	1966-03-01	US
3	Amina	Fold	1982-05-22	GB

A Closer Look at What Comprises a Table

The storage and maintenance of valuable data is the reason for any database's existence. You have just viewed the data that is used to explain SQL concepts in this book. The following sections take a closer look at the elements within a table. Remember, a table is the most common and simple form of data storage.

Fields

Every table is broken into smaller entities called fields. A *field* is a column in a table that is designed to maintain specific information about every record in the table. The fields in the `Passengers` table consist of `PassengerID`, `FirstName`, `LastName`, `BirthDate`, and `CountryCode`. These fields categorize the specific information that is maintained in a given table.

Records, or Rows of Data

A *record*, also called a *row* of data, is each horizontal entry that exists in a table. Looking at the last table, `Passengers`, consider the following first record in that table:

```
1       Adeline     Wogan      1988-09-24      CA
```

The record is obviously composed of a passenger identification, passenger last name, passenger first name, date of birth, and country code. For every distinct passenger, there should be a corresponding record in the `Passengers` table.

A *row of data* is an entire record in a relational database table.

Columns

A *column* is a vertical entity in a table that contains all information associated with a specific field in a table. For example, a column in the `Passengers` table having to do with the passenger's last name consists of the following:

```
Wogan
Mastrelli
Fold
```

This column is based on the field `LastName`, the passenger's last name. A column pulls information about a certain field from every record within a table.

Primary Keys

A primary key is a column that makes each row of data in the table unique in a relational database. The primary key in the `Passengers` table is `PassengerID`, which is typically initialized during the table creation process. The nature of the primary key is to ensure that all product identifications are unique, so each record in the `Passengers` table has its own `PassengerID`. Primary keys alleviate the possibility of a duplicate record in a table and are used in other ways, which you will read about in Hour 3.

NULL Values

`NULL` is the term used to represent a missing value. A *NULL value* in a table is a value in a field that appears to be blank. A field with a `NULL` value is a field with no value. It is important to understand that a NULL value is different from a zero value or a field that contains spaces. A field with a NULL value is one that has been left blank during record creation. For example, a table containing a column called MiddleName might allow null or missing values because every person does not necessarily have a middle name. Records in tables that do not have an entry for a particular column signify a NULL value.

Additional table elements are discussed in detail during the next two hours.

Examples and Exercises

Many exercises in this book use the MySQL, Microsoft SQL Server, and Oracle databases to generate the examples. We decided to concentrate on these three database implementations because they allow freely distributed versions of their database to be available. Also, these are the three most popular relational database implementations. This enables you to select an implementation of your choice, install it, and follow along with the exercises in the book. Note that because these databases are not 100%-compliant to SQL-2011, the exercises might present slight variations or nonadoption of the ANSI standard. However, by learning the basics of the ANSI standard, you can in most cases easily translate your skills between different database implementations.

Summary

You have been introduced to the standard language of SQL and have been given a brief history and thumbnail of how the standard has evolved over the past several years. Database systems and current technologies were also discussed, including the relational database, client/server systems, and web-based database systems, all of which are vital to your understanding of SQL. The main SQL language components and the fact that there are numerous players in the relational database market, and likewise, many different flavors of SQL, were discussed. Despite ANSI SQL variations, most vendors do comply to some extent with the current standard (SQL-2011), rendering consistency across the board and forcing the development of portable SQL applications.

The database that is used during your course of study was also introduced. The database, as you have seen it so far, has consisted of a few tables (which are related to one another) and the data that each table contains at this point (at the end of Hour 1). You should have acquired some overall background knowledge of the fundamentals of SQL and should understand the concept of a modern database. After a few refreshers in the workshop for this hour, you should feel confident about continuing to the next hour.

Q&A

Q. If I learn SQL, can I use any of the implementations that use SQL?

A. Yes, you can communicate with a database whose implementation is ANSI SQL-compliant. If an implementation is not completely compliant, you should pick it up quickly with some adjustments.

Q. In a client/server environment, is the personal computer the client or the server?

A. The personal computer is known as the client; although a server can also serve as a client.

Q. Is there an overall standard for naming conventions for database objects such as tables and columns?

A. Although not necessary, a naming convention for database objects and data should be established within each organization and should be used consistently. Consistency in naming conventions make data more easily identifiable and data easier to manage in general.

Workshop

The following workshop is composed of a series of quiz questions and practical exercises. The quiz questions are designed to test your overall understanding of the current material. The practical exercises are intended to afford you the opportunity to apply the concepts discussed during the current hour, as well as build upon the knowledge acquired in previous hours of study. Please take time to complete the quiz questions and exercises before continuing. Refer to Appendix C, "Answers to Quizzes and Exercises," for answers.

Quiz

1. What does the acronym SQL stand for?

2. What are the six main categories of SQL commands?

3. What are the four transactional control commands?

4. What is the main difference between client/server and web technologies as they relate to database access?

5. If a field is defined as NULL, does something have to be entered into that field?

Exercises

1. Identify the categories in which the following SQL commands fall:

   CREATE TABLE
   DELETE
   SELECT
   INSERT
   ALTER TABLE
   UPDATE

2. Study the following tables, and pick out the column that would be a good candidate for the primary key:

   AIRPORTS
   EMPLOYEES
   PASSENGERS
   AIRCRAFT

3. Refer to Appendix B, "Installing Oracle and Microsoft SQL." Download and install one of the three database implementations on your computer to prepare for hands-on exercises in the following hours of instruction.

HOUR 2
Defining Data Structures

What You'll Learn in This Hour:

- ▶ A look at the underlying data of a table
- ▶ An introduction to the basic data types
- ▶ Instruction on the use of various data types
- ▶ Examples depicting differences between data types

In this second hour, you learn more about the data you viewed at the end of Hour 1, "Welcome to the World of SQL." You learn the characteristics of the data and how such data is stored in a relational database. There are several data types, as you'll soon discover.

What Is Data?

Data is a collection of information stored in a database as one of several different data types. Data includes names, numbers, dollar amounts, text, graphics, decimals, figures, calculations, summarization, and just about anything else you can possibly imagine. Data can be stored in uppercase, lowercase, or mixed case. Data can be manipulated or changed; most data does not remain static for its lifetime.

Data types are used to provide rules for data for particular columns. A data type deals with the way values are stored in a column for the length allocated for a column and whether values such as alphanumeric, numeric, and date and time data are allowed. There is a data type for every possible bit or combination of data that can be stored in a particular database. These data types store data such as characters, numbers, date and time, images, and other binary data. More specifically, the data might consist of names, descriptions, numbers, calculations, images, image descriptions, documents, and so forth.

The data is the purpose of any database and must be protected. The protector of the data is normally the *database administrator (DBA)*, although it is every database user's responsibility to ensure that measures are taken to protect data. Data security is discussed in depth in Hour 18, "Managing Database Users," and Hour 19, "Managing Database Security."

Basic Data Types

The following sections discuss the basic data types supported by ANSI SQL. Data types are characteristics of the data itself, whose attributes are placed on fields within a table. For example, you can specify that a field must contain numeric values, disallowing the entering of alphanumeric strings. After all, you would not want to enter alphabetic characters in a field for a dollar amount. Defining each field in the database with a data type eliminates much of the incorrect data found in a database due to data entry errors. *Field definition* (data type definition) is a form of data validation that controls the type of data that may be entered into each given field.

Depending on your implementation of *relational database management system (RDBMS)*, certain data types can be converted automatically to other data types depending upon their format. This type of conversion in known as an *implicit conversion*, which means that the database handles the conversion for you. An example of this is taking a numeric value of 1000.92 from a numeric field and inputting it into a string field. Other data types cannot be converted implicitly by the host RDBMS and therefore must undergo an explicit conversion. This usually involves the use of a SQL function, such as CAST or CONVERT. In the following Oracle example, the current system date is retrieved from the database in the default date format, which is a date data type:

```
SELECT CAST('12/27/1974' AS DATETIME) AS MYDATE

SQL> SELECT SYSDATE FROM DUAL;

SYSDATE
---------
08-SEP-15
```

If we want to change, or display the date in a format other than the default data type, we can apply the Oracle TO_CHAR function to display the date as a character string, in the next example retrieving only the current month:

```
SQL> SELECT TO_CHAR(SYSDATE, 'Month') MONTH
  2   FROM DUAL;

MONTH
------------------------------------
September
```

The basic data types, as with most other languages, are:

- ▶ String types
- ▶ Numeric types
- ▶ Date and time types

TIP

SQL Data Types

Every implementation of SQL has its own specific set of data types. The use of implementation-specific data types is necessary to support the philosophy of each implementation on how to handle the storage of data. However, the basics are the same among all implementations.

Fixed-Length Strings

Constant characters, those strings that always have the same length, are stored using a fixed-length data type. The following is the standard for a SQL fixed-length character:

CHARACTER(n)

n represents a number identifying the allocated or maximum length of the particular field with this definition.

Some implementations of SQL use the CHAR data type to store fixed-length data. You can store alphanumeric data in this data type. An example of a constant length data type would be for a state abbreviation because all state abbreviations are two characters.

Spaces are normally used to fill extra spots when using a fixed-length data type; if a field's length were set to 10 and data entered filled only 5 places, the remaining 5 spaces would be recorded as spaces. The padding of spaces ensures that each value in a field is a fixed length.

CAUTION

Fixed-Length Data Types

Be careful not to use a fixed-length data type for fields that might contain varying-length values, such as an individual's name. If you use the fixed-length data type inappropriately, you eventually encounter problems such as the waste of available space and the inability to make accurate comparisons between data.

Always use the varying-length data type for nonconstant character strings to save database space.

Varying-Length Strings

SQL supports the use of *varying-length strings*, strings whose length is not constant for all data. The following is the standard for a SQL varying-length character:

CHARACTER VARYING(n)

n represents a number identifying the allocated or maximum length of the particular field with this definition.

Common data types for variable-length character values are the VARCHAR, VARBINARY, and VARCHAR2 data types. VARCHAR is the ANSI standard, which Microsoft SQL Server and MySQL use; Oracle uses both VARCHAR and VARCHAR2. The data stored in a character-defined column can be alphanumeric, which means that the data value may contain numeric characters. VARBINARY is similar to VARCHAR and VARCHAR2 except that it contains a variable length of bytes. Normally, you would use a type such as this to store some kind of digital data such as an image file.

Remember that fixed-length data types typically pad spaces to fill in allocated places not used by the field. The varying-length data type does not work this way. For instance, if the allocated length of a varying-length field is 10, and a string of 5 characters is entered, the total length of that particular value would be only 5. Spaces are not used to fill unused places in a column.

Large Object Types

Some variable-length data types need to hold longer lengths of data than what is traditionally reserved for a VARCHAR field. The BLOB and TEXT data types are two examples of such data types in modern database implementations. These data types are specifically made to hold large sets of data. The BLOB is a binary large object, so its data is treated as a large binary string (a byte string). A BLOB is especially useful in an implementation that needs to store binary media files in the database, such as images or MP3s.

The TEXT data type is a large character string data type that can be treated as a large VARCHAR field. It is often used when an implementation needs to store large sets of character data in the database. An example of this would be storing HTML input from the entries of a blog site. Storing this type of data in the database enables the site to be dynamically updated.

Numeric Types

Numeric values are stored in fields that are defined as some type of number, typically referred to as NUMBER, INTEGER, REAL, DECIMAL, and so on.

The following are the standards for SQL numeric values:

▶ BIT(n)

▶ BIT VARYING(n)

▶ DECIMAL(p,s)

▶ INTEGER

▶ SMALLINT

▶ BIGINT

▶ FLOAT(p,s)

▶ DOUBLE PRECISION(p,s)

▶ REAL(s)

p represents a number identifying the allocated or maximum length of the particular field for each appropriate definition.

s is a number to the right of the decimal point, such as 34.*ss*.

A common numeric data type in SQL implementations is NUMERIC, which accommodates the direction for numeric values provided by ANSI. Numeric values can be stored as zero, positive, negative, fixed, and floating-point numbers. The following is an example using NUMERIC:

```
NUMERIC(5)
```

This example restricts the maximum value entered in a particular field to 99999. Note that all the database implementations that we use for the examples support the NUMERIC type but implement it as a DECIMAL.

Decimal Types

Decimal values are numeric values that include the use of a decimal point. The standard for a decimal in SQL follows, where *p* is the precision and *s* is the decimal's scale:

```
DECIMAL(p,s)
```

The *precision* is the total length of the numeric value. In a numeric defined DECIMAL(4,2), the precision is 4, which is the total length allocated for a numeric value. The scale is the number of digits to the right of the decimal point. The scale is 2 in the previous DECIMAL(4,2) example. If a value has more places to the right side of the decimal point than the scale allows, the value is rounded; for instance, 34.33 inserted into a DECIMAL(3,1) is typically rounded to 34.3.

If a numeric value were defined as the following data type, the maximum value allowed would be 99.99:

```
DECIMAL(4,2)
```

The precision is 4, which represents the total length allocated for an associated value. The scale is 2, which represents the number of *places*, or *bytes*, reserved to the right side of the decimal point. The decimal point does not count as a character.

Allowed values for a column defined as DECIMAL(4,2) include the following:

▶ 12

▶ 12.4

▶ 12.44

▶ 12.449

The last numeric value, 12.449, is rounded off to 12.45 upon input into the column. In this case, any numbers between 12.445 and 12.449 would be rounded to 12.45.

Integers

An *integer* is a numeric value that does not contain a decimal, only whole numbers (both positive and negative).

Valid integers include the following:

- ▶ 1
- ▶ 0
- ▶ −1
- ▶ 99
- ▶ −99
- ▶ 199

Floating-Point Decimals

Floating-point decimals are decimal values whose precision and scale are variable lengths and virtually without limit. Any precision and scale is acceptable. The REAL data type designates a column with single-precision, floating-point numbers. The DOUBLE PRECISION data type designates a column that contains double-precision, floating-point numbers. To be considered a single-precision floating point, the precision must be between 1 and 21 inclusive. To be considered a double-precision floating point, the precision must be between 22 and 53 inclusive. The following are examples of the FLOAT data type:

- ▶ FLOAT
- ▶ FLOAT(15)
- ▶ FLOAT(50)

Date and Time Types

Date and time data types are quite obviously used to keep track of information concerning dates and time. Standard SQL supports DATETIME data types, which include the following specific data types:

- ▶ DATE
- ▶ TIME

▶ DATETIME

▶ TIMESTAMP

The elements of a DATETIME data type consist of the following:

▶ YEAR

▶ MONTH

▶ DAY

▶ HOUR

▶ MINUTE

▶ SECOND

NOTE

Fractions and Leap Seconds

The SECOND element can also be broken down to fractions of a second. The range is from 00.000 to 61.999, although some implementations of SQL might not support this range. The extra 1.999 seconds is used for leap seconds.

Be aware that each implementation of SQL might have its own customized data type for dates and times. The previous data types and elements are standards to which each SQL vendor should adhere, but be advised that most implementations have their own data type for date values, varying in both appearance and the way date information is actually stored internally.

A length is not normally specified for a date data type. Later in this hour, you learn more about dates—how date information is stored in some implementations and how to manipulate dates and times using conversion functions. You also study practical examples of how dates and times are used in the real world.

Literal Strings

A *literal string* is a series of characters, such as a name or a phone number, which is explicitly specified by a user or program. Literal strings consist of data with the same attributes as the previously discussed data types, but the value of the string is known. The value of a column is usually unknown because a column typically has a different value associated with each row of data in a table.

You do not actually specify data types with literal strings—you simply specify the string. Some examples of literal strings follow:

▶ `'Hello'`

▶ `45000`

▶ `"45000"`

▶ `3.14`

▶ `'November 1, 1997'`

The alphanumeric strings are enclosed by single quotation marks, whereas the number value `45000` is not. Also notice that the second numeric value of `45000` is enclosed by quotation marks. Generally speaking, character strings require quotation marks, whereas numeric strings don't.

The process that converts a number into a numeric type is known as an *implicit conversion*. This means that the database attempts to figure out what type it needs to create for the object. So if you do not have a number enclosed with single quotation marks, the SQL compiler assumes that you want a numeric type. You need to be careful when working with data to ensure that the data is being represented as you want it to be. Otherwise, it might skew your results or result in an unexpected error. You see later how literal strings are used with database queries.

NULL Data Types

As you should know from Hour 1, a NULL value is a missing value or a column in a row of data that has not been assigned a value. NULL values are used in nearly all parts of SQL, including the creation of tables, search conditions for queries, and even in literal strings.

The way a NULL value is designated is simply using the keyword NULL.

Because the following is in quotations, it does not represent a NULL value, but a literal string containing the characters N-U-L-L:

`'NULL'`

When using the NULL data type, it is important to realize that data is not required in a particular field. If data is always required for a given field, always use NOT NULL with a data type. If there is a chance that there might not always be data for a field, it is better to use NULL.

BOOLEAN Values

A BOOLEAN value is a value of TRUE, FALSE, or NULL. BOOLEAN values are used to make data comparisons. For example, when criteria are specified for a query, each condition evaluates to a TRUE, FALSE, or NULL. If the BOOLEAN value of TRUE is returned by all conditions in a query, data is returned. If a BOOLEAN value of FALSE or NULL is returned, data might not be returned.

Consider the following example:

```
WHERE NAME = 'SMITH'
```

This line might be a condition found in a query. The condition is evaluated for every row of data in the table that is queried. If the value of NAME is SMITH for a row of data in the table, the condition returns the value TRUE, thereby returning the data associated with that record.

Most database implementations do not implement a strict BOOLEAN type and instead opt to use their own methodology. MySQL contains the BOOLEAN type, but it is merely a synonym for its existing TINYINT type. Oracle prefers to direct its users to use a CHAR(1) value to denote a BOOLEAN, and Microsoft SQL Server uses a value known as BIT.

NOTE
_____

Differences in Data Type Implementations

Some of the data types mentioned during this hour might not be available by name in the implementation of SQL that you are using. Data types are often named differently among implementations of SQL, but the concept behind each data type remains. Most, if not all, data types are supported by relational databases.
_____

User-Defined Types

A *user-defined type* is a data type that the user defines. User-defined types allow users to customize their own data types to meet data storage needs and are based on existing data types. User-defined data types can assist the developer by providing greater flexibility during database application development because they maximize the number of possibilities for data storage. The CREATE TYPE statement is used to create a user-defined type.

For example, you can create a type as follows in Oracle:

```
CREATE TYPE PERSON AS OBJECT
(NAME        VARCHAR (30),
 SSN         VARCHAR (9));
```

You can reference your user-defined type as follows:

```
CREATE TABLE EMP_PAY
(EMPLOYEE    PERSON,
 SALARY      DECIMAL(10,2),
 HIRE_DATE   DATE);
```

Notice that the data type referenced for the first column EMPLOYEE is PERSON. PERSON is the user-defined type you created in the first example.

Domains

A *domain* is a set of valid data types that can be used. A domain is associated with a data type, so only certain data is accepted. After you create a domain, you can add constraints to the domain. Constraints work with data types, allowing you to further specify acceptable data for a field. The domain is used like the user-defined type.

The use of user-defined domains are not nearly as common as user-defined types and is not supported by Oracle, for example. The following syntax does not work with the implementations downloaded for this book, but is an example of a basic syntax to create a domain:

```
CREATE DOMAIN MONEY_D AS NUMBER(8,2);
```

You would add constraints to your domain as follows:

```
ALTER DOMAIN MONEY_D
ADD CONSTRAINT MONEY_CON1
CHECK (VALUE > 5);
```

You would reference the domain as follows:

```
CREATE TABLE EMP_PAY
(EMP_ID        NUMBER(9),
 EMP_NAME      VARCHAR2(30),
 PAY_RATE      MONEY_D);
```

Summary

Several data types are available with SQL. If you have programmed in other languages, you probably recognize many of the data types mentioned. Data types allow different types of data to be stored in the database, ranging from simple characters to decimal points to date and time. The concept of data types is the same in all languages, whether programming in a third-generation language such as C and passing variables or using a relational database implementation and coding in SQL. Of course, each implementation has its own names for standard data types, but they basically work the same. Also remember that an RDBMS does not have to implement all the data types in the ANSI standard to be considered ANSI compliant. Therefore, it is prudent to check with the documentation of your specific RDBMS implementation to see what options you have available.

You must take care in planning for both the near and distant future when deciding on data types, lengths, scales, and precisions in which to store your data. Business rules and how you want the end user to access the data are other factors in deciding on specific data types. You should know the nature of the data and how data in the database is related to assign proper data types.

Q&A

Q. How is it that I can enter numbers such as a person's Social Security number in fields defined as character fields?

A. Numeric values are still alphanumeric, which are allowed in string data types. The process is called an implicit conversion because the database system handles it automatically. Typically, the only data stored as numeric values are values used in computations. However, it might be helpful for some to define all numeric fields with a numeric data type to help control the data entered in that field.

Q. I still do not understand the difference between constant-length and varying-length data types. Can you explain?

A. Say you have an individual's last name defined as a constant-length data type with a length of 20 bytes. Suppose the individual's name is Smith. When the data is inserted into the table, 20 bytes are taken: 5 for the name and 15 for the extra spaces. (Remember that this is a constant-length data type.) If you use a varying-length data type with a length of 20 and insert `Smith`, only 5 bytes of space are taken. If you then imagine that you are inserting 100,000 rows of data into this system, you could possibly save 1.5 million bytes of data.

Q. Are there limits on the lengths of data types?

A. Yes, there are limits on the lengths of data types, and they do vary among the various implementations.

Workshop

The following workshop is composed of a series of quiz questions and practical exercises. The quiz questions are designed to test your overall understanding of the current material. The practical exercises are intended to afford you the opportunity to apply the concepts discussed during the current hour, as well as build upon the knowledge acquired in previous hours of study. Please take time to complete the quiz questions and exercises before continuing. Refer to Appendix C, "Answers to Quizzes and Exercises," for answers.

Quiz

1. True or false: An individual's Social Security number, entered in the format `'111111111'`, can be any of the following data types: constant-length character, varying-length character, or numeric.

2. True or false: The scale of a numeric value is the total length allowed for values.

3. Do all implementations use the same data types?

4. What are the precision and scale of the following?

```
DECIMAL(4,2)
DECIMAL(10,2)
DECIMAL(14,1)
```

5. Which numbers could be inserted into a column whose data type is `DECIMAL(4,1)`?

  A. 16.2

  B. 116.2

  C. 16.21

  D. 1116.2

  E. 1116.21

6. What is data?

Exercises

1. Take the following column titles, assign them to a data type, decide on the proper length, and give an example of the data you would enter into that column:

  A. ssn

  B. state

  C. city

  D. phone_number

  E. zip

  F. last_name

  G. first_name

  H. middle_name

  I. salary

  J. hourly_pay_rate

  K. date_hired

2. Take the same column titles and decide whether they should be NULL or NOT NULL, realizing that in some cases in which a column would normally be NOT NULL, the column could be NULL or vice versa, depending on the application:

  A. ssn

  B. state

  C. city

    D. phone_number

    E. zip

    F. last_name

    G. first_name

    H. middle_name

    I. salary

    J. hourly_pay_rate

    K. date_hired

3. We are going to set up a database to use for the subsequent hours in this book. Remember that you must have installed one of the two database implementations—Oracle or Microsoft SQL Server—before continuing.

Oracle

Open your web browser and navigate to the administration home page, which is typically located at http://127.0.0.1:8080/apex. At the login prompt, if this is the first time that you are logging into the system, use system as the username and the password that you set up during the installation. From the administration screen you can select SQL, SQL Commands, and Enter Command. Now in the command window, input the following command and click the Run button:

```
create user canaryairlines identified by canary_2015;
```

In Oracle, when you create a user, the RDMS automatically creates a schema. So with this command you not only created a user for querying the data but also a schema named canaryairlines. Oracle treats the schema in much the same way that Microsoft SQL Server treats a database. You can view your schema by simply logging out and then logging back in as the newly created user.

Microsoft

From the Start menu, type SSMS.exe into the Run box and press Enter. This brings up SQL Server Management Studio. The first dialog box to open is for your database connection. If it is not already filled in with localhost as the server name, type localhost into the box. Leave the other values such as Windows Authentication as they are, and click the Connect button. On the left side of the screen is an area called Object Explorer showing your localhost database instance. Right-click localhost and select New Query. This opens a query window in the right pane. Now type the following command and press F5:

```
Create database CanaryAirlines;
```

Then right-click the folder underneath localhost that's labeled Databases and select Refresh. Now if you expand the folder tree by clicking the + symbol, you should see your CanaryAirlines database.

Managing Database Objects

What You'll Learn in This Hour:

▶ An introduction to database objects

▶ An introduction to schemas

▶ An introduction to tables

▶ A discussion of the nature and attributes of tables

▶ Examples for the creation and manipulation of tables

▶ A discussion of table storage options

▶ Concepts on referential integrity and data consistency

In this hour, you learn about database objects: what they are, how they act, how they are stored, and how they relate to one another. Database objects are the logical units that compose the building blocks of the database. The majority of the instruction during this hour revolves around tables, but keep in mind that there are other database objects, many of which are discussed in later hours of study.

Database Objects and Schema

A *database object* is any defined object in a database that is used to store or reference data. Some examples of database objects include tables, views, clusters, sequences, indexes, and synonyms. The table is this hour's focus because it is the primary and simplest form of data storage in a relational database.

A *schema* is a collection of database objects normally associated with one particular database username. This username is called the *schema owner*, or the owner of the related group of objects. You may have one or multiple schemas in a database. The user is only associated with the schema of the same name, and often the terms are used interchangeably. Basically, any user who creates an object has just created it in her own schema unless she specifically instructs it to be created in another one. So, based on a user's privileges within the database, the user has control over objects that are created, manipulated, and deleted. A schema can consist of a single table and has no limits to the number of objects that it may contain, unless restricted by a specific database implementation.

Say you have been issued a database username and password by the database administrator. Your username is USER1. Suppose you log on to the database and then create a table called EMPLOYEE_TBL. According to the database, your table's actual name is USER1.EMPLOYEE_TBL. The schema name for that table is USER1, which is also the owner of that table. You have just created the first table of a schema.

The good thing about schemas is that when you access a table that you own (in your own schema), you do not have to refer to the schema name. For instance, you could refer to your table as either one of the following:

```
EMPLOYEE_TBL
USER1.EMPLOYEE_TBL
```

The first option is preferred because it requires fewer keystrokes. If another user were to query one of your tables, the user would have to specify the schema as follows:

```
USER1.EMPLOYEE_TBL
```

In Hour 20, "Creating and Using Views and Synonyms," you learn about the distribution of permissions so that other users can access your tables. You also learn about synonyms, which enable you to give a table another name so that you do not have to specify the schema name when accessing a table. Figure 3.1 illustrates two schemas in a relational database.

FIGURE 3.1
Schemas in a database

In Figure 3.1, two user accounts in the database own tables: USER1 and USER2. Each user account has its own schema. Some examples for how the two users can access their own tables and tables owned by the other user follow:

```
USER1 accesses own TABLE1:              TABLE1

USER1 accesses own TEST:                TEST

USER1 accesses USER2's TABLE10          USER2.TABLE10

USER1 accesses USER2's TEST             USER2.TEST
```

In this example, both users have a table called TEST. Tables can have the same names in a database as long as they belong to different schemas. If you look at it this way, table names are always unique in a database because the schema owner is actually part of the table name. For instance, USER1.TEST is a different table than USER2.TEST. If you do not specify a schema with the table name when accessing tables in a database, the database server looks for a table that you own by default. That is, if USER1 tries to access TEST, the database server looks for a USER1-owned table named TEST before it looks for other objects owned by USER1, such as synonyms to tables in another schema. Hour 21, "Working with the System Catalog," helps you fully understand how synonyms work.

You must be careful to understand the distinction between objects in your own schema and those objects in another schema. If you do not provide a schema when performing operations that alter the table, such as a DROP command, the database assumes that you mean a table in your own schema. This could possibly lead to your unintentionally dropping the wrong object. So you must always pay careful attention as to which user you are currently logged into the database with.

CAUTION

Object Naming Rules Differ Between Systems

Every database server has rules concerning how you can name objects and elements of objects, such as field names. You must check your particular implementation for the exact naming conventions or rules.

Tables: The Primary Storage for Data

The table is the primary storage object for data in a relational database. In its simplest form, a table consists of row(s) and column(s), both of which hold the data. A table takes up physical space in a database and can be permanent or temporary.

Columns

A *field*, also called a *column* in a relational database, is part of a table that is assigned a specific data type. The data type determines what kind of data the column is allowed to hold. This enables the designer of the table to help maintain the integrity of the data.

Every database table must consist of at least one column. Columns are those elements within a table that hold specific types of data, such as a person's name or address. For example, a valid column in a customer table might be the customer's name. Figure 3.2 illustrates a column in a table.

FIGURE 3.2
An example of a column

Generally, a column name must be one continuous string and can be limited to the number of characters used according to each implementation of SQL. It is typical to use underscores with names to provide separation between characters. For example, a column for the customer's name can be named CUSTOMER_NAME instead of CUSTOMERNAME. This is normally done to increase the readability of database objects. There are other naming conventions that you can utilize, such as CamelCase, to fit your specific preferences. As such, it is important for a database development team to agree upon a standard naming convention and stick to it so that order is maintained within the development process.

The most common form of data stored within a column is string data. This data can be stored as either uppercase or lowercase for character-defined fields. The case that you use for data is simply a matter of preference, which should be based on how the data will be used. In many cases, data is stored in uppercase for simplicity and consistency. However, if data is stored in different case types throughout the database (uppercase, lowercase, and mixed case), functions can be applied to convert the data to either uppercase or lowercase if needed. These functions are covered in Hour 11, "Restructuring the Appearance of Data."

Columns also can be specified as NULL or NOT NULL, meaning that if a column is NOT NULL, something must be entered. If a column is specified as NULL, nothing has to be entered. NULL is different from an empty set, such as an empty string, and holds a special place in database design. As such, you can relate a NULL value to a lack of any data in the field.

Rows

A *row* is a record of data in a database table. For example, a row of data in a customer table might consist of a particular customer's identification number, name, address, phone number, and fax number. A row is composed of fields that contain data from one record in a table. A table can contain as little as one row of data and as many as several million rows of data or records. Figure 3.3 illustrates a row within a table.

EMP_ID	LAST_NAME	FIRST_NAME	MIDDLE_NAME
213764555	GLASS	BRANDON	SCOTT
220984332	WALLACE	MARIAH	
311549902	STEPHENS	TINA	DAWN
313782439	GLASS	JACOB	
442346889	PLEW	LINDA	CAROL
443679012	SPURGEON	TIFFANY	

FIGURE 3.3
Example of a table row

The CREATE TABLE Statement

The CREATE TABLE statement in SQL is used to create a table. Although the act of creating a table is quite simple, much time and effort should be put into planning table structures before the actual execution of the CREATE TABLE statement. Carefully planning your table structure before implementation saves you from having to reconfigure things after they are in production.

NOTE

Types We Use in This Hour

In this hour's examples, we use the popular data types CHAR (constant-length character), VARCHAR (variable-length character), NUMBER (numeric values, decimal, and nondecimal), and DATE (date and time values).

Some elementary questions need to be answered when creating a table:

▶ What type of data will be entered into the table?

▶ What will be the table's name?

▶ What column(s) will compose the primary key?

▶ What names shall be given to the columns (fields)?

▶ What data type will be assigned to each column?

▶ What will be the allocated length for each column?

▶ Which columns in a table can be left as a null value?

NOTE

Existing Systems Often Have Existing Naming Rules

Be sure to check your implementation for rules when naming objects and other database elements. Often database administrators adopt a *naming convention* that explains how to name the objects within the database so that you can easily discern how they are used.

After these questions are answered, the actual CREATE TABLE statement is simple. The basic syntax to create a table follows:

```
CREATE TABLE table_name
( field1   data_type   [ not null ],
  field2   data_type   [ not null ],
  field3   data_type   [ not null ],
  field4   data_type   [ not null ],
  field5   data_type   [ not null ] );
```

Note that a semicolon is the last character in the previous statement. Also, brackets indicate portions that are optional. Most SQL implementations have some character that terminates a statement or submits a statement to the database server. Oracle, Microsoft SQL Server, and MySQL use the semicolon. Although Transact-SQL, Microsoft SQL Server's ANSI SQL version, has no such requirement, it is considered best practice to use it. This book uses the semicolon.

Create a table called EMPLOYEE_TBL in the following example using the syntax for MySQL:

```
CREATE TABLE EMPLOYEE_TBL
(EMP_ID         VARCHAR (9)    NOT NULL,
EMP_NAME        VARCHAR (40)   NOT NULL,
EMP_ST_ADDR     VARCHAR (20)   NOT NULL,
EMP_CITY        VARCHAR (15)   NOT NULL,
EMP_ST          VARCHAR (2)    NOT NULL,
EMP_ZIP         INTEGER(5)     NOT NULL,
EMP_PHONE       INTEGER(10)    NULL,
EMP_PAGER       INTEGER(10)    NULL);
```

The following code would be the compatible code for both Microsoft SQL Server and Oracle:

```
CREATE TABLE EMPLOYEE_TBL
(EMP_ID         VARCHAR (9)    NOT NULL,
EMP_NAME        VARCHAR (40)   NOT NULL,
EMP_ST_ADDR     VARCHAR (20)   NOT NULL,
EMP_CITY        VARCHAR (15)   NOT NULL,
EMP_ST          VARCHAR (2)    NOT NULL,
EMP_ZIP         INTEGER        NOT NULL,
EMP_PHONE       INTEGER        NULL,
EMP_PAGER       INTEGER        NULL);
```

Eight different columns make up this table. Notice the use of the underscore character to break up the column names into what appears to be separate words. (EMPLOYEE ID is stored as EMP_ID.) This technique makes the table or column name more readable. Each column has been assigned a specific data type and length, and by using the NULL/NOT NULL constraint, you have specified which columns require values for every row of data in the table. The EMP_PHONE is defined as NULL, meaning that NULL values are allowed in this column because there might be individuals without a telephone number. The information concerning each column is separated by a comma, with parentheses surrounding all columns (a left parenthesis before the first column and a right parenthesis following the information on the last column).

CAUTION

Limitations on Data Types Vary

Check your particular implementation for name length limits and characters that are allowed; they could differ from implementation to implementation.

Each record, or row of data, in this table consists of the following:

EMP_ID, EMP_NAME, EMP_ST_ADDR, EMP_CITY, EMP_ST, EMP_ZIP, EMP_PHONE, EMP_PAGER

In this table, each field is a column. The column EMP_ID could consist of one employee's identification number or many employees' identification numbers, depending on the requirements of a database query or transaction.

Naming Conventions

When selecting names for objects, specifically tables and columns, make sure the name reflects the data that is to be stored. For example, the name for a table pertaining to employee information could be named EMPLOYEE_TBL. Names for columns should follow the same logic. When storing an employee's phone number, an obvious name for that column would be PHONE_NUMBER.

The ALTER TABLE Command

You can modify a table after the table has been created by using the ALTER TABLE command. You can add column(s), drop column(s), change column definitions, add and drop constraints, and, in some implementations, modify table STORAGE values. The standard syntax for the ALTER TABLE command follows:

```
alter table table_name [modify] [column column_name] [datatype | null not null]
[restrict|cascade]
[drop]    [constraint constraint_name]
[add]     [column] column definition
```

Modifying Elements of a Table

The *attributes* of a column refer to the rules and behavior of data in a column. You can modify the attributes of a column with the `ALTER TABLE` command. The word *attributes* here refers to the following:

► The data type of a column

► The length, precision, or scale of a column

► Whether the column can contain `NULL` values

The following example uses the `ALTER TABLE` command on `EMPLOYEE_TBL` to modify the attributes of the column `EMP_ID`:

```
ALTER TABLE EMPLOYEE_TBL MODIFY
EMP_ID VARCHAR(10);
Table altered.
```

The column was already defined as data type `VARCHAR` (a varying-length character), but you increased the maximum length from 9 to 10.

Adding Mandatory Columns to a Table

One of the basic rules for adding columns to an existing table is that the column you are adding cannot be defined as `NOT NULL` if data currently exists in the table. `NOT NULL` means that a column must contain some value for every row of data in the table. So, if you are adding a column defined as `NOT NULL`, you are contradicting the `NOT NULL` constraint from the beginning if the preexisting rows of data in the table do not have values for the new column.

There is, however, a way to add a mandatory column to a table:

1. Add the column and define it as `NULL`. (The column does not have to contain a value.)

2. Insert a value into the new column for every row of data in the table.

3. Alter the table to change the column's attribute to `NOT NULL`.

Adding Auto-Incrementing Columns to a Table

Sometimes, it is necessary to create a column that auto-increments itself to give a unique sequence number for a particular row. You could do this for many reasons, such as not having a natural key for the data or wanting to use a unique sequence number to sort the data. Creating an auto-incrementing column is generally easy. In MySQL, the implementation provides the `SERIAL` method to produce a truly unique value for the table. Following is an example:

```
CREATE TABLE TEST_INCREMENT(
        ID              SERIAL,
        TEST_NAME    VARCHAR(20));
```

Using NULL for Table Creation

NULL is a default attribute for a column; therefore, it does not have to be entered in the CREATE TABLE statement. NOT NULL must always be specified.

In Microsoft SQL Server, we are provided with an IDENTITY column type. The following is an example for the SQL Server implementation:

```
CREATE TABLE TEST_INCREMENT(
        ID      INT IDENTITY(1,1) NOT NULL,
        TEST_NAME    VARCHAR(20));
```

Oracle does not provide a direct method for an auto-incrementing column. However, one method using an object called a SEQUENCE and a TRIGGER simulates the effect in Oracle. This technique is discussed when we talk about TRIGGERs in Hour 22, "Advanced SQL Topics."

Now we can insert values into the newly created table without specifying a value for our auto-incrementing column:

```
INSERT INTO TEST_INCREMENT(TEST_NAME)
VALUES ('FRED'),('JOE'),('MIKE'),('TED');
SELECT * FROM TEST_INCREMENT;
| ID |     TEST_NAME |
|  1 |     FRED      |
|  2 |     JOE       |
|  3 |     MIKE      |
|  4 |     TED       |
```

Modifying Columns

You need to consider many things when modifying existing columns of a table. Following are some common rules for modifying columns:

► The length of a column can be increased to the maximum length of the given data type.

► The length of a column can be decreased only if the largest value for that column in the table is less than or equal to the new length of the column.

► The number of digits for a number data type can always be increased.

► The number of digits for a number data type can be decreased only if the value with the most number of digits for that column is less than or equal to the new number of digits specified for the column.

▶ The number of decimal places for a number data type can either be increased or decreased.

▶ The data type of a column can normally be changed.

Some implementations might actually restrict you from using certain ALTER TABLE options. For example, you might not be allowed to drop columns from a table. To do this, you have to drop the table itself and then rebuild the table with the wanted columns. You could run into problems by dropping a column in one table that is dependent on a column in another table or dropping a column that is referenced by a column in another table. Be sure to refer to your specific implementation documentation.

NOTE

Creating Tables for Exercises

You create the tables that you see in these examples at the end of this hour in the "Exercises" section. In Hour 5, "Manipulating Data," you populate the tables you create in this hour with data.

Creating a Table from an Existing Table

You can create a copy of an existing table using a combination of the CREATE TABLE statement and the SELECT statement. The new table has the same column definitions. You can select any or all columns. New columns that you create via functions or a combination of columns automatically assume the size necessary to hold the data. The basic syntax for creating a table from another table follows:

```
create table new_table_name as
select [ *|column1, column2 ]
from table_name
[ where ]
```

CAUTION

Altering or Dropping Tables Can Be Dangerous

Take heed when altering and dropping tables. If you make logical or typing mistakes when issuing these statements, you can lose important data.

Notice some new keywords in the syntax, particularly the SELECT keyword. SELECT is a database query and is discussed in more detail in Chapter 7, "Introduction to Database Queries." However, it is important to know that you can create a table based on the results from a query.

Both MySQL and Oracle support the CREATE TABLE AS SELECT method of creating a table based on another table. Microsoft SQL Server, however, uses a different statement. For that database implementation, you use a SELECT ... INTO statement. This statement is used like this:

```
select [ *|column1, column2]
into new_table_name
from table_name
[ where ]
```

Here you can examine some examples of using this method.

First, do a simple query to view the data in the FlightStatuses table:

select * from FlightStatuses;


```
STATUSCODE      STATUSNAME
-------------------------
CAN             Cancelled
COM             Completed
DEL             Delayed
ONT             On-Time
```

Next, create a table called FlightStatusesNew based on the previous query:

```
create table FlightStatusesNew as
select * from FlightStatuses;

Table created.
```

In SQL Server, the same statement would be written as such:

```
select *
into FlightStatusesNew
from FlightStatuses;

Table created.
```

Now if you run a query on the FlightStatusesNew table, your results appear the same as if you had selected data from the original table:

select *
```
from FlightStatusNew;

STATUSCODE      STATUSNAME
-------------------------
CAN             Cancelled
COM             Completed
DEL             Delayed
ONT             On-Time
```

TIP

What the * Means

`SELECT` `*` selects data from all fields in the given table. The * represents a complete row of data, or record, in the table.

Dropping Tables

Dropping a table is actually one of the easiest things to do. When the `RESTRICT` option is used and the table is referenced by a view or constraint, the `DROP` statement returns an error. When the `CASCADE` option is used, the drop succeeds and all referencing views and constraints are dropped. The syntax to drop a table follows:

```
drop table table_name [ restrict | cascade ]
```

SQL Server does not allow for the use of the `CASCADE` option. So for that particular implementation, you must ensure that you drop all objects that reference the table you are removing to ensure that you are not leaving an invalid object in your system.

In the following example, you drop the table that you just created:

```
drop table products_tmp;

Table dropped.
```

CAUTION

Be Specific When Dropping a Table

Whenever you drop a table, be sure to specify the schema name or owner of the table before submitting your command. You could drop the incorrect table. If you have access to multiple user accounts, ensure that you are connected to the database through the correct user account before dropping tables.

Integrity Constraints

Integrity constraints ensure accuracy and consistency of data in a relational database. Data integrity is handled in a relational database through the concept of referential integrity. Many types of integrity constraints play a role in *referential integrity (RI)*. Referential integrity consists of rules that are in place in the database to ensure that the data in tables remain consistent.

Primary Key Constraints

Primary key is the term that identifies one or more columns in a table that make a row of data unique. Although the primary key typically consists of one column in a table, more than one column can comprise the primary key. For example, either the employee's Social Security number or an assigned employee identification number is the logical primary key for an employee table. The objective is for every record to have a unique primary key or value for the employee's identification number. Because there is probably no need to have more than one record for each employee in an employee table, the employee identification number makes a logical primary key. The primary key is assigned at table creation.

The following example identifies the EMP_ID column as the PRIMARY KEY for the EMPLOYEES table:

```
CREATE TABLE EMPLOYEE_TBL
(EMP_ID           VARCHAR(9)       NOT NULL PRIMARY KEY,
EMP_NAME         VARCHAR(40)      NOT NULL,
EMP_ST_ADDR      VARCHAR(20)      NOT NULL,
EMP_CITY         VARCHAR(15)      NOT NULL,
EMP_ST           VARCHAR(2)       NOT NULL,
EMP_ZIP          INTEGER(5)       NOT NULL,
EMP_PHONE        INTEGER(10)      NULL,
EMP_PAGER        INTEGER(10)      NULL);
```

This method of defining a primary key is accomplished during table creation. The primary key in this case is an implied constraint. You can also specify a primary key explicitly as a constraint when setting up a table, as follows:

```
CREATE TABLE EMPLOYEE_TBL
(EMP_ID           VARCHAR(9)       NOT NULL,
EMP_NAME         VARCHAR(40)      NOT NULL,
EMP_ST_ADDR      VARCHAR(20)      NOT NULL,
EMP_CITY         VARCHAR(15)      NOT NULL,
EMP_ST           VARCHAR(2)       NOT NULL,
EMP_ZIP          INTEGER(5)       NOT NULL,
EMP_PHONE        INTEGER(10)      NULL,
EMP_PAGER        INTEGER(10)      NULL,
PRIMARY KEY (EMP_ID));
```

The primary key constraint in this example is defined after the column comma list in the CREATE TABLE statement.

You can define a primary key that consists of more than one column by either of the following methods, which demonstrate creating a primary key in an Oracle table:

```
CREATE TABLE PRODUCT_TST
(PROD_ID          VARCHAR (10)     NOT NULL,
VEND_ID          VARCHAR (10)     NOT NULL,
PRODUCT          VARCHAR (30)     NOT NULL,
COST             NUMBER(8,2)      NOT NULL,
PRIMARY KEY (PROD_ID, VEND_ID));
ALTER TABLE PRODUCTS_TST
ADD CONSTRAINT PRODUCTS_PK PRIMARY KEY (PROD_ID, VEND_ID);
```

Unique Constraints

A *unique column constraint* in a table is similar to a primary key where each value in a column must be a unique value. Although a primary key constraint is placed on one column, you can place a unique constraint on another column even though it is not actually for use as the primary key.

Study the following example:

```
CREATE TABLE EMPLOYEE_TBL
(EMP_ID          VARCHAR (9)     NOT NULL       PRIMARY KEY,
EMP_NAME        VARCHAR (40)    NOT NULL,
EMP_ST_ADDR     VARCHAR (20)    NOT NULL,
EMP_CITY        VARCHAR (15)    NOT NULL,
EMP_ST          VARCHAR (2)     NOT NULL,
EMP_ZIP         INTEGER(5)      NOT NULL,
EMP_PHONE       INTEGER(10)     NULL           UNIQUE,
EMP_PAGER       INTEGER(10)     NULL);
```

The primary key in this example is `EMP_ID`, meaning that the employee identification number is the column ensuring that every record in the table is unique. The primary key is a column that is normally referenced in queries, particularly to join tables. The column `EMP_PHONE` has been designated as a `UNIQUE` value, meaning that no two employees can have the same telephone number. There is not a lot of difference between the two, except that the primary key provides an order to data in a table and, in the same respect, joins related tables.

Foreign Key Constraints

A *foreign key* is a column in a child table that references a primary key in the parent table. A *foreign key constraint* is the main mechanism that enforces referential integrity between tables in a relational database. A column defined as a foreign key references a column defined as a primary key in another table.

Study the creation of the foreign key in the following example:

```
CREATE TABLE EMPLOYEE_PAY_TST
(EMP_ID            VARCHAR (9)    NOT NULL,
POSITION          VARCHAR (15)   NOT NULL,
DATE_HIRE         DATE           NULL,
PAY_RATE          NUMBER(4,2)    NOT NULL,
DATE_LAST_RAISE   DATE           NULL,
CONSTRAINT EMP_ID_FK FOREIGN KEY (EMP_ID) REFERENCES EMPLOYEE_TBL (EMP_ID));
```

The `EMP_ID` column in this example has been designated as the foreign key for the `EMPLOYEE_PAY_TBL` table. This foreign key, as you can see, references the `EMP_ID` column in the `EMPLOYEE_TBL` table. This foreign key ensures that for every `EMP_ID` in the

EMPLOYEE_PAY_TBL, there is a corresponding EMP_ID in the EMPLOYEE_TBL. This is called a *parent/child relationship*. The parent table is the EMPLOYEE_TBL table, and the child table is the EMPLOYEE_PAY_TBL table. Study Figure 3.4 for a better understanding of the parent table/child table relationship.

FIGURE 3.4
The parent/child table relationship

In this figure, the EMP_ID column in the child table references the EMP_ID column in the parent table. For a value to be inserted for EMP_ID in the child table, a value for EMP_ID in the parent table must exist. Likewise, for a value to be removed for EMP_ID in the parent table, all corresponding first values for EMP_ID must be removed from the child table. This is how referential integrity works.

You can add a foreign key to a table using the ALTER TABLE command, as shown in the following example:

```
alter table employee_pay_tbl
add constraint id_fk foreign key (emp_id)
references employee_tbl (emp_id);
```

NOTE

ALTER TABLE Variations

The options available with the ALTER TABLE command differ among implementations of SQL, particularly when dealing with constraints. In addition, the actual use and definitions of constraints vary, but the concept of referential integrity should be the same with all relational databases.

NOT NULL Constraints

Previous examples use the keywords NULL and NOT NULL listed on the same line as each column and after the data type. NOT NULL is a constraint that you can place on a table's column. This constraint disallows the entrance of NULL values into a column; in other words, data is required in a NOT NULL column for each row of data in the table. NULL is generally the default for a column if NOT NULL is not specified, allowing NULL values in a column.

Check Constraints

You can utilize check (CHK) constraints to test the validity of data entered into particular table columns. Check constraints provide back-end database edits; although edits are commonly found in the front-end application as well. General edits restrict values that can be entered into columns or objects, whether within the database or on a front-end application. The check constraint is a way of providing another protective layer for the data.

The following example illustrates the use of a check constraint in Oracle:

```
CREATE TABLE EMPLOYEE_CHECK_TST
(EMP_ID          VARCHAR (9)     NOT NULL,
EMP_NAME         VARCHAR (40)    NOT NULL,
EMP_ST_ADDR      VARCHAR (20)    NOT NULL,
EMP_CITY         VARCHAR (15)    NOT NULL,
EMP_ST           VARCHAR (2)     NOT NULL,
EMP_ZIP          NUMBER(5)       NOT NULL,
EMP_PHONE        NUMBER(10)      NULL,
EMP_PAGER        NUMBER(10)      NULL,
PRIMARY KEY (EMP_ID),
CONSTRAINT CHK_EMP_ZIP CHECK ( EMP_ZIP = '46234'));
```

The check constraint in this table has been placed on the EMP_ZIP column, ensuring that all employees entered into this table have a ZIP code of '46234'. Perhaps that is a little restricting. Nevertheless, you can see how it works.

If you wanted to use a check constraint to verify that the ZIP code is within a list of values, your constraint definition could look like the following:

```
CONSTRAINT CHK_EMP_ZIP CHECK ( EMP_ZIP in ('46234','46227','46745') );
```

If there is a minimum pay rate that can be designated for an employee, you could have a constraint that looks like the following:

```
CREATE TABLE EMPLOYEE_PAY_TBL
(EMP_ID          VARCHAR (9)     NOT NULL,
POSITION         VARCHAR (15)    NOT NULL,
DATE_HIRE        DATE            NULL,
PAY_RATE         NUMBER(4,2)     NOT NULL,
```

```
DATE_LAST_RAISE    DATE          NULL,
CONSTRAINT  EMP_ID_FK FOREIGN KEY (EMP_ID) REFERENCES EMPLOYEE_TBL (EMP_ID),
CONSTRAINT CHK_PAY CHECK ( PAY_RATE > 12.50 ) );
```

In this example, any employee entered into this table must be paid more than $12.50 an hour. You can use just about any condition in a check constraint, as you can with an SQL query. You learn more about these conditions in Hours 5 and 7.

Dropping Constraints

Using the ALTER TABLE command with the DROP CONSTRAINT option, you can drop any constraint that you have defined. For example, to drop the primary key constraint in the EMPLOYEES table, you can use the following command:

```
ALTER TABLE EMPLOYEES DROP CONSTRAINT EMPLOYEES_PK;

Table altered.
```

Some implementations provide shortcuts for dropping certain constraints. For example, to drop the primary key constraint for a table in MySQL, you can use the following command:

```
ALTER TABLE EMPLOYEES DROP PRIMARY KEY;

Table altered.
```

TIP

Other Ways of Dealing with Constraints

Instead of permanently dropping a constraint from the database, some implementations allow you to temporarily disable constraints and then enable them later.

Summary

You have learned a little about database objects in general, but you have specifically learned about tables. The table is the simplest form of data storage in a relational database. Tables contain groups of logical information, such as employee, customer, or product information. A table is composed of various columns, with each column having attributes; those attributes mainly consist of data types and constraints, such as NOT NULL values, primary keys, foreign keys, and unique values.

You learned about the CREATE TABLE command and options, such as storage parameters, that might be available with this command. You also learned how to modify the structure of existing tables using the ALTER TABLE command. Although the process of managing database tables might not be the most basic process in SQL, if you first learn the structure and nature of tables, you will more easily grasp the concept of accessing the tables, whether through data manipulation operations or database queries. In later hours, you learn about the management of other objects in SQL, such as indexes on tables and views.

Q&A

Q. When I name a table that I am creating, is it necessary to use a suffix such as _TBL?

A. Absolutely not. You do not have to use anything. For example, a table that holds employee information could be named something similar to the following, or anything else that would refer to what type of data is to be stored in that particular table:

```
EMPLOYEE
EMP_TBL
EMPLOYEE_TBL
EMPLOYEE_TABLE
WORKER
```

Q. Why is it so important to use the schema name when dropping a table?

A. Here's a true story about a new DBA who dropped a table. A programmer had created a table under his schema with the same name as a production table. That particular programmer left the company. His database account was being deleted from the database, but the DROP USER statement returned an error because he owned outstanding objects. After some investigation, it was determined that his table was not needed, so a DROP TABLE statement was issued.

It worked like a charm, but the problem was that the DBA was logged in as the production schema when the DROP TABLE statement was issued. The DBA should have specified a schema name, or owner, for the table to be dropped. Yes, the wrong table in the wrong schema was dropped. It took approximately 8 hours to restore the production database.

Workshop

The following workshop is composed of a series of quiz questions and practical exercises. The quiz questions are designed to test your overall understanding of the current material. The practical exercises are intended to afford you the opportunity to apply the concepts discussed during the current hour, as well as build upon the knowledge acquired in previous hours of study. Please take time to complete the quiz questions and exercises before continuing. Refer to Appendix C, "Answers to Quizzes and Exercises," for answers.

Quiz

1. Does the following CREATE TABLE statement work? If not, what needs to be done to correct the problem(s)? Are there limitations as to what database implementation it works in (MySQL, Oracle, or SQL Server)?

```
Create table EMPLOYEE_TABLE as:
    ( ssn              number(9)      not null,
      last_name        varchar(20)    not null,
      first_name       varchar(20)    not null,
      middle_name      varchar(20)    not null,
      st address       varchar(30)    not null,
      city             varchar(20)    not null,
      state            varchar(2)     not null,
      zip              number(4)      not null,
      date hired       date);
```

2. Can you drop a column from a table?

3. What statement would you issue to create a primary key constraint on the preceding EMPLOYEE_TABLE?

4. What statement would you issue on the preceding EMPLOYEE_TABLE to allow the MIDDLE_NAME column to accept NULL values?

5. What statement would you use to restrict the people added into the preceding EMPLOYEE_TABLE to reside only in the state of New York ('NY')?

6. What statement would you use to add an auto-incrementing column called EMPID to the preceding EMPLOYEE_TABLE using both the MySQL and SQL Server syntax?

Exercises

In this exercise, you create all the tables in the database to set up the environment for later. In addition, you execute several commands that allow you to investigate the table structure in an existing database. For thoroughness we have provided instructions for each of the implementations (Microsoft SQL Server and Oracle) because each is slightly different in its approach.

Microsoft SQL Server

Bring up a command prompt and use the following syntax to log on to your local SQL Server instance, replacing username with your username and password with your password. Ensure that you do not leave a space between -p and your password.

```
SQLCMD  -S localhost -U username  -Ppassword
```

At the 1> command prompt, enter the following command to tell SQL Server that you want to use the database you created previously. Remember that with SQLCMD you must use the keyword GO to tell the command tool that you want the previous lines to execute.

```
1>use learnsql;
2>GO
```

Now go to Appendix D, "Bonus Exercises," to get the DDL for the tables used in this book. At the 1> prompt, enter each CREATE TABLE statement. Be sure to include a semicolon at the end of each CREATE TABLE statement and follow up with the keyword GO to have your statement execute. The tables that you create are used throughout the book.

At the `1>` prompt, enter the following command to get a list of your tables. Follow this command with the keyword `GO`:

```
Select name from sys.tables;
```

At the `1>` prompt, use the `sp_help` stored procedure to list the columns and their attributes for each one of the tables you created. For example:

```
Sp_help_ trips;
Sp_help flights;
```

If you have errors or typos, simply re-create the appropriate table(s). If the table was successfully created but has typos (perhaps you did not properly define a column or forgot a column), drop the table and issue the `CREATE TABLE` command again. The syntax of the `DROP TABLE` command follows:

```
drop table flights;
```

Oracle

Bring up a command prompt, and use the following syntax to log on to your local Oracle instance. You are prompted to enter your username and password.

```
sqlplus
```

Now go to Appendix D to get the DDL for the tables used in this book. At the `SQL>` prompt, enter each `CREATE TABLE` statement. Be sure to include a semicolon at the end of each `CREATE TABLE` statement. The tables that you create are used throughout the book.

At the `SQL>` prompt, enter the following command to get a list of your tables:

```
Select * from cat;
```

If all tables were successfully created, you should see the following output:

```
SQL> SELECT * FROM CAT;

TABLE_NAME                        TABLE_TYPE
------------------------------    -----------
TRIPS                             TABLE
TRIPITINERARY                     TABLE
ROUTES                            TABLE
RICH_EMPLOYEES                    TABLE
PASSENGERS                        TABLE
HIGH_SALARIES                     TABLE
FLIGHTSTATUSES                    TABLE
FLIGHTS                           TABLE
EMPLOYEE_MGR                      TABLE
EMPLOYEES                         TABLE
EMPLOYEEPOSITIONS                 TABLE
COUNTRIES                         TABLE
```

```
AIRPORTS                     TABLE
AIRCRAFTFLEET                TABLE
AIRCRAFT                     TABLE
```

15 rows selected.

At the SQL> prompt, use the DESCRIBE command (desc for short) to list the columns and their attributes for each one of the tables you created. For example:

DESCRIBE FLIGHTS;

returns the following output:

```
Name                                    Null?     Type
--------------------------------------- --------- ----------------------------
FLIGHTID                                NOT NULL  NUMBER(10)
FLIGHTSTART                                       DATE
FLIGHTEND                                         DATE
FLIGHTDURATION                                    NUMBER(5)
ROUTEID                                           NUMBER(10)
AIRCRAFTFLEETID                                   NUMBER(10)
STATUSCODE                                        CHAR(3 CHAR)
```

If you have errors or typos, simply re-create the appropriate table(s). If the table was successfully created but has typos (perhaps you did not properly define a column or forgot a column), drop the table, and issue the CREATE TABLE command again. The syntax of the DROP TABLE command follows:

DROP TABLE FLIGHTS;

The Normalization Process

What You'll Learn in This Hour:

▶ Definition of normalization
▶ Benefits of normalization
▶ Advantages of denormalization
▶ Normalization techniques
▶ Guidelines of normalization
▶ The three normal forms
▶ Database design

In this hour, you learn the process of taking a raw database and breaking it into a logical table structure. This process is referred to as normalization. The normalization process is used by database developers to design databases in which it is easy to organize and manage data while ensuring the accuracy of data throughout the database. The great thing is that the process is the same regardless of which *relational database management system (RDBMS)* you use.

The advantages and disadvantages of both normalization and denormalization of a database are discussed in this hour, as well as data integrity versus performance issues that pertain to normalization.

Normalizing a Database

Normalization is a process of reducing redundancies of data in a database. A technique that is used when designing and redesigning a database, normalization optimally designs a database to reduce redundant data. The actual guidelines of normalization, called *normal forms*, are discussed later in this hour. It was a difficult decision to cover normalization in this book because of the complexity involved. Understanding the rules of the normal forms can be difficult this early in your SQL journey. However, normalization is an important process that, if understood, increases your understanding of SQL.

The Raw Database

A database that is not normalized might include data that is contained in one or more tables for no apparent reason. This could be bad for security reasons, disk space usage, speed of queries, efficiency of database updates, and, maybe most important, data integrity. A database before normalization is one that has not been broken down logically into smaller, more manageable tables. Figure 4.1 illustrate an example of a much simpler database than is used in this book before it was normalized.

COMPANY_DATABASE	
emp_id	cust_id
last_name	cust_name
first_name	cust_address
middle_name	cust_city
address	cust_state
city	cust_zip
state	cust_phone
zip	cust_fax
phone	ord_num
pager	qty
position	ord_date
date_hire	prod_id
pay_rate	prod_desc
bonus	cost
date_last_raise	

FIGURE 4.1
The raw database

Determining the set of information that the raw database consists of is one of the first and most important steps in logical database design. You must know all the data elements that comprise your database to effectively apply the techniques discussed in this hour. Taking the time to perform the due diligence of gathering the set of required data keeps you from having to backtrack your database design scheme because of missing data elements.

Logical Database Design

Any database should be designed with the end user in mind. Logical database design, also referred to as the *logical model*, is the process of arranging data into logical, organized groups of objects that can easily be maintained. The logical design of a database should reduce data repetition or go so far as to completely eliminate it. After all, why store the same data twice? In addition, the logical database design should strive to make the database easy to maintain and update. Naming conventions used in a database should also be standard and logical to aid in this endeavor.

The End User's Needs

The needs of the end user should be one of the top considerations when designing a database. Remember that the end user is the person who ultimately uses the database. There should be ease of use through the user's *front-end tool* (a client program that enables a user access to a database), but this, along with optimal performance, cannot be achieved if the user's needs are not considered.

Some user-related design considerations include the following:

- ▶ What data should be stored in the database?

- ▶ How does the user access the database?

- ▶ What privileges does the user require?

- ▶ How should the data be grouped in the database?

- ▶ What data is the most commonly accessed?

- ▶ How is all data related in the database?

- ▶ What measures should be taken to ensure accurate data?

- ▶ What measures can be taken to reduce redundancy of data?

- ▶ What measures can be taken to ensure ease of use for the end user who is maintaining the data?

Data Redundancy

Data should not be redundant; the duplication of data should be kept to a minimum for several reasons. For example, it is unnecessary to store an employee's home address in more than one table. With duplicate data, unnecessary space is used. Confusion is always a threat when, for instance, an address for an employee in one table does not match the address for the same employee in another table. Which table is correct? Do you have documentation to verify the employee's current address? As if data management were not difficult enough, redundancy of data could prove to be a disaster.

Reducing redundancy also ensures that updating the data within the database is relatively simple. If you have a single table for the employees' addresses and you update that table with new addresses, you can rest assured that it is updated for everyone who is viewing the data.

Normal Forms

The next sections discuss normal forms, an integral concept involved in the process of database normalization.

Normal form is a way of measuring the levels, or depth, to which a database has been normalized. A database's level of normalization is determined by the normal form.

The following are the three most common normal forms in the normalization process:

▶ The first normal form

▶ The second normal form

▶ The third normal form

There are normal forms beyond these, but they are used far less often than the three major ones noted here. Of the three major normal forms, each subsequent normal form depends on normalization steps taken in the previous normal form. For example, to normalize a database using the second normal form, the database must be in the first normal form.

First Normal Form

The objective of the first normal form is to divide the base data into tables. When each table has been designed, a primary key is assigned to most or all tables. Remember from Hour 3, "Managing Database Objects," that your primary key must be a unique value, so try to select a data element for the primary key that naturally uniquely identifies a specific piece of data. Examine Figure 4.2, which illustrates how the raw database shown in Figure 4.1 has been redeveloped using the first normal form.

You can see that to achieve the first normal form, data had to be broken into logical units of related information, each having a primary key and ensuring that there are no repeated groups in any of the tables. Instead of one large table, there are now smaller, more manageable tables: EMPLOYEE_TBL, CUSTOMER_TBL, and PRODUCTS_TBL. The primary keys are normally the first columns listed in a table; in this case, EMP_ID, CUST_ID, and PROD_ID. This is a normal convention that you should use when diagramming your database to ensure that it is easily readable.

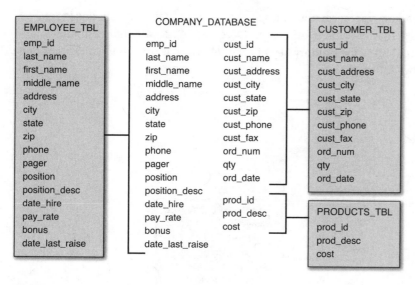

FIGURE 4.2
The first normal form

However, your primary key could also be made up of more than one of the columns in the data set. Often, these values are not simple database-generated numbers but logical points of data such as a product's name or a book's ISBN. These are commonly referred to as natural keys because they would uniquely define a specific object regardless of whether it was in a database. The main thing that you need to remember in picking out your primary key for a table is that it must uniquely identify a single row. Without this, you introduce the possibility of adding duplication into your results of queries and prevent yourself from doing even simple things such as removing a particular row of data based solely on the key.

Second Normal Form

The objective of the second normal form is to take data that is only partly dependent on the primary key and enter that data into another table. Figure 4.3 illustrates the second normal form.

As shown in the figure, the second normal form is derived from the first normal form by further breaking two tables into more specific units.

EMPLOYEE_TBL is split into two tables called EMPLOYEE_TBL and EMPLOYEE_PAY_TBL. Personal employee information is dependent on the primary key (EMP_ID) so that information remained in the EMPLOYEE_TBL (EMP_ID, LAST_NAME, FIRST_NAME, MIDDLE_NAME, ADDRESS, CITY, STATE, ZIP, PHONE, and PAGER). However, the information that is only partly dependent on the EMP_ID (each individual employee) populates EMPLOYEE_PAY_TBL (EMP_ID, POSITION, POSITION_DESC, DATE_HIRE, PAY_RATE, and DATE_LAST_RAISE). Notice that both tables contain the column EMP_ID. This is the primary key of each table and is used to match corresponding data between the two tables.

FIRST NORMAL FORM   SECOND NORMAL FORM

FIGURE 4.3
The second normal form

CUSTOMER_TBL is split into two tables called CUSTOMER_TBL and ORDERS_TBL. What took place is similar to what occurred in the EMPLOYEE_TBL. Columns that were partly dependent on the primary key were directed to another table. The order of the information for a customer depends on each CUST_ID but does not directly depend on the general customer information in the original table.

Third Normal Form

The third normal form's objective is to remove data from a table that is not dependent on the primary key. Figure 4.4 illustrates the third normal form.

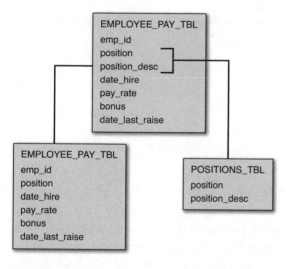

FIGURE 4.4
The third normal form

Another table was created to display the use of the third normal form. EMPLOYEE_PAY_TBL is split into two tables: one table containing the actual employee pay information and the other containing the position descriptions, which do not need to reside in EMPLOYEE_PAY_TBL. The POSITION_DESC column is totally independent of the primary key, EMP_ID. As you can see, the normalization process is a series of steps that breaks down the data from your raw database into discrete tables of related data.

Naming Conventions

Naming conventions are one of the foremost considerations when you normalize a database. Names are how you refer to objects in the database. You want to give your tables names that are descriptive of the type of information they contain so that the data you look for is easy to find. Descriptive table names are especially important for users who had no part in the database design but who need to query the database.

Companies should have a company-wide naming convention to provide guidance in the naming of not only tables within the database, but also users, filenames, and other related objects. Naming conventions also help in database administration by making it easier to discern the purpose of tables and locations of files within a database system. Designing and enforcing naming conventions is one of a company's first steps toward a successful database implementation.

Benefits of Normalization

Normalization provides numerous benefits to a database. Some of the major benefits include the following:

- ▶ Greater overall database organization

- ▶ Reduction of redundant data

- ▶ Data consistency within the database

- ▶ A much more flexible database design

- ▶ A better handle on database security

- ▶ Reinforcement of the concept of referential integrity

Organization is brought about by the normalization process, making everyone's job easier, from the user who accesses tables to the *database administrator (DBA)* who is responsible for the overall management of every object in the database. Data redundancy is reduced, which simplifies data structures and conserves disk space. Because duplicate data is minimized, the possibility of inconsistent data is greatly reduced. For example, in one table an individual's name could read STEVE SMITH, whereas the name of the same individual might read STEPHEN R. SMITH in another table. Reducing duplicate data increases *data integrity*, or the assurance of consistent and accurate data within a database. Because the database has been normalized and broken into smaller tables, you have more flexibility in modifying existing structures. It is much easier to modify a small table with little data than to modify one big table that holds all the vital data in the database. Lastly, security is provided in the sense that the DBA can grant access to a limited number of tables to certain users. Security is easier to control when normalization has occurred because data has been grouped into neatly organized sets.

Referential integrity simply means that the values of one column in a table depend on the values of a column in another table. For instance, for a trip to have a record in the TRIPS table, there must first be a record for a passenger that is going to take the trip in the PASSENGERS table. Integrity constraints can also control values by restricting a range of values for a column. For example, if a passenger's date of birth is required for travel, then we would need to ensure that it always contains a valid value. Referential integrity is typically controlled through the use of primary and foreign keys. The integrity constraint should be created at the table's creation so that you can be confident that all the data entered into a table is consistent. Otherwise, constraints placed on a table after creation and load of data may require a data cleanup operation.

In a table, a foreign key, normally a *single field*, directly references a primary key in another table to enforce referential integrity. In the preceding paragraph, the PASSENGERID in TRIPS is a foreign key that references PASSENGERID in PASSENGER. Normalization helps to enhance and enforce these constraints by logically breaking down data into subsets that are referenced by a primary key.

Drawbacks of Normalization

Although most successful databases are normalized to some degree, there is one substantial drawback of a normalized database: reduced database performance. The acceptance of reduced performance requires the knowledge that when a query or transaction request is sent to the database, there are factors involved such as CPU usage, memory usage, and input/output (I/O). To make a long story short, a normalized database requires much more CPU, memory, and I/O to process transactions and database queries than a denormalized database. A normalized database must locate the requested tables and then join the data from the tables to either get the requested information or to process the wanted data. A more in-depth discussion concerning database performance occurs in Hour 18, "Managing Database Users."

Denormalizing a Database

Denormalization is the process of taking a normalized database and modifying table structures to allow controlled redundancy for increased database performance. Attempting to improve performance is the only reason to denormalize a database. A denormalized database is not the same as a database that has not been normalized. Denormalizing a database is the process of taking the level of normalization within the database down a notch or two. Remember, normalization can actually slow performance with its frequently occurring table join operations. (Table joins are discussed during Hour 13, "Joining Tables in Queries.")

Denormalization might involve recombining separate tables or creating duplicate data within tables to reduce the number of tables that need to be joined to retrieve the requested data, which results in less I/O and CPU time. This is normally advantageous in larger data warehousing applications in which aggregate calculations are made across millions of rows of data within tables.

There are costs to denormalization, however. Data redundancy is increased in a denormalized database, which can improve performance but requires more extraneous efforts to keep track of related data. Application coding renders more complications because the data has been spread across various tables and might be more difficult to locate. In addition, referential integrity is more of a chore; related data has been divided among a number of tables.

There is a happy medium in both normalization and denormalization, but both require a thorough knowledge of the actual data and the specific business requirements of the pertinent company. If you do look at denormalizing parts of your database structure, carefully document the process so that you can see exactly how you are handling issues such as redundancy to maintain data integrity within your systems.

Summary

A difficult decision has to be made concerning database design: to normalize or not to normalize. You always want to normalize a database to some degree. How much do you normalize a database without destroying performance? The real decision relies on the application. How large is the database? What is its purpose? What types of users are going to access the data? This hour covered the three most common normal forms, the concepts behind the normalization process, and the integrity of data. The normalization process involves many steps, most of which are optional but vital to the functionality and performance of your database. Regardless of how deep you decide to normalize, there is almost always a trade-off, either between simple maintenance and questionable performance or complicated maintenance and better performance. In the end, the individual (or team of individuals) designing the database must decide, and that person or team is responsible.

Q&A

Q. Why should I be so concerned with the end users' needs when designing the database?

A. The end users are the actual data experts who use the database, and, in that respect, they should be the focus of any database design effort. The database designer only helps organize the data.

Q. Is normalization more advantageous than denormalization?

A. It can be more advantageous. However, denormalization, to a point, could be more advantageous. Remember, many factors help determine which way to go. You will probably normalize your database to reduce repetition in the database, but you might denormalize to a certain extent to improve performance.

Workshop

The following workshop is composed of a series of quiz questions and practical exercises. The quiz questions are designed to test your overall understanding of the current material. The practical exercises are intended to afford you the opportunity to apply the concepts discussed during the current hour, as well as build upon the knowledge acquired in previous hours of study. Please take time to complete the quiz questions and exercises before continuing. Refer to Appendix C, "Answers to Quizzes and Exercises," for answers.

Quiz

1. True or false: Normalization is the process of grouping data into logical related groups.

2. True or false: Having no duplicate or redundant data in a database and having everything in the database normalized is always the best way to go.

3. True or false: If data is in the third normal form, it is automatically in the first and second normal forms.

4. What is a major advantage of a denormalized database versus a normalized database?

5. What are some major disadvantages of denormalization?

6. How do you determine if data needs to be moved to a separate table when normalizing your database?

7. What are the disadvantages of over-normalizing your database design?

Exercises

1. You are developing a new database for a small company. Take the following data and normalize it. Keep in mind that there would be many more items for a small company than you are given here.

Employees:

Angela Smith, secretary, 317-545-6789, RR 1 Box 73, Greensburg, Indiana, 47890, $9.50 per hour, date started January 22, 2006, SSN is 323149669.

Jack Lee Nelson, salesman, 3334 N. Main St., Brownsburg, IN, 45687, 317-852-9901, salary of $35,000.00 per year, SSN is 312567342, date started 10/28/2005.

Customers:

Robert's Games and Things, 5612 Lafayette Rd., Indianapolis, IN, 46224, 317-291-7888, customer ID is 432A.

Reed's Dairy Bar, 4556 W 10th St., Indianapolis, IN, 46245, 317-271-9823, customer ID is 117A.

Customer Orders:

Customer ID is 117A, date of last order is December 20, 2009, the product ordered was napkins, and the product ID is 661.

2. Log in to your new database instance just as you did in Hour 3. Ensure that you are in the `CanaryAirlines` database by using the following statement:

```
USE CanaryAirlines;
```

In Oracle this is known as a schema; by default you create items in your user schema when you use Oracle.

Now that you are in the database, run the following select statements to look at the data in the tables `FLIGHTS`, `AIRCRAFTFLEET`, `AIRCRAFT`, and `FLIGHTSTATUSES`. How can you denormalize these into a single table?

```
SELECT * FROM FLIGHTS;
SELECT * FROM FLIGHTSTATUSES;
SELECT * FROM AIRCRAFTFLEET;
SELECT * FROM AIRCRAFT;
```

Manipulating Data

What You'll Learn in This Hour:

▶ An overview of DML

▶ Instruction on how to manipulate data in tables

▶ Concepts behind table population of data

▶ How to delete data from tables

▶ How to change or modify data in tables

In this hour, you learn the piece of SQL known as *Data Manipulation Language (DML)*. You use DML to change data and tables in a relational database.

Overview of Data Manipulation

DML is the part of SQL that enables a database user to actually propagate changes among data in a relational database. With DML, the user can populate tables with new data, update existing data in tables, and delete data from tables. Simple database queries can also be performed within a DML command.

The three basic DML commands in SQL are:

▶ INSERT

▶ UPDATE

▶ DELETE

The SELECT command, which can be used with DML commands, is discussed in more detail in Hour 7, "Introduction to Database Queries." The SELECT command is the basic query command that you can use after you enter data into the database with the INSERT command. So in this hour we concentrate on getting the data into our tables so that we have something interesting to use the SELECT command on.

Populating Tables with New Data

Populating a table with data is simply the process of entering new data into a table, whether through a manual process using individual commands or through batch processes using programs or other related software. *Manual population of data* refers to data entry via a keyboard. *Automated population* normally deals with obtaining data from an external data source (such as another database or possibly a flat file) and loading the obtained data into the database.

Many factors can affect what data and how much data can be put into a table when populating tables with data. Some major factors include existing table constraints, the physical table size, column data types, the length of columns, and other integrity constraints, such as primary and foreign keys. The following sections help you learn the basics of inserting new data into a table, in addition to offering some Do's and Don'ts.

Inserting Data into a Table

Use the INSERT statement to insert new data into a table. There are a few options with the INSERT statement; look at the following basic syntax to begin:

```
INSERT INTO TABLE_NAME
VALUES ('value1', 'value2', [ NULL ] );
```

CAUTION

Data Is Case-Sensitive

Do not forget that SQL statements can be in uppercase or lowercase. However, data is sometimes case-sensitive. For example, if you enter data into the database as uppercase, depending on your database you might have to reference that data in uppercase. These examples use both lowercase and uppercase statements just to show that it does not affect the outcome.

Using this INSERT statement syntax, you must include every column in the specified table in the VALUES list. Notice that each value in this list is separated by a comma. Enclose the values inserted into the table by single quotation marks for character and date/time data types. Single quotation marks are not required for numeric data types or NULL values using the NULL keyword. A value should be present for each column in the table, and those values must be in the same order as the columns are listed in the table. In later sections, you learn how to specify the column ordering, but for now just know that the SQL engine you are working with assumes that you want to enter the data in the same order in which the columns were created.

In the following example, you insert a new record into the COUNTRIES table.

Here is the table structure:

```
Countries
COLUMN Name                          Null?      DATA Type
------------------------------------------------------
CountryCode                          NOT NULL CHAR(3)
Country                              NOT NULL VARCHAR(50)
CountryGeoCodeID                     NOT NULL VARCHAR(100)
WorldAreaCode                        NOT NULL INT
```

Here is the sample INSERT statement:

```
INSERT INTO Countries
VALUES ('UTO','Utopia', '11111',0);
1 row created.
```

In this example, four values were inserted into a table with four columns. The inserted values are in the same order as the columns listed in the table. The first three values are inserted using single quotation marks because the data types of the corresponding columns are character data types. The fourth value's associated column, WORLDAREACODE, is a numeric data type and does not require quotation marks; although you can use them without fear of affecting the outcome of the statement.

NOTE
_____

When to Use Quotation Marks

Although single quotation marks are not required around numeric data that is inserted, they may be used with any data type. Said another way, single quotation marks are optional when referring to numeric data values in the database, but they are required for all other data values (data types). Although usually a matter of preference, most SQL users choose not to use quotation marks with numeric values because their queries are more readable without them.

_____

Inserting Data into Limited Columns of a Table

There is a way you can insert data into specified columns. For instance, suppose you want to insert all values for a passenger. In this case, the first column PASSENGERID is referred to as an identity or auto incrementing column. This means that the value is a numeric number that will increment on its own (for example, 1, 2, 3, ...). You must, in this case, leave out the PASSENGERID column by specifying a column list as well as a VALUES list in your INSERT statement:

```
INSERT INTO PASSENGERS
(FIRSTNAME, LASTNAME, BIRTHDATE, COUNTRYCODE)
VALUES
('John', 'Doe', '1990-10-12', 'US');
1 row created.
```

The syntax for inserting values into a limited number of columns in a table follows:

```
INSERT INTO TABLE_NAME ('COLUMN1', 'COLUMN2')
VALUES ('VALUE1', 'VALUE2');
```

You use `AIRCRAFT` and insert values into only specified columns in the following example.

Here is the table structure:

```
AIRCRAFT
COLUMN NAME                          Null?     DATA TYPE
-----------------------------------------------------------
AIRCRAFTCODE                         NULL      VARCHAR(3)
AIRCRAFTTYPE                         NULL      VARCHAR(75)
FREIGHTONLY                          NULL      VARCHAR2(10)
SEATING                              NULL      NUMERIC(18,0)
```

Here is the sample `INSERT` statement:

```
INSERT INTO AIRCRAFT(AIRCRAFTCODE, AIRCRAFTTYPE, FREIGHTONLY)
VALUES('AAA','Big Boeing',0);
1 row created.
```

You have specified a column list enclosed by parentheses after the table name in the `INSERT` statement. You have listed all columns into which you want to insert data. `SEATING` is the only excluded column. If you look at the table definition, you can see that `SEATING` does not require data for every record in the table. You know that `SEATING` does not require data because `NULL` is specified in the table definition. `NULL` tells us that `NULL` values are allowed in the column. Furthermore, the list of values must appear in the same order as the column list.

TIP

Column List Ordering Can Differ

The column list in the `INSERT` statement does not have to reflect the same order of columns as in the definition of the associated table, but the list of values must be in the order of the associated columns in the column list. In addition, you can leave off the `NULL` syntax for a column because the defaults for most RDBMSs specify that columns allow `NULL` values.

Inserting Data from Another Table

You can insert data into a table based on the results of a query from another table using a combination of the `INSERT` statement and the `SELECT` statement. Briefly, a *query* is an inquiry to the database that either expects or does not expect data to be returned. See Hour 7 for more information on queries. A query is a question that the user asks the database, and the data returned is the answer. When combining the `INSERT` statement with the `SELECT` statement, you can insert the data retrieved from a query into a table.

The syntax for inserting data from another table is

```
insert into table_name [('column1', 'column2')]
select [*|('column1', 'column2')]
from table_name
[where condition(s)];
```

You see three new keywords in this syntax, which are covered here briefly. These keywords are SELECT, FROM, and WHERE. SELECT is the main command used to initiate a query in SQL. FROM is a clause in the query that specifies the names of tables in which the target data should be found. The WHERE clause, also part of the query, places conditions on the query. A *condition* is a way of placing criteria on data affected by a SQL statement. A sample condition might state this: WHERE LASTNAME = 'SMITH'. These three keywords are covered extensively during Hour 7 and Hour 8, "Using Operators to Categorize Data."

The following example uses a simple query to view all data in the FLIGHTSTATUSES table. SELECT * tells the database server that you want information on all columns of the table. Because no WHERE clause is used, you see all records in the table as well.

```
SELECT * FROM FLIGHTSTATUSES;

StatusCode StatusName
---------- -----------------------------------------------------
CAN        Cancelled
COM        Completed
DEL        Delayed
ONT        On-Time

(4 row(s) affected)
```

Now insert values into the STATUSES_TMP table based on the preceding query. For this we use a special SELECT statement that uses the INTO clause to push those rows into a new table. You can see that four rows are created in the temporary table:

```
SELECT * INTO STATUSES_TMP
FROM FLIGHTSTATUSES;

(4 rows(s) affected)
```

You must ensure that the columns returned from the SELECT query are in the same order as the columns that you have in your table or INSERT statement. In addition, double-check that the data from the SELECT query is compatible with the data type of the column that it is inserting into the table. For example, trying to insert a VARCHAR field with 'ABC' into a numeric column would cause your statement to fail.

The following query shows all data in the STATUSES_TMP table that you just inserted:

```
SELECT * FROM STATUSES_TMP;

StatusCode StatusName
---------- -------------------------------------------------
CAN        Cancelled
COM        Completed
DEL        Delayed
ONT        On-Time

(4 row(s) affected)
```

Inserting NULL Values

Inserting a NULL value into a column of a table is a simple matter. You might want to insert a NULL value into a column if the value of the column in question is unknown. For instance, not every trip at an airport would have a return flight, so it would be inaccurate to enter an erroneous return flight number—not to mention, you would not be efficiently budgeting space. You can insert a NULL value into a column of a table using the keyword NULL.

The syntax for inserting a NULL value follows:

```
insert into schema.table_name values
('column1', NULL, 'column3');
```

Use the NULL keyword in the proper sequence of the associated column that exists in the table. That column does not have data in it for that row if you enter NULL. In the syntax, a NULL value is entered in the place of COLUMN2.

Study the two following examples.

In this first example, all columns in which to insert values are listed, which also happen to be every column in the AIRCRAFT table:

```
INSERT INTO AIRCRAFT(AIRCRAFTCODE, AIRCRAFTTYPE, FREIGHTONLY, SEATING)
VALUES('BBB','Boeing',0,NULL);
  (1 row(s) affected)
```

You inserted a NULL value for the SEATING column, meaning that you either do not know the seating capacity, or there is no information at this time.

Now look at the second example:

```
INSERT INTO AIRCRAFT
VALUES('CCC','Boeing',0, NULL);
  (1 row(s) affected)
```

This example contains a slight difference from the first statement. There is not a column list. A column list is not required if you insert data into all columns of a table. Remember that a NULL value signifies an absence of value from a field and is different from an empty string.

Lastly, consider an example in which our FLIGHTSTATUSES table allowed NULL values and you wanted to insert values into the STATUSES_TMP table using it:

```
INSERT INTO FLIGHSTATUSES(STATUSCODE, STATUSNAME)
VALUES('UNK',NULL);

(1 row(s) affected)

SELECT * FROM FLIGHTSTATUSES ;
StatusCode StatusName
---------- --------------------------------------------------
CAN        Cancelled
COM        Completed
DEL        Delayed
ONT        On-Time
UNK        NULL

(5 row(s) affected)



SELECT * INTO STATUSES_TMP;

(5 row(s) affected)
```

In this case the NULL values would be inserted without intervention needed on your part as long as the column that the data is inserted into allows NULL values. Later this book addresses the need to specify a DEFAULT value for a column that allows you to automatically substitute a value for any NULLs that are inserted.

Updating Existing Data

You can modify pre-existing data in a table using the UPDATE command. This command does not add new records to a table, nor does it remove records—UPDATE simply updates existing data. The update is generally used to update one table at a time in a database, but you can use it to update multiple columns of a table at the same time. An individual row of data in a table can be updated, or numerous rows of data can be updated in a single statement, depending on what's needed.

Updating the Value of a Single Column

The simplest use of the UPDATE statement is to update a single column in a table. Either a single row of data or numerous records can be updated when updating a single column in a table.

The syntax for updating a single column follows:

```
update table_name
set column_name = 'value'
[where condition];
```

The following example updates the QTY column in the ORDERS_TBL table to the new value 1 for the ORD_NUM 23A16, which you have specified using the WHERE clause:

```
UPDATE AIRCRAFT
SET SEATING = 105
WHERE AIRCRAFTCODE = 'BBB';
```

```
(1 row(s) affected)
```

The following example is identical to the previous example, except for the absence of the WHERE clause. (Do not run this.)

```
UPDATE AIRCRAFT
SET SEATING = 105;
```

```
(40 row(s) affected)
```

Notice that in this example, 40 rows of data were updated. You set the SEATING to 105, which updated the seating column in the AIRCRAFT table for all rows of data. Is this actually what you wanted to do? Perhaps in some cases, but rarely do you issue an UPDATE statement without a WHERE clause. An easy way to check to see whether you are going to be updating the correct data-set is to write a SELECT statement for the same table with your WHERE clause that you are using in the INSERT statement. Then you can physically verify that these are the rows you want to update.

CAUTION

Test Your UPDATE and DELETE Statements

Use extreme caution when using the UPDATE statement without a WHERE clause. The target column is updated for all rows of data in the table if conditions are not designated using the WHERE clause. In most situations, the use of the WHERE clause with a DML command is appropriate.

Updating Multiple Columns in One or More Records

Next, you see how to update multiple columns with a single UPDATE statement. Study the following syntax:

```
update table_name
set column1 = 'value',
   [column2 = 'value',]
   [column3 = 'value']
[where condition];
```

Notice the use of SET in this syntax—there is only one SET, but multiple columns. Each column is separated by a comma. You should start to see a trend in SQL. The comma usually separates different types of arguments in SQL statements. In the following code, a comma separates the two columns being updated. Again, the WHERE clause is optional, but it's usually necessary.

```
UPDATE AIRCRAFT
SET SEATING = 105,
    AIRCRAFTTYPE = 'AAA AIRCRAFT'
WHERE AIRCRAFTCODE = 'CCC';

(1 row(s) affected)
```

NOTE

When to Use the SET Keyword

The SET keyword is used only once for each UPDATE statement. If you want to update more than one column, use a comma to separate the columns to be updated.

Later in this book you learn how to write more complex statements through a construct known as a JOIN so that you can update values in one table using values from one or more outside tables.

Deleting Data from Tables

The DELETE command removes entire rows of data from a table. It does not remove values from specific columns; a full record, including all columns, is removed. Use the DELETE statement with caution.

To delete a single record or selected records from a table, use the DELETE statement with the following syntax:

```
delete from table_name
[where condition];

DELETE FROM AIRCRAFT
WHERE AIRCRAFTCODE = 'CCC';

(1 row(s) affected)
```

Notice the use of the WHERE clause. It is an essential part of the DELETE statement if you want to remove selected rows of data from a table. You rarely issue a DELETE statement without the use of the WHERE clause. If you do, your results are similar to the following example:

```
DELETE FROM AIRCRAFT;

(40 row(s) affected)
```

CAUTION
_____

Don't Omit the WHERE Clause

If the WHERE clause is omitted from the DELETE statement, all rows of data are deleted from the table. As a general rule, always use a WHERE clause with the DELETE statement. In addition, first test your WHERE clause with a SELECT statement.

Also, remember that the DELETE command might have a permanent effect on the database. Ideally, it should be possible to recover erroneously deleted data via a backup, but in some cases, it might be difficult or even impossible to recover data. If you cannot recover data, you must re-enter it into the database—trivial if dealing with only one row of data, but not so trivial if dealing with thousands of rows of data. Hence, the importance of the WHERE clause.

_____

The temporary table that was populated from the original table earlier in this hour can be useful for testing the DELETE and UPDATE commands before issuing them against the original table. Also, remember the technique discussed earlier when we talked about the UPDATE command. Write a SELECT statement using the same WHERE clause that you want to use for the DELETE statement. That way you can verify that the data being deleted is actually the data you want.

Summary

You have learned about the three basic commands in DML: the INSERT, UPDATE, and DELETE statements. As you have seen, data manipulation is a powerful part of SQL, allowing the database user to populate tables with new data, update existing data, and delete data.

An important lesson when updating or deleting data from tables in a database is sometimes learned when neglecting the use of the WHERE clause. Remember that the WHERE clause places conditions on a SQL statement—particularly in the case of UDPATE and DELETE operations, when you specify specific rows of data that are affected during a transaction. All target table data rows are affected if the WHERE clause is not used, which could be disastrous to the database. Protect your data, and be cautious during data manipulation operations.

Q&A

Q. With all the warnings about DELETE and UPDATE, I'm a little afraid to use them. If I accidentally update all the records in a table because I didn't use the WHERE clause, can I reverse the changes?

A. There is no reason to be afraid because there is not much you can do to the database that cannot be corrected; although considerable time and work might be involved. Hour 6, "Managing Database Transactions," discusses the concept of transactional control, which allows data manipulation operations to be finalized or undone.

Q. Is the INSERT statement the only way to enter data into a table?

A. No, but remember that the INSERT statement is an ANSI standard. The various implementations have their tools to enter data into tables. For example, Oracle has a SQL*Loader utility, whereas SQL Server has a SQL Server Integration Services (SSIS) utility. Many other implementations have IMPORT utilities called that can insert data.

Workshop

The following workshop is composed of a series of quiz questions and practical exercises. The quiz questions are designed to test your overall understanding of the current material. The practical exercises are intended to afford you the opportunity to apply the concepts discussed during the current hour, as well as build upon the knowledge acquired in previous hours of study. Please take time to complete the quiz questions and exercises before continuing. Refer to Appendix C, "Answers to Quizzes and Exercises," for answers.

Quiz

1. Do you always need to supply a column list for the table that you use an INSERT statement on?

2. What would you do if you did not want to enter in a value for one particular column?

3. Why is it important to use a WHERE clause with UPDATE and DELETE?

4. What would be an easy way to check that an UPDATE or DELETE will affect the rows that you want?

Exercises

1. Use an imaginary PASSENGER_TBL with the following structure:

```
Column          data type       (not)null
LAST_NAME       varchar2(20)     not null
FIRST_NAME      varchar2(20)     not null
SSN             char(9)          not null
PHONE           number(10)       null
```

Include the following data already in the table:

```
LAST_NAME     FIRST_NAME      SSN           PHONE
-----------   -------------   ---------     ----------
SMITH         JOHN            312456788     3174549923
ROBERTS       LISA            232118857     3175452321
SMITH         SUE             443221989     3178398712
PIERCE        BILLY           310239856     3176763990
```

What would happen if the following statements were run?

a. `INSERT INTO PASSENGER_TBL VALUES`
   `('JACKSON', 'STEVE', '313546078', '3178523443');`

b. `INSERT INTO PASSENGER_TBL VALUES`
   `('JACKSON', 'STEVE', '313546078', '3178523443');`

c. `INSERT INTO PASSENGER_TBL VALUES`
   `('MILLER', 'DANIEL', '230980012', NULL);`

d. `INSERT INTO PASSENGER_TBL VALUES`
   `('TAYLOR', NULL, '445761212', '3179221331');`

e. `DELETE FROM PASSENGER_TBL;`

f. `DELETE FROM PASSENGER_TBL`
   `WHERE LAST_NAME = 'SMITH';`

g. `DELETE FROM PASSENGER_TBL`
   `WHERE LAST_NAME = 'SMITH'`
   `AND FIRST_NAME = 'JOHN';`

h. `UPDATE PASSENGER_TBL`
   `SET LAST_NAME = 'CONRAD';`

i. `UPDATE PASSENGER_TBL`
   `SET LAST_NAME = 'CONRAD'`
   `WHERE LAST_NAME = 'SMITH';`

j. `UPDATE PASSENGER_TBL`
   `SET LAST_NAME = 'CONRAD',`
   `FIRST_NAME = 'LARRY';`

k. `UPDATE PASSENGER_TBL`
   `SET LAST_NAME = 'CONRAD'`
   `FIRST_NAME = 'LARRY'`
   `WHERE SSN = '313546078';`

2. Use the `AIRCRAFT` table for this exercise.

Remove the two aircrafts that were added earlier in the chapter with the `AIRCRAFTCODE` of `'BBB'` and `'CCC'`.

Add the following products to the product table:

AIRCRAFTCODE	AIRCRAFTTYPE	FREIGHTONLY	SEATING
A11	Lockheed Superliner	0	600
B22	British Aerospace X11	0	350
C33	Boeing Freightmaster	1	0

Write DML to correct the seating associated with the Lockheed Superliner. The correct seating should be 500.

An error was made with C33; this should not have been labeled for `FREIGHTONLY` and should have a seating capacity of 25. Write the DML to correct this entry.

Now suppose you decide to cut your supported aircraft line. Remove the three products you just added.

Before you executed the statements to remove the products you added, what should you have done to ensure that you delete only the desired rows?

Managing Database Transactions

What You'll Learn in This Hour:

▶ The definition of a transaction

▶ The commands used to control transactions

▶ The syntax and examples of transaction commands

▶ When to use transactional commands

▶ The consequences of poor transactional control

In manipulating data inside of a database, so far we have discussed all-or-nothing scenarios. However, in more complicated processes you must have the ability to isolate changes so that they can be applied or rolled back to an original state at will. This is where transactions come in. Transactions give you the additional flexibility to isolate database changes into discrete batches and undo those changes if something goes wrong. In this hour, you learn the concepts behind the management of database transactions, how to implement them, and how to properly control transactions.

What Is a Transaction?

A *transaction* is a unit of work that is performed against a database. Transactions are units or sequences of work accomplished in a logical order, whether in a manual fashion by a user or automatically by some sort of a database program. In a relational database using SQL, transactions are accomplished using the *Data Manipulation Language (DML)* commands that were discussed during Hour 5, "Manipulating Data" (INSERT, UPDATE, and DELETE). A transaction is the propagation of one or more changes to the database. For instance, you are performing a transaction if you perform an UPDATE statement on a table to change an individual's name.

A transaction can either be one DML statement or a group of statements. When managing transactions, each designated transaction (group of DML statements) must be successful as one entity, or none of them will be successful.

The following list describes the nature of transactions:

▶ All transactions have a beginning and an end.

▶ A transaction can be saved or undone.

▶ If a transaction fails in the middle, no part of the transaction can be saved to the database.

Controlling Transactions

Transactional control is the capability to manage various transactions that might occur within a *relational database management system (RDBMS)*. When you speak of transactions, you are referring to the INSERT, UPDATE, and DELETE commands, which were covered during the previous hour.

NOTE
_____

Transactions Are Implementation-Specific

Starting or executing transactions is implementation-specific. You must check your particular implementation for how to begin transactions.
_____

When a transaction is executed and completes successfully, the target table is not immediately changed; although, it might appear so according to the output. When a transaction successfully completes, transactional control commands are used to finalize the transaction, either saving the changes made by the transaction to the database or reversing the changes made by the transaction. During the execution of the transaction, the information is stored either in an allocated area or in a temporary rollback area in the database. All changes are held in this temporary rollback area until a transactional control command is issued. When a transactional control command is issued, changes are either made to the database or discarded; then the temporary rollback area is emptied. Figure 6.1 illustrates how changes are applied to a relational database.

Three commands are used to control transactions:

▶ COMMIT

▶ ROLLBACK

▶ SAVEPOINT

Each of these is discussed in detail in the following sections.

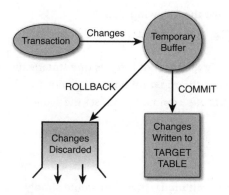

FIGURE 6.1
Rollback area

The COMMIT Command

The COMMIT command is the transactional command used to save changes invoked by a transaction to the database. The COMMIT command saves all transactions to the database since the last COMMIT or ROLLBACK command.

The syntax for this command is

```
commit [ work ];
```

The keyword COMMIT is the only mandatory part of the syntax, along with the character or command that terminates a statement according to each implementation. WORK is a keyword that is completely optional; its only purpose is to make the command user-friendly.

In the following example, you begin by creating a copy of the AIRCRAFT table called the AIRCRAFT_TMP table:

```
SELECT * INTO AIRCRAFT_TMP FROM AIRCRAFT;
(40 row(s) affected)
```

Next, you delete all records from the table where the seating for the aircraft is less than 300:

```
DELETE FROM AIRCRAFT_TMP
WHERE SEATING < 300;
(26 row(s) affected)
```

A COMMIT statement is issued to save the changes to the database, completing the transaction:

```
COMMIT;
Commit complete.
```

If you issue a COMMIT statement and use SQL Server, you get the following error:

```
The COMMIT TRANSACTION request has no corresponding BEGIN TRANSACTION.
```

This is because SQL Server uses an auto-commit. This simply means that it treats any statement as a transaction and automatically issues a commit if successful and a rollback if it is not. To change this you need to issue a SET IMPLICIT_TRANSACTIONS command and set the mode to ON:

```
SET IMPLICIT_TRANSACTIONS ON;
Command(s) completed successfully.
```

If you want your current connection to go back to auto-commit mode, then you would simply issue the same statement and set the mode to OFF:

```
SET IMPLICIT_TRANSACTIONS OFF;
Command(s) completed successfully.
```

Frequent COMMIT statements in large loads or unloads of the database are highly recommended; however, too many COMMIT statements cause the job to take a lot of extra time to complete. Remember that all changes are sent to the temporary rollback area first. If this temporary rollback area runs out of space and cannot store information about changes made to the database, the database will probably halt, disallowing further transactional activity.

You should realize that when an UPDATE, INSERT, or DELETE is issued, most RDBMSs use a form of transaction in the background so that if the query is canceled or runs into an error, changes are not committed. Therefore, issuing a transaction is more of an action to ensure that a set of transactions is run and is commonly referred to as a *unit of work*. In a real-world example, you might process a bank transaction at an ATM with a client wanting to withdraw money. In such a situation, you need to both insert a transaction for the money being withdrawn as well as update the client's balance to reflect the new total. Obviously, you would want either both of these statements to be successful or both of them to fail. Otherwise, the system's data integrity is compromised. So in this instance, you would wrap your unit of work in a transaction to ensure that you could control the outcome of both statements.

CAUTION
_____

Some Implementations Treat the COMMIT Differently

In some implementations, transactions are committed without issuing the COMMIT command; instead, merely signing out of the database causes a commit to occur. However, in some implementations, such as MySQL, after you perform a SET TRANSACTION command, the auto-commit functionality does not resume until it has received a COMMIT or ROLLBACK statement. In addition, in other implementations such as Microsoft SQL Server, statements are auto-committed unless a transaction is specifically used. Ensure that you check the documentation of your particular RDBMS to understand exactly how transactions and committing of statements are handled.

_____

The ROLLBACK Command

The ROLLBACK command is the transactional control command that undoes transactions that have not already been saved to the database. You can use the ROLLBACK command only to undo transactions since the last COMMIT or ROLLBACK command was issued.

The syntax for the ROLLBACK command follows:

```
rollback [ work ];
```

Again, as in the COMMIT statement, the WORK keyword is an optional part of the ROLLBACK syntax.

For the rest of the exercise, if you use SQL Server, you need to turn on IMPLICIT_TRANSACTIONS to make the examples easier to follow:

```
SET IMPLICIT_TRANSACTIONS ON;
Command(s) completed successfully.
```

In the following example, you begin by selecting all records from the AIRCRAFT_TMP table since the previous deletion of 26 records:

```
SELECT * FROM AIRCRAFT_TMP;
AircraftCode AircraftType                                       FreightOnly Seating
------------ -------------------------------------------------- ----------- -------
330          Airbus 330 (200 & 300) series                      0           335
742          Boeing 747-200                                     0           420
743          Boeing 747-300                                     0           420
744          Boeing 747-400                                     0           400
747          Boeing 747 (all series)                            0           420
74L          Boeing 747SP                                       0           314
772          Boeing 777-200                                     0           375
773          Boeing 777-300                                     0           420
777          Boeing 777                                         0           375
BBB          Boeing                                             0           NULL
CCC          Boeing                                             0           NULL
D10          McDonnell Douglas DC10                             0           399
L10          Lockheed L/1011 TR                                 0           400
M11          McDonnell Douglas MD-11                            0           323

(14 row(s) affected)
```

Next, you update the table, changing the seating capacity to 150 for the planes that have NULL for their seating value:

```
UPDATE AIRCRAFT_TMP
SET SEATING=150
WHERE SEATING IS NULL;
(2 row(s) affected)
```

Notice the WHERE clause and the use of IS instead of the = sign. When comparing against NULL you use either IS NULL or IS NOT NULL instead of the traditional = sign. If you perform a quick query on the table, the change appears to have occurred:

```
SELECT * FROM AIRCRAFT_TMP WHERE SEATING=150;
AircraftCode AircraftType                          FreightOnly Seating
------------ ------------------------------------- ----------- -------------------------
BBB          Boeing                                0           150
CCC          Boeing                                0           150

(2 row(s) affected)
```

Now issue the ROLLBACK statement to undo the last change:

```
rollback;
Command(s) completed successfully.
```

Finally, verify that the change was not committed to the database:

```
SELECT * FROM AIRCRAFT_TMP WHERE SEATING IS NULL;
AircraftCode AircraftType                          FreightOnly Seating
------------ ------------------------------------- ----------- -------------------------
BBB          Boeing                                0           NULL
CCC          Boeing                                0           NULL

(2 row(s) affected)
```

The SAVEPOINT Command

A *savepoint* is a point in a transaction where you can roll the transaction back to without rolling back the entire transaction.

The syntax for the SAVEPOINT command is

```
savepoint savepoint_name
```

This command serves only to create a savepoint among transactional statements. The ROLLBACK command undoes a group of transactions. The savepoint is a way of managing transactions by breaking large numbers of transactions into smaller, more manageable groups.

Microsoft SQL Server uses a slightly different syntax. In SQL Server, you would use the statement SAVE TRANSACTION instead of SAVEPOINT, as is shown in the following statement:

```
save transaction savepoint_name
```

Otherwise, the procedure works exactly as the other implementations.

The ROLLBACK TO SAVEPOINT Command

The syntax for rolling back to a savepoint follows:

```
ROLLBACK TO SAVEPOINT_NAME;
```

In this example, you delete the remaining three records from the PRODUCTS_TMP table. You want to issue a SAVEPOINT command before each delete, so you can issue a ROLLBACK command to any savepoint at any time to return the appropriate data to its original state. In SQL Server the SAVEPOINT command is actually a SAVE TRANSACTION command, but the objective is still the same. In Oracle you would use the following:

```
SAVEPOINT sp1;
Savepoint created.
DELETE FROM AIRCRAFT_TMP WHERE AIRCRAFTCODE = 'BBB';
1 row deleted.
SAVEPOINT sp2;
Savepoint created.
DELETE FROM AIRCRAFT_TMP WHERE AIRCRAFTCODE = 'CCC';
1 row deleted.
SAVEPOINT sp3;
Savepoint created.
DELETE FROM AIRCRAFT_TMP WHERE AIRCRAFTCODE = '777';
1 row deleted.
```

In SQL Server the syntax would be slightly different:

```
SAVE TRANSACTION sp1;
Command(s) completed successfully.
DELETE FROM AIRCRAFT_TMP WHERE AIRCRAFTCODE = 'BBB';
(1 row(s) affected)
SAVE TRANSACTION sp2;
Command(s) completed successfully.
DELETE FROM AIRCRAFT_TMP WHERE AIRCRAFTCODE = 'CCC';
(1 row(s) affected)
SAVE TRANSACTION sp3;
Command(s) completed successfully.
DELETE FROM AIRCRAFT_TMP WHERE AIRCRAFTCODE = '777';
(1 row(s) affected)
```

NOTE

SAVEPOINT Names Need to Be Unique

A savepoint's name must be unique to the associated group of transactions. However, it can have the same name as a table or other object. Refer to specific implementation documentation for more details on naming conventions. Otherwise, savepoint names are a matter of personal preference and are used only by the database application developer to manage groups of transactions.

Now that the three deletions have taken place, say you change your mind and decide to issue a ROLLBACK command to the savepoint that you identify as SP2. Because SP2 was created after the first deletion, the last two deletions are undone. In Oracle you would use

```
ROLLBACK TO sp2;
Rollback complete.
```

In SQL Server use the following:

```
ROLLBACK TRANSACTION sp2;
Command(s) completed successfully.
```

Notice that only the first deletion took place because you rolled back to SP2:

```
SELECT * FROM AIRCRAFT_TMP;
```

AircraftCode	AircraftType	FreightOnly	Seating
330	Airbus 330 (200 & 300) series	0	335
742	Boeing 747-200	0	420
743	Boeing 747-300	0	420
744	Boeing 747-400	0	400
747	Boeing 747 (all series)	0	420
74L	Boeing 747SP	0	314
772	Boeing 777-200	0	375
773	Boeing 777-300	0	420
777	Boeing 777	0	375
CCC	Boeing	0	NULL
D10	McDonnell Douglas DC10	0	399
L10	Lockheed L/1011 TR	0	400
M11	McDonnell Douglas MD-11	0	323

```
(13 row(s) affected)
```

Remember, the ROLLBACK command by itself rolls back to the last COMMIT or ROLLBACK statement. You have not yet issued a COMMIT, so all deletions are undone, as in the following example:

```
ROLLBACK;
Command(s) completed successfully.
```

```
SELECT * FROM AIRCRAFT_TMP;
```

AircraftCode	AircraftType	FreightOnly	Seating
330	Airbus 330 (200 & 300) series	0	335
742	Boeing 747-200	0	420
743	Boeing 747-300	0	420
744	Boeing 747-400	0	400
747	Boeing 747 (all series)	0	420
74L	Boeing 747SP	0	314

```
772            Boeing 777-200              0        375
773            Boeing 777-300              0        420
777            Boeing 777                  0        375
BBB            Boeing                      0        NULL
CCC            Boeing                      0        NULL
D10            McDonnell Douglas DC10      0        399
L10            Lockheed L/1011 TR          0        400
M11            McDonnell Douglas MD-11     0        323
```

(14 row(s) affected)

Now if you use SQL Server, you want to put the database into the standard auto-commit setting by issuing the following command:

SET IMPLICIT_TRANSACTIONS ON;
Command(s) completed successfully.

The RELEASE SAVEPOINT Command

The RELEASE SAVEPOINT command removes a savepoint that you have created. After a savepoint has been released, you can no longer use the ROLLBACK command to undo transactions performed since the savepoint. You might want to issue a RELEASE SAVEPOINT command to avoid the accidental rollback to a savepoint that is no longer needed:

RELEASE SAVEPOINT savepoint_name;

Microsoft SQL Server does not support the RELEASE SAVEPOINT syntax; instead, all SAVEPOINTs are released when the transaction is completed. This is either by the COMMIT or the ROLLBACK of the transaction. Remember this point when you structure your transactions within your environment.

The SET TRANSACTION Command

You can use the SET TRANSACTION command to initiate a database transaction. This command specifies characteristics for the transaction that follows. For example, you can specify a transaction to be read-only or read/write:

SET TRANSACTION READ WRITE;
SET TRANSACTION READ ONLY;

READ WRITE is used for transactions that are allowed to query and manipulate data in the database. READ ONLY is used for transactions that require query-only access. READ ONLY is useful for generating reports and for increasing the speed at which transactions are accomplished. If a transaction is READ WRITE, the database must create locks on database objects to maintain data integrity if multiple transactions are happening concurrently. If a transaction is READ ONLY, no locks are established by the database, thereby improving transaction performance.

Poor Transactional Control

Poor transactional control can hurt database performance and even bring the database to a halt. Repeated poor database performance might be due to a lack of transactional control during large inserts, updates, or deletes. Large batch processes also cause temporary storage for rollback information to grow until either a COMMIT or a ROLLBACK command is issued.

When a COMMIT is issued, rollback transactional information is written to the target table, and the rollback information in temporary storage is cleared. When a ROLLBACK is issued, no changes are made to the database, and the rollback information in the temporary storage is cleared. If neither a COMMIT nor ROLLBACK is issued, the temporary storage for rollback information continues to grow until there is no more space left, thus forcing the database to stop all processes until space is freed. Although space usage is ultimately controlled by the database administrator (DBA), a lack of transactional control can still cause database processing to stop, sometimes forcing the DBA to take action that might consist of killing running user processes.

Summary

During this hour, you learned the preliminary concepts of transactional management through the use of three transactional control commands: COMMIT, ROLLBACK, and SAVEPOINT. You use COMMIT to save a transaction to the database. You use ROLLBACK to undo a transaction you performed. You use SAVEPOINT to break a transaction or transactions into groups, which allows you to roll back to specific logical points in transaction processing.

Remember that you should frequently use the COMMIT and ROLLBACK commands when running large transactional jobs to keep space free in the database. Also, keep in mind that these transactional commands are used only with the three DML commands (INSERT, UPDATE, and DELETE).

Q&A

Q. Is it necessary to issue a commit after every INSERT statement?

A. No, absolutely not. Some systems such as SQL Server would automatically issue a commit after your INSERT statement. However, if you have large inserts or updates, you may consider doing them in batches as large updates to tables could negatively affect performance.

Q. How does the ROLLBACK command undo a transaction?

A. The ROLLBACK command clears all changes from the rollback area.

Q. **If I issue a transaction and 99% of the transaction completes but the other 1% errs, can I redo only the error part?**

A. No, the entire transaction must succeed; otherwise, data integrity is compromised. Therefore, you should always perform a `ROLLBACK` on an error unless there is a compelling reason not to.

Q. **A transaction is permanent after I issue a `COMMIT`, but can I change data with an `UPDATE` command?**

A. The word *permanent* used in this matter means that it is now a part of the database. You can always use the `UPDATE` statement to make modifications or corrections to the data.

Workshop

The following workshop is composed of a series of quiz questions and practical exercises. The quiz questions are designed to test your overall understanding of the current material. The practical exercises are intended to afford you the opportunity to apply the concepts discussed during the current hour, as well as build upon the knowledge acquired in previous hours of study. Please take time to complete the quiz questions and exercises before continuing. Refer to Appendix C, "Answers to Quizzes and Exercises," for answers.

Quiz

1. True or false: If you have committed several transactions, have several more transactions that have not been committed, and issue a `ROLLBACK` command, all your transactions for the same session are undone.

2. True or false: A `SAVEPOINT` or `SAVE TRANSACTION` command actually saves transactions after a specified number of transactions have executed.

3. Briefly describe the purpose of each one of the following commands: `COMMIT`, `ROLLBACK`, and `SAVEPOINT`.

4. What are some differences in the implementation of transactions in Microsoft SQL Server?

5. What are some performance implications when using transactions?

6. When using several `SAVEPOINT` or `SAVE TRANSACTION` commands, can you roll back more than one?

Exercises

1. Take the following transactions and create a `SAVEPOINT` or a `SAVE TRANSACTION` command after the first three transactions. Then create a `ROLLBACK` statement for your savepoint at the end. Try to determine what the `PASSENGERS` table will look like after you are done.

```
INSERT INTO PASSENGERS(FIRSTNAME,LASTNAME,BIRTHDATE,COUNTRYCODE)
VALUES('George','Allwell','1981-03-23','US');
INSERT INTO PASSENGERS(FIRSTNAME,LASTNAME,BIRTHDATE,COUNTRYCODE)
VALUES('Steve','Schuler','1974-09-11','US');
INSERT INTO PASSENGERS(FIRSTNAME,LASTNAME,BIRTHDATE,COUNTRYCODE)
VALUES('Mary','Ellis','1990-11-12','US');
UPDATE PASSENGERS SET FIRSTNAME='Peter' WHERE LASTNAME='Allwell'
AND BIRTHDATE='1981-03-23';
UPDATE PASSENGERS SET COUNTRYCODE='AU' WHERE FIRSTNAME='Mary'
AND LASTNAME='Ellis';
UPDATE PASSENGERS SET BIRTHDATE='1964-09-11' WHERE LASTNAME='Schuler';
```

2. Take the following group of transactions and create a savepoint after the first transactions. Then place a COMMIT statement at the end, followed by a ROLLBACK statement to your savepoint. What do you think should happen?

```
UPDATE PASSENGERS SET BIRTHDATE='Stephen' WHERE LASTNAME='Schuler';
DELETE FROM PASSENGERS WHERE LASTNAME='Allwell' AND BIRTHDATE='1981-03-23';
DELETE FROM PASSENGERS WHERE LASTNAME='Schuler' AND BIRTHDATE='1964-09-11';
DELETE FROM PASSENGERS WHERE  LASTNAME='Ellis' AND BIRTHDATE='1990-11-12';
```

Introduction to Database Queries

What You'll Learn in This Hour:

▶ Definition of a database query
▶ How to use the SELECT statement
▶ Adding conditions to queries using the WHERE clause
▶ Using column aliases
▶ Selecting data from another user's table

In this hour, you learn about database queries, which involve the use of the SELECT statement. The SELECT statement is the most frequently used of all SQL commands after a database's establishment. The SELECT statement enables you to view data that is stored in the database.

The SELECT Statement

The SELECT statement, which is known as the Data Query Language (DQL) command, is the basic statement used to construct database queries. A *query* is an inquiry into the database to extract data from the database in a readable format according to the user's request. For instance, in the sample database where you have a passengers table, you might issue an SQL statement that returns the oldest passengers on a flight so that you could have them board first. This request to the database for usable passenger information is a typical query that can be performed in a relational database.

The SELECT statement is by far one of the most powerful statements in SQL. The SELECT statement is not a standalone statement, which means that one or more additional clauses (elements) are required for a syntactically correct query. In addition to the required clauses, optional clauses increase the overall functionality of the SELECT statement. The FROM clause is a mandatory clause and must always be used with the SELECT statement.

Four keywords, or *clauses*, are valuable parts of a SELECT statement:

- ▶ SELECT

- ▶ FROM

- ▶ WHERE

- ▶ ORDER BY

Each of these clauses is covered in detail in the following sections.

The SELECT Clause

The SELECT statement is used with the FROM clause to extract data from the database in an organized, readable format. The SELECT clause of the query is for selecting the data you want to see according to the columns in which they are stored in a table.

The syntax for a simple SELECT statement follows:

```
SELECT [ * | ALL | DISTINCT COLUMN1, COLUMN2 ]
FROM TABLE1 [ , TABLE2 ];
```

The SELECT clause in a query is followed by a comma delimited list of column names that you want displayed as part of the query output. The asterisk (*) denotes that all columns in a table should display as part of the output. Check your particular implementation for its usage. The ALL option displays all values for a column, including duplicates. The DISTINCT option suppresses duplicate rows from displaying in the output. The ALL option is an inferred option. It is thought of as the default; therefore, it does not necessarily need to be used in the SELECT statement. The FROM keyword is followed by a list of one or more tables from which you want to select data. Notice that the columns following the SELECT clause are separated by commas, as is the table list following the FROM clause.

NOTE

Constructing Lists

Commas separate arguments in a list in SQL statements. *Arguments* are values that are either required or optional to the syntax of a SQL statement or command. Some common lists include lists of columns in a query, lists of tables to be selected from in a query, values to be inserted into a table, and values grouped as a condition in a query's WHERE clause.

The basic capabilities of the SELECT statement are explored in the following examples. First, perform a simple query from our AIRCRAFT_TMP table from the previous chapter:

```
SELECT * FROM AIRCRAFT_TMP;
```

```
AircraftCode AircraftType                                      FreightOnly Seating
------------ ------------------------------------------------- ----------- -------
330          Airbus 330 (200 & 300) series                     0           335
742          Boeing 747-200                                    0           420
743          Boeing 747-300                                    0           420
744          Boeing 747-400                                    0           400
747          Boeing 747 (all series)                           0           420
74L          Boeing 747SP                                      0           314
772          Boeing 777-200                                    0           375
773          Boeing 777-300                                    0           420
777          Boeing 777                                        0           375
BBB          Boeing                                            0           NULL
CCC          Boeing                                            0           NULL
D10          McDonnell Douglas DC10                            0           399
L10          Lockheed L/1011 TR                                0           400
M11          McDonnell Douglas MD-11                           0           323
```

```
(14 row(s) affected)
```

The asterisk represents all columns in the table, which, as you can see, display in the form AircraftCode, AircraftType, FreightOnly, and Seating. Each column in the output displays in the order that it appears in the table. There are 14 records in this table, identified by the feedback (14 row(s) affected). This feedback differs among implementations; for example, another feedback for the same query would be 14 rows selected. Although the asterisk is a helpful piece of shorthand when writing SQL queries, it is considered best practice to explicitly name the columns that you are returning.

Now select data from another table, PASSENGERS. List the column name after the SELECT keyword to display only one column in the table:

```
SELECT COUNTRYCODE FROM PASSENGERS;
```

```
CountryCode
-----------
CA
US
GB
US
US
US
US
GB
US
CA
US
```

```
GB
US
US
US
 .
 .
 .

(135001 row(s) affected)
```

As you can see, this returned 135001 rows of country codes here, and by looking at the sample of the results here, it is evident that there is a lot of duplication in the results. The DISTINCT option is used in the following statement to suppress the display of duplicate records. Notice that there are only seven rows in this example.

```
SELECT DISTINCT COUNTRYCODE
FROM PASSENGERS;
CountryCode
-----------
US
FR
MX
JP
DE
CA
GB

(7 row(s) affected)
```

You can also use DISTINCT with parentheses enclosing the associated column, as follows. Parentheses are often used in SQL—as well as many other languages—to improve readability.

```
SELECT DISTINCT(COUNTRYCODE)
FROM PASSENGERS;
CountryCode
-----------
US
FR
MX
JP
DE
CA
GB

(7 row(s) affected)
```

The FROM Clause

The FROM clause must be used with the SELECT statement. It is a required element for any query. The FROM clause's purpose is to tell the database what table(s) to access to retrieve the wanted data for the query. The FROM clause may contain one or more tables. The FROM clause must always list at least one table.

The syntax for the FROM clause follows:

```
from table1 [ , table2 ]
```

The WHERE Clause

A *condition* is part of a query that displays selective information as specified by the user. The value of a condition is either TRUE or FALSE, thereby limiting the data received from the query. The WHERE clause places conditions on a query by eliminating rows that would normally be returned by a query without conditions.

You can have more than one condition in the WHERE clause. If more than one condition exists, the conditions connect by the AND and OR operators, which are discussed during Hour 8, "Using Operators to Categorize Data." As you also learn during the next hour, several conditional operators exist that can specify conditions in a query. This hour deals with only a single condition for each query.

An *operator* is a character or keyword in SQL that combines elements in a SQL statement.

The syntax for the WHERE clause follows:

```
select [ all | * | distinct column1, column2 ]
from table1 [ , table2 ]
where [ condition1 | expression1 ]
[ and|OR condition2 | expression2 ]
```

The following is a simple SELECT statement without conditions specified by the WHERE clause:

```
SELECT AIRPORTID, AIRPORTNAME, CITY, COUNTRYCODE
FROM AIRPORTS;
```

AIRPORTID	AIRPORTNAME	CITY	COUNTRYCODE
1	Bamiyan	Bamiyan	AF
2	Bost	Bost	AF
3	Chakcharan	Chakcharan	AF
4	Darwaz	Darwaz	AF
5	Faizabad	Faizabad	AF
6	Farah	Farah	AF
7	Gardez	Gardez	AF

```
8              Ghazni              Ghazni              AF
9              Herat               Herat               AF
10             Jalalabad           Jalalabad           AF
.
.
.

(9185 row(s) affected)
```

Obviously, you may not need all 9185 rows of airports, so you need to trim that listing down. Now add a condition for the same query so that you can see only the airports in Hungary:

```
SELECT AIRPORTID, AIRPORTNAME, CITY, COUNTRYCODE
FROM AIRPORTS
WHERE COUNTRYCODE='HU';
```

```
AIRPORTID   AIRPORTNAME                 CITY                          COUNTRYCODE
----------- --------------------------- ----------------------------- ---------
7695        Debrecen                    Debrecen                      HU
7696        Deli Railway                Budapest                      HU
7697        Ferihegy                    Budapest                      HU
7698        Gyor-Per                    Per                           HU
7699        Miskolc                     Miskolc                       HU
7700        Pecs-Pogany                 Pecs                          HU
7701        Saarmelleek/balaton         Saarmelleek                   HU

(7 row(s) affected)
```

The only records that display are those where the country code is 'HU,' which is Hungary.

Conditions do not always have to be exact matches of exact terms. Sometimes, you want a range of values. The following query displays the passenger names and birthdates that have passenger identification numbers greater than 134995:

```
SELECT PASSENGERID, FIRSTNAME, LASTNAME, BIRTHDATE
FROM PASSENGERS
WHERE PASSENGERID>134995;
```

```
PASSENGERID FIRSTNAME             LASTNAME                    BirthDate
----------- --------------------- ------- ----------------    -----------------------
134996      Mozell                Scullen                     1962-04-07 00:00:00.000
134997      Lien                  Filippo                     1951-04-10 00:00:00.000
134998      Ann                   Cornford                    1978-06-06 00:00:00.000
134999      Nita                  Stott                       1971-04-16 00:00:00.000
135000      Maddie                Guzman                      1987-03-01 00:00:00.000
135001      John                  Doe                         1990-10-12 00:00:00.000

(6 row(s) affected)
```

The ORDER BY Clause

You usually want your output to have some kind of order. Data can be sorted by using the ORDER BY clause. The ORDER BY clause arranges the results of a query in a listing format you specify. The default ordering of the ORDER BY clause is an *ascending order;* the sort displays in the order A–Z if it's sorting output names alphabetically. A *descending order* for alphabetical output would be displayed in the order Z–A. Ascending order for output for numeric values between 1 and 9 would be displayed 1–9; descending order would be displayed as 9–1.

The syntax for the ORDER BY clause is as follows:

```
select [ all· | * | distinct column1, column2 ]
from table1 [ , table2 ]
where [ condition1 | expression1 ]
[ and|OR condition2 | expression2 ]
ORDER BY column1|integer [ ASC|DESC ]
```

Begin your exploration of the ORDER BY clause with an extension of one of the previous statements, as follows. You order the passenger list in ascending order or alphabetical order. Note the use of the ASC option. You can specify ASC after any column in the ORDER BY clause.

```
SELECT PASSENGERID, FIRSTNAME, LASTNAME, BIRTHDATE
FROM PASSENGERS
WHERE PASSENGERID>134995
ORDER BY LASTNAME ASC;
```

PASSENGERID	FIRSTNAME	LASTNAME	BirthDate
134998	Ann	Cornford	1978-06-06 00:00:00.000
135001	John	Doe	1990-10-12 00:00:00.000
134997	Lien	Filippo	1951-04-10 00:00:00.000
135000	Maddie	Guzman	1987-03-01 00:00:00.000
134996	Mozell	Scullen	1962-04-07 00:00:00.000
134999	Nita	Stott	1971-04-16 00:00:00.000

(6 row(s) affected)

NOTE

Rules for Sorting

SQL sorts are ASCII, character-based sorts. The numeric values 0–9 would be sorted as character values and sorted before the characters A–Z. Because numeric values are treated like characters during a sort, an example list of numeric values would be sorted in the following order: 1, 12, 2, 255, 3.

You can use DESC, as in the following statement, if you want the same output to be sorted in reverse alphabetical order:

```
SELECT PASSENGERID, FIRSTNAME, LASTNAME, BIRTHDATE
FROM PASSENGERS
WHERE PASSENGERID>134995
ORDER BY LASTNAME DESC;
```

PASSENGERID	FIRSTNAME	LASTNAME	BirthDate
134999	Nita	Stott	1971-04-16 00:00:00.000
134996	Mozell	Scullen	1962-04-07 00:00:00.000
135000	Maddie	Guzman	1987-03-01 00:00:00.000
134997	Lien	Filippo	1951-04-10 00:00:00.000
135001	John	Doe	1990-10-12 00:00:00.000
134998	Ann	Cornford	1978-06-06 00:00:00.000

(6 row(s) affected)

TIP

There Is a Default for Ordering
Because ascending order for output is the default, you do not have to specify ASC.

Shortcuts do exist in SQL. A column listed in the ORDER BY clause can be abbreviated with an integer. An *integer* is a substitution for the actual column name (an alias for the purpose of the sort operation), identifying the position of the column after the SELECT keyword.

An example of using an integer as an identifier in the ORDER BY clause follows:

```
SELECT PASSENGERID, FIRSTNAME, LASTNAME, BIRTHDATE
FROM PASSENGERS
WHERE PASSENGERID>134995
ORDER BY 3 ASC;
```

PASSENGERID	FIRSTNAME	LASTNAME	BirthDate
134998	Ann	Cornford	1978-06-06 00:00:00.000
135001	John	Doe	1990-10-12 00:00:00.000
134997	Lien	Filippo	1951-04-10 00:00:00.000
135000	Maddie	Guzman	1987-03-01 00:00:00.000
134996	Mozell	Scullen	1962-04-07 00:00:00.000
134999	Nita	Stott	1971-04-16 00:00:00.000

(6 row(s) affected)

In this query, the integer 3 represents the column LASTNAME. The integer 1 represents the PASSENGERID column, 2 represents the FIRSTNAME column, and so on.

You can order by multiple columns in a query, using either the column name or the associated number of the column in the SELECT:

```
ORDER BY 1,2,3
```

Columns in an ORDER BY clause are not required to appear in the same order as the associated columns following the SELECT, as shown by the following example:

```
ORDER BY 1,3,2
```

The order in which the columns are specified within the ORDER BY clause is the manner in which the ordering process is done. So the statement that follows first orders by the LASTNAME column and then by the FIRSTNAME column:

```
ORDER BY LASTNAME,FIRSTNAME
```

Case-Sensitivity

Case-sensitivity is an important concept to understand when coding with SQL. Typically, SQL commands and keywords are not case-sensitive, which enables you to enter your commands and keywords in either uppercase or lowercase—whatever you prefer. The case may also be mixed (both uppercase and lowercase for a single word or statement), which is often referred to as *CamelCase*. See Hour 5, "Manipulating Data," on case-sensitivity.

Collation is the mechanism that determines how the *relational database management system (RDBMS)* interprets data. This includes methods of ordering the data as well as case-sensitivity. Case-sensitivity in relation to your data is important because it determines how your WHERE clauses, among other things, interpret matches. You need to check with your specific RDBMS implementation to determine what the default collation is on your system. Some systems, such as MySQL and Microsoft SQL Server, have a default collation that is case-insensitive. This means that it matches strings without considering their case. Other systems, such as Oracle, have a default collation that is case-sensitive. This means that strings are matched with case taken into account. Because case-sensitivity is a factor at the database level, its importance as a factor in your queries varies.

CAUTION

Use a Standard Case in Your Queries

It is a good practice to use the same case in your query as the data that is stored in your database. Moreover, it is good to implement a corporate policy to ensure that data entry is handled in the same manner across an enterprise.

Case-sensitivity is, however, a factor in maintaining data consistency within your RDBMS. For instance, your data would not be consistent if you arbitrarily enter your data using random case:

▶ SMITH

▶ Smith

▶ smith

If the last name is stored as smith and you issue a query as follows in an RDBMS such as Oracle, which is case-sensitive, no rows return:

```
SELECT *
FROM PASSENGERS
WHERE LASTNAME = 'SMITH';
SELECT *
FROM PASSENGERS
WHERE UPPER(LASTNAME) = UPPER('Smith');
```

Fundamentals of Query Writing

This section provides several examples of queries based on the concepts that have been discussed. It begins with the simplest query you can issue and builds upon the initial query progressively. You use the EMPLOYEE_TBL table.

Select all records from a table and display all columns:

```
SELECT * FROM EMPLOYEE_TBL;
```

Select all records from a table and display a specified column:

```
SELECT EMP_ID
FROM EMPLOYEE_TBL;
```

Select all records from a table and display a specified column. You can enter code on one line or use a carriage return as wanted:

```
SELECT EMP_ID FROM EMPLOYEE_TBL;
```

Select all records from a table and display multiple columns separated by commas:

```
SELECT EMP_ID, LAST_NAME
FROM EMPLOYEE_TBL;
```

Display data for a given condition:

```
SELECT EMP_ID, LAST_NAME
FROM EMPLOYEE_TBL
WHERE EMP_ID = '333333333';
```

Ensure That Your Queries Are Constrained

When selecting all rows of data from a large table, the results could return a substantial amount of data. In highly transactional databases this can cause a slowdown in performance not only of the query that is executed but also of the system. Use WHERE clauses whenever possible to work on the smallest subset of your data as possible. This will limit the affect your query has on precious database resources.

Display data for a given condition and sort the output:

```
SELECT EMP_ID, LAST_NAME
FROM EMPLOYEE_TBL
WHERE CITY = 'INDIANAPOLIS'
ORDER BY EMP_ID;
```

Display data for a given condition and sort the output on multiple columns, with one column sorted in reverse order. In the instance that follows, the EMP_ID column is sorted in ascending order, whereas the LAST_NAME column is sorted in descending order:

```
SELECT EMP_ID, LAST_NAME
FROM EMPLOYEE_TBL
WHERE CITY = 'INDIANAPOLIS'
ORDER BY EMP_ID, LAST_NAME DESC;
```

Display data for a given condition and sort the output using an integer in the place of the spelled-out column name:

```
SELECT EMP_ID, LAST_NAME
FROM EMPLOYEE_TBL
WHERE CITY = 'INDIANAPOLIS'
ORDER BY 1;
```

Display data for a given condition and sort the output by multiple columns using integers. The order of the columns in the sort is different from their corresponding order after the SELECT keyword:

```
SELECT EMP_ID, LAST_NAME
FROM EMPLOYEE_TBL
WHERE CITY = 'INDIANAPOLIS'
ORDER BY 2, 1;
```

Counting the Records in a Table

You can issue a simple query on a table to get a quick count of the number of records in the table or the number of values for a column in the table. A count is accomplished by the function COUNT. Although functions are not discussed until later in this book, this function should be introduced here because it is often a part of one of the simplest queries that you can create.

The syntax of the COUNT function follows:

```
SELECT COUNT(*)
FROM TABLE_NAME;
```

The COUNT function is used with parentheses, which enclose the target column or the asterisk to count all rows of data in the table.

TIP

Counting Basics

Counting the number of values for a column is the same as counting the number of records in a table if the column being counted is NOT NULL (a required column). However, COUNT(*) is typically used for counting the number of rows for a table.

You would use the following to count the number of records in the PASSENGERS table:

```
SELECT COUNT(*) FROM PASSENGERS;


-----------
135001

(1 row(s) affected)
```

The following counts the number of values for COUNTRYCODE in the PASSENGERS table:

```
SELECT COUNT(COUNTRYCODE) FROM PASSENGERS;


-----------
135001

(1 row(s) affected)
```

If you want to count only the unique values that show up within a table, you would use the DISTINCT syntax within the COUNT function. For example, if you want to get the distinct states represented in the STATE column of the EMPLOYEE_TBL, use a query such as the one that follows:

```
SELECT COUNT(DISTINCT COUNTRYCODE) FROM PASSENGERS;


-----------
7

(1 row(s) affected)
```

Selecting Data from Another User's Table

Permission must be granted to a user to access another user's table. If no permission has been granted, access is not allowed. You can select data from another user's table after access has been granted. (The GRANT command is discussed in Hour 20, "Creating and Using Views and Synonyms.") To access another user's table in a SELECT statement, precede the table name with the schema name or the username that owns (created) the table, as in the following example:

```
SELECT EMPLOYEEID
FROM DBO.EMPLOYEES;
```

Using Column Aliases

Column aliases temporarily rename a table's columns for the purpose of a particular query. The following syntax illustrates the use of column aliases:

```
SELECT COLUMN_NAME ALIAS_NAME
FROM TABLE_NAME;
```

The following example displays the airport name twice, giving the second column an alias named AIRPORT. Notice the column headers in the output.

```
SELECT
AIRPORTNAME,
AIRPORTNAME AS AIRPORT
FROM AIRPORTS
WHERE COUNTRYCODE='HU';
```

AIRPORTNAME	AIRPORT
Debrecen	Debrecen
Deli Railway	Deli Railway
Ferihegy	Ferihegy
Gyor-Per	Gyor-Per
Miskolc	Miskolc
Pecs-Pogany	Pecs-Pogany
Saarmelleek/balaton	Saarmelleek/balaton

(7 row(s) affected)

NOTE

Using Synonyms in Queries

If a *synonym* exists in the database for the table to which you want access, you do not have to specify the schema name for the table. Synonyms are alternative names for tables, which are discussed in Hour 21, "Working with the System Catalog."

Column aliases can be used to customize names for column headers and reference a column with a shorter name in some SQL implementations.

TIP

Aliasing a Column in a Query

When a column is renamed in a SELECT statement, the name is not a permanent change. The change is only for that particular SELECT statement.

Summary

This hour introduced you to the database query, a means for obtaining useful information from a relational database. The SELECT statement creates queries in SQL. You must include the FROM clause with every SELECT statement. You have learned how to place a condition on a query using the WHERE clause and how to sort data using the ORDER BY clause. You have also learned the fundamentals of writing queries. After a few exercises, you should be prepared to learn more about queries during the next hour.

Q&A

Q. Why won't the SELECT clause work without the FROM clause?

A. The SELECT clause merely tells the database what data you want to see. The FROM clause tells the database where to get the data.

Q. What is the purpose of using the DISTINCT option?

A. The DISTINCT option causes the query to suppress duplicate rows of columns from appearing in the result set.

Q. When I use the ORDER BY clause and choose the descending option, what does that actually do to the data?

A. Say that you use the ORDER BY clause and have selected LASTNAME from the PASSENGERS table. If you use the descending option, the order starts with the letter *Z* and finishes with the letter *A*. Now, say that you have used the ORDER BY clause and have selected the BIRTHDATE from the PASSENGERS. If you use the descending option, the order starts with the most recent date and goes down to the oldest date.

Q. If I have a DISTINCT option, WHERE clause, and an ORDER BY clause, in which order are they performed?

A. The WHERE clause is applied first to constrain the results, then the DISTINCT is applied, and lastly the ORDER BY clause is used to order the finalized result set.

Q. What advantage is there to renaming columns?

A. The new column name could fit the description of the returned data more closely for a particular report.

Q. What would be the ordering of the following statement?

```
SELECT FIRSTNAME,LASTNAME,BIRTHDATE FROM PASSENGERS
ORDER BY 3,1
```

A. The query would be ordered by the BIRTHDATE column and then by the FIRSTNAME column. Because no ordering preference was specified, they would both be in ascending order.

Workshop

The following workshop is composed of a series of quiz questions and practical exercises. The quiz questions are designed to test your overall understanding of the current material. The practical exercises are intended to afford you the opportunity to apply the concepts discussed during the current hour, as well as build upon the knowledge acquired in previous hours of study. Please take time to complete the quiz questions and exercises before continuing. Refer to Appendix C, "Answers to Quizzes and Exercises," for answers.

Quiz

1. Name the required parts for any SELECT statement.
2. In the WHERE clause, are single quotation marks required for all the data?
3. Can multiple conditions be used in the WHERE clause?
4. Is the DISTINCT option applied before or after the WHERE clause?
5. Is the ALL option required?
6. How are numeric characters treated when ordering based upon a character field?
7. How does Oracle handle its default case-sensitivity differently from Microsoft SQL Server?
8. How is the ordering of the fields in the ORDER BY clause important?
9. How is the ordering determined in the ORDER BY clause when you use numbers instead of column names?

Exercises

1. Invoke your RDBMS query editor on your computer. Using your `CanaryAirlines` database, enter the following `SELECT` statements. Determine whether the syntax is correct. If the syntax is incorrect, make corrections to the code as necessary. Use the `PASSENGERS` table for this exercise.

   a. `SELECT PASSENGERID, LASTNAME, FIRSTNAME,`
   `FROM PASSENGERS;`

   b. `SELECT PASSENGERID, LASTNAME`
   `ORDER BY PASSENGERS`
   `FROM PASSENGERS;`

   c. `SELECT PASSENGERID, LASTNAME, FIRSTNAME`
   `FROM PASSENGERS`
   `WHERE PASSENGERID = '134996'`
   `ORDER BY PASSENGERID;`

   d. `SELECT PASSENGERID BIRTHDATE, LASTNAME`
   `FROM PASSENGERS`
   `WHERE PASSENGERID = '134996'`
   `ORDER BY 1;`

   e. `SELECT PASSENGERID, LASTNAME, FIRSTNAME`
   `FROM PASSENGERS`
   `WHERE PASSENGERID = '134996'`
   `ORDER BY 3, 1, 2;`

2. Write a `SELECT` statement to get a passenger's `LASTNAME`, `FIRSTNAME`, and `BIRTHDATE` by her `PASSENGERID` number. Does it matter if you use a string value instead of a number? Is the string `'99999999'` a valid value to use in the `WHERE` clause?

   `SELECT LASTNAME, FIRSTNAME, BIRTHDATE`
   `FROM PASSENGERS`
   `WHERE PASSENGERID = '99999999';`

3. Write a `SELECT` statement that returns the name and seating capacity of each airplane from the `AIRCRAFT` table. Which type of plane has the largest capacity? How many planes are freight planes? Where do the freight-only planes show up in your ordered results?

4. Write a query that generates a list of all passengers who were born after 2015-01-01.

5. Write a simple query to return a list of passengers with a particular last name. Try using a `WHERE` clause with the name in mixed case and uppercase. What case-sensitivity is your RDBMS set to?

Using Operators to Categorize Data

What You'll Learn in This Hour:

▶ What is an operator?

▶ An overview of operators in SQL

▶ How are operators used singularly?

▶ How are operators used in combinations?

Operators are used with the SELECT command's WHERE clause to place extended constraints on data that a query returns. Various operators are available to the SQL user that support all data querying needs. This hour shows you what operators are available for you to use as well as how to utilize them properly within the WHERE clause.

What Is an Operator in SQL?

An operator is a reserved word or a character used primarily in a SQL statement's WHERE clause to perform operation(s), such as comparisons and arithmetic operations. *Operators* are used to specify conditions in a SQL statement and to serve as conjunctions for multiple conditions in a statement.

The operators discussed during this hour are

▶ Comparison operators

▶ Logical operators

▶ Operators used to negate conditions

▶ Arithmetic operators

Comparison Operators

Comparison operators test single values in a SQL statement. The comparison operators discussed consist of =, <>, <, and >.

These operators are used to test

- ▶ Equality
- ▶ Non-equality
- ▶ Less than
- ▶ Greater than

These comparison operators, including examples, are covered in the following sections.

Equality

The *equal operator* compares single values to one another in a SQL statement. The equal sign (=) symbolizes equality. When testing for equality, the compared values must match exactly, or no data is returned. If two values are equal during a comparison for equality, the returned value for the comparison is TRUE; the returned value is FALSE if equality is not found. This Boolean value (TRUE/FALSE) is used to determine whether data is returned according to the condition.

You can use the = operator by itself or combine it with other operators. Remember from the previous chapter that character data comparisons can either be case-sensitive or case-insensitive depending on how your relational database management system (RDBMS) is set up. So remember to ensure that you understand how exactly your values are compared by the query engine.

The following example shows that seating is equal to 400:

```
WHERE SEATING = 400
```

The following query returns all rows of data where the PROD_ID is equal to 2345:

```
SELECT *
FROM AIRCRAFT
WHERE SEATING=400;
```

AircraftCode	AircraftType	FreightOnly	Seating
744	Boeing 747-400	0	400
L10	Lockheed L/1011 TR	0	400

(2 row(s) affected)

Non-Equality

For every equality, there are multiple non-equalities. In SQL, the operator used to measure non-equality is <> (the less than sign combined with the greater than sign). The condition returns TRUE if the condition finds non-equality; FALSE is returned if equality is found.

The following example shows that seating is not equal to 400:

```
WHERE SEATING<>400
```

TIP

Options for Non-Equality

Another option for non-equality is !=. Many of the major implementations have adopted != to represent not-equal. Microsoft SQL Server, MySQL, and Oracle support both versions of the operator. Oracle actually supports a third, ^=, as another version, but it is rarely used because most people are accustomed to using the earlier two versions.

The following example shows all the aircraft information from the AIRCRAFT table that does not have the FreightOnly column of 0:

```
SELECT *
FROM AIRCRAFT
WHERE FREIGHTONLY <> 0;
```

```
AircraftCode AircraftType                          FreightOnly Seating
------------ ------------------------------------- ----------- ---------------------------
74F          Boeing 747 Freighter                  1           0
M1F          McDonnell Douglas MD-11 Freigh        1           0
WWF          Westwind Freighter                    1           0

(3 row(s) affected)
```

Again, remember that your collation and specifically whether your system is set up as case-sensitive or case-insensitive plays a critical role in these comparisons. If your system is case-sensitive, then WESTWIND, WestWind, and westwind would be considered different values, which might or might not be your intention.

Less Than and Greater Than

Two of the most widely used comparison operators are greater than and less than. Greater than works the opposite of less than. You can use the symbols < (less than) and > (greater than) by themselves or in combination with each other or other operators to perform a comparison of non-null values. The results of both are a Boolean value that shows whether the comparison is accurate.

The following examples show that seating is less than or greater than 400:

```
WHERE SEATING < 400
WHERE SEATING > 400
```

In the following example, anything less than and not equal to 400 returns TRUE. Any value of 400 or more returns FALSE:

```
SELECT *
FROM AIRCRAFT
WHERE SEATING>400;
```

AircraftCode	AircraftType	FreightOnly	Seating
742	Boeing 747-200	0	420
743	Boeing 747-300	0	420
747	Boeing 747 (all series)	0	420
773	Boeing 777-300	0	420

(4 row(s) affected)

In the next example, notice that the Boeing 737 with seating for 100 was not included in the query's result set. This is because the less than operator is not inclusive of the value it is compared against.

```
SELECT *
FROM AIRCRAFT
WHERE SEATING < 100;
```

AircraftCode	AircraftType	FreightOnly	Seating
146	British Aerospace BAe146-100	0	82
74F	Boeing 747 Freighter	1	0
AR7	British Aerospace RJ70	0	76
BEH	Beachcraft 1900D	0	18
BEK	Beach 200	0	13
CV5	Convair 500	0	36
DH8	Bombardier DE HA	0	37
E12	Embraer (EMB) 120	0	30
EM2	Embraer 120	0	26
F10	Fokker F100	0	95
F28	Fokker F28-1000	0	65
M1F	McDonnell Douglas MD-11 Freigh	1	0
WWF	Westwind Freighter	1	0

(13 row(s) affected)

Combinations of Comparison Operators

The equal operator can be combined with the less than and greater than operators to have them include the value that they are compared against.

The following example shows that seating is less than or equal to 400:

```
WHERE SEATING <= 400
```

The next example shows that seating is greater than or equal to 400:

```
WHERE SEATING >= 400
```

Less than or equal to 400 includes 400 and all values less than 400. Any value in that range returns TRUE; any value greater than 400 returns FALSE. Greater than or equal to also includes the value 400 in this case and works the same as the <= operator. The following example demonstrates how to use the combined operator to find all aircraft that have 100 seats or less capacity:

```
SELECT *
FROM AIRCRAFT
WHERE SEATING <= 100;
```

AircraftCode	AircraftType	FreightOnly	Seating
146	British Aerospace BAe146-100	0	82
737	Boeing 737	0	100
74F	Boeing 747 Freighter	1	0
AR7	British Aerospace RJ70	0	76
BEH	Beachcraft 1900D	0	18
BEK	Beach 200	0	13
CV5	Convair 500	0	36
DH8	Bombardier DE HA	0	37
E12	Embraer (EMB) 120	0	30
EM2	Embraer 120	0	26
F10	Fokker F100	0	95
F28	Fokker F28-1000	0	65
M1F	McDonnell Douglas MD-11 Freigh	1	0
WWF	Westwind Freighter	1	0

```
(14 row(s) affected)
```

Logical Operators

Logical operators are those operators that use SQL keywords instead of symbols to make comparisons. Following are the logical operators in SQL, which are covered in the following subsections:

▶ IS NULL

▶ BETWEEN

▶ IN

▶ LIKE

▶ EXISTS

▶ UNIQUE

▶ ALL, SOME, and ANY

IS NULL

The IS NULL operator compares a value with a NULL value. For example, you might look for passengers who do not have a birthdate entered by searching for NULL values in the BIRTHDATE column of the PASSENGERS table.

The following example compares a value to a NULL value; here, birthdate has no value:

```
WHERE BIRTHDATE IS NULL
```

The following example demonstrates finding all the passengers from the PASSENGERS table who do not have a birthdate listed in the table:

```
SELECT PASSENGERID, LASTNAME, FIRSTNAME, BIRTHDATE
FROM PASSENGERS
WHERE BIRTHDATE IS NULL;
```

```
PASSENGERID LASTNAME                        FIRSTNAME                     BIRTHDATE
----------- ------------------------------- ----------------------------- ---------
124309      Copsey                          Merle                         NULL
124310      Alsaqri                         Leann                         NULL
```

(2 row(s) affected)

Understand that the literal word *null* is different from a NULL value. Examine the following example; observe that you cannot interchange the string value 'NULL' because it does not mean the same thing as a NULL value:

```
SELECT PASSENGERID, LASTNAME, FIRSTNAME, BIRTHDATE
FROM PASSENGERS
WHERE BIRTHDATE='NULL';
```

```
PASSENGERID LASTNAME                        FIRSTNAME                    BIRTHDATE
----------- ------------------------------- ------------------------- --------------
Msg 241, Level 16, State 1, Line 1
Conversion failed when converting date and/or time from character string.
```

BETWEEN

The BETWEEN operator searches for values that are within a set of values, given the minimum value and the maximum value. The minimum and maximum values are included as part of the conditional set.

The following example shows that seating must fall between 200 and 300, including the values 200 and 300:

```
WHERE SEATING BETWEEN 200 AND 300
```

TIP

Proper Use of Between

BETWEEN is inclusive and therefore includes the minimum and maximum values in the query results.

The following example shows all the aircraft that have seating between 200 and 300:

```
SELECT *
FROM AIRCRAFT
WHERE SEATING BETWEEN 200 AND 300;
```

AircraftCode	AircraftType	FreightOnly	Seating
313	Airbus A310-300	0	218
343	Airbus 340-300	0	230
74M	Boeing 747 Combi	0	246
762	Boeing 767-200	0-	200
763	Boeing 763-300	0	228
AB6	Airbus 600 Series E	0	226

(6 row(s) affected)

Notice that the value 200 is included in the output.

IN

The IN operator compares a value to a list of literal values that have been specified. For TRUE to be returned, the compared value must match at least one of the values in the list.

The following example shows that seating must match one of the values 200, 300, or 400:

```
WHERE SEATING IN(200, 300, 400)
```

The following example uses the IN operator to match all the aircraft that have a seating capacity within a certain range of values:

```
SELECT *
FROM AIRCRAFT
WHERE SEATING IN (200, 300, 400);
```

```
AircraftCode AircraftType                          FreightOnly Seating
------------ ------------------------------------- ----------- ---------------------------
744          Boeing 747-400                        0           400
762          Boeing 767-200                        0           200
L10          Lockheed L/1011 TR                    0           400
```

```
(3 row(s) affected)
```

Using the IN operator can achieve the same results as using the OR operator, but it can return the results quicker because it is optimized in the database.

LIKE

The LIKE operator compares a value to similar values using wildcard operators. Two wildcards are used with the LIKE operator:

▶ The percent sign (%)

▶ The underscore (_)

The percent sign represents zero, one, or multiple characters. The underscore represents a single number or character. The symbols can be used in combinations.

The following could find any values that start with B:

```
WHERE AIRCRAFTTYPE LIKE 'B%'
```

The following example finds any values that have DOUGLAS in any position:

```
WHERE AIRCRAFTTYPE LIKE '%DOUGLAS%'
```

The following example finds any values that have ir in the second and third positions:

```
WHERE AIRCRAFTTYPE LIKE '_ir%'
```

The following example finds any values that start with A and are at least three characters in length:

```
WHERE AIRCRAFTTYPE LIKE 'A_%_%'
```

The following example finds any values that end with 0:

```
WHERE AIRCRAFTTYPE LIKE '%0'
```

The following example finds any values that have a c in the second position and end with a 1:

```
WHERE AIRCRAFTTYPE LIKE '_c%1'
```

The following example finds any values in a five-digit number that start with 2 and end with 3:

```
WHERE PASSENGERID LIKE '2___3'
```

The following example shows all aircraft types that end with the letter *P* in uppercase:

```
SELECT AIRCRAFTTYPE
FROM AIRCRAFT
WHERE AIRCRAFTTYPE LIKE '%P';
```

```
AIRCRAFTTYPE
-----------------------------
Boeing 747SP


(1 row(s) affected)
```

The following example shows all product descriptions whose second character is the letter *c* in lowercase:

```
SELECT AIRCRAFTTYPE
FROM AIRCRAFT
WHERE AIRCRAFTTYPE LIKE '_c%';
```

```
AIRCRAFTTYPE
-----------------------------
McDonnell Douglas DC10
McDonnell Douglas MD-11
McDonnell Douglas MD-11 Freight


(3 row(s) affected)
```

EXISTS

The EXISTS operator searches for the presence of a row in a specified table that meets certain criteria.

The following example searches to see whether the PASSENGERID 3333333333 is in the PASSENGERS table:

```
EXISTS (SELECT * FROM PASSENGERS WHERE PASSENGERID =333333333)
```

The following example is a form of a subquery, which is further discussed during Hour 14, "Using Subqueries to Define Unknown Data":

```
SELECT SEATING
FROM AIRCRAFT A
WHERE EXISTS ( SELECT *
               FROM AIRCRAFT
               WHERE AIRCRAFTCODE=A.AIRCRAFTCODE AND SEATING > 500 );
No rows selected.
----------
```

There were no rows selected because no records existed where the seating was greater than 500. The AIRCRAFTCODE=A.AIRCRAFTCODE portion of the subquery is what maps rows from the EXISTS query to the table in the FROM clause. Because AIRCRAFTCODE is the column that uniquely identifies rows in the AIRCRAFT table, it is the best field to use for the mapping.

Consider the following example:

```
SELECT SEATING
FROM AIRCRAFT A
WHERE EXISTS ( SELECT *
               FROM AIRCRAFT
               WHERE AIRCRAFTCODE=A.AIRCRAFTCODE AND SEATING > 400 );
SEATING
-----------------------------
420
420
420
420

(4 row(s) affected)
```

The seating was displayed for records in the table because records existed where the aircraft seating capacity was greater than 400. What if we had not used the AIRCRAFTCODE to tie the EXISTS subquery back to the AIRCRAFT table? Try the following and compare the number of rows returned. Why do you think you got these results?

```
SELECT SEATING
FROM AIRCRAFT A
WHERE EXISTS ( SELECT *
               FROM AIRCRAFT
               WHERE SEATING > 400 );
```

ALL, SOME, and ANY

The ALL operator is used to compare a value to all values in another value set.

The following example tests seating to see whether it is greater than the seating capacity of the Boeing 777 aircraft type:

```
WHERE SEATING > ALL SEATING (SELECT SEATING FROM AIRCRAFT
                                 WHERE AIRCRAFTTYPE = 'Boeing 777')
```

The following example shows how the ALL operator is used with a subquery:

```
SELECT *
FROM AIRCRAFT
WHERE SEATING > ALL ( SELECT SEATING
               FROM AIRCRAFT
               WHERE AIRCRAFTTYPE='Boeing 777' );
```

AircraftCode	AircraftType	FreightOnly	Seating
742	Boeing 747-200	0	420
743	Boeing 747-300	0	420
744	Boeing 747-400	0	400
747	Boeing 747 (all series)	0	420
773	Boeing 777-300	0	420
D10	McDonnell Douglas DC10	0	399
L10	Lockheed L/1011 TR	0	400

```
(7 row(s) affected)
```

In this output, seven records had a seating capacity greater than the Boeing 777.

The ANY operator compares a value to any applicable value in the list according to the condition. SOME is an alias for ANY, so you can use them interchangeably.

The following example tests seating to see whether it is greater than any of the seating capacities of aircraft having greater than 375 seats:

```
WHERE SEATING > ANY SEATING (SELECT SEATING FROM AIRCRAFT
                                 WHERE SEATING > 375)
```

The following example shows the use of the ANY operator used with a subquery:

```
SELECT *
FROM AIRCRAFT
WHERE SEATING > ANY (SELECT SEATING
               FROM AIRCRAFT
               WHERE SEATING > 375);
```

AircraftCode	AircraftType	FreightOnly	Seating
742	Boeing 747-200	0	420
743	Boeing 747-300	0	420
744	Boeing 747-400	0	400
747	Boeing 747 (all series)	0	420

```
773              Boeing 777-300                   0        420
L10,             Lockheed L/1011 TR               0        400
```

```
(6 row(s) affected)
```

In this output, fewer records were returned than when using ALL because the seating had to be greater than any of the values for seating above 375. The one record that was not displayed had a seating capacity of 399, which was not greater than any of the values greater than 375 (which the lowest value was, in fact, 399). It should also be noted that ANY is not a synonym for IN because the IN operator can take an expression list of the form shown here, whereas ANY cannot:

```
IN (<Item#1>,<Item#2>,<Item#3>)
```

In addition, the negation of IN, discussed later in the section "Negative Operators," would be NOT IN, and its alias would be <>ALL instead of <>ANY.

Conjunctive Operators

What if you want to use multiple conditions to narrow data in a SQL statement? You must be able to combine the conditions, and you would do this with the following conjunctive operators:

- ▶ AND
- ▶ OR

Conjunctive operators provide a means to make multiple comparisons with different operators in the same SQL statement. The following sections describe each operator's behavior.

AND

The AND operator allows the existence of multiple conditions in a SQL statement's WHERE clause. For an action to be taken by the SQL statement, whether it be a transaction or query, all conditions separated by the AND must be TRUE.

The following example shows that the PASSENGERID must match 333333333 and the BIRTHDATE must be greater than 1990-01-01:

```
WHERE PASSENGERID = 333333333 AND BIRTHDATE > '1990-01-01'
```

The following example shows the use of the AND operator to find the aircraft with seating capacity between two limiting values:

```
SELECT *
FROM AIRCRAFT
WHERE SEATING > 300
  AND SEATING < 400;
```

AircraftCode	AircraftType	FreightOnly	Seating
330	Airbus 330 (200 & 300) series	0	335
74L	Boeing 747SP	0	314
772	Boeing 777-200	0	375
777	Boeing 777	0	375
D10	McDonnell Douglas DC10	0	399
M11	McDonnell Douglas MD-11	0	323

```
(6 row(s) affected)
```

In this output, the value for seating had to be both greater than 300 and less than 400 for data to be retrieved.

This statement retrieves no data because each row of data has only one aircraft code:

```
SELECT *
FROM AIRCRAFT
WHERE AIRCRAFTCODE = '772'
  AND AIRCRAFTCODE = '777';
```

```
no rows selected
```

OR

The OR operator combines multiple conditions in a SQL statement's WHERE clause. For an action to be taken by the SQL statement, whether it is a transaction or query, at least one of the conditions that are separated by OR must be TRUE.

The following example shows that seating must match either 200 or 300:

```
WHERE SEATING = 200 OR SEATING = 300
```

The following example shows the use of the OR operator to limit a query on the PASSENGERS table:

```
SELECT PASSENGERID, FIRSTNAME, LASTNAME
FROM PASSENGERS
WHERE PASSENGERID = 20
  OR PASSENGERID = 134991;
```

```
PASSENGERID FIRSTNAME                          LASTNAME
----------- ----------------------------- -----------------------------
20          Odilia                         Moros
134991      Tana                           Lehnortt

(2 row(s) affected)
```

In this output, either one of the conditions had to be TRUE for data to be retrieved.

Two records that met either one or the other condition were found.

In the next example, notice the use of the AND and two OR operators. In addition, notice the logical placement of the parentheses to make the statement more readable.

```
SELECT PASSENGERID, FIRSTNAME, LASTNAME
FROM PASSENGERS
WHERE
LASTNAME LIKE 'M%'
AND ( PASSENGERID = 20
   OR PASSENGERID = 134991 );
```

```
PASSENGERID FIRSTNAME                          LASTNAME
----------- ----------------------------- -----------------------------
20          Odilia                         Moros

(1 row(s) affected)
```

The passenger record returned needed a last name beginning with M, and the PASSENGERID had to be any one of the two listed. A row was not returned for PASSENGERID 134991 because the last name of the passenger did not begin with M. Parentheses are not used just to make your code more readable but to ensure that logical grouping of conjunctive operators is evaluated properly. By default, operators are parsed from left to right in the order that they are listed.

If you remove the parentheses, the result is much different, as you can see in the following example:

```
SELECT PASSENGERID, FIRSTNAME, LASTNAME
FROM PASSENGERS
WHERE
LASTNAME LIKE 'M%'
AND PASSENGERID = 20
   OR PASSENGERID = 134991;
```

```
PASSENGERID FIRSTNAME                      LASTNAME
----------- ----------------------------- -----------------------------
20          Odilia                        Moros
134991      Tana                          Lehnortt
```

```
(2 row(s) affected)
```

The passenger name Tana Lehnortt gets returned now because this SQL query asks to return a PASSENGERID equal to 20 and LASTNAME starting with M or any rows with PASSENGERID equal to 134991. Use parentheses properly within your WHERE clause to ensure that you are returning the correct logical result set. Otherwise, remember that your operators are evaluated in a certain order, which is normally from left to right.

Negative Operators

There is a way to negate each logical operator to change the tested condition's viewpoint.

The NOT operator reverses the meaning of the logical operator with which it is used. NOT can be used with other operators to form the following methods:

- ► <>, != (NOT EQUAL)
- ► NOT BETWEEN
- ► NOT IN
- ► NOT LIKE
- ► IS NOT NULL
- ► NOT EXISTS
- ► NOT UNIQUE

Each method is discussed in the following sections. First, look at how to test for inequality.

NOT EQUAL

Earlier this hour you learned how to test for inequality using the <> operator. To test for inequality, you actually negate the equality operator. Here we cover a second method for testing inequality available in some SQL implementations.

The following examples show that seating is not equal to 200:

```
WHERE SEATING <> 200
WHERE SEATING != 200
```

In the second example, you can see that the exclamation mark negates the equality comparison. The use of the exclamation mark is allowed in addition to the standard operator for inequality <> in some implementations.

NOTE

Check Your Implementation

Check your particular implementation for the use of the exclamation mark to negate the inequality operator. The other operators mentioned are almost always the same if compared between different SQL implementations.

NOT BETWEEN

The BETWEEN operator is negated with the NOT operator as follows:

```
WHERE SEATING NOT BETWEEN 100 AND 400
```

The value for seating cannot fall between 100 and 400 or include the values 100 and 400. Now see how this works on the AIRCRAFT table:

```
SELECT *
FROM AIRCRAFT
WHERE SEATING NOT BETWEEN 100 AND 400;
```

AircraftCode	AircraftType	FreightOnly	Seating
146	British Aerospace BAe146-100	0	82
742	Boeing 747-200	0	420
743	Boeing 747-300	0	420
747	Boeing 747 (all series)	0	420
74F	Boeing 747 Freighter	1	0
773	Boeing 777-300	0	420
AR7	British Aerospace RJ70	0	76
BEH	Beachcraft 1900D	0	18
BEK	Beach 200	0	13
CV5	Convair 500	0	36
DH8	Bombardier DE HA	0	37

E12	Embraer (EMB) 120	0	30
EM2	Embraer 120	0	26
F10	Fokker F100	0	95
F28	Fokker F28-1000	0	65
M1F	McDonnell Douglas MD-11 Freigh	1	0
WWF	Westwind Freighter	1	0

(17 row(s) affected)

NOT IN

The IN operator is negated as NOT IN. All seating in the following example that are not in the
listed values, if any, are returned:

```
WHERE SEATING NOT IN (100, 150, 200, 250, 300, 375, 400, 420)
```

The following example demonstrates using the negation of the IN operator:

```
SELECT *
FROM AIRCRAFT
```

```
WHERE SEATING NOT IN (100, 150, 200, 250, 300, 375, 400, 420);
```

AircraftCode	AircraftType	FreightOnly	Seating
146	British Aerospace BAe146-100	0	82
310	Airbus A310	0	198
313	Airbus A310-300	0	218
330	Airbus 330 (200 & 300) series	0	335
343	Airbus 340-300	0	230
72S	Boeing 727	0	153
733	Boeing 737-300	0	106
734	Boeing 737-400	0	129
735	Boeing 737-500	0	108
738	Boeing 737-800	0	114
74F	Boeing 747 Freighter	1	0
74L	Boeing 747SP	0	314
74M	Boeing 747 Combi	0	246
763	Boeing 763-300	0	228
AB6	Airbus 600 Series E	0	226
AR7	British Aerospace RJ70	0	76
BEH	Beachcraft 1900D	0	18
BEK	Beach 200	0	13
CV5	Convair 500	0	36
D10	McDonnell Douglas DC10	0	399
DH8	Bombardier DE HA	0	37
E12	Embraer (EMB) 120	0	30
EM2	Embraer 120	0	26
F10	Fokker F100	0	95
F28	Fokker F28-1000	0	65

```
M11          McDonnell Douglas MD-11        0        323
M1F          McDonnell Douglas MD-11 Freigh 1        0
WWF          Westwind Freighter             1        0
```

(28 row(s) affected)

In this output, records were not displayed for the listed identifications after the NOT IN operator.

NOT LIKE

The LIKE, or wildcard, operator is negated as NOT LIKE. When NOT LIKE is used, only values that are not similar are returned.

The following finds values that do not start with BOE:

```
WHERE AIRCRAFTTYPE NOT LIKE 'BOE%'
```

The following finds values that do not have BOE in any position:

```
WHERE SALARY NOT LIKE '%737%'
```

The following finds values that do not have cD starting in the second position:

```
WHERE SALARY NOT LIKE '_cD%'
```

The following finds any values that are not a 5-digit number that starts with 2 and ends with 3:

```
WHERE PASSENGERID NOT LIKE '2___3'
```

The following example demonstrates using the NOT LIKE operator to display a list of values:

```
SELECT AIRCRAFTTYPE
FROM AIRCRAFT
WHERE AIRCRAFTTYPE NOT LIKE 'B%';

AIRCRAFTTYPE
------------------------------
Airbus A310
Airbus A310-300
Airbus 330 (200 & 300) series
Airbus 340-300
Airbus 600 Series E
Convair 500
McDonnell Douglas DC10
Embraer (EMB) 120
Embraer 120
Fokker F100
Fokker F28-1000
Lockheed L/1011 TR
```

```
McDonnell Douglas MD-11
McDonnell Douglas MD-11 Freigh
Westwind Freighter
```

```
(15 row(s) affected)
```

In this output, the aircraft descriptions starting with the letter *B* were not displayed.

IS NOT NULL

The IS NULL operator is negated as IS NOT NULL to test for values that are not NULL. The following example returns only NOT NULL rows:

```
WHERE SEATING IS NOT NULL
```

The following example demonstrates using the IS NOT NULL operator to retrieve a list of aircraft whose seating is NOT NULL:

```
SELECT *
FROM AIRCRAFT_TMP
WHERE SEATING IS NOT NULL;
```

AircraftCode	AircraftType	FreightOnly	Seating
330	Airbus 330 (200 & 300) series	0	335
742	Boeing 747-200	0	420
743	Boeing 747-300	0	420
744	Boeing 747-400	0	400
747	Boeing 747 (all series)	0	420
74L	Boeing 747SP	0	314
772	Boeing 777-200	0	375
773	Boeing 777-300	0	420
777	Boeing 777	0	375
D10	McDonnell Douglas DC10	0	399
L10	Lockheed L/1011 TR	0	400
M11	McDonnell Douglas MD-11	0	323

```
(12 row(s) affected)
```

NOT EXISTS

EXISTS is negated as NOT EXISTS.

The following example searches to see whether the PASSENGERID 3333333333 is not in PASSENGERS:

```
WHERE NOT EXISTS (SELECT EMP_ID FROM EMPLOYEE_TBL WHERE EMP_ID = '3333333333')
```

The following example demonstrates the use of the NOT EXISTS operator with a subquery:

```
SELECT MAX(SEATING)
FROM AIRCRAFT A
WHERE NOT EXISTS ( SELECT *
                   FROM AIRCRAFT
                   WHERE AIRCRAFTCODE=A.AIRCRAFTCODE AND SEATING < 350 );


-----------------------------
420
Warning: Null value is eliminated by an aggregate or other SET operation.

(1 row(s) affected)
```

The maximum seating for the table displays in this output because we are looking for records that don't exist below 350.

Arithmetic Operators

Arithmetic operators perform mathematical functions in SQL—the same as in most other languages. The four conventional operators for mathematical functions are

- ▶ + (addition)
- ▶ - (subtraction)
- ▶ * (multiplication)
- ▶ / (division)

Addition

Addition is performed through the use of the plus (+) symbol.

The following example adds the TRAVELTIME column with the 30 minute delay for a total for each row of data:

```
SELECT TRAVELTIME + 30 AS DELAY_TIME FROM ROUTES;
```

This example returns all rows where the total of the TRAVELTIME and 30 minute delay together makes the travel time greater than 18 hours:

```
SELECT * FROM ROUTES WHERE (TRAVELTIME + 30) > 1080;
```

Subtraction

Subtraction is performed using the minus (-) symbol.

The following example subtracts a bonus value of $10,000.00 from the SALARY column for the difference:

```
SELECT SALARY - 10000 FROM EMPLOYEES;
```

This example returns all rows where the SALARY minus the bonus is greater than 40000:

```
SELECT SALARY FROM EMPLOYEES WHERE SALARY - 10000 > '40000';
```

Multiplication

Multiplication is performed using the asterisk (*) symbol.

The following example multiplies the TRAVELTIME column by FUELCOSTPERMINUTE:

```
SELECT TRAVELTIME * FUELCOSTPERMINUTE AS TOTAL_FUEL_COST FROM ROUTES;
```

The next example returns all rows where the product of the TRAVELTIME multiplied by FUELCOSTPERMINUTE is greater than $240,000.00:

```
SELECT ROUTEID, ROUTECODE, AIRPLANECODE, DISTANCE, TRAVELTIME,
TRAVELTIME * FUELCOSTPERMINUTE AS TOTAL_COST
FROM ROUTES
WHERE (TRAVELTIME * FUELCOSTPERMINUTE)>240000.00;
```

ROUTEID	ROUTECODE	AIRPLANECODE	DISTANCE	TRAVELTIME	TOTAL_COST
2719	SQL-MKF	EM2	16729	1079	242775.00
2720	MKF-SQL	EM2	16729	1079	242775.00
3223	MKF-LAX	E12	16786	1083	243675.00
3224	LAX-MKF	E12	16786	1083	243675.00

```
(4 row(s) affected)
```

Division

Division is performed through the use of the slash (/) symbol.

The following example divides the TRAVELTIME column by 60:

```
SELECT TRAVELTIME / 60 AS TRAVEL_HOURS FROM ROUTES;
```

This example returns all rows where the hours of the trip is greater than 17:

```
SELECT * FROM ROUTES WHERE (TRAVELTIME / 60) > 17;
```

Arithmetic Operator Combinations

You can use the arithmetic operators in combination with one another. Remember the rules of precedence in basic mathematics. Multiplication and division operations are performed first and then addition and subtraction operations. The only way the user has control over the order of the mathematical operations is through the use of parentheses. Parentheses surrounding an expression cause that expression to be evaluated as a block.

Precedence is the order in which expressions are resolved in a mathematical expression or with embedded functions in SQL. The following table shows some simple examples of how operator precedence can affect the outcome of a calculation:

Expression	Result
1 + 1 * 5	6
(1 + 1) * 5	10
10 – 4 / 2 +1	9
(10 – 4) / (2 + 1)	2

In the following examples, notice that the placement of parentheses in an expression does not affect the outcome if only multiplication and division are involved.

CAUTION

Ensure Your Math Is Correct

When combining arithmetic operators, remember to consider the rules of precedence. The absence of parentheses in a statement could render inaccurate results. Although the syntax of a SQL statement is correct, a logical error might result.

The following are some more examples of adding a $25 surcharge to the fuel cost per minute:

```
SELECT TRAVELTIME * FUELCOSTPERMINUTE + 25 AS TOTAL_COST
FROM ROUTES
WHERE (TRAVELTIME * FUELCOSTPERMINUTE + 25) > 240000;
SELECT TRAVELTIME * (FUELCOSTPERMINUTE + 25) AS TOTAL_COST
FROM ROUTES
WHERE (TRAVELTIME * (FUELCOSTPERMINUTE + 25)) > 240000;
```

Because parentheses are not used, mathematical precedence takes effect, altering the value for TOTAL_COST tremendously for the condition.

Summary

This hour introduced you to various operators available in SQL. You have learned the "hows" and "whys" of operators. You have also seen examples of operators used by themselves and in various combinations with one another, using the conjunctive-type operators AND and OR. You have learned the basic arithmetic functions: addition, subtraction, multiplication, and division. Comparison operators test equality, inequality, less than values, and greater than values. Logical operators include BETWEEN, IN, LIKE, EXISTS, ANY, and ALL. You can now see how elements are added to SQL statements to further specify conditions and better control the processing and retrieving capabilities provided with SQL.

Q&A

Q. Can I have more than one AND in the WHERE clause?

A. Yes. In fact, you can use all the operators multiple times. An example would be

```
SELECT *
     FROM AIRCRAFT
     WHERE SEATING < 300
     AND FREIGHTONLY=0
     AND AIRCRAFTTYPE LIKE 'B%'
```

Q. What happens if I use single quotation marks around a NUMBER data type in a WHERE clause?

A. Your query still processes, but quotation marks are not necessary for NUMBER fields.

Workshop

The following workshop is composed of a series of quiz questions and practical exercises. The quiz questions are designed to test your overall understanding of the current material. The practical exercises are intended to afford you the opportunity to apply the concepts discussed during the current hour, as well as build upon the knowledge acquired in previous hours of study. Please take time to complete the quiz questions and exercises before continuing. Refer to Appendix C, "Answers to Quizzes and Exercises," for answers.

Quiz

1. True or false: Both conditions when using the OR operator must be TRUE.
2. True or false: All specified values must match when using the IN operator.
3. True or false: The AND operator can be used in the SELECT and the WHERE clauses.
4. True or false: The ANY operator can accept an expression list.
5. What is the logical negation of the IN operator?
6. What is the logical negation of the ANY and ALL operators?
7. What, if anything, is wrong with the following SELECT statements?

    a. `SELECT AIRCRAFTTYPE`
       `FROM AIRCRAFT`
       `WHERE SEATING BETWEEN 200, 300;`

    b. `SELECT DISTANCE + AIRPLANECODE`
       `FROM ROUTES;`

    c. `SELECT FIRSTNAME, LASTNAME`
       `FROM PASSENGERS`
       `WHERE BIRTHDATE BETWEEN 1980-01-01`
       `AND 1990-01-01`
       `AND COUNTRYCODE = 'US'`
       `OR COUNTRYCODE = 'GB'`
       `AND PASSENGERID LIKE '%55%';`

Exercises

1. Using the `ROUTES` table, write a `SELECT` statement that returns all routes originating from Indianapolis, with route codes starting with 'IND'. Order your results based on the route name in alphabetical order and then the distance of the route going from largest to smallest.

2. Rewrite the query from Exercise 1 to show only those flights that are between 1000 and 2000 miles long.

3. Assuming that you used the `BETWEEN` operator in Exercise 2, rewrite your SQL statement to achieve the same results using different operators. If you did not use the `BETWEEN` operator, do so now.

4. Rewrite your query so that instead of showing results where the distance is between 1000 and 2000 miles, you show all distances except that range. Show at least two ways that you could achieve this result.

5. Write a `SELECT` statement that returns the route code, distance, and travel time, and then calculates a cost column by multiplying travel time by the fuel cost per minute value for all routes originating from Indianapolis. Order your results from most expensive routes to least expensive.

6. Rewrite your statement from Exercise 5 to include a 10% fuel surcharge added onto the cost.

7. Enhance your statement from Exercise 6 by including those routes with route codes IND-MFK, IND-MYR, and IND-MDA. There are at least two ways to write this constraint.

8. Now rewrite your statement from Exercise 7, include an additional column called `COST_PER_MILE`, and use the distance column that is in miles to calculate the resulting value. Pay special attention to parentheses in your answer.

Summarizing Data Results from a Query

What You'll Learn in This Hour:

► Definition of functions
► Using aggregate functions
► Summarizing data with aggregate functions
► Results from using functions

In this hour, you learn about SQL's aggregate functions. You can perform a variety of useful functions with aggregate functions, such as getting the highest total of a sale or counting the number of orders processed on a given day. The real power of aggregate functions will be discussed in the next hour when you tackle the GROUP BY clause.

Aggregate Functions

Functions are keywords in SQL used to manipulate values within columns for output purposes. A *function* is a command normally used with a column name or expression that processes the incoming data to produce a result. SQL contains several types of functions. This hour covers aggregate functions. An *aggregate function* provides summarization information for a SQL statement, such as counts, totals, and averages.

The basic set of aggregate functions discussed in this hour are

► COUNT

► SUM

► MAX

► MIN

► AVG

The following query lists the employee information from the EMPLOYEES table. Note that some of the employees do not have data assigned in some of the columns. We use this data for most of this hour's examples.

```
SELECT TOP 10 EMPLOYEEID,LASTNAME,
  CITY,STATE,PAYRATE,SALARY
  FROM EMPLOYEES;
```

EMPLOYEEID	LASTNAME	CITY	STATE	PAYRATE	SALARY
1	Iner	Red Dog	NULL		54000.00
2	Denty	Errol	NH	22.24	NULL
3	Sabbah	Errol	NH	15.29	NULL
4	Loock	Errol	NH	12.88	NULL
5	Sacks	Errol	NH	23.61	NULL
6	Arcoraci	Alexandria	LA	24.79	NULL
7	Astin	Espanola	NM	18.03	NULL
8	Contreraz	Espanola	NM	NULL	60000.00
9	Capito	Espanola	NM	NULL	52000.00
10	Ellamar	Espanola	NM	15.64	NULL

```
(10 row(s) affected)
```

COUNT

You use the COUNT function to count rows or values of a column that do not contain a NULL value. When used within a query, the COUNT function returns a numeric value. You can also use the COUNT function with the DISTINCT command to only count the distinct rows of a dataset. ALL (opposite of DISTINCT) is the default; it is not necessary to include ALL in the syntax. Duplicate rows are counted if DISTINCT is not specified. One other option with the COUNT function is to use it with an asterisk. COUNT(*) counts all the rows of a table including duplicates, regardless of whether a NULL value is contained in a column.

NOTE

DISTINCT Can Be Used Only in Certain Circumstances

You cannot use the DISTINCT command with COUNT(*), only with COUNT(*column_name*).

The syntax for the COUNT function follows:

```
COUNT [ (*) | (DISTINCT | ALL) ] (COLUMN NAME)
```

This example counts all employee IDs:

```
SELECT COUNT(EMPLOYEEID) FROM EMPLOYEES
```

This example counts only the distinct rows:

```
SELECT COUNT(DISTINCT SALARY) FROM EMPLOYEES
```

This example counts all rows for SALARY:

```
SELECT COUNT(ALL SALARY) FROM EMPLOYEES
```

This final example counts all rows of the EMPLOYEES table:

```
SELECT COUNT(*) FROM EMPLOYEES
```

COUNT(*) is used in the following example to get a count of all records in the EMPLOYEES table. There are 5,611 employees.

```
SELECT COUNT(*)
FROM EMPLOYEES;
-----------
5611

(1 row(s) affected)
```

CAUTION

COUNT(*) Is Different from Other Count Variations

COUNT(*) produces slightly different calculations than other count variations. This is because when the COUNT function is used with the asterisk, it counts the rows in the returned result set without regard to duplicates and NULL values. This is an important distinction. If you need your query to return a count of a particular field and include NULLs, you need to use a function such as ISNULL to replace the NULL values.

COUNT(EMPLOYEEID) is used in the next example to get a count of all the employee identification IDs that exist in the table. The returned count is the same as the last query because all employees have an identification number.

```
SELECT COUNT(EMPLOYEEID)
FROM EMPLOYEES;
-----------
5611

(1 row(s) affected)
```

COUNT([STATE]) is used in the following example to get a count of all the employee records that have a state assigned. Look at the difference between the two counts. The difference is the number of employees who have NULL in the STATE column.

```
SELECT COUNT([STATE])
FROM EMPLOYEES;
-----------
5147
Warning: Null value is eliminated by an aggregate or other SET operation.

(1 row(s) affected)
```

The following examples obtain a count of all salary amounts and then all the distinct salary amounts in the EMPLOYEES table.

```
SELECT COUNT(SALARY )
FROM EMPLOYEES;
-----------
1359
Warning: Null value is eliminated by an aggregate or other SET operation.

(1 row(s) affected)
```

```
SELECT COUNT(DISTINCT SALARY )
FROM EMPLOYEES;
-----------
45
Warning: Null value is eliminated by an aggregate or other SET operation.

(1 row(s) affected)
```

The SALARY column had a lot of matching amounts, so the DISTINCT values make the counts drop dramatically.

NOTE

Data Types Do Not Use COUNT

Because the COUNT function counts the rows, data types do not play a part. The rows can contain columns with any data type. The only thing that actually counts is whether the value is NULL.

SUM

The SUM function returns a total on the values of a column for a group of rows. You can also use the SUM function with DISTINCT. When you use SUM with DISTINCT, only the distinct rows are totaled, which might not have much purpose. Your total is not accurate in that case because rows of data are omitted.

The syntax for the SUM function follows:

```
SUM ([ DISTINCT ] COLUMN NAME)
```

CAUTION

SUM Must Be Numeric

The value of an argument must be numeric to use the SUM function. You cannot use the SUM function on columns that have a data type other than numeric, such as character or date.

This example totals the salaries:

```
SELECT SUM(SALARY) FROM EMPLOYEES
```

This example totals the distinct salaries:

```
SELECT SUM(DISTINCT SALARY) FROM EMPLOYEES
```

In the following query, the sum, or total amount, of all salary values is retrieved from the EMPLOYEES table:

```
SELECT SUM(SALARY)
FROM EMPLOYEES;.
---------------------------
70791000.00
Warning: Null value is eliminated by an aggregate or other SET operation.

(1 row(s) affected)
```

Observe the way the DISTINCT command in the following example skews the previous results by 68 million dollars. This is why it is rarely useful.

```
SELECT SUM(DISTINCT COST)
FROM EMPLOYEES;
---------------------------
2340000.00
Warning: Null value is eliminated by an aggregate or other SET operation.

(1 row(s) affected)
```

The following query demonstrates that although some aggregate functions require numeric data, this is only limited to the type of data. Here the ZIP column of the EMPLOYEES table shows that the implicit conversion of the VARCHAR data to a numeric type is supported in Oracle:

```
SELECT SUM(ZIP)
FROM EMPLOYEES;
SUM(ZIP)
-----------
280891448
```

Some aggregate functions require numeric data; this is only limited to the type of data. If the data can be converted implicitly, for example, the string `'12345'` to an integer, then you can use the aggregate function. When you use a type of data that cannot be implicitly converted to a numeric type, such as the `POSITION` column, it results in an error, as in the following example:

```
SELECT SUM(POSITION)
FROM EMPLOYEES;
Msg 8117, Level 16, State 1, Line 1
Operand data type varchar is invalid for sum operator.
```

AVG

The `AVG` function finds the average value for a given group of rows. When used with the `DISTINCT` command, the `AVG` function returns the average of the distinct rows. The syntax for the `AVG` function follows:

```
AVG ([ DISTINCT ] COLUMN NAME)
```

NOTE

AVG Must Be Numeric

The value of the argument must be numeric for the `AVG` function to work.

The average value for all values in the `EMPLOYEES` table's `SALARY` column is retrieved in the following example:

```
SELECT AVG(SALARY)
FROM EMPLOYEES;
------------------------------
52090.507726
Warning: Null value is eliminated by an aggregate or other SET operation.

(1 row(s) affected)
```

This example returns the distinct average salary:

```
SELECT AVG(DISTINCT SALARY)
FROM EMPLOYEES;
------------------------------
52000.000000
Warning: Null value is eliminated by an aggregate or other SET operation.

(1 row(s) affected)
```

Sometimes Your Data Is Truncated

In some implementations, the results of your query might be truncated to the precision of the data type. You need to review your database system's documentation to ensure you understand what the normal precision for the various data types is. This will prevent you from unnecessarily truncating data and possibly getting an unexpected result due to the data not being of the proper precision.

The next example uses two aggregate functions in the same query. Because some employees are paid hourly and others are on salary, you want to retrieve the average value for both PAYRATE and SALARY.

```
SELECT AVG(PAYRATE) AS AVG_PAYRATE, AVG(SALARY) AS AVG_SALARY
FROM EMPLOYEES;
AVG_PAYRATE                     AVG_SALARY
----------------------------    ----------------------------
18.473012                       52090.507726
Warning: Null value is eliminated by an aggregate or other SET operation.

(1 row(s) affected)
```

Notice how the use of aliases makes the output more readable with multiple aggregate values. Also remember that the aggregate function can work on any numeric data. So you can perform calculations within the parentheses of the function as well. So if you need to get the average hourly rate of salaried employees to compare to the average rate of hourly employees, you could write the following:

```
SELECT AVG(PAYRATE) AS AVG_PAYRATE, AVG(SALARY/2040) AS AVG_SALARY_RATE
FROM EMPLOYEES;
AVG_PAYRATE                     AVG_SALARY_RATE
----------------------------    ----------------------------
18.473012                       25.5345625
Warning: Null value is eliminated by an aggregate or other SET operation.

(1 row(s) affected)
```

MAX

The MAX function returns the maximum value from the values of a column in a group of rows. NULL values are ignored when using the MAX function. Using MAX with the DISTINCT command is an option. However, because the maximum value for all the rows is the same as the distinct maximum value, DISTINCT is useless.

The syntax for the MAX function is

```
MAX([ DISTINCT ] COLUMN NAME)
```

The following example returns the highest SALARY in the EMPLOYEES table:

```
SELECT MAX(SALARY)
FROM EMPLOYEES;
-----------------------------
74000.00
Warning: Null value is eliminated by an aggregate or other SET operation.

(1 row(s) affected)
```

This example returns the highest distinct salary:

```
SELECT MAX(DISTINCT SALARY)
FROM EMPLOYEES;
-----------------------------
74000.00
Warning: Null value is eliminated by an aggregate or other SET operation.

(1 row(s) affected)
```

You can also use aggregate functions such as MAX and MIN (covered in the next section) on character data. In the case of these values, collation of your database comes into play again. Most commonly your database collation is set to a dictionary order, so the results are ranked according to that. For example, say you perform a MAX on the CITY column of the employees table:

```
SELECT MAX(CITY) AS MAX_CITY
FROM EMPLOYEES;
MAX_CITY
-----------------------------
Zwara

(1 row(s) affected)
```

In this instance, the function returned the largest value according to a dictionary ordering of the data in the column.

MIN

The MIN function returns the minimum value of a column for a group of rows. NULL values are ignored when using the MIN function. Using MIN with the DISTINCT command is an option. However, because the minimum value for all rows is the same as the minimum value for distinct rows, DISTINCT is useless.

The syntax for the MIN function is

```
MIN([ DISTINCT ] COLUMN NAME)
```

The following example returns the lowest `SALARY` in the `EMPLOYEES` table:

```
SELECT MIN(SALARY)
FROM EMPLOYEES;
-----------------------------
30000.00
Warning: Null value is eliminated by an aggregate or other SET operation.

(1 row(s) affected)
```

This example returns the lowest distinct salary:

```
SELECT MIN(DISTINCT SALARY)
FROM EMPLOYEES;
-----------------------------
30000.00
Warning: Null value is eliminated by an aggregate or other SET operation.

(1 row(s) affected)
```

NOTE

DISTINCT and Aggregate Functions Don't Always Mix

One important thing to keep in mind when using aggregate functions with the `DISTINCT` command is that your query might not return the wanted results. The purpose of aggregate functions is to return summarized data based on all rows of data in a table. When `DISTINCT` is used it is applied first to the results and then those results are passed on to the aggregate function, which can dramatically alter the results. You need to ensure that when you work with `DISTINCT` with aggregate functions that you understand this.

As with the `MAX` function, the `MIN` function can work against character data and returns the minimum value according to the dictionary ordering of the data.

```
SELECT MIN(CITY) AS MIN_CITY
FROM EMPLOYEES;
MIN_CITY
-----------------------------
 AFB MunicipalCharleston SC

(1 row(s) affected)
```

Summary

Aggregate functions can be useful and are quite simple to use. In this hour you learned how to count values in columns, count rows of data in a table, get the maximum and minimum values for a column, figure the sum of the values in a column, and figure the average value for values in a column. Remember that NULL values are not considered when using aggregate functions, except when using the COUNT function in the format COUNT(*).

Aggregate functions are the first functions in SQL that you have learned in this book, but more follow in the coming hours. You can also use aggregate functions for group values, which are discussed during the next hour. As you learn about other functions, you see that the syntaxes of most functions are similar to one another and that their concepts of use are relatively easy to understand.

Q&A

Q. Why are NULL values ignored when using the MAX or MIN function?

A. A NULL value means that nothing is there, so there would be no maximum or minimum value.

Q. Why don't data types matter when using the COUNT function?

A. The COUNT function counts only rows.

Q. Does the data type matter when using the SUM or AVG function?

A. Not exactly. If the data can be implicitly converted to numeric data, then it will still work. It's less a function of what the data type is and more about what data is stored in it.

Q. Are you limited to using only column names inside of aggregate functions?

A. No, you can use any type of calculation or formula as long as the output corresponds to the proper type of data that the function is expecting to use.

Workshop

The following workshop is composed of a series of quiz questions and practical exercises. The quiz questions are designed to test your overall understanding of the current material. The practical exercises are intended to afford you the opportunity to apply the concepts discussed during the current hour, as well as build upon the knowledge acquired in previous hours of study. Please take time to complete the quiz questions and exercises before continuing. Refer to Appendix C, "Answers to Quizzes and Exercises," for answers.

Quiz

1. True or false: The `AVG` function returns an average of all rows from a `SELECT` column, including any `NULL` values.

2. True or false: The `SUM` function adds column totals.

3. True or false: The `COUNT(*)` function counts all rows in a table.

4. True or false: The `COUNT([column name])` function counts `NULL` values.

5. Will the following `SELECT` statements work? If not, what fixes the statements?

   a. `SELECT COUNT *`
   `FROM EMPLOYEES;`

   b. `SELECT COUNT(EMPLOYEEID), SALARY`
   `FROM EMPLOYEES;`

   c. `SELECT MIN(PAYRATE), MAX(SALARY)`
   `FROM EMPLOYEES`
   `WHERE SALARY > 50000;`

   d. `SELECT COUNT(DISTINCT EMPLOYEEID) FROM EMPLOYEES;`

   e. `SELECT AVG(LASTNAME) FROM EMPLOYEES;`

   f. `SELECT AVG(CAST(ZIP AS INT)) FROM EMPLOYEES;`

Exercises

1. Use the `EMPLOYEES` table to construct SQL statements to solve the following exercises:

   a. What is the average salary?

   b. What is the maximum pay rate for hourly employees?

   c. What are the total salaries?

   d. What is the minimum pay rate?

   e. How many rows are in the table?

2. Write a query to determine how many employees are in the company whose last names begin with a *G*.

3. Write a query to determine the minimum and maximum salary and pay rates per city for employees.

4. Write two sets of queries to find the first employee name and last employee name when they are listed in alphabetical order.

5. Write a query to perform an `AVG` function on the employee names. Does the statement work? Determine why it is that you got that result.

6. Write a query to display the average value of employees' salaries that takes `NULL` values into account. Hint: You won't be using the `AVG` function.

Sorting and Grouping Data

What You'll Learn in This Hour:

▶ Why you would want to group data

▶ How to group results with the GROUP BY clause

▶ Group value functions

▶ The how and why of group functions

▶ Grouping by columns

▶ GROUP BY versus ORDER BY

▶ Reducing groups with the HAVING clause

You have learned how to query the database and return data in an organized fashion. You have also learned how to sort data from a query. During this hour, you learn how to break returned data from a query into groups for improved readability.

Why Group Data?

Grouping data is the process of combining columns with duplicate values in a logical order. For example, a database might contain information about employees; many employees live in different cities, but some employees live in the same city. You might want to execute a query that shows employee information for each particular city. You would group employee information by city and create a summarized report.

Or perhaps you want to figure the average salary paid to employees according to each city. You can do this by using the aggregate function AVG on the SALARY column, as you learned in the previous hour, and by using the GROUP BY clause to group the output by city.

Grouping data is accomplished through the use of the GROUP BY clause of a SELECT statement (query). In Hour 9, "Summarizing Data Results from a Query," you learned how to use aggregate functions. In this lesson, you see how to use aggregate functions with the GROUP BY clause to display results more effectively.

The GROUP BY Clause

The GROUP BY clause is used in collaboration with the SELECT statement to arrange identical data into groups. This clause follows the WHERE clause in a SELECT statement and precedes the ORDER BY clause.

The position of the GROUP BY clause in a query follows:

```
SELECT
FROM
WHERE
GROUP BY
ORDER BY
```

The following is the SELECT statement's syntax, including the GROUP BY clause:

```
SELECT COLUMN1, COLUMN2
FROM TABLE1, TABLE2
WHERE CONDITIONS
GROUP BY COLUMN1, COLUMN2
ORDER BY COLUMN1, COLUMN2
```

This ordering normally takes a little getting used to when writing your first queries with the GROUP BY clause; however, it is logical. The GROUP BY clause is normally a much more CPU-intensive operation, and if you do not constrain the rows provided to it, you are grouping unnecessary data that would later be discarded. So you intentionally reduce the data set with the WHERE clause so that you perform your grouping only on the rows you need.

You can use the ORDER BY statement, but normally the relational database management system (RDBMS) also orders the results by the column ordering in the GROUP BY clause, which is discussed more in depth later in this hour. So unless you need to order the values in a different pattern than the GROUP BY clause, the ORDER BY clause is redundant. However, sometimes it is provided because you use aggregate functions in the SELECT statement that are not in the GROUP BY clause or because your particular RDBMS functions slightly differently from the standard.

The following sections explain how to use the GROUP BY clause and provide examples of using it in a variety of situations.

Group Functions

Typical group functions—those that the GROUP BY clause uses to arrange data in groups—include AVG, MAX, MIN, SUM, and COUNT. These are the aggregate functions that you learned about in Hour 9. Remember that the aggregate functions were used for single values in Hour 9; now you use the aggregate functions for group values.

Grouping Selected Data

Grouping data is simple. The selected columns (the column list following the SELECT keyword in a query) are the columns you can reference in the GROUP BY clause. If a column is not in the SELECT statement, you cannot use it in the GROUP BY clause. How can you group data on a report if the data is not displayed?

If the column name has been qualified, the qualified name must go into the GROUP BY clause. The column name can also be represented by a number, which is discussed later in the "Representing Column Names with Numbers" section. When grouping the data, the order of columns grouped does not have to match the column order in the SELECT clause.

Creating Groups and Using Aggregate Functions

The SELECT clause has conditions that must be met when using GROUP BY. Specifically, whatever columns are selected must appear in the GROUP BY clause, except for any aggregate values. Should the columns in the SELECT clause be qualified, the qualified names of the columns must be used in the GROUP BY clause. Some examples of syntax for the GROUP BY clause are shown next.

The following SQL statement selects the DISTANCE and the SOURCECITY from the EMPLOYEE_TBL and groups the data returned by SOURCECITY and then DISTANCE:

```
SELECT DISTANCE, SOURCECITY
FROM VW_FLIGHTINFO
GROUP BY SOURCECITY, DISTANCE;
```

This SQL statement returns the SOURCECITY and the total of the DISTANCE column. Then it groups the results by the SOURCECITY:

```
SELECT SOURCECITY, SUM(DISTANCE)
FROM VW_FLIGHTINFO
GROUP BY SOURCECITY;
```

This SQL statement returns the distance traveled for flights that took off during the month of May 2013:

```
SELECT SUM(DISTANCE) AS TOTAL_DISTANCE
FROM VW_FLIGHTINFO
WHERE FLIGHTSTART BETWEEN '2013-05-01' AND '2013-06-01';

TOTAL_DISTANCE
--------------
62587932

(1 row(s) affected)
```

This SQL statement returns the totals for the different groups of distances:

```
SELECT SUM(DISTANCE) AS TOTAL_DISTANCE
FROM VW_FLIGHTINFO
GROUP BY SOURCECITY;
TOTAL_DISTANCE
--------------
1111579
1145224
1825544
276003
617604
.
.
.


(166 row(s) affected)
```

Practical examples using real data follow. In this first example, you can see three distinct cities in the VW_FLIGHTINFO view. A view is just like a table in terms of selecting data from it. We'll go into greater depth about views in later chapters.

```
SELECT DISTINCT SOURCECITY
FROM VW_FLIGHTINFO;

SOURCECITY
------------------------------
Niagara Falls
Taylor
Fayetteville
Chicago
Hattiesburg/Laurel MS
Clovis
```

In the following example, you select the city and a count of all records for each city. You receive a count on each of the three distinct cities because you use a GROUP BY clause:

```
SELECT SOURCECITY, COUNT(*)
FROM VW_FLIGHTINFO
WHERE SOURCECITY LIKE 'A%'
GROUP BY SOURCECITY;

SOURCECITY
------------------------------ -----------
Albany                         453
Algona                         135
Arcata                         253
Augusta GA                     211
```

```
Ardmore                        225
Athens                         427
Anchorage                      123
Atlanta                        61
Austin                         576
Alexandria                     810
Aiken                          396
```

(11 row(s) affected)

In the following example, you retrieve the average pay rate and salary on each distinct city using the aggregate function AVG from the EMPLOYEES table. There is no average salary for ADRIAN because there are no employees living there who are paid salary:

```
SELECT CITY, AVG(PAYRATE) AS AVG_PAYRATE, AVG(SALARY) AS AVG_SALARY
FROM EMPLOYEES
GROUP BY CITY;
```

```
CITY                           AVG_PAYRATE                    AVG_SALARY
------------------------------ ------------------------------ ---------------------
AFB MunicipalCharleston SC     NULL                           51000.000000
Downtown MemorialSpartanburg   19.320000                      56000.000000
Aberdeen                       19.326000                      63000.000000
Abilene                        13.065000                      66000.000000
Abingdon                       20.763333                      31000.000000
Adak Island                    20.545000                      56000.000000
Adrian                         21.865000                      NULL
  .
  .
  .
```

Warning: Null value is eliminated by an aggregate or other SET operation.

(1865 row(s) affected)

In the next example, you combine the use of multiple components in a query to return grouped data. You still want to see the average pay rate and salary, but only for cities like INDIANAPOLIS, CHICAGO, and NEW_YORK. You are forced to group the data by CITY because you use aggregate functions on the other columns. Lastly, you want to order the report by 2 and then 3, which are the average pay rate and then average salary, respectively:

```
SELECT CITY, AVG(PAYRATE) AS AVG_PAYRATE, AVG(SALARY) AS AVG_SALARY
FROM EMPLOYEES
WHERE CITY LIKE 'INDIANAPOLIS%'
OR CITY LIKE 'CHICAGO%'
OR CITY LIKE 'NEW YORK%'
GROUP BY CITY
ORDER BY 2,3;
```

CITY	AVG_PAYRATE	AVG_SALARY
Chicago	19.642142	35333.333333
New York	19.701904	42666.666666
Indianapolis IN	21.445000	NULL
Chicago Il	22.040000	32000.000000
New York NY	23.740000	NULL

Warning: Null value is eliminated by an aggregate or other SET operation.

```
(5 row(s) affected)
40000
```

Values are sorted before NULL values; therefore, the record for CHICAGO is displayed first. If the order of the columns of the ORDER BY was switched, then NEW YORK would be first and then INDIANAPOLIS, and NEW YORK NY would be pushed to the bottom of the list.

The last example in this section shows the use of the MAX and MIN aggregate functions with the GROUP BY clause to get the maximum PAYRATE and the minimum SALARY for the cities of INDIANAPOLIS, CHICAGO, and NEW YORK grouped by CITY:

```
SELECT CITY, MAX(PAYRATE) AS MAX_PAYRATE, MIN(SALARY) AS MIN_SALARY
FROM EMPLOYEES
WHERE CITY LIKE 'INDIANAPOLIS%'
OR CITY LIKE 'CHICAGO%'
OR CITY LIKE 'NEW YORK%'
GROUP BY CITY;
```

CITY	MAX_PAYRATE	MIN_SALARY
Chicago	24.31	31000.00
Chicago Il	22.04	32000.00
Indianapolis IN	23.15	NULL
New York	24.69	33000.00
New York NY	23.74	NULL

Warning: Null value is eliminated by an aggregate or other SET operation.

```
(5 row(s) affected)
```

GROUP BY Versus ORDER BY

You should understand that the GROUP BY clause works the same as the ORDER BY clause in that both sort data. Specifically, you use the ORDER BY clause to sort data from a query. The GROUP BY clause also sorts data from a query to properly group the data.

However, there are some differences and disadvantages of using GROUP BY instead of ORDER BY for sorting operations:

▶ All non-aggregate columns selected must be listed in the GROUP BY clause.

▶ The GROUP BY clause is generally not necessary unless you use aggregate functions.

An example of performing sort operations utilizing the GROUP BY clause in place of the ORDER BY clause is shown next:

```
SELECT LASTNAME, FIRSTNAME, CITY
FROM EMPLOYEES
GROUP BY LASTNAME;

Msg 8120, Level 16, State 1, Line 1
```

The column EMPLOYEES.FirstName is invalid in the select list because it is not contained in either an aggregate function or the GROUP BY clause.

NOTE

Error Messages Differ

Different SQL implementations return errors in different formats.

In this example, a SQL Server database server received an error stating that FIRSTNAME is invalid and that this was not a proper GROUP BY expression. Remember that all columns and expressions in the SELECT statement must be listed in the GROUP BY clause, with the exception of aggregate columns (those columns targeted by an aggregate function).

In the next example, the previous problem is solved by adding all the expressions in the SELECT statement to the GROUP BY clause:

```
SELECT LASTNAME, FIRSTNAME, CITY
FROM EMPLOYEES
GROUP BY LASTNAME, FIRSTNAME, CITY;
```

LASTNAME	FIRSTNAME	CITY
Aarant	Sidney	Columbia
Abbas	Gail	Port Hueneme CA
Abbay	Demetrice	Shangri-la
Abbington	Gaynelle	Forrest City
Abbington	Gaynelle	Sparta
Abdelal	Marcelo	Benson
.		
.		
.		

```
(5611 row(s) affected)
```

In this example, the same columns were selected from the same table, but all columns in the GROUP BY clause are listed as they appeared after the SELECT keyword. The results are ordered by LASTNAME first, FIRSTNAME second, and CITY third. These results could have been accomplished easier with the ORDER BY clause; however, it might help you better understand how the GROUP BY clause works if you can visualize how it must first sort data to group data results.

The following example shows a SELECT statement from EMPLOYEES and uses the GROUP BY clause to order by CITY:

```
SELECT CITY, LASTNAME
FROM EMPLOYEES
GROUP BY CITY, LASTNAME;


CITY                          LASTNAME
----------------------------- -----------------------------
 AFB MunicipalCharleston SC   Tobey
 Downtown MemorialSpartanburg Bovey
 Downtown MemorialSpartanburg Fawbush
 Downtown MemorialSpartanburg Sundin
 Downtown MemorialSpartanburg Vignaux
Aberdeen                      Apkin
Aberdeen                      Blystone
 .
 .
 .

(5611 row(s) affected)
```

Notice the order of data in the previous results, as well as the LASTNAME of the individual for each CITY.

In the following example, all employee records in the EMPLOYEES table are now counted, and the results are grouped by CITY but ordered by the count on each city first:

```
SELECT CITY, COUNT(*)
FROM EMPLOYEES
GROUP BY CITY
ORDER BY 2 DESC,1;


CITY
----------------------------- -----------
New York                      27
Columbus                      24
Greenville                    20
San Diego                     18
Chicago                       17
 .
 .
 .

(1865 row(s) affected)
```

Check out the order of the results. The results were first sorted by the count on each city in descending order and then sorted by city.

Although GROUP BY and ORDER BY perform a similar function, there is one major difference. The GROUP BY clause is designed to group identical data, whereas the ORDER BY clause is designed merely to put data into a specific order. You can use GROUP BY and ORDER BY in the same SELECT statement, but you must follow a specific order.

TIP

You Can't Use the ORDER BY Clause in a View

You can use the GROUP BY clause in the CREATE VIEW statement to sort data, but the ORDER BY clause is not allowed in the CREATE VIEW statement. The CREATE VIEW statement is discussed in depth in Hour 20, "Creating and Using Views and Synonyms."

CUBE and ROLLUP Expressions

Sometimes, it is advantageous to get summary totals within a certain group. For instance, you might want to have a breakdown of the SUM of sales per year, country, and product type but also want to see the totals in each year and country. Luckily, the ANSI SQL standard provides for such functionality using the CUBE and ROLLUP expressions.

The ROLLUP expression is used to get subtotals, or what is commonly referred to as *super-aggregate* rows, along with a grand total row. The ANSI syntax follows:

```
GROUP BY ROLLUP(ordered column list of grouping sets)
```

The way the ROLLUP expression works is that for every change in the LAST column provided for the grouping set, an additional row is inserted into the result set with a NULL value for that column and the subtotal of the values in the set. In addition, a row is inserted at the end of the result set with NULL values for each of the group columns and a grand total for the aggregate information. Both Microsoft SQL Server and Oracle follow the ANSI-compliant format.

First, examine a result set of a simple GROUP BY statement in which you examine average employee pay by CITY and ZIP for the city of INDIANAPOLIS:

```
SELECT CITY,LASTNAME, AVG(PAYRATE) AS AVG_PAYRATE, AVG(SALARY) AS AVG_SALARY
FROM EMPLOYEES
WHERE CITY LIKE 'INDIANAPOLIS%'
GROUP BY CITY,LASTNAME
ORDER BY CITY,LASTNAME;
```

```
CITY                         LASTNAME             AVG_PAYRATE          AVG_SALARY
-------------------------    --------------------  --------------------  ----------
Indianapolis IN              Maddry               19.740000            NULL
Indianapolis IN              Wahl                 23.150000            NULL
Warning: Null value is eliminated by an aggregate or other SET operation.

(2 row(s) affected)
```

The following is an example of using the ROLLUP expression to get subtotals of pay rates and salaries:

```
SELECT CITY,LASTNAME, AVG(PAYRATE) AS AVG_PAYRATE, AVG(SALARY) AS AVG_SALARY
FROM EMPLOYEES
WHERE CITY LIKE 'INDIANAPOLIS%'
GROUP BY ROLLUP(CITY,LASTNAME);
```

```
CITY                         LASTNAME             AVG_PAYRATE              AVG_SALARY
-------------------------    --------------------  ------------------------  ----------
Indianapolis IN              Maddry               19.740000                      NULL
Indianapolis IN              Wahl                 23.150000                      NULL
Indianapolis IN              NULL                 21.445000                      NULL
NULL                         NULL                 21.445000                      NULL
Warning: Null value is eliminated by an aggregate or other SET operation.

(4 row(s) affected)
```

Notice how you now get an average super-aggregate row for each one of the cities and an overall average for the entire set as the last row.

The CUBE expression is different. It returns a single row of data with every combination of the columns in the column list along with a row for the grand total of the whole set. The syntax for the CUBE expression follows:

```
GROUP BY CUBE(column list of grouping sets)
```

CUBE is often used to create crosstab reports due to its unique nature. For instance, if you want to have sales use the following columns in the GROUP BY CUBE expression list, CITY, STATE, and REGION, you receive rows for each of the following:

```
CITY
CITY, STATE
CITY, REGION
CITY, STATE, REGION
REGION
STATE,REGION
STATE
<grand total row>
```

The following statement shows an example of using the CUBE expression:

```
SELECT CITY,LASTNAME, AVG(PAYRATE) AS AVG_PAYRATE, AVG(SALARY) AS AVG_SALARY
FROM EMPLOYEES
WHERE CITY LIKE 'INDIANAPOLIS%'
GROUP BY CUBE(CITY,LASTNAME);
```

CITY	LASTNAME	AVG_PAYRATE	AVG_SALARY
Indianapolis IN	Maddry	19.740000	NULL
NULL	Maddry	19.740000	NULL
Indianapolis IN	Wahl	23.150000	NULL
NULL	Wahl	23.150000	NULL
NULL	NULL	21.445000	NULL
Indianapolis IN	NULL	21.445000	NULL

```
Warning: Null value is eliminated by an aggregate or other SET operation.
```

```
(6 row(s) affected)
```

Now you can see that with the CUBE expression, there are even more rows because the statement needs to return each combination of columns within the column set that we provided.

The HAVING Clause

The HAVING clause when used with the GROUP BY clause in a SELECT statement tells GROUP BY which groups to include in the output. HAVING is to GROUP BY as WHERE is to SELECT. In other words, the WHERE clause places conditions on the selected columns, and the HAVING clause places conditions on groups created by the GROUP BY clause. Therefore, when you use the HAVING clause, you are effectively including or excluding, as the case might be, whole groups of data from the query results.

The following shows the position of the HAVING clause in a query:

```
SELECT
FROM
WHERE
GROUP BY
HAVING
ORDER BY
```

The following is the syntax of the SELECT statement, including the HAVING clause:

```
SELECT COLUMN1, COLUMN2
FROM TABLE1, TABLE2
WHERE CONDITIONS
GROUP BY COLUMN1, COLUMN2
HAVING CONDITIONS
ORDER BY COLUMN1, COLUMN2
```

In the following example, you select the average pay rate and salary for all cities. You group the output by CITY, but you want to display only those groups (cities) that have an average salary equal to $71,000. You sort the results by average salary for each city:

```
SELECT CITY, AVG(PAYRATE) AS AVG_PAYRATE, AVG(SALARY) AS AVG_SALARY
FROM EMPLOYEES
GROUP BY CITY
HAVING AVG(SALARY) =71000
ORDER BY 3;
```

CITY	AVG_PAYRATE	AVG_SALARY
Amarillo	14.070000	71000.000000
Anaheim	16.250000	71000.000000
Butler	15.730000	71000.000000
Hidden Falls	23.690000	71000.000000
Hoffman	NULL	71000.000000
King Of Prussia	22.553333	71000.000000
Kuparuk	18.856666	71000.000000
Linden	19.003333	71000.000000
Marquette	17.350000	71000.000000
Neosho	16.565000	71000.000000
New Haven	15.236666	71000.000000
Rome NY	21.140000	71000.000000
Sheffield	NULL	71000.000000
West Yellowstone	16.893333	71000.000000

Warning: Null value is eliminated by an aggregate or other SET operation.

(14 row(s) affected)

Summary

You have learned in this hour how to group the results of a query using the GROUP BY clause. The GROUP BY clause is primarily used with aggregate SQL functions, such as SUM, AVG, MAX, MIN, and COUNT. The nature of GROUP BY is like that of ORDER BY in that both sort query results. The GROUP BY clause must sort data to group results logically, but you can also use it exclusively to sort data. However, an ORDER BY clause is much simpler for this purpose.

The HAVING clause, an extension to the GROUP BY clause, places conditions on the established groups of a query. The WHERE clause places conditions on a query's SELECT clause. During the next hour, you learn a new arsenal of functions that enable you to further manipulate query results.

Q&A

Q. Is using the ORDER BY clause mandatory when using the GROUP BY clause in a SELECT statement?

A. No, using the ORDER BY clause is strictly optional, but it can be helpful when used with GROUP BY.

Q. What is a group value?

A. Take the CITY column from the EMPLOYEES table. If you select the employee's name and city and then group the output by city, all the cities that are identical are arranged together.

Q. Must a column appear in the SELECT statement to use a GROUP BY clause on it?

A. Yes, a column must be in the SELECT statement to use a GROUP BY clause on it.

Q. Must all columns that appear in the SELECT statement be used in the GROUP BY clause?

A. Yes, every column that appears in the SELECT statement except for aggregate functions must be used in the GROUP BY clause or you will get an error.

Workshop

The following workshop is composed of a series of quiz questions and practical exercises. The quiz questions are designed to test your overall understanding of the current material. The practical exercises are intended to afford you the opportunity to apply the concepts discussed during the current hour, as well as build upon the knowledge acquired in previous hours of study. Please take time to complete the quiz questions and exercises before continuing. Refer to Appendix C, "Answers to Quizzes and Exercises," for answers.

Quiz

1. Will the following SQL statements work?

a.
```
SELECT SUM(SALARY) AS TOTAL_SALARY, EMPLOYEEID
FROM EMPLOYEES
GROUP BY 1 and 2;
```

b.
```
SELECT EMPLOYEEID, MAX(SALARY)
FROM EMPLOYEES
GROUP BY SALARY, EMPLOYEEID;
```

c.
```
SELECT EMPLOYEEID, COUNT(SALARY)
FROM EMPLOYEES
ORDER BY EMPLOYEEID
GROUP BY SALARY;
```

    d. `SELECT YEAR(DATE_HIRE) AS YEAR_HIRED,SUM(SALARY)`
       `FROM EMPLOYEES`
       `GROUP BY 1`
       `HAVING SUM(SALARY)>20000;`

2. What is the purpose of the `HAVING` clause and which other clause is it closest to?

3. True or false: You must also use the `GROUP BY` clause when using the `HAVING` clause.

4. True or false: The following SQL statement returns a total of the salaries by groups:

`SELECT SUM(SALARY)`
`FROM EMPLOYEES;`

5. True or false: The columns selected must appear in the `GROUP BY` clause in the same order.

6. True or false: The `HAVING` clause tells the `GROUP BY` clause which groups to include.

Exercises

1. Invoke the database and enter the following query to show all cities in `EMPLOYEES`:

`SELECT CITY`
`FROM EMPLOYEES;`

2. Enter the following query and compare the results to the query in Exercise 1:

`SELECT CITY, COUNT(*)`
`FROM EMPLOYEES`
`GROUP BY CITY;`

3. The `HAVING` clause works like the `WHERE` clause in that it enables the user to specify conditions on data returned. The `WHERE` clause is the main filter on the query, and the `HAVING` clause is the filter used after groups of data have been established using the `GROUP BY` clause. Enter the following query to see how the `HAVING` clause works:

`SELECT CITY, COUNT(*) AS CITY_COUNT`
`FROM EMPLOYEES`
`GROUP BY CITY`
`HAVING COUNT(*) > 15;`

4. Modify the query in Exercise 3 to order the results in descending order, from highest count to lowest.

5. Write a query to list the average pay rate and salary by position from the `EMPLOYEES` table.

6. Write a query to list the average salary by position from the `EMPLOYEES` table where the average salary is greater than `40000`.

7. Write the same query you used for Exercise 6, but find the average salary only for those people making more than 40000 grouped by city and position and compare the results. Explain the difference.

HOUR 11

Restructuring the Appearance of Data

What You'll Learn in This Hour:

- ▶ Introduction to character functions
- ▶ How and when to use character functions
- ▶ Examples of ANSI SQL functions
- ▶ Examples of common implementation-specific functions
- ▶ Overview of conversion functions
- ▶ How and when to use conversion functions

In this hour, you learn how to restructure the appearance of output results using some American National Standards Institute (ANSI) standard functions, other functions based on the standard, and several variations used by some major SQL implementations.

NOTE

The ANSI Standard Is Not Rigid

The ANSI concepts discussed in this book are just that—concepts. Standards provided by ANSI are simply guidelines for how the use of SQL in a relational database should be implemented. With that thought, keep in mind that the specific functions discussed in this hour are not necessarily the exact functions that you might use in your particular implementation. Yes, the concepts are the same, and the way the functions work are generally the same, but function names and actual syntax might differ.

ANSI Character Functions

Character functions are functions that transform strings in SQL into formats different from the way they are stored in the table. The first part of this hour discusses the concepts for character functions as covered by ANSI. The second part of this hour shows real-world examples using functions that are specific to various SQL implementations. The most common forms of ANSI character functions deal with operations for concatenation, substrings, and TRANSLATE.

Concatenation is the process of combining two strings into one. For example, you might want to concatenate an individual's first and last names into a single string for the complete name. JOHN concatenated with SMITH produces JOHN SMITH.

The concept of substring is the capability to extract part of a string, or a "sub" of the string. For example, the following values are substrings of JOHNSON:

- ▶ J

- ▶ JOHN

- ▶ JO

- ▶ ON

- ▶ SON

The TRANSLATE function translates a string, character by character, into another string. There are normally three arguments with the TRANSLATE function: the string to be converted, a list of the characters to convert, and a list of the substitution characters. Implementation examples are shown in the next part of this hour.

Common Character Functions

You use character functions mainly to compare, join, search, and extract a segment of a string or a value in a column. Several character functions are available to the SQL programmer.

The following sections illustrate the application of ANSI concepts in some of the leading implementations of SQL, such as Microsoft SQL Server, MySQL, and Oracle.

The CONCAT Function

The CONCAT function, along with most other functions, is represented slightly differently among various implementations. The following examples show the use of concatenation in Oracle and SQL Server.

Say you want to concatenate JOHN and SON to produce JOHNSON. In Oracle, your code looks like this:

```
SELECT 'JOHN' | | 'SON'
```

In SQL Server, your code appears as follows:

```
SELECT 'JOHN' + 'SON'
```

In SQL Server or Oracle, your code using the CONCAT looks like this:

```
SELECT CONCAT('JOHN' , 'SON')
```

Now for an overview of the syntaxes. The syntax for Oracle is

```
COLUMN_NAME | | [ '' | | ] COLUMN_NAME [ COLUMN_NAME ]
```

The syntax for SQL Server is

```
COLUMN_NAME + [ '' + ] COLUMN_NAME [ COLUMN_NAME ]
```

The syntax for the CONCAT function is

```
CONCAT(COLUMN_NAME , [ '' , ] COLUMN_NAME [ COLUMN_NAME ])
```

Both SQL Server as well as Oracle employ the CONCAT function. You can use it to get the concatenation of pairs of strings just like the shortened syntax of + for SQL Server and the double pipe (| |) for Oracle. The main difference between the two versions is that the Oracle version is limited to two values to be concatenated, whereas you can use the MySQL version for many values. In addition, remember that because this operation is for string values, any numeric values must be converted to strings before concatenation. Some examples of utilizing concatenation in its various formats are shown next.

This SQL Server statement concatenates the values for city and state into one value:

```
SELECT CITY + STATE FROM EMPLOYEES;
```

This Oracle statement concatenates the values for city and state into one value, placing a comma between the values for city and state:

```
SELECT CITY | |', '| | STATE FROM EMPLOYEES;
```

Alternatively for Oracle, if you want to use the CONCAT statement to achieve the preceding result, you cannot do so because you are concatenating more than two values.

NOTE

Use of Quotation Marks for Special Characters

Notice the use of single quotation marks and a comma in the preceding SQL statement. Most characters and symbols are allowed if they're enclosed by single quotations marks. Some implementations might use double quotation marks for literal string values.

This SQL Server statement concatenates the values for city and state into one value, placing a space between the two original values:

```
SELECT CITY + '' + STATE FROM EMPLOYEES;
```

This SQL Server statement concatenates the last name with the first name and inserts a comma between the two original values:

```
SELECT LASTNAME + ', ' + FIRSTNAME NAME
FROM EMPLOYEES
ORDER BY LASTNAME;

NAME
------------------------------
Aarant, Sidney
Abbas, Gail
Abbay, Demetrice
Abbington, Gaynelle
Abbington, Gaynelle
Abdelal, Marcelo
Abdelal, Marcelo
Abdelwahed, Scarlet
.
.
.
.

(5611 row(s) affected)
```

The UPPER Function

Most implementations have a way to control the case of data by using functions. The UPPER function converts lowercase letters to uppercase letters for a specific string.

The syntax is as follows:

```
UPPER(character string)
```

This SQL statement converts all characters in the column to uppercase:

```
SELECT DISTINCT UPPER(CITY) AS CITY
FROM EMPLOYEES
WHERE STATE='IN'
AND ( CITY LIKE 'A%'
OR CITY LIKE 'B%'
OR CITY LIKE 'C%'
);

CITY
------------------------------
ANDERSON
ANDREWS
ANGOLA
```

```
BATESVILLE
BEDFORD
BLOOMINGTON
COATESVILLE
CONNERSVILLE
CRANE

(9 row(s) affected)
```

Microsoft SQL Server, MySQL, and Oracle all support this syntax. In addition, MySQL supports an alternative to the UPPER function called UCASE. Because both functions accomplish the same task, you are better served to follow the ANSI syntax.

The LOWER Function

The converse of the UPPER function, the LOWER function, converts uppercase letters to lowercase letters for a specific string.

The syntax follows:

```
LOWER(character string)
```

This SQL statement converts all characters in the column to lowercase:

```
SELECT DISTINCT LOWER(CITY) AS CITY
FROM EMPLOYEES
WHERE STATE='IN'
AND ( CITY LIKE 'A%'
OR CITY LIKE 'B%'
OR CITY LIKE 'C%'
);

CITY
----------------------------
anderson
andrews
angola
batesville
bedford
bloomington
coatesville
connersville
crane

(9 row(s) affected)
```

The LOWER function is supported in Microsoft SQL Server, Oracle, and MySQL. Like the UPPER function, MySQL supports an alternative, LCASE, but as discussed with the UPPER function, it is often better to follow the ANSI standard.

The SUBSTR Function

Taking an expression's substring is common in most implementations of SQL, but the function name might differ, as shown in the following Oracle and SQL Server examples.

The syntax for Oracle is

```
SUBSTR(COLUMN NAME, STARTING POSITION, LENGTH)
```

The syntax for SQL Server is

```
SUBSTRING(COLUMN NAME, STARTING POSITION, LENGTH)
```

The only difference between the two implementations is the spelling of the function name.

This SQL statement returns the first three characters of LASTNAME:

```
SELECT SUBSTRING(LASTNAME,1,3) FROM EMPLOYEES
```

This SQL statement returns the fourth and fifth characters of LASTNAME:

```
SELECT SUBSTRING(LASTNAME,4,2) FROM EMPLOYEES
```

This SQL statement returns the sixth through the ninth characters of LASTNAME:

```
SELECT SUBSTRING(LASTNAME,6,4) FROM EMPLOYEES
```

The following is an example that is compatible with Microsoft SQL Server and MySQL:

```
SELECT TOP 10 EMPLOYEEID, SUBSTRING(UPPER(LASTNAME),1,3)
FROM EMPLOYEES;

EMPLOYEEID
----------- ----
1           INE
2           DEN
3           SAB
4           LOO
5           SAC
6           ARC
7           AST
8           CON
9           CAP
10          ELL

(10 row(s) affected)
```

The following SQL statement is what you use for Oracle:

```
SELECT EMPLOYEEID, SUBSTR(UPPER(LASTNAME),1,3)
FROM EMPLOYEES
WHERE ROWNUM<=10;
```

```
EMPLOYEEID
----------- ----
1           INE
2           DEN
3           SAB
4           LOO
5           SAC
6           ARC
7           AST
8           CON
9           CAP
10          ELL

10 rows selected.
```

NOTE

Output Statements Differ Between Implementations

Notice the difference in the feedback of the two queries. The first example returns the feedback `10 row(s) affected`, and the second returns `10 rows selected`. You will see differences such as this between the various implementations.

The TRANSLATE Function

The TRANSLATE function searches a string of characters and checks for a specific character, makes note of the position found, searches the replacement string at the same position, and then replaces that character with the new value. The syntax is

```
TRANSLATE(CHARACTER SET, VALUE1, VALUE2)
```

The next SQL statement substitutes every occurrence of I in the string with A, every occurrence of N with B, and all occurrences of D with C:

```
SELECT TRANSLATE (CITY,'IND','ABC' FROM EMPLOYEES) CITY_TRANSLATION
```

The following example illustrates the use of TRANSLATE with real data:

```
SELECT DISTINCT UPPER(CITY) CITY, TRANSLATE(UPPER(CITY),'ACE','XYZ') CITY_
TRANSLATION
FROM EMPLOYEES
WHERE CITY LIKE ('C%');
```

```
CITY            CITY_TRANSLATION
----------      ----------------
COATESVILLE     YOXTZSVILLZ
CONNERSVILLE    YONNZRSVILLZ
CRANE           YRXNZ
```

3 rows selected.

Notice in this example that all occurrences of A were replaced with X, C with Y, and E with Z.

Both MySQL and Oracle support the use of the TRANSLATE function. Microsoft SQL Server does not currently support the use of TRANSLATE.

The REPLACE Function

The REPLACE function replaces every occurrence of a character or string with another specified character or string. The use of this function is similar to the TRANSLATE function except only one specific character or string is replaced within another string. The syntax is

REPLACE('VALUE', 'VALUE', [NULL] 'VALUE')

This statement returns all the first names and changes any occurrence of T to B:

SELECT REPLACE(FIRSTNAME,'T', 'B') FROM EMPLOYEES

This statement returns all the cities in EMPLOYEES and returns the same cities with each I replaced with a Z:

SELECT TOP 10 CITY, REPLACE(CITY,'I','Z') AS REPLACE_CITY
FROM EMPLOYEES
WHERE CITY LIKE '%I%';

```
CITY                            REPLACE_CITY
-----------------------------   -----------------------------
Alexandria                      AlexandrZa
Eunice                          EunZce
Eunice                          EunZce
Eunice                          EunZce
Evansville IN                   EvansvZlle ZN
Evansville IN                   EvansvZlle ZN
Evansville IN                   EvansvZlle ZN
Union City                      UnZon CZty
Union City                      UnZon CZty
Union City                      UnZon CZty
```

(10 row(s) affected)

Microsoft SQL Server, MySQL, and Oracle all support the ANSI version of the syntax.

The LTRIM Function

The LTRIM function is another way of clipping part of a string. This function and SUBSTRING are in the same family. LTRIM trims characters from the left of a string. The syntax is

```
LTRIM(CHARACTER STRING [ ,'set' ])
```

In SQL Server, however, you do not provide the set of characters to trim. Instead the LTRIM function works to trim spaces only from the left of a string. So the SQL Server syntax is

```
LTRIM(CHARACTER STRING)
```

This SQL statement trims the characters KIM from the left of all names that begin with KIM:

```
SELECT LTRIM(UPPER(FIRSTNAME),'KIM') FROM CUSTOMERS WHERE UPPER(FIRSTNAME)
LIKE 'KIM%';
```

This SQL statement returns the first name of the employees with the prefix of KIM trimmed from the left side of the character string in Oracle:

```
SELECT FIRSTNAME, LTRIM(UPPER(FIRSTNAME),'KIM') TRIMMED
FROM EMPLOYEES
WHERE ROWNUM<=10;
```

```
FIRSTNAME                        TRIMMED
-------------------------------  -------------------------------
Kimberly                         BERLY
Kimbra                           BRA
Kimiko                           IKO
Kimberli                         BERLI
Kimberlie                        BERLIE
Kimberlee                        BERLEE
Kimberlie                        BERLIE
Kimbery                          BERY
Kim
Kimiko                           IKO

10 rows selected.
```

The same query run in SQL Server would trim only the blank characters from the left side of the strings:

```
SELECT TOP 10 FIRSTNAME, LTRIM(UPPER(FIRSTNAME)) TRIMMED
FROM EMPLOYEES;
```

```
FIRSTNAME                      TRIMMED
----------------------------   ----------------------------
Kimberly                       KIMBERLY
Kimbra                         KIMBRA
Kimiko                         KIMIKO
Kimberli                       KIMBERLI
Kimberlie                      KIMBERLIE
Kimberlee                      KIMBERLEE
Kimberlie                      KIMBERLIE
Kimbery                        KIMBERY
Kim                            KIM
Kimiko                         KIMIKO

(10 row(s) affected)
```

The LTRIM function is supported in Microsoft SQL Server, MySQL, and Oracle.

The RTRIM Function

Like LTRIM, the RTRIM function trims characters, but this time from the right of a string. The syntax is

```
RTRIM(CHARACTER STRING [ ,'set' ])
```

Remember that the SQL Server version removes only the blank spaces from the right side of the string and therefore doesn't require the [, 'set'] portion of the syntax.

```
RTRIM(CHARACTER STRING)
```

This SQL statement for Oracle returns the first name STEPHEN and trims the HEN, leaving STEP as a result:

```
SELECT FIRSTNAME,LASTNAME,RTRIM(UPPER(FIRSTNAME), 'HEN') TRIMMED
FROM EMPLOYEES
WHERE UPPER(FIRSTNAME) = 'STEPHEN';
```

```
FIRSTNAME                      LASTNAME                      TRIMMED
----------------------------   ----------------------------  ---------------------
---------
Stephen                        Carrick                       STEP
Stephen                        Basurto                       STEP

2 rows selected.
```

The string HEN was trimmed from the right of all applicable strings.

The RTRIM function is supported in Microsoft SQL Server, MySQL, and Oracle.

Miscellaneous Character Functions

The following sections show a few other character functions worth mentioning. Again, these are functions that are fairly common among major implementations.

The LENGTH Function

The LENGTH function is a common one that finds the length of a string, number, date, or expression in bytes. The syntax is

```
LENGTH(CHARACTER STRING)
```

This SQL statement run in Oracle returns the product description and its corresponding length:

```
SELECT AIRCRAFTTYPE, LENGTH(AIRCRAFTTYPE)
FROM AIRCRAFT
WHERE ROWNUM<=10;
```

```
AIRCRAFTTYPE                    NAMELENGTH
------------------------------  -----------
British Aerospace BAe146-100    28
Airbus A310                     11
Airbus A310-300                 15
Airbus 330 (200 & 300) series   29
Airbus 340-300                  14
Boeing 727                      10
Boeing 737-300                  14
Boeing 737-400                  14
Boeing 737-500                  14
Boeing 737                      10

10 rows selected.
```

The LENGTH function is supported in both MySQL and Oracle. Microsoft SQL Server uses a shortened version LEN instead, but the functionality is the same.

The ISNULL Function (NULL Value Checker)

The ISNULL function returns data from one expression if another expression is NULL. You can use ISNULL with most data types; however, the value and the substitute must be the same data type. The syntax is

```
ISNULL('VALUE', 'SUBSTITUTION')
```

This SQL statement finds NULL values and substitutes ZZ for them:

```
SELECT TOP 10 CITY, IFNULL(STATE,'ZZ') STATE
FROM EMPLOYEES;
```

```
CITY                              STATE
------------------------------    ----------
Red Dog                           ZZ
Falls Bay                         ZZ
False Island                      ZZ
False Island                      ZZ
Sandy River                       ZZ
Sandy River                       ZZ
Sandy River                       ZZ
Sandy River                       ZZ
Fin Creek                         ZZ
Fin Creek                         ZZ

(10 row(s) affected)
```

Only NULL values are now represented as ZZ.

ISNULL is supported only in the SQL Server implementation. Oracle utilizes the COALESCE function, which is discussed next.

The COALESCE Function

The COALESCE function is similar to the ISNULL function in that it specifically replaces NULL values within the result set. The COALESCE function, however, can accept a whole set of values and checks each one in order until it finds a non-NULL result. If a non-NULL result is not present, COALESCE returns a NULL value.

The following example demonstrates the COALESCE function by giving us the first non-NULL value of STATE or the string value of ZZ:

```
SELECT TOP 10 CITY, COALESCE(STATE,'ZZ') STATE
FROM EMPLOYEES;
```

```
CITY                              STATE
------------------------------    ----------
Red Dog                           ZZ
Falls Bay                         ZZ
False Island                      ZZ
False Island                      ZZ
Sandy River                       ZZ
Sandy River                       ZZ
Sandy River                       ZZ
```

```
Sandy River                    ZZ
Fin Creek                      ZZ
Fin Creek                      ZZ

(10 row(s) affected)
```

The COALESCE function is supported in Microsoft SQL Server, Oracle, and MySQL.

The LPAD Function

LPAD (left pad) is used to add characters or spaces to the left of a string. The syntax is

LPAD(*CHARACTER SET*)

The following example pads periods to the left of each product description, totaling 30 characters between the actual value and padded periods:

```
SELECT DISTINCT LPAD(UPPER(CITY),20,'.') CITY
FROM EMPLOYEES WHERE STATE='RI';
```

```
CITY
-----------------------------
........BLOCK ISLAND
........PAWTUCKET RI
..........PROVIDENCE
............WESTERLY

4 rows selected.
```

The LPAD function is supported in both MySQL and Oracle. Unfortunately, no alternative is available for Microsoft SQL Server.

The RPAD Function

The RPAD (right pad) function adds characters or spaces to the right of a string. The syntax is

RPAD(*CHARACTER SET*)

The following example pads periods to the right of each product description, totaling 30 characters between the actual value and padded periods:

```
SELECT DISTINCT RPAD(UPPER(CITY),20,'.') CITY
FROM EMPLOYEES WHERE STATE='RI';
```

```
CITY
------------------------------
BLOCK ISLAND........
PAWTUCKET RI........
PROVIDENCE.........
WESTERLY...........
```

```
4 rows selected.
```

The RPAD function is available in both MySQL and Oracle. Unfortunately, no substitute is available for Microsoft SQL Server.

The ASCII Function

The ASCII function returns the ASCII representation of the leftmost character of a string. The syntax is

ASCII(*CHARACTER SET*)

Following are some examples:

- ▶ ASCII('A') returns 65

- ▶ ASCII('B') returns 66

- ▶ ASCII('C') returns 67

- ▶ ASCII('a') returns 97

For more information, you may refer to the ASCII chart located at www.asciitable.com.

The ASCII function is supported in Microsoft SQL Server, MySQL, and Oracle.

Mathematical Functions

Mathematical functions are standard across implementations. Mathematical functions enable you to manipulate numeric values in a database according to mathematical rules.

The most common functions include the following:

- ▶ Absolute value (ABS)

- ▶ Rounding (ROUND)

- ▶ Square root (SQRT)

- ▶ Sign values (SIGN)

- ▶ Power (`POWER`)

- ▶ Ceiling and floor values (`CEIL(ING)`, `FLOOR`)

- ▶ Exponential values (`EXP`)

- ▶ `SIN`, `COS`, `TAN`

The general syntax of most mathematical functions is

`FUNCTION(EXPRESSION)`

All the mathematical functions are supported in Microsoft SQL Server, MySQL, and Oracle.

Conversion Functions

Conversion functions convert a data type into another data type. For example, perhaps you have data that is normally stored in character format, but occasionally you want to convert the character format to numeric to make calculations. Mathematical functions and computations are not allowed on data that is represented in character format.

The following are general types of data conversions:

- ▶ Character to numeric

- ▶ Numeric to character

- ▶ Character to date

- ▶ Date to character

The first two types of conversions are discussed in this hour. The remaining conversion types are discussed in Hour 12, "Understanding Dates and Times."

Converting Character Strings to Numbers

You should notice two things regarding the differences between numeric data types and character string data types:

- ▶ You can use arithmetic expressions and functions on numeric values.

- ▶ Numeric values are right-justified in the output results, whereas character string data types are left-justified.

NOTE

Converting to Numeric Values

For a character string to be converted to a number, the characters must typically be 0 through 9. The addition symbol (+), minus symbol (–), and period (.) can also be used to represent positive numbers, negative numbers, and decimals. For example, the string STEVE cannot be converted to a number, whereas an individual's Social Security number can be stored as a character string but can easily be converted to a numeric value via use of a conversion function.

When a character string is converted to a numeric value, the value takes on the two attributes just mentioned.

Some implementations might not have functions to convert character strings to numbers, whereas others have such conversion functions. In either case, consult your implementation documentation for specific syntax and rules for conversions.

NOTE

Some Systems Do the Conversions for You

Some implementations might implicitly convert data types when necessary. This means that the system makes the conversion for you when changing between data types. In these cases, the use of conversion functions is unnecessary. Check your implementation's documentation to see which types of implicit conversions are supported.

The following is an example of a numeric conversion using an Oracle conversion function:

```
SELECT EMPLOYEEID, TO_CHAR(EMPLOYEEID) AS CONVERTEDNUM
FROM EMPLOYEES
WHERE EMPLOYEEID<=10;


EMPLOYEEID   CONVERTEDNUM
----------- ------------
1            1
2            2
3            3
4            4
5            5
6            6
7            7
8            8
9            9
10           10

10 rows selected.
```

The employee identification is right-justified following the conversion.

Converting Numbers to Character Strings

Converting numeric values to character strings is precisely the opposite of converting characters to numbers.

The following is an example of converting a numeric value to a character string using two different Transact-SQL conversion functions for Microsoft SQL Server:

```
SELECT TOP 10 PAY = PAYRATE, NEW_PAY = STR(PAYRATE), NEWER_PAY = CAST(PAYRATE AS
VARCHAR(10))
FROM EMPLOYEES
WHERE PAYRATE IS NOT NULL;
```

PAY	NEW_PAY	NEWER_PAY
22.24	22	22.24
15.29	15	215.29
12.88	13	212.88
23.61	24	223.61
24.79	25	224.79
18.03	18	218.03
15.64	16	215.64
23.09	23	223.09
21.25	21	221.25
14.94	15	214.94

```
(10 row(s) affected)
```

TIP

Different Data Is Output in Different Ways

The data's justification is the simplest way to identify a column's data type. Character data is most often left-justified whereas numeric data is often right-justified. This enables you to determine what kind of data is returned from a given query quickly.

The following is the same example using an Oracle conversion function:

```
SELECT PAYRATE, TO_CHAR(PAYRATE)
FROM EMPLOYEES
WHERE PAY_RATE IS NOT NULL
AND ROWNUM<=10;
```

PAYRATE	TO_CHAR(PAYRATE)
22.24	22.24
15.29	15.29
12.88	12.88

```
23.61              23.61
24.79              24.79
18.03              18.03
15.64              15.64
23.09              23.09
21.25              21.25
14.94              14.94
```

10 rows selected.

Combining Character Functions

You can combine most functions in a SQL statement. SQL would be far too limited if function combinations were not allowed. The following example combines two functions in the query: concatenation with substring. By expanding the EMPLOYEEID to 9 characters and then pulling the column apart into three pieces, you can concatenate those pieces with dashes to render a readable Social Security number. This example uses the CONCAT function to combine the strings for output:

```
SELECT CONCAT(LASTNAME,', ',FIRSTNAME) NAME,
       CONCAT(SUBSTRING(CAST(100000000 + EMPLOYEEID AS VARCHAR(9)),1,3),'-',
       SUBSTRING(CAST(100000000 + EMPLOYEEID AS VARCHAR(9)),4,2),'-',
       SUBSTRING(CAST(100000000 + EMPLOYEEID AS VARCHAR(9)),6,4)) AS ID
FROM EMPLOYEES
WHERE EMPLOYEEID BETWEEN 4000 AND 4009;
```

```
NAME                              ID
------------------------------    -----------
Waltermire, Jessie                100-00-4000
Calcao, Kitty                     100-00-4001
Aracena, Fabian                   100-00-4002
Neason, Hana                      100-00-4003
Vanner, Tonie                     100-00-4004
Usina, Annabell                   100-00-4005
Tegenkamp, Thanh                  100-00-4006
Stage, Laure                      100-00-4007
Allam, Irma                       100-00-4008
Saulters, Ruby                    100-00-4009
```

(10 row(s) affected)

The following example uses the LEN function and the addition arithmetic operator (+) to add the length of the first name to the length of the last name for each column; the SUM function then finds the total length of all first and last names:

```
SELECT SUM(LEN(LASTNAME) + LEN(FIRSTNAME)) TOTAL
FROM EMPLOYEES;

TOTAL
-----------
71571


(1 row(s) affected)
```

NOTE

How Embedded Functions Are Resolved

When embedding functions within functions in a SQL statement, remember that the innermost function is resolved first, and then each function is subsequently resolved from the inside out.

Summary

This hour introduced you to various functions used in a SQL statement—usually a query—to modify or enhance the way output is represented. Those functions include character, mathematical, and conversion functions. It is important to realize that the ANSI standard is a guideline for how SQL should be implemented by vendors, but it does not dictate the exact syntax or necessarily place limits on vendors' innovations. Most vendors have standard functions and conform to the ANSI concepts, but each vendor has its own specific list of available functions. The function name might differ and the syntax might differ, but the concepts with all functions are the same.

Q&A

Q. Are all functions in the ANSI standard?

A. No, not all functions are exactly ANSI SQL. Functions, like data types, are often implementation-dependent. Most implementations contain supersets of the ANSI functions; many have a wide range of functions with extended capability, whereas other implementations seem to be somewhat limited. Several examples of functions from selected implementations are included in this hour. However, because so many implementations use similar functions (although they might slightly differ), check your particular implementation for available functions and their usage.

Q. Is the data actually changed in the database when using functions?

A. No, data is not changed in the database when using functions. Functions are typically used in queries to manipulate the output's appearance.

Workshop

The following workshop is composed of a series of quiz questions and practical exercises. The quiz questions are designed to test your overall understanding of the current material. The practical exercises are intended to afford you the opportunity to apply the concepts discussed during the current hour, as well as build upon the knowledge acquired in previous hours of study. Please take time to complete the quiz questions and exercises before continuing. Refer to Appendix C, "Answers to Quizzes and Exercises," for answers.

Quiz

1. Match the descriptions with the possible functions:

Descriptions	Functions
a. Used to select a portion of a character string	||
	RPAD
b. Used to trim characters from either the right or left of a string	LPAD
	UPPER
c. Used to change all letters to lowercase	RTRIM
d. Used to find the length of a string	LTRIM
	LENGTH
e. Used to combine strings	LOWER
	SUBSTR
	LEN

2. True or false: Using functions in a SELECT statement to restructure the appearance of data in output also affects the way the data is stored in the database.

3. True or false: The outermost function is always resolved first when functions are embedded within other functions in a query.

Exercises

1. Type the following code to concatenate each employee's last name and first name in SQL Server:

    ```
    SELECT CONCAT(LASTNAME, ', ', FIRSTNAME) AS FULLNAME
    FROM EMPLOYEES;
    ```

    How would the same statement be applied in Oracle?

2. Type the following MySQL code to print each employee's concatenated name and his or her area code:

    ```
    SELECT CONCAT(LASTNAME, ', ', FIRSTNAME) AS FULLNAME, SUBSTRING(LASTNAME, 1,
    3) AS SUBNAME
    FROM EMPLOYEES;
    ```

    Try writing the same code in Oracle.

3. Write a SQL statement that lists employee email addresses. Email is not a stored column. The email address for each employee should be as follows:

`FIRST.LAST@PERPTECH.COM`

For example, John Smith's email address is `JOHN.SMITH@PERPTECH.COM`.

4. Write a SQL statement that lists each employee's name, employee ID, and phone number in the following formats:

    a. The name should be displayed as `SMITH, JOHN`.

    b. The employee ID should be displayed as the first three letters of their last name in uppercase, a dash, and then the employee number. Example: SMI-4203

    c. The phone number should be displayed as `(999)999-9999`.

HOUR 12
Understanding Dates and Times

What You'll Learn in This Hour:

▶ How the date and time are stored

▶ Typical date and time formats

▶ How to use date functions

▶ How to use date conversions

In this hour, you learn about the nature of dates and times in SQL. Not only does this hour discuss the DATETIME data type in more detail, but you also see how some implementations use dates, how to extract the date and time in a wanted format, and some of the common rules.

NOTE

Variations in the SQL Syntax

As you know by now, there are many different SQL implementations. This book shows the American National Standards Institute (ANSI) standard and the most common nonstandard functions, commands, and operators. MySQL is used for the examples. Even in MySQL, the date can be stored in different formats. You must check your particular implementation for the date storage. No matter how it is stored, your implementation should have functions that convert date formats.

How Is a Date Stored?

Each implementation has a default storage format for the date and time. This default storage often varies among different implementations, as do other data types for each implementation. The following sections begin by reviewing the standard format of the DATETIME data type and its elements. Then you see the data types for date and time in some popular implementations of SQL, including Oracle, MySQL, and Microsoft SQL Server.

Standard Data Types for the Date and Time

There are three standard SQL data types for date and time (DATETIME) storage:

▶ **DATE–** Stores date literals. DATE is formatted as YYYY-MM-DD and ranges from 0001-01-01 to 9999-12-31.

▶ **TIME–** Stores time literals. TIME is formatted as HH:MI:SS.nn... and ranges from 00:00:00... to 23:59:61.999....

▶ **TIMESTAMP–** Stores date and time literals. TIMESTAMP is formatted as YYYY-MM-DD HH:MI:SS.nn... and ranges from 0001-01-01 00:00:00... to 9999-12-31 23:59:61.999....

DATETIME Elements

DATETIME elements are those elements pertaining to the date and time that are included as part of a DATETIME definition. The following is a list of the constrained DATETIME elements and a valid range of values for each element:

DATETIME Element	Valid Ranges
YEAR	0001 to 9999
MONTH	01 to 12
DAY	01 to 31
HOUR	00 to 23
MINUTE	00 to 59
SECOND	00.000... to 61.999...

Each of these is an element of time that you deal with on a daily basis. Seconds can be represented as a decimal, allowing the expression of tenths of a second, hundredths of a second, milliseconds, and so on. You might question that a minute can contain more than 60 seconds. According to the ANSI standard, this 61.999 seconds is due to the possible insertion or omission of a leap second in a minute, which is a rare occurrence. Refer to your implementation on the allowed values because date and time storage might vary widely.

TIP

Databases Handle Leap Years

Date variances such as leap seconds and leap years are handled internally by the database if the data is stored in a DATETIME data type.

Implementation-Specific Data Types

As with other data types, each implementation provides its own representation and syntax. Table 12.1 shows how three products (Microsoft SQL Server, MySQL, and Oracle) have been implemented with a date and time.

TABLE 12.1   DATETIME Types Across Platforms

Product	Data Type	Use
Oracle	DATE	Stores both date and time information
SQL Server	DATETIME	Stores both date and time information
	SMALLDATETIME	Same as DATETIME except it has a small range
	DATE	Stores a date value
	TIME	Stores a time value
MySQL	DATETIME	Stores both date and time information
	TIMESTAMP	Stores both date and time information
	DATE	Stores a date value
	TIME	Stores a time value
	YEAR	One byte type that represents the year

TIP

Even Date and Time Types Can Differ

Each implementation has its own specific data type(s) for date and time information. However, most implementations comply with the ANSI standard; all elements of the date and time are included in their associated data types. The way the date is internally stored is implementation-dependent.

Date Functions

Date functions are available in SQL depending on the options with each specific implementation. *Date functions*, similar to character string functions, manipulate the representation of date and time data. Available date functions are often used to format the output of dates and time in an appealing format, compare date values with one another, compute intervals between dates, and so on.

The Current Date

You might have already raised the question, "How do I get the current date from the database?" The need to retrieve the current date from the database might originate from several situations, but the current date is normally returned either to compare it to a stored date or to return the value of the current date as some sort of timestamp.

The current date is ultimately stored on the host computer for the database and is called the *system date*. The database, which interfaces with the appropriate operating system, has the capability to retrieve the system date for its own purpose or to resolve database requests, such as queries.

Take a look at a couple methods of attaining the system date based on commands from two different implementations.

Microsoft SQL Server uses a function called GETDATE() to return the system date. This function is used in a query as follows:

```
SELECT GETDATE()
2015-06-01 19:23:38.167
```

MySQL uses the NOW function to retrieve the current date and time. NOW is called a *pseudocolumn* because it acts as any other column in a table and can be selected from any table in the database; although it is not actually part of the table's definition.

The following MySQL statement returns the output if today were June 01, 2015:

```
SELECT NOW ();
01-JUN-15 13:41:45
```

Oracle uses a function known as SYSDATE and looks like this if using the DUAL table, which is a dummy table in Oracle:

```
SELECT SYSDATE FROM DUAL;
01-JUN-15 13:41:45
```

Time Zones

The use of time zones might be a factor when dealing with date and time information. For instance, a time of 6:00 p.m. in the central United States does not equate to the same time in Australia; although the actual point in time is the same. Some of us who live within the daylight saving time zone are used to adjusting our clocks twice a year. If time zones are considerations when maintaining data in your case, you might find it necessary to consider time zones and perform time conversions, if available with your SQL implementation.

The following are some common time zones and their abbreviations:

Abbreviation	Time Zone
AST, ADT	Atlantic standard time, Atlantic daylight time
BST, BDT	Bering standard time, Bering daylight time
CST, CDT	Central standard time, Central daylight time
EST, EDT	Eastern standard time, Eastern daylight time
GMT	Greenwich mean time
HST, HDT	Alaska/Hawaii standard time, Alaska/Hawaii daylight time
MST, MDT	Mountain standard time, Mountain daylight time
NST	Newfoundland standard time, Newfoundland daylight time
PST, PDT	Pacific standard time, Pacific daylight time
YST, YDT	Yukon standard time, Yukon daylight time

The following shows examples of time zone differences based on a given time:

Time Zone	Time
AST	June 12, 2015 at 1:15 p.m.
BST	June 12, 2015 at 6:15 a.m.
CST	June 12, 2015 at 11:15 a.m.
EST	June 12, 2015 at 12:15 p.m.
GMT	June 12, 2015 at 5:15 p.m.
HST	June 12, 2015 at 7:15 a.m.
MST	June 12, 2015 at 10:15 a.m.
NST	June 12, 2015 at 1:45 p.m.
PST	June 12, 2015 at 9:15 a.m.
YST	June 12, 2015 at 8:15 a.m.

NOTE

Handling Time Zones

Some implementations have functions that enable you to deal with different time zones. However, not all implementations support the use of time zones. Be sure to verify the use of time zones in your particular implementation, as well as the need to deal with them in the case of your database.

Adding Time to Dates

Days, months, and other parts of time can be added to dates for the purpose of comparing dates or to provide more specific conditions in the WHERE clause of a query.

Intervals can be used to add periods of time to a DATETIME value. As defined by the standard, intervals can manipulate the value of a DATETIME value, as in the following examples:

```
DATE '2015-12-31' + INTERVAL '1' DAY
'2016-01-01'
DATE '2015-12-31' + INTERVAL '1' MONTH
'2016-01-31'
```

The following is an example using the SQL Server function DATEADD:

```
SELECT FLIGHTSTART, DATEADD(MONTH, 1, FLIGHTSTART) AS MONTHADDED
FROM FLIGHTS
WHERE FLIGHTID<=10;


FLIGHTSTART              MONTHADDED
----------------------   -----------------------
2013-05-01 07:00:00.000  2013-06-01 07:00:00.000
2013-05-01 07:00:00.000  2013-06-01 07:00:00.000
2013-05-01 07:00:00.000  2013-06-01 07:00:00.000
2013-05-01 07:00:00.000  2013-06-01 07:00:00.000
2013-05-01 07:00:00.000  2013-06-01 07:00:00.000
2013-05-01 07:00:00.000  2013-06-01 07:00:00.000
2013-05-01 07:00:00.000  2013-06-01 07:00:00.000
2013-05-01 07:00:00.000  2013-06-01 07:00:00.000
2013-05-01 07:00:00.000  2013-06-01 07:00:00.000
2013-05-01 07:00:00.000  2013-06-01 07:00:00.000


(10 row(s) affected)
```

The following example uses the Oracle function ADD_MONTHS:

```
SELECT FLIGHTSTART, ADD_MONTHS(FLIGHTSTART,1)
FROM FLIGHTS
WHERE FLIGHTID<=10;


FLIGHTSTART                   MONTHADDED
-----------------------------  ----------------------------
01-MAY-13                     01-JUN-13
01-MAY-13                     01-JUN-13
01-MAY-13                     01-JUN-13
01-MAY-13                     01-JUN-13
01-MAY-13                     01-JUN-13
```

```
01-MAY-13                           01-JUN-13
01-MAY-13                           01-JUN-13
01-MAY-13                           01-JUN-13
01-MAY-13                           01-JUN-13
01-MAY-13                           01-JUN-13

10 rows selected.
```

To add one day to a date in Oracle, use the following:

```
SELECT FLIGHTSTART, FLIGHTSTART + 1 AS DAYADDED
FROM FLIGHTS
WHERE FLIGHTID=1;


FLIGHTSTART                    DAYADDED
-----------------------------  -------------------------------

01-MAY-13                      02-MAY-13

1 row selected.
```

If you want to do the same query in MySQL, use the ANSI standard INTERVAL command, as follows. Otherwise, MySQL would convert the date to an integer and try to perform the operation.

```
SELECT FLIGHTSTART, DATE_ADD(FLIGHTSTART, INTERVAL 1 DAY) AS DAYADDED,
FLIGHTSTART + 1 AS ALTDATE
FROM FLIGHTS
WHERE FLIGHTID=1;


FLIGHTSTART          DAYADDED              ALTDATE
-----------          ---------------       ----------------

01-MAY-13            02-MAY-13             2013602

1 row selected.
```

Notice that these examples in MySQL, SQL Server, and Oracle, although they differ syntactically from the ANSI examples, derive their results based on the same concept as described by the SQL standard.

Miscellaneous Date Functions

Table 12.2 shows some powerful date functions that exist in the implementations for SQL Server, Oracle, and MySQL.

TABLE 12.2   Date Functions by Platform

Product	Date Function	Use
SQL Server	DATEPART	Returns the integer value of a DATEPART for a date
	DATENAME	Returns the text value of a DATEPART for a date
	GETDATE()	Returns the system date
	DATEDIFF	Returns the difference between two dates for specified date parts, such as days, minutes, and seconds
Oracle	NEXT_DAY	Returns the next day of the week as specified (for example, FRIDAY) since a given date
	MONTHS_BETWEEN	Returns the number of months between two given dates
MySQL	DAYNAME(date)	Displays day of week
	DAYOFMONTH(date)	Displays day of month
	DAYOFWEEK(date)	Displays day of week
	DAYOFYEAR(date)	Displays day of year

Date Conversions

The conversion of dates can take place for any number of reasons. Conversions are mainly used to alter the data type of values defined as a DATETIME value or any other valid data type of a particular implementation.

Typical reasons for date conversions are as follows:

▶ To compare date values of different data types

▶ To format a date value as a character string

▶ To convert a character string into a date format

The ANSI CAST operator converts data types into other data types. The basic syntax follows:

```
CAST ( EXPRESSION AS NEW_DATA_TYPE )
```

Specific syntax examples of some implementations are illustrated in the following subsections, covering

▶ The representation of parts of a DATETIME value

▶ Conversions of dates to character strings

▶ Conversions of character strings to dates

Date Pictures

A *date picture* is composed of formatting elements used to extract date and time information from the database in a wanted format. Date pictures might not be available in all SQL
implementations.

Without the use of a date picture and some type of conversion function, the date and time information is retrieved from the database in a default format, such as

```
2010-12-31
31-DEC-10
2010-12-31 23:59:01.11
. . .
```

What if you want the date to display as the following?

```
December 31, 2010
```

You would have to convert the date from a DATETIME format into a character string format. This
is accomplished by implementation-specific functions for this purpose, further illustrated in the
following sections.

Table 12.3 displays some of the common date parts used in various implementations. This aids
you in using the date picture in the following sections to extract the proper DATETIME information from the database.

TABLE 12.3 Date Parts by Platform

Product	Syntax	Date Part
SQL Server	yy	Year
	qq	Quarter
	mm	Month
	dy	Day of year
	wk	Week
	dw	Weekday
	hh	Hour
	mi	Minute
	ss	Second
	ms	Millisecond
Oracle	AD	Anno Domini
	AM	Ante meridian

Product	Syntax	Date Part
Oracle	BC	Before Christ
	CC	Century
	D	Number of the day in the week
	DD	Number of the day in the month
	DDD	Number of the day in the year
	DAY	The day spelled out (MONDAY)
	Day	The day spelled out (Monday)
	day	The day spelled out (monday)
	DY	The three-letter abbreviation of the day (MON)
	Dy	The three-letter abbreviation of the day (Mon)
	dy	The three-letter abbreviation of the day (mon)
	HH	Hour of the day
	HH12	Hour of the day
	HH24	Hour of the day for a 24-hour clock
	J	Julian days since 12-31-4713 B.C.
	MI	Minute of the hour
	MM	The number of the month
	MON	The three-letter abbreviation of the month (JAN)
	Mon	The three-letter abbreviation of the month (Jan)
	mon	The three-letter abbreviation of the month (jan)
	MONTH	The month spelled out (JANUARY)
	Month	The month spelled out (January)
	month	The month spelled out (january)
	PM	Post meridian
	Q	The number of the quarter
	RM	The Roman numeral for the month
	RR	The two digits of the year
	SS	The second of a minute
	SSSSS	The seconds since midnight
	SYYYY	The signed year; if B.C. 500, B.C. = −500
	W	The number of the week in a month

Product	Syntax	Date Part
Oracle	WW	The number of the week in a year
	Y	The last digit of the year
	YY	The last two digits of the year
	YYY	The last three digits of the year
	YYYY	The year
	YEAR	The year spelled out (TWO-THOUSAND-TEN)
	Year	The year spelled out (Two-Thousand-Ten)
	year	The year spelled out (two-thousand-ten)
MySQL	SECOND	Seconds
	MINUTE	Minutes
	HOUR	Hours
	DAY	Days
	MONTH	Months
	YEAR	Years
	MINUTE_SECOND	Minutes and seconds
	HOUR_MINUTE	Hours and minutes
	DAY_HOUR	Days and hours
	YEAR_MONTH	Years and months
	HOUR_SECOND	Hours, minutes, and seconds
	DAY_MINUTE	Days and minutes
	DAY_SECOND	Days and seconds

NOTE

Date Parts in MySQL

These are some of the most common date parts for MySQL. Other date parts might be available depending on the version of MySQL.

Converting Dates to Character Strings

DATETIME values are converted to character strings to alter the appearance of output from a query. A conversion function achieves this. Two examples of converting date and time data into a character string as designated by a query follow. The first uses SQL Server:

```
SELECT DISTINCT FLIGHTSTART = DATENAME(MONTH, FLIGHTSTART)
FROM FLIGHTS;

FLIGHTSTART
------------------------------
June
August
May
September
July

(5 row(s) affected)
```

The second example is an Oracle date conversion using the TO_CHAR function:

```
SELECT DISTINCT FLIGHTSTART, TO_CHAR(FLIGHTSTART,'Month dd, yyyy') FLIGHT
FROM FLIGHTS
WHERE FLIGHTID<=10;

FLIGHTSTART                    FLIGHT
------------------------------ ------------------------------
01-MAY-13                      May 01, 2013
02-MAY-13                      May 02, 2013
03-MAY-13                      May 03, 2013
04-MAY-13                      May 04, 2013
05-MAY-13                      May 05, 2013
06-MAY-13                      May 06, 2013
07-MAY-13                      May 07, 2013

(7 row(s) affected)
```

Converting Character Strings to Dates

The following example illustrates a method from a MySQL or Oracle implementation of converting a character string into a date format. When the conversion is complete, the data can be stored in a column defined as having some form of a DATETIME data type.

```
SELECT STR_TO_DATE('01/01/2010 12:00:00 AM', '%m/%d/%Y %h:%i:%s %p') AS FORMAT_DATE
FROM FLIGHTS
WHERE FLIGHTID<=6;

FORMAT_DATE
-----------
01-JAN-10
01-JAN-10
01-JAN-10
01-JAN-10
```

```
01-JAN-10
01-JAN-10

6 rows selected.
```

You might wonder why six rows were selected from this query when only one date value was provided. It's because the conversion of the literal string was selected from the FLIGHTS table which we asked to have all rows with a FLIGHTID less than or equal to 6 returned. Hence, the conversion of the literal string was selected against each record that was returned from our query.

In Microsoft SQL Server we instead use the CONVERT function:

```
SELECT CONVERT(DATETIME,'02/25/2010 12:00:00 AM') AS FORMAT_DATE
FROM FLIGHTS
WHERE FLIGHTID<=6;

FORMAT_DATE
-----------------------
2010-02-25 00:00:00.000
2010-02-25 00:00:00.000
2010-02-25 00:00:00.000
2010-02-25 00:00:00.000
2010-02-25 00:00:00.000
2010-02-25 00:00:00.000

6 rows selected.
```

Summary

You now should have an understanding of DATETIME values. ANSI provided a standard; however, as with many SQL elements, most implementations have deviated from the exact functions and syntax of standard SQL commands; although the concepts remain the same as far as the basic representation and manipulation of date and time information. In Hour 11, "Restructuring the Appearance of Data," you saw how functions varied depending on each implementation. This hour, you have seen some of the differences between date and time data types, functions, and operators. Keep in mind that not all examples discussed in this hour work with your particular implementation, but the concepts of dates and times are the same and should be applicable to any implementation.

Q&A

Q. Why do implementations choose to deviate from a single standard set of data types and functions?

A. Implementations differ as far as the representation of data types and functions mainly because of the way each vendor has chosen to internally store data and provide the most efficient means of data retrieval. However, all implementations should provide the same means for the storage of date and time values based on the required elements prescribed by ANSI, such as the year, month, day, hour, minute, second, and so on.

Q. What if I want to store date and time information differently than what is available in my implementation?

A. Dates can be stored in nearly any type of format if you choose to define the column for a date as a variable length character. The main thing to remember is that when comparing date values to one another, you are usually required to first convert the character string representation of the date to a valid DATETIME format for your implementation—that is, if appropriate conversion functions are available.

Workshop

The following workshop is composed of a series of quiz questions and practical exercises. The quiz questions are designed to test your overall understanding of the current material. The practical exercises are intended to afford you the opportunity to apply the concepts discussed during the current hour, as well as build upon the knowledge acquired in previous hours of study. Please take time to complete the quiz questions and exercises before continuing. Refer to Appendix C, "Answers to Quizzes and Exercises," for answers.

Quiz

1. From where is the system date and time normally derived?

2. What are the standard internal elements of a DATETIME value?

3. What could be a major factor concerning the representation and comparison of date and time values if your company is an international organization?

4. Can a character string date value be compared to a date value defined as a valid DATETIME data type?

5. What would you use in SQL Server and Oracle to get the current date and time?

Exercises

1. Type the following SQL code into the `sql` prompt in each of the implementations to display the current date from the database:

   ```
   For SQL Server: SELECT GETDATE();
   For Oracle: SELECT SYSDATE FROM DUAL;
   ```

2. Type the following SQL code to display each employee's hire date:

   ```
   SELECT EMPLOYEEID, HIREDATE
   FROM EMPLOYEES;
   ```

3. In SQL Server, dates can be segmented into various parts by using functions like YEAR and MONTH. Type the following code to display the year and month that each employee was hired:

   ```
   SELECT EMPLOYEEID, YEAR(HIREDATE) AS YEAR_HIRED, MONTH(HIREDATE) AS MONTH_
   HIRED
   FROM EMPLOYEES;
   ```

4. Type in a statement similar to this SQL Server implementation to display each of the employees' hire dates along with today's date:

   ```
   SELECT EMPLOYEEID, HIREDATE, GETDATE() as TODAYSDATE
   FROM EMPLOYEES;
   ```

5. Using Exercise 4, determine what day of the week each employee was hired.

6. Write a query like Exercise 4 except use a function to show how many days the employee has worked for the company. Could you also estimate years?

7. Write a query to determine today's Julian date (day of year).

Joining Tables in Queries

What You'll Learn in This Hour:

▶ An introduction to table joins

▶ The different types of joins

▶ How and when joins are used

▶ Numerous practical examples of table joins

▶ The effects of improperly joined tables

▶ Renaming tables in a query using an alias

To this point, all database queries you have executed in this book have extracted data from a single table. During this hour, you learn how to join tables in a query so that you can retrieve data from multiple tables.

Selecting Data from Multiple Tables

Having the capability to select data from multiple tables is one of SQL's most powerful features. Without this capability, the entire relational database concept would not be feasible. Single-table queries are sometimes quite informative, but in the real world, the most practical queries are those whose data is acquired from multiple tables within the database.

As you witnessed in Hour 4, "The Normalization Process," a relational database is broken into smaller, more manageable tables for simplicity and the sake of overall management ease. As tables are divided into smaller tables, the related tables are created with common columns: *primary keys* and *foreign keys*. These keys are used to join related tables to one another.

You might ask why you should normalize tables if, in the end, you are going to rejoin the tables to retrieve the data you want. You rarely select all data from all tables, so it is better to pick and choose according to the needs of each query. Although performance might suffer slightly due to a normalized database, overall coding and maintenance are much simpler. Remember that you generally normalize the database to reduce redundancy and increase data integrity. Your over-reaching task as a database administrator is to ensure the safeguarding of data.

Understanding Joins

A *join* combines two or more tables to retrieve data from multiple tables. Although different implementations have many ways of joining tables, you concentrate on the most common joins in this lesson. The types of joins that you learn are

▶ Equijoins or inner joins

▶ Non-equijoins

▶ Outer joins

▶ Self joins

As you have learned from previous hours, both the SELECT and FROM clauses are required SQL statement elements; the WHERE clause is a required element of an SQL statement when joining tables. The tables joined are listed in the FROM clause. The join is performed in the WHERE clause. Several operators can be used to join tables, such as =, <, >, <>, <=, >=, !=, BETWEEN, LIKE, and NOT. However, the most common operator is the equal symbol.

Joins of Equality

Perhaps the most used and important of the joins is the equijoin, also referred to as an *inner join*. The equijoin joins two tables with a common column in which each is usually the primary key.

The syntax for an equijoin is

```
SELECT TABLE1.COLUMN1, TABLE2.COLUMN2...
FROM TABLE1, TABLE2 [, TABLE3 ]
WHERE TABLE1.COLUMN_NAME = TABLE2.COLUMN_NAME
[ AND TABLE1.COLUMN_NAME = TABLE3.COLUMN_NAME ]
```

Look at the following example:

```
SELECT EMPLOYEES.EMPLOYEEID,EMPLOYEES.FIRSTNAME,EMPLOYEES.LASTNAME,
       AIRPORTS.AIRPORTID,AIRPORTS.AIRPORTNAME
FROM EMPLOYEES,
       AIRPORTS
WHERE EMPLOYEES.AIRPORTID = AIRPORTS.AIRPORTID;
```

This SQL statement returns the employees' identification, name, and the name of the airport at which they work. You need to tell the query how the tables are related, which is the purpose of the WHERE clause. Here you specify that the two tables are linked via the AIRPORTID column. Because the AIRPORTID exists in both tables, you must justify both columns with the table name in your column listing. By justifying the columns with the table names, you tell the database server where to get the data.

Data in the following example is selected from EMPLOYEES and AIRPORTS because wanted data resides in each of the two tables. An equijoin is used.

```
SELECT EMPLOYEES.EMPLOYEEID,EMPLOYEES.FIRSTNAME,EMPLOYEES.LASTNAME,
       AIRPORTS.AIRPORTID,AIRPORTS.AIRPORTNAME
FROM EMPLOYEES,
       AIRPORTS
WHERE EMPLOYEES.AIRPORTID = AIRPORTS.AIRPORTID
AND EMPLOYEEID<=10;
```

```
EMPLOYEEID  FIRSTNAME               LASTNAME                 AIRPORTID    AIRPORTNAME
----------- ----------------------  ----------------------   ------------ -----------
1           Erlinda                 Iner                     27           Red Dog
2           Nicolette               Denty                    1209         Errol
3           Arlen                   Sabbah                   1209         Errol
4           Yulanda                 Loock                    1209         Errol
5           Tena                    Sacks                    1209         Errol
6           Inocencia               Arcoraci                 1210         Esler Field
7           Christa                 Astin                    1211         Espanola
8           Tamara                  Contreraz                1211         Espanola
9           Michale                 Capito                   1211         Espanola
10          Kimberly                Ellamar                  1211         Espanola
```

(10 row(s) affected)

Notice that each column in the SELECT clause is preceded by the associated table name to iden-tify each column. This is called *qualifying columns* in a query. Qualifying columns is only neces-sary for columns that exist in more than one table referenced by a query. You usually qualify all columns for consistency and to avoid questions when debugging or modifying SQL code.

In addition, the SQL syntax provides for a more readable version of the previous syntax by intro-ducing the JOIN syntax. The JOIN syntax follows:

```
SELECT TABLE1.COLUMN1, TABLE2.COLUMN2...
FROM TABLE1
INNER JOIN TABLE2 ON TABLE1.COLUMN_NAME = TABLE2.COLUMN_NAME
```

As you can see, the JOIN operator is removed from the WHERE clause and instead replaced with the JOIN syntax. The table joined is added after the JOIN syntax, and then the JOIN operators are placed after the ON qualifier. In the following example, the previous query for employee identification and hire date is rewritten to use the JOIN syntax:

```
SELECT EMPLOYEES.EMPLOYEEID,EMPLOYEES.FIRSTNAME,EMPLOYEES.LASTNAME,
       AIRPORTS.AIRPORTID,AIRPORTS.AIRPORTNAME
FROM EMPLOYEES
     INNER JOIN AIRPORTS
ON EMPLOYEES.AIRPORTID = AIRPORTS.AIRPORTID
WHERE EMPLOYEEID<=10;
```

Notice that this query returns the same set of data as the previous version, even though the syntax is different. So you may use either version of the syntax without fear of coming up with different results.

Using Table Aliases

You use *table aliases* to rename a table in a particular SQL statement. Renaming is temporary; the actual table name does not change in the database. As you learn later in the "Self Joins" section, giving the tables aliases is a necessity for the self join. Aliases are most often used to save keystrokes, which results in a shorter and easier-to-read SQL statement. In addition, fewer keystrokes means fewer keystroke errors. Also, programming errors are typically less frequent if you can refer to an alias, which is often shorter in length and more descriptive of the data with which you are working. Giving tables aliases also means that the columns selected must be qualified with the table alias. The following are some examples of table aliases and the corresponding columns:

```
SELECT E.EMPLOYEEID,E.FIRSTNAME,E.LASTNAME,
       A.AIRPORTNAME, E.SALARY
FROM EMPLOYEES E
     INNER JOIN  AIRPORTS A
ON E.AIRPORTID = A.AIRPORTID
WHERE E.SALARY=73000
AND A.AIRPORTNAME LIKE 'N%';
```

In the preceding SQL statement, EMPLOYEES has been renamed E. and AIRPORTS has been renamed A. The choice of what to rename the tables is arbitrary. These letters were chosen because EMPLOYEES starts with E and AIRPORTS starts with A. The selected columns were justified with the corresponding table alias. Note that SALARY was used in the WHERE clause and was justified with the table alias.

Joins of Non-Equality

A *non-equijoin* joins two or more tables based on a specified column value not equaling a specified column value in another table. The syntax for the non-equijoin follows:

```
FROM TABLE1, TABLE2 [, TABLE3 ]
WHERE TABLE1.COLUMN_NAME != TABLE2.COLUMN_NAME
[ AND TABLE1.COLUMN_NAME != TABLE2.COLUMN_NAME ]
```

An example follows:

```
SELECT A.AIRPORTID, A.AIRPORTNAME, A.COUNTRYCODE
FROM AIRPORTS A
     INNER JOIN EMPLOYEES E
ON A.AIRPORTID<>E.AIRPORTID;
```

The preceding SQL statement returns the airport information for all airports that do not have a corresponding record in both tables. The following example is a join of non-equality:

```
SELECT TOP 10 A.AIRPORTID, A.AIRPORTNAME, A.COUNTRYCODE
FROM AIRPORTS A
      INNER JOIN EMPLOYEES E
ON A.AIRPORTID<>E.AIRPORTID;
```

```
AIRPORTID    AIRPORTNAME                        COUNTRYCODE
-----------  ---------------------------------  -----------
1            Bamiyan                            AF
2            Bost                               AF
3            Chakcharan                         AF
4            Darwaz                             AF
5            Faizabad                           AF
6            Farah                              AF
7            Gardez                             AF
8            Ghazni                             AF
9            Herat                              AF
10           Jalalabad                          AF

(10 row(s) affected)
```

CAUTION

Non-Equijoins Can Add Data

When using non-equijoins, you might receive several rows of data that are of no use to you. Check your results carefully.

You might be curious and want to remove the TOP 10 clause on the SELECT statement to see how many rows are actually returned. You might be surprised when it returns more than 51 million rows of data. Because it is a non-equality match we are looking for, each row in the AIRPORTS table returns a row for each row in the EMPLOYEES table that *does not* match. So with 9100+ airports and 5600+ employees, a lot of non-matching rows exist.

In the earlier section's test for equality example, each of the rows in the first table were paired with only one row in the second table (each row's corresponding row).

Outer Joins

An *outer join* returns all rows that exist in one table, even though corresponding rows do not exist in the joined table. The (+) symbol denotes an outer join in a query and is placed at the end of the table name in the WHERE clause. The table with the (+) should be the table that does not have matching rows. In many implementations, the outer join is broken into joins called *left outer join*, *right outer join*, and *full outer join*. The outer join in these implementations is normally optional.

CAUTION
___

Join Syntax Varies Widely

You must check your particular implementation for exact usage and syntax of the outer join. The (+) symbol is used by some major implementations, but it is nonstandard. This varies somewhat between versions of implementations. For example, Microsoft SQL Server 2000 supports this type of join syntax, but SQL Server 2005 and newer versions do not. Be sure to carefully consider using this syntax before implementing.
___

The general syntax for an outer join is

```
FROM TABLE1
{RIGHT | LEFT | FULL} [OUTER] JOIN
ON TABLE2
```

The Oracle syntax is

```
FROM TABLE1, TABLE2 [, TABLE3 ]
WHERE TABLE1.COLUMN_NAME[(+)] = TABLE2.COLUMN_NAME[(+)]
[ AND TABLE1.COLUMN_NAME[(+)] = TABLE3.COLUMN_NAME[(+)]]
```

First, create a temporary table to use called HIGH_SALARIES using the following query. The idea is to get a listing of the distinct salaries that are equal to or greater than $70,000.00.

In SQL Server this would be

```
SELECT DISTINCT Salary
INTO HIGH_SALARIES
FROM Employees
WHERE Salary>=70000;


(5 row(s) affected)
```

In Oracle this would be

```
INSERT INTO HIGH_SALARIES
SELECT DISTINCT Salary
FROM Employees
WHERE Salary>=70000;

5 rows selected
```

The concept of the outer join is explained in the next two examples. In the first example, the employee name, city, and high salary amount are selected; both values are extracted from two separate tables. One important factor to keep in mind is that there might not be a corresponding record in HIGH_SALARIES for every employee. A regular join of equality is performed:

```
SELECT E.FIRSTNAME,E.LASTNAME,E.CITY,H.SALARY AS HIGH_SALARY
FROM EMPLOYEES E ,
     HIGH_SALARIES H
```

```
WHERE E.SALARY=H.SALARY
AND E.STATE='IN';
```

FIRSTNAME	LASTNAME	CITY	HIGH_SALARY
Carletta	Farrelly	Rensselaer	71000.00
Latashia	Trussell	Crane	72000.00

```
(2 row(s) affected)
```

Only two rows were selected with only two salaries listed, but there are many more employees that work in Indiana. You want to display all employees, regardless if they make what is considered a high salary.

The next example accomplishes the wanted output through the use of an outer join. Oracle's syntax is used here:

```
SELECT E.FIRSTNAME,E.LASTNAME,E.CITY,H.SALARY AS HIGH_SALARY
FROM EMPLOYEES E ,
     HIGH_SALARIES H
WHERE E.SALARY=H.SALARY(+)
AND E.STATE='IN'
ORDER BY H.SALARY DESC;
```

FIRSTNAME	LASTNAME	CITY	HIGH_SALARY
Latashia	Trussell	Crane	72000.00
Carletta	Farrelly	Rensselaer	71000.00
Nelle	Mocco	Rensselaer	NULL
Caterina	Bourgeault	Richmond IN	NULL
Lannie	Geldmacher	Richmond IN	NULL
Neil	Golda	Andrews	NULL
.			
.			
.			
.			

```
94 rows selected.
```

You can also use the more verbose standard join syntax discussed earlier to achieve the same result, which makes it easier to read:

```
SELECT E.FIRSTNAME,E.LASTNAME,E.CITY,H.SALARY AS HIGH_SALARY
FROM EMPLOYEES E ,
     LEFT OUTER JOIN HIGH_SALARIES H
     ON E.SALARY=H.SALARY
WHERE   E.STATE='IN'
ORDER BY H.SALARY DESC;
```

```
FIRSTNAME              LASTNAME              CITY                  HIGH_SALARY
-------------------    -------------------   -------------------   -------------------
Latashia               Trussell              Crane                 72000.00
Carletta               Farrelly              Rensselaer            71000.00
Nelle                  Mocco                 Rensselaer            NULL
Caterina               Bourgeault            Richmond IN           NULL
Lannie                 Geldmacher            Richmond IN           NULL
Neil                   Golda                 Andrews               NULL
.
.
.
.

(94 row(s) affected)
```

All employees in Indiana were returned by the query, even though they might not have had a salary that matched our table's criteria of a high salary. The outer join is inclusive of all rows of data in EMPLOYEES, regardless whether a corresponding row exists in HIGH_SALARIES.

TIP

Use of Outer Joins

You can use the outer join on only one side of a JOIN condition; however, you can use an outer join on more than one column of the same table in the JOIN condition.

Self Joins

A *self join* joins a table to itself, as if the table were two tables, temporarily renaming at least one table in the SQL statement using a table alias. The syntax follows:

```
SELECT A.COLUMN_NAME, B.COLUMN_NAME, [ C.COLUMN_NAME ]
FROM TABLE1 A, TABLE2 B [, TABLE3 C ]
WHERE A.COLUMN_NAME = B.COLUMN_NAME
[ AND A.COLUMN_NAME = C.COLUMN_NAME ]
```

Following is an example:

```
SELECT A.LASTNAME, B.LASTNAME, A.FIRSTNAME
FROM EMPLOYEES A,
     EMPLOYEES B
WHERE A.LASTNAME = B.LASTNAME;
```

The preceding SQL statement returns the employees' first names for all the employees with the same last name from EMPLOYEES. Self joins are useful when all the data you want to retrieve resides in one table, but you must somehow compare records in the table to other records in the table.

You may also use the alternative INNER JOIN syntax as shown here to obtain the same result:

```
SELECT A.LASTNAME, B.LASTNAME, A.FIRSTNAME
FROM EMPLOYEES A
INNER JOIN EMPLOYEES B
ON A.LASTNAME = B.LASTNAME;
```

Another common example used to explain a self join follows: Suppose you create a table that stores an employee identification number, the employee's name, and the employee identification number of the employee's manager. You might want to produce a list of all employees and their managers' names. The problem is that the manager's name does not exist as a category in the table:

```
SELECT E.EmployeeID,E.FirstName,E.LastName,
CASE WHEN E.EmployeeID%3=0 THEN 3 WHEN E.EmployeeID%2=0 THEN 2 ELSE 1 END AS MGR_ID
INTO EMPLOYEE_MGR
FROM EMPLOYEES E
WHERE E.EmployeeID<=10;
```

```
(10 row(s) affected)
```

```
SELECT * FROM EMPLOYEE_MGR;
```

EmployeeID	FirstName	LastName	MGR_ID
1	Erlinda	Iner	1
2	Nicolette	Denty	2
3	Arlen	Sabbah	3
4	Yulanda	Loock	2
5	Tena	Sacks	1
6	Inocencia	Arcoraci	3
7	Christa	Astin	1
8	Tamara	Contreraz	2
9	Michale	Capito	3
10	Kimberly	Ellamar	2

```
(10 row(s) affected)
```

In the following example, we have included the table EMPLOYEE_MGR twice in the FROM clause of the query, giving the table two aliases for the purpose of the query. By providing two aliases, it is as if you are selecting from two distinct tables. All managers are also employees, so the JOIN condition between the two tables compares the value of the employee identification number from the first table with the manager identification number in the second table. The first table acts as a table that stores employee information, whereas the second table acts as a table that stores manager information:

```
SELECT E1.FIRSTNAME, E2.FIRSTNAME
FROM EMPLOYEE_MGR E1, EMPLOYEE_MGR E2
WHERE E1.MGR_ID = E2.EMPLOYEEID;

FIRSTNAME                        FIRSTNAME
------------------------------   ------------------------------
Erlinda                          Erlinda
Nicolette                        Nicolette
Arlen                            Arlen
Yulanda                          Nicolette
Tena                             Erlinda
Inocencia                        Arlen
Christa                          Erlinda
Tamara                           Nicolette
Michale                          Arlen
Kimberly                         Nicolette

(10 row(s) affected)
```

Joining on Multiple Keys

Most join operations involve the merging of data based on a key in one table and a key in another table. Depending on how your database has been designed, you might have to join on more than one key field to accurately depict that data in your database. You might have a table that has a primary key that is composed of more than one column. You might also have a foreign key in a table that consists of more than one column, which references the multiple column primary key.

Consider the following Oracle tables that are used here for examples only:

```
SQL> desc prod
Name                                     Null?    Type
--------------------------------------   -------  ----------------------------
SERIAL_NUMBER                            NOT NULL NUMBER(10)
VENDOR_NUMBER                            NOT NULL NUMBER(10)
PRODUCT_NAME                             NOT NULL VARCHAR2(30)
COST                                     NOT NULL NUMBER(8,2)
SQL> desc ord
Name                                     Null?    Type
--------------------------------------   -------  ----------------------------
ORD_NO                                   NOT NULL NUMBER(10)
PROD_NUMBER                              NOT NULL NUMBER(10)
VENDOR_NUMBER                            NOT NULL NUMBER(10)
QUANTITY                                 NOT NULL NUMBER(5)
ORD_DATE                                 NOT NULL DATE
```

The primary key in PROD is the combination of the columns SERIAL_NUMBER and VENDOR_NUMBER. Perhaps two products can have the same serial number within the distribution company, but each serial number is unique per vendor.

The foreign key in ORD is also the combination of the columns SERIAL_NUMBER and VENDOR_NUMBER.

When selecting data from both tables (PROD and ORD), the join operation might appear as follows:

```
SELECT P.PRODUCT_NAME, O.ORD_DATE, O.QUANTITY
FROM PROD P, ORD O
WHERE P.SERIAL_NUMBER = O.SERIAL_NUMBER
  AND P.VENDOR_NUMBER = O.VENDOR_NUMBER;
```

Similarly, if you were using the INNER JOIN syntax, you would merely list the multiple join operations after the ON keyword, as shown here:

```
SELECT P.PRODUCT_NAME, O.ORD_DATE, O.QUANTITY
FROM PROD P,
INNER JOIN ORD O ON P.SERIAL_NUMBER = O.SERIAL_NUMBER
  AND P.VENDOR_NUMBER = O.VENDOR_NUMBER;
```

Join Considerations

You should consider several things before using joins: what columns(s) to join on, whether there is no common column to join on, and what the performance issues are. More joins in a query means the database server has to do more work, which means that more time is taken to retrieve data. You cannot avoid joins when retrieving data from a normalized database, but it is imperative to ensure that joins are performed correctly from a logical standpoint. Incorrect joins can result in serious performance degradation and inaccurate query results. Performance issues are discussed in more detail in Hour 18, "Managing Database Users."

Using a Base Table

What should you join on? Should you have the need to retrieve data from two tables that do not have a common column to join, you must join on another table that has a common column or columns to both tables. That table becomes the *base table*. A base table joins one or more tables that have common columns, or joins tables that do not have common columns.

Say you have a need to use FLIGHTS and AIRPORTS. There is no common column in which to join the tables. Now look at ROUTES. ROUTES has a ROUTEID column to join with FLIGHTS. AIRPORTS has an AIRPORTID column, which is also in ROUTES under the name of

SOURCEAIRPORTID and DESTINATIONAIRPORTID. The JOIN conditions and results would look like the following:

```
SELECT F.FLIGHTID,A.AIRPORTNAME,F.FLIGHTSTART
FROM FLIGHTS F
INNER JOIN ROUTES R ON F.RouteID=R.RouteID
INNER JOIN Airports A ON R.SourceAirportID=A.AirportID
WHERE F.FlightID=1;


FLIGHTID     AIRPORTNAME                    FLIGHTSTART
-----------  -----------------------------  ----------------------
1            Blue Grass                     2013-05-01 07:00:00.000

(1 row(s) affected)
```

Note the use of table aliases and their use on the columns in the WHERE clause.

The Cartesian Product

The *Cartesian product* is a result of a Cartesian join or "no join." If you select from two or more tables and do not join the tables, your output is all possible rows from all the tables selected. If your tables were large, the result could be hundreds of thousands, or even millions, of rows of data. A WHERE clause is highly recommended for SQL statements retrieving data from two or more tables. The Cartesian product is also known as a *cross join*.

The syntax is

```
FROM TABLE1, TABLE2 [, TABLE3 ]
WHERE TABLE1, TABLE2 [, TABLE3 ]
```

Following is an example of a cross join, or the dreaded Cartesian product:

```
SELECT E.EMPLOYEEID, E.LASTNAME, A.AIRPORTNAME
FROM EMPLOYEES E,
     AIRPORTS A;


EMPLOYEEID   LASTNAME                       AIRPORTNAME
-----------  -----------------------------  -----------------------------
1            Iner                           Bamiyan
1            Iner                           Bost
1            Iner                           Chakchara
.
.
.
.

(51537035 row(s) affected)
```

Data is selected from two separate tables, yet no JOIN operation is performed. Because you have not specified how to join rows in the first table with rows in the second table, the database server pairs every row in the first table with every row in the second table. Because each table has several thousand rows of data each, the product of 51537035 rows selected is achieved from 5611 rows multiplied by 9185 rows.

To fully understand exactly how the Cartesian product is derived, study the following example:

```
SQL> SELECT X FROM TABLE1;

X
-
A
B
C
D

4 rows selected.

SQL> SELECT V FROM TABLE2;

X
-
A
B
C
D

4 rows selected.

SQL> SELECT TABLE1.X, TABLE2.X
  2* FROM TABLE1, TABLE2;

X X
- -
A A
B A
C A
D A
A B
B B
C B
D B
A C
B C
C C
D C
A D
```

```
B D
C D
D D
```

16 rows selected.

CAUTION

Ensure That All Tables Are Joined

Be careful to join all tables in a query. If two tables in a query have not been joined and each table contains 1,000 rows of data, the Cartesian product consists of 1,000 rows multiplied by 1,000 rows, which results in a total of 1,000,000 rows of data returned. Cartesian products when dealing with large amounts of data can cause the host computer to stall or crash in some cases based on resource usage on the host computer. Therefore, it is important for the database administrator (DBA) and system administrator to closely monitor for long-running queries.

Summary

This hour introduced you to one of the most robust features of SQL: the table join. Imagine the limits if you could not extract data from more than one table in a single query. You were shown several types of joins, each serving its own purpose depending on conditions placed on the query. Joins are used to link data from tables based on equality and non-equality. Outer joins are powerful, allowing data to be retrieved from one table, even though associated data is not found in a joined table. Self joins are used to join a table to itself. Beware of the cross join, more commonly known as the Cartesian product. The Cartesian product is the resultset of a multiple table query without a join, often yielding a large amount of unwanted output. When selecting data from more than one table, be sure to properly join the tables according to the related columns (normally primary keys). Failure to properly join tables could result in incomplete or inaccurate output.

Q&A

Q. When joining tables, must they be joined in the same order that they appear in the FROM clause?

A. No, they do not have to appear in the same order; however, performance might benefit depending on the order of tables in the FROM clause and the order in which tables are joined.

Q. When using a base table to join unrelated tables, must I select any columns from the base table?

A. No, the use of a base table to join unrelated tables does not mandate that columns from the base table be selected.

Q. Can I join on more than one column between tables?

A. Yes, some queries might require you to join on more than one column per table to provide a complete relationship between rows of data in the joined tables.

Workshop

The following workshop is composed of a series of quiz questions and practical exercises. The quiz questions are designed to test your overall understanding of the current material. The practical exercises are intended to afford you the opportunity to apply the concepts discussed during the current hour, as well as build upon the knowledge acquired in previous hours of study. Please take time to complete the quiz questions and exercises before continuing. Refer to Appendix C, "Answers to Quizzes and Exercises," for answers.

Quiz

1. What type of join would you use to return records from one table, regardless of the existence of associated records in the related table?

2. The JOIN conditions are located in which parts of the SQL statement?

3. What type of JOIN do you use to evaluate equality among rows of related tables?

4. What happens if you select from two different tables but fail to join the tables?

5. Use the following tables to answer the next questions:

```
ORDERS_TBL
ORD_NUM       VARCHAR(10)      NOT NULL      primary key
CUST_ID       VARCHAR(10)      NOT NULL
PROD_ID       VARCHAR(10)      NOT NULL
QTY           Integer(6)       NOT NULL
ORD_DATE      DATETIME
PRODUCTS_TBL
PROD_ID       VARCHAR(10)      NOT NULL      primary key
PROD_DESC     VARCHAR(40)      NOT NULL
COST          DECIMAL(,2)      NOT NULL
```

Is the following syntax correct for using an outer join?

```
SELECT C.CUST_ID, C.CUST_NAME, O.ORD_NUM
FROM CUSTOMER_TBL C, ORDERS_TBL O
WHERE C.CUST_ID(+) = O.CUST_ID(+)
```

What would the query look like if you used the verbose JOIN syntax?

Exercises

1. Type the following code into the database and study the resultset (Cartesian product):

```
SELECT E.LASTNAME, E.FIRSTNAME, A.AIRPORTNAME
FROM EMPLOYEES E,
     AIRPORTS A
WHERE E.STATE='IN';
```

2. Type the following code to properly join EMPLOYEES and AIRPORTS:

```
SELECT E.LASTNAME, E.FIRSTNAME, A.AIRPORTNAME
FROM EMPLOYEES E,
     AIRPORTS A
WHERE E.AIRPORTID=A.AIRPORTID
AND E.STATE='IN';
```

3. Rewrite the SQL query from Exercise 2, using the INNER JOIN syntax.

4. Write a SQL statement to return the FLIGHTID, AIRPORTNAME, and CITY columns from AIRPORTS and FLIGHTDURATION and FLIGHTSTART columns from FLIGHTS. Use both types of INNER JOIN techniques. When that's completed, use the queries to determine the average flight duration per city during the month of May, 2013.

5. Write a few queries with join operations on your own.

Using Subqueries to Define Unknown Data

What You'll Learn in This Hour:

▶ Definition of a subquery

▶ The justifications of using subqueries

▶ Examples of subqueries in regular database queries

▶ Using subqueries with data manipulation commands

▶ Using correlated subqueries to make subqueries specific

In this hour, you are introduced to the concept of subqueries. Subqueries are a means by which you can perform additional queries of information from within the same SQL statement. Using subqueries enables you to easily preform complex queries that may rely on complex subsets of data in your database.

What Is a Subquery?

A *subquery*, also known as a *nested query*, is a query embedded within the WHERE clause of another query to further restrict data returned by the query. A subquery returns data that is used in the main query as a condition to further restrict the data to be retrieved. Subqueries are employed with the SELECT, INSERT, UPDATE, and DELETE statements.

You can use a subquery in some cases in place of a join operation by indirectly linking data between the tables based on one or more conditions. When you have a subquery in a query, the subquery is resolved first, and then the main query is resolved according to the condition(s) resolved by the subquery. The results of the subquery process expressions in the WHERE clause of the main query. You can use the subquery either in the WHERE clause or the HAVING clause of the main query. You can use logical and relational operators, such as =, >, <, <>,!=, IN, NOT IN, AND, OR, and so on within the subquery as well as to evaluate a subquery in the WHERE or HAVING clause.

Subqueries must follow a few rules:

▶ Subqueries must be enclosed within parentheses.

▶ A subquery can have only one column in the SELECT clause, unless multiple columns are in the main query for the subquery to compare its selected columns.

▶ You cannot use an ORDER BY clause in a subquery; although the main query can use an ORDER BY clause. You can use the GROUP BY clause to perform the same function as the ORDER BY clause in a subquery.

▶ You can use only subqueries that return more than one row with multiple value operators, such as the IN operator.

▶ The SELECT list cannot include references to values that evaluate to a BLOB, ARRAY, CLOB, or NCLOB.

▶ You cannot immediately enclose a subquery in a SET function.

▶ You cannot use the BETWEEN operator with a subquery; however, you can use the BETWEEN operator within the subquery.

NOTE

The Rules of Using Subqueries

The same rules that apply to standard queries also apply to subqueries. You can use join operations, functions, conversions, and other options within a subquery.

The basic syntax for a subquery follows:

```
SELECT COLUMN_NAME
FROM TABLE
WHERE COLUMN_NAME = (SELECT COLUMN_NAME
                     FROM TABLE
                     WHERE CONDITIONS);
```

The following examples show how you can and cannot use the BETWEEN operator with a subquery. Here is an example of a correct use of BETWEEN in the subquery:

```
SELECT COLUMN_NAME
FROM TABLE_A
WHERE COLUMN_NAME OPERATOR (SELECT COLUMN_NAME
                           FROM TABLE_B)
                           WHERE VALUE BETWEEN VALUE)
```

You cannot use BETWEEN as an operator outside the subquery. The following is an example of an illegal use of BETWEEN with a subquery:

```
SELECT  COLUMN_NAME
FROM  TABLE_A
WHERE  COLUMN_NAME  BETWEEN  VALUE  AND  (SELECT  COLUMN_NAME
                                         FROM  TABLE_B)
```

Subqueries with the SELECT Statement

Subqueries are most frequently used with the SELECT statement; although you can use them within a data manipulation statement as well. The subquery when employed with the SELECT statement retrieves data for the main query to use.

The basic syntax follows:

```
SELECT  COLUMN_NAME  [,  COLUMN_NAME ]
FROM  TABLE1  [,  TABLE2 ]
WHERE  COLUMN_NAME  OPERATOR
                  (SELECT  COLUMN_NAME  [,  COLUMN_NAME ]
                   FROM  TABLE1  [,  TABLE2 ]
                   [ WHERE ])
```

Following is an example:

```
SELECT  E.EMPLOYEEID,E.LASTNAME,
        A.AIRPORTNAME,  E.SALARY
FROM  EMPLOYEES  E
    INNER  JOIN   AIRPORTS  A
ON  E.AIRPORTID  =  A.AIRPORTID
WHERE  E.SALARY=
              ( SELECT  SALARY
                FROM  EMPLOYEES
                WHERE  EMPLOYEEID=3908);
```

The preceding SQL statement returns the employee identification, last name, and salary for all employees who have a salary equal to that of the employee with the identification 3908. In this case, you do not necessarily know (or care) what the exact pay rate is for this particular employee; you care only about the pay rate for the purpose of getting a list of employees who bring home pay equal to the employee specified in the subquery.

TIP

Using Subqueries for Unknown Values

Subqueries are frequently used to place conditions on a query when the exact conditions are unknown. The salary for 3908 in the previous example was unknown, but the subquery was designed to do the footwork for you.

The next query selects the pay rate for a particular employee:

```
SELECT SALARY
FROM EMPLOYEES
WHERE EMPLOYEEID=3908;
SALARY
------------------------------
71000.00


(1 row(s) affected)
```

The previous query is then used as a subquery in the WHERE clause of the following query:

```
SELECT E.EMPLOYEEID,E.LASTNAME,
       A.AIRPORTNAME, E.SALARY
FROM EMPLOYEES E
    INNER JOIN  AIRPORTS A
ON E.AIRPORTID = A.AIRPORTID
WHERE E.SALARY=
            ( SELECT SALARY
              FROM EMPLOYEES
              WHERE EMPLOYEEID=3908);
```

EMPLOYEEID	LASTNAME	AIRPORTNAME	SALARY
407	Graaf	Greater Wilmington	71000.00
438	Bueckers	Griffiss AFB	71000.00
581	Mazon	Hidden Falls	71000.00
912	Glory	Kern County	71000.00
934	Pion	King Of Prussia	71000.00
991	Mateen	Kuparuk	71000.00
1075	Otukolo	Lawrence J Timmerman	71000.00
1138	Yarrito	Linden	71000.00
1231	Saxby	Mackall AAF	71000.00
2216	Zahri	Neosho	71000.00
2239	Ylonen	New Haven Rail	71000.00
2406	Almos	Orange County Steel Salvage He	71000.00
2470	Eblen	Palm Beach County Park	71000.00
2863	Farrelly	Rensselaer	71000.00
2889	Lebeck	Richards-Gebaur	71000.00
3628	Cocco	Butler County - Kenny Scholter	71000.00
3908	Withers	City Of Industry H/P	71000.00
4112	Deltufo	Dade Collier	71000.00
4575	Weisenfluh	Sawyer International	71000.00
4906	Mccollum	State	71000.00
5110	Sammis	Tradewind	71000.00
5572	Dentremont	Yellowstone	71000.00

```
(22 row(s) affected)
```

The result of the subquery is `71000` (shown in the last example), so the last condition of the
WHERE clause is evaluated as

```
AND EP.PAY_RATE = 71000
```

You did not know the value of the pay rate for the given individual when you executed the
query. However, the main query compared each individual's pay rate to the subquery results.

Subqueries with the INSERT Statement

You can also use subqueries with Data Manipulation Language (DML) statements. The INSERT
statement is the first instance you examine. It uses the data returned from the subquery to insert
into another table. You can modify the selected data in the subquery with any of the character,
date, or number functions.

NOTE

Always Remember to COMMIT Your DML

Remember to use the COMMIT and ROLLBACK commands when using DML commands such as the
INSERT statement.

The basic syntax follows:

```
INSERT INTO TABLE_NAME [ (COLUMN1 [, COLUMN2 ]) ]
SELECT [ *|COLUMN1 [, COLUMN2 ]
FROM TABLE1 [, TABLE2 ]
[ WHERE VALUE OPERATOR ]
```

Following is an example of the INSERT statement with a subquery:

```
INSERT INTO RICH_EMPLOYEES
SELECT E.EMPLOYEEID,E.LASTNAME,E.FIRSTNAME,
       A.AIRPORTNAME, E.SALARY
FROM EMPLOYEES E
     INNER JOIN  AIRPORTS A
ON E.AIRPORTID = A.AIRPORTID
WHERE E.SALARY>
            ( SELECT SALARY
              FROM EMPLOYEES
              WHERE EMPLOYEEID=3908);
```

```
(89 row(s) affected)
```

This INSERT statement inserts the EMPLOYEEID, LASTNAME, FIRSTNAME, and SALARY into a table
called RICH_EMPLOYEES for all records of employees who have a pay rate greater than the pay
rate of the employee with identification 3908.

Subqueries with the UPDATE Statement

You can use subqueries with the UPDATE statement to update single or multiple columns in a table. The basic syntax is as follows:

```
UPDATE TABLE
SET COLUMN_NAME [, COLUMN_NAME) ] =
    (SELECT ]COLUMN_NAME [, COLUMN_NAME) ]
    FROM TABLE
    [ WHERE ]
```

Examples showing the use of the UPDATE statement with a subquery follow. The first query returns the employee identification of all employees who reside in Indianapolis. You can see that two individuals meet this criterion.

```
SELECT EMPLOYEEID
FROM EMPLOYEES
WHERE CITY = 'Indianapolis IN';


EMPLOYEEID
-----------
681
682


(2 row(s) affected)
```

The previous query is used as the subquery in the following UPDATE statement; it proves how many employee identifications are returned by the subquery:

```
UPDATE EMPLOYEES
SET PAYRATE = PAYRATE * 1.1
WHERE EMPLOYEEID IN (SELECT EMPLOYEEID
                FROM EMPLOYEES
                WHERE CITY = 'Indianapolis IN');
```

```
(2 row(s) affected)
```

As expected, two rows are updated. One important thing to notice is that unlike the example in the first section, this subquery returns multiple rows of data. Because you expect multiple rows to be returned, you use the IN operator instead of the equal sign. Remember that IN compares an expression to values in a list. If you had used the equal sign, an error would have been returned.

Subqueries with the DELETE Statement

You can also use subqueries with the DELETE statement. The basic syntax follows:

```
DELETE FROM TABLE_NAME
[ WHERE OPERATOR [ VALUE ]
```

```
(SELECT COLUMN_NAME
FROM TABLE_NAME)
[ WHERE) ]
```

In the following example, you delete the `Heather Vanzee`'s record from `RICH_EMPLOYEES`. You do not know Heather's employee identification number, but you can use a subquery to get her identification number from `EMPLOYEES`, which contains the `FIRSTNAME` and `LASTNAME` columns.

```
DELETE FROM RICH_EMPLOYEES
WHERE EMPLOYEEID IN (SELECT EMPLOYEEID
            FROM EMPLOYEES
            WHERE LASTNAME = 'Vanzee'
              AND FIRSTNAME = 'Heather');
```

```
1 row deleted.
```

What is interesting is that only one row was deleted even though your subquery that searches `EMPLOYEES` by first and last name returns two rows. Remember, the subquery gets only a set of data and then passes it to be used by the main query. Because the `RICH_EMPLOYEES` table had only one of the two entries, then only that single entry is removed.

Embedded Subqueries

You can embed a subquery within another subquery, just as you can embed the subquery within a regular query. When a subquery is used, that subquery is resolved before the main query. Likewise, the lowest level subquery is resolved first in embedded or nested subqueries, working out to the main query.

NOTE

Check the Limits of Your System

You must check your particular implementation for limits on the number of subqueries, if any, that you can use in a single statement. It might differ between vendors.

The basic syntax for embedded subqueries follows:

```
SELECT COLUMN_NAME [, COLUMN_NAME ]
FROM TABLE1 [, TABLE2 ]
WHERE COLUMN_NAME OPERATOR (SELECT COLUMN_NAME
                    FROM TABLE
                    WHERE COLUMN_NAME OPERATOR
                        (SELECT COLUMN_NAME
                        FROM TABLE
                        [ WHERE COLUMN_NAME OPERATOR VALUE ]))
```

The following example uses two subqueries, one embedded within the other. You want to determine what airports have employees working at them that have more than the average salary of the rich employees.

```
SELECT AIRPORTNAME,CITY
FROM AIRPORTS
WHERE AIRPORTID IN (SELECT AIRPORTID
                    FROM EMPLOYEES E
                    WHERE E.SALARY > (SELECT AVG(SALARY)
                                      FROM
                                      RICH_EMPLOYEES));
```

```
AIRPORTNAME                      CITY
---------------------------      ---------------------------
Holy Cross                       Holy Cross
Huntsville International - Car    Huntsville AL
Marin County                     Sausalito CA
Mountain Home                    Mountain Home
Mt Pocono                        Mt Pocono
Municipal                        Macomb
Municipal                        Sumter
Municipal                        Troy
North Bend                       North Bend
North Shore                      Umnak Island
Onion Bay                        Onion Bay
Ontario International            Ontario
Parker County                    Weatherford
Pecos County                     Fort Stockton
Pedro Bay                        Pedro Bay
Pike County                      Mccomb
Preston-Glenn Field              Lynchburg
Princeton
Atqasuk                          Atqasuk
Berz-Macomb                      Utica
Beverly Municiple Airport        Beverly
Blythe                           Blythe
Cabin Creek                      Cabin Creek
Chan Gurney                      Yankton
Cortland                         Cortland
Culberson County                 Van Horn
Dobbins Afb                      Marietta
Downtown                         Ardmore
Salina                           Salina
Sioux Gateway                    Sioux City
Skagit Regional                  Mount Vernon
Telfair-Wheeler                  Mc Rae
Wash. County Regional            Hagerstown
Yampa Valley                     Hayden

(34 row(s) affected)
```

Thirty-four rows that meet the criteria of both subqueries were selected.

The following two examples show the results of each of the subqueries to aid your understanding of how the main query was resolved:

```
SELECT AVG(SALARY) FROM RICH_EMPLOYEES;


------------------------------
73125.000000

(1 row(s) affected)
```

```
SELECT AIRPORTID
        FROM EMPLOYEES E
        WHERE E.SALARY >73125.00;
```

```
AIRPORTID
-----------
1446
1467
1731
1861
1865
1981
2037
2040
2132
2140
2173
2174
2214
2227
2228
2252
2313
2314
3139
3203
3206
3240
3310
3369
3460
3484
3539
3550
3645
3721
```

```
3725
3853
3971
4059
```

```
(34 row(s) affected)
```

In essence, the main query, after the substitution of the second subquery, is evaluated as shown in the following example:

```
SELECT AIRPORTNAME,CITY
FROM AIRPORTS
WHERE AIRPORTID IN (SELECT AIRPORTID
                    FROM EMPLOYEES E
                    WHERE E.SALARY > 73125.00);
```

The following shows how the main query is evaluated after the substitution of the first subquery:

```
SELECT AIRPORTNAME, CITY
FROM AIRPORTS
WHERE AIRPORTID IN (1446,1467,1731,1861,1865,1981,2037,2040,2132,2140,2173,
                    2174,2214,2227,2228,2252,2313,2314,3139,3203,3206,3240,
                    3310,3369,3460,3484,3539,3550,3645,3721,3725,3853,3971,
                    4059);
```

The following is the final result:

```
AIRPORTNAME                          CITY
------------------------------------ ------------------------------
Holy Cross                           Holy Cross
Huntsville International - Car        Huntsville AL
Marin County                         Sausalito CA
Mountain Home                        Mountain Home
Mt Pocono                            Mt Pocono
Municipal                            Macomb
Municipal                            Sumter
Municipal                            Troy
North Bend                           North Bend
North Shore                          Umnak Island
Onion Bay                            Onion Bay
Ontario International                 Ontario
Parker County                        Weatherford
Pecos County                         Fort Stockton
Pedro Bay                            Pedro Bay
Pike County                          Mccomb
Preston-Glenn Field                  Lynchburg
Princeton                            Princeton
```

Atqasuk	Atqasuk
Berz-Macomb	Utica
Beverly Municiple Airport	Beverly
Blythe	Blythe
Cabin Creek	Cabin Creek
Chan Gurney	Yankton
Cortland	Cortland
Culberson County	Van Horn
Dobbins Afb	Marietta
Downtown	Ardmore
Salina	Salina
Sioux Gateway	Sioux City
Skagit Regional	Mount Vernon
Telfair-Wheeler	Mc Rae
Wash. County Regional	Hagerstown
Yampa Valley	Hayden

(34 row(s) affected)

CAUTION

Multiple Subqueries Can Cause Problems

The use of multiple subqueries results in slower response time and might result in reduced accuracy of the results due to possible mistakes in the statement coding.

Correlated Subqueries

Correlated subqueries are common in many SQL implementations. The concept of correlated subqueries is discussed as an ANSI-standard SQL topic and is covered briefly in this hour. A correlated subquery is a subquery that is dependent upon information in the main query. This means that tables in a subquery can be related to tables in the main query.

In the following example, the table join between AIRCRAFTFLEET and FLIGHTS in the subquery is dependent on the alias for AIRCRAFTFLEET (AF) in the main query. This query returns the aircraft code and designator of all aircraft that have flown more than 120,000 minutes. This might be important to discover for a maintenance requirement involving older aircraft.

```
SELECT AF.AircraftCode,AF.AircraftDesignator
FROM AircraftFleet AF
WHERE 120000 <=
    (SELECT SUM(F.FlightDuration) FROM  Flights F
    WHERE AF.AircraftFleetID=F.AircraftFleetID
    );
```

```
AircraftCode AircraftDesignator
------------ ------------------
E12          MMEK-270
E12          BIOA-249
F28          AGTX-691
F28          LXUT-830
EM2          IEQF-918
BEK          SKQU-790
M11          CIVG-217

(7 row(s) affected)
```

You can extract and slightly modify the subquery from the previous statement as follows to show the total minutes flown for each aircraft, allowing the previous results to be verified:

```
SELECT AF.AircraftCode,AF.AircraftDesignator,SUM(F.FlightDuration) as MinutesFlown
FROM AircraftFleet AF
INNER JOIN Flights F ON AF.AircraftFleetID=F.AircraftFleetID
GROUP BY AF.AircraftCode,AF.AircraftDesignator
HAVING SUM(F.FlightDuration)>120000;
```

```
AircraftCode AircraftDesignator MinutesFlown
------------ ------------------- ------------
F28          AGTX-691            138231
E12          BIOA-249            122138
M11          CIVG-217            123374
EM2          IEQF-918            129297
F28          LXUT-830            127180
E12          MMEK-270            133764
BEK          SKQU-790            149810

(7 row(s) affected)
```

The GROUP BY clause in this example is required because another column is selected with the aggregate function SUM. This gives you a sum for each aircraft. In the original subquery, a GROUP BY clause is not required because SUM achieves a total for the entire query, which is run against the record for each aircraft in the fleet.

NOTE
_____

Proper Use of Correlated Subqueries

For a correlated subquery, you must reference the table in the main query before you can resolve the subquery.
_____

Subquery Performance

Subqueries do have performance implications when used within a query. You must consider those implications prior to implementing them in a production environment. Consider that a subquery must be evaluated prior to the main part of the query, so the time that it takes to execute the subquery has a direct effect on the time it takes for the main query to execute. Now look at the previous example:

```
SELECT AirportID, AirportName
FROM Airports
WHERE AirportID IN (SELECT AF.HomeAirportID
                    FROM AircraftFleet AF
                    WHERE 120000 <= (SELECT SUM(F.FlightDuration)
                                     FROM Flights F
                                     WHERE AF.AircraftFleetID=F.AircraftFleetID
                    ));
```

Imagine what would happen if AIRCRAFTFLEET contained a couple thousand aircraft and FLIGHTS contained a few million lines of flight data over the last several years. The resulting effect of having to do a SUM across the FLIGHTS table and then join it with AIRCRAFTFLEET could slow the query down quite considerably. So always remember to evaluate the effect that using a subquery has on performance when deciding on a course of action to take for getting information out of the database.

Summary

By simple definition and general concept, a subquery is a query that is performed within another query to place further conditions on a query. You can use a subquery in a SQL statement's WHERE clause or HAVING clause. Queries are typically used within other queries (Data Query Language), but you can also use them in the resolution of DML statements such as INSERT, UPDATE, and DELETE. All basic rules for DML apply when using subqueries with DML commands.

The subquery's syntax is virtually the same as that of a standalone query, with a few minor restrictions. One of these restrictions is that you cannot use the ORDER BY clause within a subquery; you can use a GROUP BY clause, however, which renders virtually the same effect. Subqueries are used to place conditions that are not necessarily known for a query, providing more power and flexibility with SQL.

Q&A

Q. Is there a limit on the number of embedded subqueries that can be used in a single query?

A. Limitations such as the number of embedded subqueries allowed and the number of tables joined in a query are specific to each implementation. Some implementations might not have limits; although the use of too many embedded subqueries could drastically hinder SQL statement performance. Most limitations are affected by the actual hardware, CPU speed, and system memory available; however, there are many other considerations.

Q. It seems that debugging a query with subqueries can prove to be confusing, especially with embedded subqueries. What is the best way to debug a query with subqueries?

A. The best way to debug a query with subqueries is to evaluate the query in sections. First, evaluate the lowest-level subquery, and then work your way to the main query (the same way the database evaluates the query). When you evaluate each subquery individually, you can substitute the returned values for each subquery to check your main query's logic. An error with a subquery often results from the use of the operator that evaluates the subquery, such as `(=)`, `IN`, `>`, `<`, and so on.

Workshop

The following workshop is composed of a series of quiz questions and practical exercises. The quiz questions are designed to test your overall understanding of the current material. The practical exercises are intended to afford you the opportunity to apply the concepts discussed during the current hour, as well as build upon the knowledge acquired in previous hours of study. Please take time to complete the quiz questions and exercises before continuing. Refer to Appendix C, "Answers to Quizzes and Exercises," for answers.

Quiz

1. What is the function of a subquery when used with a `SELECT` statement?

2. Can you update more than one column when using the `UPDATE` statement with a subquery?

3. Do the following have the correct syntax? If not, what is the correct syntax?

   a.
```
SELECT PASSENGERID, FIRSTNAME, LASTNAME, COUNTRYCODE
     FROM PASSENGERS
     WHERE PASSENGERID IN
                     (SELECT PASSENGERID
                      FROM TRIPS
                      WHERE TRIPID BETWEEN 2390 AND 2400);
```

   b. `SELECT EMPLOYEEID, SALARY`
           `FROM EMPLOYEES`
           `WHERE SALARY BETWEEN '20000'`
                   `AND (SELECT SALARY`
                        `FROM EMPLOYEES`
                        `WHERE SALARY = '40000');`

   c. `UPDATE PASSENGERS`
           `SET COUNTRYCODE = 'NZ'`
           `WHERE PASSENGERID =`
                   `(SELECT PASSENGERID`
                   `FROM TRIPS`
                   `WHERE TRIPID = 2405);`

4. What would happen if you ran the following statement?

```
DELETE FROM EMPLOYEES
WHERE EMPLOYEEID IN
          (SELECT EMPLOYEEID
          FROM RICH_EMPLOYEES);
```

Exercises

1. Write the SQL code for the requested subqueries, and compare your results to ours.

2. Using a subquery, write a SQL statement to update the PASSENGERS table. Find the passenger with the TripID `3120`, and change the passenger's name to RYAN STEPHENS.

3. Using a subquery, write a query that returns the counts of passengers by country that are leaving on July, 4, 2013.

4. Using a subquery, write a query that lists all passenger information for those passengers that are taking trips that are less than 21 days from beginning to end.

Combining Multiple Queries into One

What You'll Learn in This Hour:

▶ An overview of the operators that combine queries

▶ When to use the commands to combine queries

▶ Using the GROUP BY clause with the compound operators

▶ Using the ORDER BY clause with the compound operators

▶ How to retrieve accurate data

In this hour, you learn how to combine SQL queries using the UNION, UNION ALL, INTERSECT, and EXCEPT operators. Because SQL is meant to work on data in sets, you need to combine and compare various sets of query data. The UNION, INSERSECT, and EXCEPT operators enable you to work with different SELECT statements and combine and compare the results in different ways. Again, you must check your particular implementation for any variations in the use of these operators.

Single Queries Versus Compound Queries

A single query uses one SELECT statement, whereas a compound query includes two or more SELECT statements.

You form compound queries using some type of operator to join the two queries. The UNION operator in the following examples joins two queries.

A single SQL statement could be written as follows:

```
SELECT EmployeeID, Salary, PayRate
FROM Employees
WHERE Salary IS NOT NULL OR
PayRate IS NOT NULL;
```

This is the same statement using the UNION operator:

```
SELECT EmployeeID, Salary
FROM Employees
WHERE Salary IS NOT NULL
UNION
SELECT EmployeeID, PayRate
FROM Employees
WHERE PayRate IS NOT NULL;
```

The previous statements return pay information for all employees who are paid either hourly or on a salary.

Compound operators combine and restrict the results of two SELECT statements. You can use these operators to return or suppress the output of duplicate records. Compound operators can bring together similar data that is stored in different fields.

NOTE
_____

How UNION Works

If you executed the second query, the output has two column headings: EmployeeID and Salary. Each individual's pay rate is listed under the Salary column. When using the UNION operator, column headings are determined by column names or column aliases used in the first SELECT statement.

_____

Compound queries enable you to combine the results of more than one query to return a single set of data. This type of query is often simpler to write than a single query with complex conditions. These queries also allow for more flexibility regarding the never-ending task of data retrieval.

Compound Query Operators

Compound query operators vary among database vendors. The American National Standards Institute (ANSI) standard includes the UNION, UNION ALL, EXCEPT, and INTERSECT operators, all of which are discussed in the following sections.

The UNION Operator

The UNION operator combines the results of two or more SELECT statements without returning duplicate rows. In other words, if a row of output exists in the results of one query, the same row is not returned, even though it exists in the second query. To use the UNION operator, each SELECT statement must have the same number of columns selected, the same number of column expressions, the same data type, and the same order—but they do not have to be the same length.

The syntax follows:

```
SELECT COLUMN1 [, COLUMN2 ]
FROM TABLE1 [, TABLE2 ]
[ WHERE ]
UNION
SELECT COLUMN1 [, COLUMN2 ]
FROM TABLE1 [, TABLE2 ]
[ WHERE ]
```

Look at the following example:

```
SELECT EmployeeID FROM Employees
UNION
SELECT EmployeeID FROM Employees;
```

Those employee IDs appear only once in the results even though we selected from the Employees table twice.

This hour's examples begin with a simple SELECT statement from two tables:

```
SELECT DISTINCT Position FROM Employees;

Position
------------------------------
Ground Operations
Security Officer
Ticket Agent
Baggage Handler

(4 row(s) affected)

SELECT Position FROM EmployeePositions;

Position
------------------------------
Baggage Handler
Ground Operations
Security Officer
Ticket Agent

(4 row(s) affected)
```

Now, combine the same two queries with the UNION operator, making a compound query:

```
SELECT DISTINCT Position FROM Employees
UNION
SELECT Position FROM EmployeePositions;
```

```
Position
------------------------------
Baggage Handler
Ground Operations
Security Officer
Ticket Agent

(4 row(s) affected)
```

In the first query, four rows of data were returned, and four rows of data were returned from the second query. Four rows of data are returned when the UNION operator combines the two queries. Only four rows are returned because duplicate rows of data are not returned when using the UNION operator.

The following code shows an example of combining two unrelated queries with the UNION operator:

```
SELECT Position FROM EmployeePositions
UNION
SELECT Country FROM Countries WHERE Country LIKE 'Z%';

Position
------------------------------
Baggage Handler
Ground Operations
Security Officer
Ticket Agent
Zambia
Zimbabwe

(6 row(s) affected)
```

The Position and Country values are listed together, and the column heading is taken from the column name in the first query.

The UNION ALL Operator

You use the UNION ALL operator to combine the results of two SELECT statements, including duplicate rows. The same rules that apply to UNION apply to the UNION ALL operator. The UNION and UNION ALL operators are the same; although one returns duplicate rows of data where the other does not.

The syntax follows:

```
SELECT COLUMN1 [, COLUMN2 ]
FROM TABLE1 [, TABLE2 ]
[ WHERE ]
```

```
UNION ALL
SELECT COLUMN1 [, COLUMN2 ]
FROM TABLE1 [, TABLE2 ]
[ WHERE ]
```

The following SQL statement returns all employee IDs from both tables and shows duplicates:

```
SELECT DISTINCT Position FROM Employees
UNION ALL
SELECT Position FROM EmployeePositions;
```

The following is the same compound query in the previous section with the UNION ALL operator:

```
SELECT DISTINCT Position FROM Employees
UNION ALL
SELECT Position FROM EmployeePositions;

Position
------------------------------
Ground Operations
Security Officer
Ticket Agent
Baggage Handler
Baggage Handler
Ground Operations
Security Officer
Ticket Agent

(8 row(s) affected)
```

Notice that there were 8 rows returned in this query (4+4) because duplicate records are retrieved with the UNION ALL operator.

The INTERSECT Operator

You use the INTERSECT operator to combine two SELECT statements, but it returns only rows from the first SELECT statement that are identical to rows in the second SELECT statement. The same rules apply when using the INTERSECT operator as when you used the UNION operator.

The syntax follows:

```
SELECT COLUMN1 [, COLUMN2 ]
FROM TABLE1 [, TABLE2 ]
[ WHERE ]
INTERSECT
SELECT COLUMN1 [, COLUMN2 ]
FROM TABLE1 [, TABLE2 ]
[ WHERE ]
```

The following SQL statement returns the customer identification for those customers who have placed an order:

```
SELECT PassengerID FROM Passengers
INTERSECT
SELECT PassengerID FROM Trips;
```

The following example illustrates the INTERSECT operator using the two original queries in this hour:

```
SELECT DISTINCT Position FROM Employees
INTERSECT
SELECT Position FROM EmployeePositions;


Position
-----------------------------
Ground Operations
Security Officer
Ticket Agent
Baggage Handler


(4 row(s) affected)
```

Only 4 rows are returned because only 4 rows were identical between the output of the two single queries.

The EXCEPT Operator

The EXCEPT operator combines two SELECT statements and returns rows from the first SELECT statement that are not returned by the second SELECT statement. Again, the same rules that apply to the UNION operator also apply to the EXCEPT operator. In Oracle the EXCEPT operator is referenced by using the term MINUS but it performs the same functionality.

The syntax follows:

```
SELECT COLUMN1 [, COLUMN2 ]
FROM TABLE1 [, TABLE2 ]
[ WHERE ]
EXCEPT
SELECT COLUMN1 [, COLUMN2 ]
FROM TABLE1 [, TABLE2 ]
[ WHERE ]
```

Study the following example, which would work in a SQL Server implementation:

```
SELECT DISTINCT Position FROM Employees
EXCEPT
SELECT Position FROM EmployeePositions WHERE PositionID<=2;
```

```
Position
-----------------------------
Security Officer
Ticket Agent

(2 row(s) affected)
```

According to the results, two rows of data were returned by the first query that were not returned by the second query.

The following example demonstrates the use of the MINUS operator as a replacement for the EXCEPT operator:

```
SELECT DISTINCT Position FROM Employees
MINUS
SELECT Position FROM EmployeePositions WHERE PositionID<=2;

Position
-----------------------------
Security Officer
Ticket Agent

2 rows selected.
```

Using ORDER BY with a Compound Query

You can use the ORDER BY clause with a compound query. However, you can use the ORDER BY clause only to order the results of both queries. Therefore, there can be only one ORDER BY clause in a compound query, even though the compound query might consist of multiple individual queries or SELECT statements. The ORDER BY clause must reference the columns ordered by an alias or by the column number.

The syntax follows:

```
SELECT COLUMN1 [, COLUMN2 ]
FROM TABLE1 [, TABLE2 ]
[ WHERE ]
OPERATOR{UNION | EXCEPT | INTERSECT | UNION ALL}
SELECT COLUMN1 [, COLUMN2 ]
FROM TABLE1 [, TABLE2 ]
[ WHERE ]
[ ORDER BY ]
```

The following SQL statement returns the employee ID from Employees and EMPLOYEE_MGR tables, but it does not show duplicates and it orders by EmployeeID:

```
SELECT EmployeeID FROM Employees
UNION
SELECT EmployeeID FROM EMPLOYEE_MGR
ORDER BY 1;
```

NOTE

Using Numbers in the ORDER BY Clause

The column in the ORDER BY clause is referenced by the number 1 instead of the actual column name.

The results of the compound query are sorted by the first column of each query. Sorting compound queries lets you easily recognize duplicate records.

The following example shows the use of the ORDER BY clause with a compound query. You can use the column name in the ORDER BY clause if the column sorted by has the same name in all individual queries of the statement.

```
SELECT DISTINCT Position FROM Employees
UNION
SELECT Position FROM EmployeePositions
ORDER BY Position;

Position
-------------------------------
Baggage Handler
Ground Operations
Security Officer
Ticket Agent

(4 row(s) affected)
```

The following query uses a numeric value in place of the actual column name in the ORDER BY clause:

```
SELECT DISTINCT Position FROM Employees
UNION
SELECT Position FROM EmployeePositions
ORDER BY 1;

Position
-------------------------------
Baggage Handler
Ground Operations
Security Officer
Ticket Agent

(4 row(s) affected)
```

Using GROUP BY with a Compound Query

Unlike ORDER BY, you can use GROUP BY in each SELECT statement of a compound query, but you also can use it following all individual queries. In addition, you can use the HAVING clause (sometimes used with the GROUP BY clause) in each SELECT statement of a compound statement.

The syntax follows:

```
SELECT COLUMN1 [, COLUMN2 ]
FROM TABLE1 [, TABLE2 ]
[ WHERE ]
[ GROUP BY ]
[ HAVING ]
OPERATOR {UNION | EXCEPT | INTERSECT | UNION ALL}
SELECT COLUMN1 [, COLUMN2 ]
FROM TABLE1 [, TABLE2 ]
[ WHERE ]
[ GROUP BY ]
[ HAVING ]
[ ORDER BY ]
```

In the following Oracle example, you select a literal string to represent passenger records, employee records, and aircraft records. Each query is simply a count of all records in each appropriate table. The GROUP BY clause groups the results of the entire report by the numeric value 1, which represents the first column in each query.

```
SELECT 'PASSENGERS' AS RECORDTYPE, COUNT(*)
FROM Passengers
UNION
SELECT 'EMPLOYEES' AS RECORDTYPE, COUNT(*)
FROM Employees
UNION
SELECT 'AIRCRAFT' AS RECORDTYPE, COUNT(*)
FROM AircraftFleet
GROUP BY 1;

RECORDTYPE COUNT(*)
---------- -----------
PASSENGERS 135001
EMPLOYEES  5611
AIRCRAFT   350

3 rows selected.
```

In SQL Server because you use a literal value there is no requirement for the GROUP BY clause:

```
SELECT 'PASSENGERS' AS RECORDTYPE, COUNT(*)
FROM Passengers
UNION
SELECT 'EMPLOYEES' AS RECORDTYPE, COUNT(*)
FROM Employees
UNION
SELECT 'AIRCRAFT' AS RECORDTYPE, COUNT(*)
FROM AircraftFleet;


RECORDTYPE
---------- -----------
PASSENGERS 135001
EMPLOYEES  5611
AIRCRAFT   350


(3 row(s) affected)
```

The following query is identical to the previous query, except that the ORDER BY clause is used as well:

```
SELECT 'PASSENGERS' AS RECORDTYPE, COUNT(*)
FROM Passengers
UNION
SELECT 'EMPLOYEES' AS RECORDTYPE, COUNT(*)
FROM Employees
UNION
SELECT 'AIRCRAFT' AS RECORDTYPE, COUNT(*)
FROM AircraftFleet
ORDER BY 2;


RECORDTYPE COUNT(*)
---------- -----------
AIRCRAFT   350
EMPLOYEES  5611
PASSENGERS 135001


3 rows selected.
```

This is sorted by column 2, which was the count on each table. Hence, the final output is sorted by the count from least to greatest.

Retrieving Accurate Data

Be cautious when using the compound operators. Incorrect or incomplete data might be returned if you use the INTERSECT operator and you use the wrong SELECT statement as the first individual query. In addition, consider whether you want duplicate records when using the UNION and UNION ALL operators. What about EXCEPT? Do you need any of the rows that the second query did not return? As you can see, the wrong compound query operator or the wrong order of individual queries in a compound query can easily cause misleading data to be returned.

Summary

This hour introduced you to compound queries. All SQL statements previous to this hour have consisted of a single query. Compound queries allow multiple individual queries to be used together as a single query to achieve the data resultset wanted as output. The compound query operators discussed included UNION, UNION ALL, INTERSECT, and EXCEPT (MINUS). UNION returns the output of two single queries without displaying duplicate rows of data. UNION ALL simply displays all output of single queries, regardless of existing duplicate rows. INTERSECT returns identical rows between two queries. EXCEPT (MINUS in Oracle) returns the results of one query that do not exist in another query. Compound queries provide greater flexibility when trying to satisfy the requirements of various queries, which, without the use of compound operators, could result in complex queries.

Q&A

Q. How are the columns referenced in the GROUP BY clause in a compound query?

A. The columns can be referenced by the actual column name or by the number of the column placement in the query if the column names are not identical in the two queries.

Q. I understand what the EXCEPT operator does, but would the outcome change if I were to reverse the SELECT statements?

A. Yes, the order of the individual queries is important when using the EXCEPT or MINUS operator. Remember that all rows are returned from the first query that are not returned by the second query. Changing the order of the two individual queries in the compound query could definitely affect the results.

Q. Must the data type and the length of columns in a compound query be the same in both queries?

A. No, only the data type must be the same. The length can differ.

Q. What determines the column names when using the UNION operator?

A. The first query set determines the column names for the data returned when using a UNION operator.

Workshop

The following workshop is composed of a series of quiz questions and practical exercises. The quiz questions are designed to test your overall understanding of the current material. The practical exercises are intended to afford you the opportunity to apply the concepts discussed during the current hour, as well as build upon the knowledge acquired in previous hours of study. Please take time to complete the quiz questions and exercises before continuing. Refer to Appendix C, "Answers to Quizzes and Exercises," for answers.

Quiz

1. Is the syntax correct for the following compound queries? If not, what would correct the syntax? Use the PASSENGERS and TRIPS tables.

   a. ```
      SELECT PASSENGERID, BIRTHDATE, FIRSTNAME
      FROM PASSENGERS
      UNION
      SELECT PASSENGERID, LEAVING, RETURNING
      FROM TRIPS;
      ```

   b. ```
      SELECT PASSENGERID FROM PASSENGERS
      UNION ALL
      SELECT PASSENGERID FROM TRIPS
      ORDER BY PASSENGERID;
      ```

   c. ```
      SELECT PASSENGERID FROM TRIPS
      INTERSECT
      SELECT PASSENGERID FROM PASSENGERS
      ORDER BY 1;
      ```

2. Match the correct operator to the following statements:

| Statement | Operator |
|---|---|
| a. Show duplicates. | UNION |
| b. Return only rows from the first query that match those in the second query. | INTERSECT |
| c. Return no duplicates. | UNION ALL |
| d. Return only rows from the first query not returned by the second. | EXCEPT |
      ```

Exercises

1. Use the PASSENGERS and TRIPS tables to write a compound query to find the passengers who have scheduled a trip.

2. Write a compound query to find the passengers who have not scheduled a trip.

3. Write a query that uses EXCEPT to list all the passengers who have taken a trip except those that originated in Albany.

Using Indexes to Improve Performance

What You'll Learn in This Hour:

▶ How indexes work

▶ How to create an index

▶ The different types of indexes

▶ When to use indexes

▶ When not to use indexes

In this hour, you learn how to improve SQL statement performance by creating and using indexes. You begin with the CREATE INDEX command and learn how to use indexes that have been created on tables.

What Is an Index?

Simply put, an *index* is a pointer to data in a table. An index in a database is similar to an index in the back of a book. For example, if you want to reference all pages in a book that discuss a certain topic, you first refer to the index, which lists all topics alphabetically, and it refers you to one or more specific page numbers. An index in a database works the same way in that a query is pointed to the exact physical location of data in a table. You are actually directed to the data's location in an underlying file of the database, but as far as you are concerned, you are referring to a table.

Which would be faster, looking through a book page by page for some information or searching the book's index and getting a page number? Of course, using the book's index is the most efficient method. It can save a lot of time, especially if the book is large. If you have a book of just a few pages, however, it might be faster to flip through the chapters for the information than to flip back and forth between the index and chapters. When a database does not use an index, it is performing what is typically called a full table scan, the same as flipping through a book page by page. Full table scans are discussed in Hour 17, "Improving Database Performance."

An index is typically stored separately from the table for which the index was created. An index's main purpose is to improve the performance of data retrieval. Indexes can be created or dropped with no effect on the data. However, after an index is dropped, performance of data retrieval might be slowed. Indexes do take up physical space and can often grow larger than the table. Therefore, you should consider them when estimating your database storage needs.

How Do Indexes Work?

When an index is created, it records the location of values in a table that are associated with the column that is indexed. Entries are added to the index when new data is added to the table. When a query is executed against the database and a condition is specified on a column in the WHERE clause that is indexed, the index is first searched for the values specified in the WHERE clause. If the value is found in the index, the index returns the exact location of the searched data in the table. Figure 16.1 illustrates the functioning of an index.

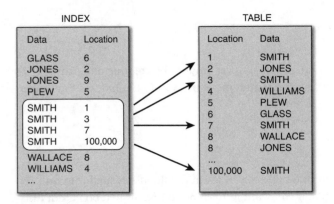

FIGURE 16.1
Table access using an index

Suppose the following query was issued:

```
SELECT *
FROM TABLE_NAME
WHERE NAME = 'SMITH';
```

As shown in Figure 16.1, the NAME index is referenced to resolve the location of all names equal to SMITH. After the location is determined, the data can quickly be retrieved from the table. The data, names in this case, is alphabetized in the index.

Variations of Index Creation

Indexes can be created during table creation in certain implementations. Most implementations accommodate a command, aside from the CREATE TABLE command, used to create indexes. Check your particular implementation for the exact syntax for the command, if any, which is available to create an index.

A full table scan occurs if there is no index on the table and the same query is executed, which means that every row of data in the table is read to retrieve information pertaining to all individuals with the name SMITH.

An index is faster because it typically stores information in an orderly tree-like format. Consider if we have a list of books upon which we place an index. The index has a root node, which is the beginning point of each query. Then it is split into branches. Maybe in our case there are two branches, one for letters A–L and the other for letters M–Z. Now if you ask for a book with a name that starts with the letter M, you enter the index at the root node and immediately travel to the branch containing letters M–Z. This effectively cuts your time to find the book by eliminating close to one-half the possibilities.

The CREATE INDEX Command

The CREATE INDEX statement, as with many other statements in SQL, varies greatly among different relational database vendors. It is used to create the various types of indexes available for a table. Most relational database implementations use the CREATE INDEX statement:

```
CREATE INDEX INDEX_NAME ON TABLE_NAME
```

The syntax for the CREATE INDEX statement varies greatly among vendors. Some implementations allow the specification of a storage clause (as with the CREATE TABLE statement), ordering (DESC||ASC), and the use of clusters. You must check your particular implementation for its correct syntax.

Types of Indexes

You can create different types of indexes on tables in a database, all of which serve the same goal: to improve database performance by expediting data retrieval. This hour discusses single-column indexes, composite indexes, and unique indexes.

Single-Column Indexes

Indexing on a single column of a table is the simplest and most common manifestation of an index. Obviously, a *single-column index* is one that is created based on only one table column. The basic syntax follows:

```
CREATE INDEX INDEX_NAME_IDX
ON TABLE_NAME (COLUMN_NAME)
```

For example, if you want to create an index on EMPLOYEES for employees' last names, the command used to create the index looks like the following:

```
CREATE INDEX NAME_IDX
ON EMPLOYEES (LASTNAME);
```

TIP

Best Places for Single-Column Indexes

Single-column indexes are most effective when used on columns that are frequently used alone in the WHERE clause as query conditions. Good candidates for a single-column index are an individual identification number, a serial number, or a system-assigned key.

Unique Indexes

You use *unique indexes* for performance and data integrity. A unique index does not allow duplicate values to be inserted into the table. Otherwise, the unique index performs the same way a regular index performs. The syntax follows:

```
CREATE UNIQUE INDEX INDEX_NAME
ON TABLE_NAME (COLUMN_NAME)
```

If you want to create a unique index on EMPLOYEES for an employee's last name, the command looks like the following:

```
CREATE UNIQUE INDEX NAME_IDX
ON EMPLOYEES (LASTNAME);
```

The only problem with this index is that every individual's last name in EMPLOYEES must be unique, which is impractical. However, a unique index should be created for a column, such as an individual's identification number, because that number would be unique for each individual.

You might be wondering, "What if an employee's identification number is the primary key for a table?" An index is usually implicitly created when you define a primary key for a table. So normally you do not also have to create a unique index on the table.

When working with objects such as unique indexes, it is often beneficial to create the indexes on empty tables during the creation of the database structure. This ensures that the data going into the structure already meets the demand of the constraints you want to place on it. If you work with existing data, you want to analyze the impact of whether the data needs to be adjusted to properly apply the index.

TIP

Unique Index Constraints

You can create a unique index only on a column in a table whose values are unique. In other words, you cannot create a unique index on an existing table with data that already contains records on the indexed key that are non-unique. Similarly, you cannot create a unique index on a column that allows for NULL values. If you attempt to create a unique index on a column that violates one of these principles, the statement fails.

Composite Indexes

A composite index is an index on two or more columns of a table. You should consider performance when creating a composite index because the order of columns in the index has a measurable effect on the data retrieval speed. Generally, the most restrictive value should be placed first for optimum performance. However, the columns that are always specified in your queries should be placed first. The syntax follows:

```
CREATE INDEX INDEX_NAME
ON TABLE_NAME (COLUMN1, COLUMN2)
```

An example of a composite index follows:

```
CREATE INDEX FLIGHT_IDX
ON FLIGHTS (ROUTEID, AIRCRAFTFLEETID);
```

In this example, you create a composite index based on two columns in the FLIGHTS table: ROUTEID and AIRCRAFTFLEETID. You assume that these two columns are frequently used together as conditions in the WHERE clause of a query.

In deciding whether to create a single-column index or a composite index, consider the column(s) that you might use frequently in a query's WHERE clause as filter conditions. If only one column is used, choose a single-column index. If two or more columns are frequently used in the WHERE clause as filters, a composite index would be the best choice.

Implicit Indexes

Implicit indexes are indexes that are automatically created by the database server when an object is created. Indexes are automatically created for primary key constraints and unique constraints.

Why are indexes automatically created for these constraints? Imagine a database server. Now say a user adds a new product to the database. The product identification is the primary key on the table, which means that it must be a unique value. To efficiently make sure the new value is unique among hundreds or thousands of records, the product identifications in the table must be indexed. Therefore, when you create a primary key or unique constraint, an index is automatically created for you.

When Should Indexes Be Considered?

Unique indexes are implicitly used with a primary key for the primary key to work. Foreign keys are also excellent candidates for an index because you often use them to join the parent table. Most, if not all, columns used for table joins should be indexed.

Columns that you frequently reference in the ORDER BY and GROUP BY clauses should be considered for indexes. For example, if you are sorting on an individual's name, it is quite beneficial to have an index on the name column. It renders an automatic alphabetical order on every name, thus simplifying the actual sort operation and expediting the output results.

Furthermore, you should create indexes on columns with a high number of unique values, or columns that, when used as filter conditions in the WHERE clause, return a low percentage of rows of data from a table. This is where trial and error might come into play. Just as you should always test production code and database structures before implementing them into production, so should you test indexes. Your testing should center on trying different combinations of indexes, no indexes, single-column indexes, and composite indexes. There is no cut-and-dried rule for using indexes. The effective use of indexes requires a thorough knowledge of table relationships, query and transaction requirements, and the data itself.

NOTE

Plan for Indexing Accordingly

You should plan your tables and indexes. Don't assume that because an index has been created, all performance issues are resolved. The index might not help at all. It might actually hinder performance and might just take up disk space.

When Should Indexes Be Avoided?

Although indexes are intended to enhance a database's performance, sometimes you should avoid them. The following guidelines indicate when you should reconsider using an index:

▶ You should not use indexes on small tables. This is because indexes have an overhead associated with them in terms of query time to access them. In the case of small tables, it is usually faster for the query engine to do a quick scan over the table rather than look at an index first.

▶ You should not use indexes on columns that return a high percentage of data rows when used as a filter condition in a query's WHERE clause. For instance, you would not have an entry for the words the or and in the index of a book.

▶ You can index tables that have frequent, large batch update jobs run. However, the batch job's performance is slowed considerably by the index. You can correct the conflict of having an index on a table that is frequently loaded or manipulated by a large batch process by dropping the index before the batch job and then re-creating the index after the job has completed. This is because the indexes are also updated as the data is inserted, causing additional overhead.

▶ You should not use indexes on columns that contain a high number of NULL values. This is because indexes operate best on columns that have a higher uniqueness of data between rows. If there are a lot of NULL values, the index will be skewed toward the NULL values and might affect performance.

▶ You should not index columns that are frequently manipulated. Maintenance on the index can become excessive.

You can see in Figure 16.2 that an index on a column, such as gender, might not prove beneficial. For example, suppose the following query was submitted to the database:

```
SELECT *
FROM TABLE_NAME
WHERE GENDER = 'FEMALE';
```

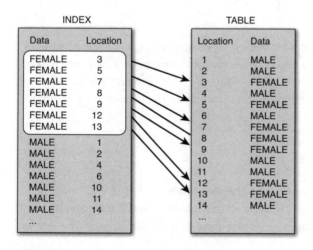

FIGURE 16.2
An example of an ineffective index

By referring to Figure 16.2, which is based on the previous query, you can see that there is constant activity between the table and its index. Because a high number of data rows is returned for `WHERE GENDER = 'FEMALE'` (or `'MALE'`), the database server constantly has to read the index, then the table, then the index, then the table, and so on. In this case, it might be more efficient for a full table scan to occur because a high percentage of the table must be read anyway.

CAUTION

Indexes Can Sometimes Lead to Performance Problems

Caution should be taken when creating indexes on a table's extremely long keys because performance is inevitably slowed by high I/O costs.

As a general rule, do not use an index on a column used in a query's condition that returns a high percentage of data rows from the table. In other words, do not create an index on a column such as gender or any column that contains few distinct values. This is often referred to as a column's *cardinality,* or the uniqueness of the data. High cardinality means very unique and describes things such as identification numbers. Low-cardinality values are not very unique and refer to columns such as gender.

Altering an Index

You can alter an index after it has been created using syntax that is similar to the `CREATE INDEX` syntax. The types of alterations that you can manage with the statement differ between implementations but handle all the basic variations of an index in terms of columns, ordering, and such. The syntax follows:

```
ALTER INDEX INDEX_NAME
```

You should take care when altering an existing index on production systems. This is because in most cases the index is immediately rebuilt, which obviously creates an overhead in terms of resources. In addition, on most basic implementations, while the index is being rebuilt it cannot be utilized for queries. This might put an additional hindrance upon the performance of your system.

Dropping an Index

An index can be dropped rather simply. Check your particular implementation for the exact syntax, but most major implementations use the `DROP` command. You should take care when dropping an index because performance might be slowed drastically (or improved!). The syntax follows:

```
DROP INDEX INDEX_NAME
```

MySQL uses a slightly different syntax; you also specify the table name of the table that you are dropping the index from:

```
DROP INDEX INDEX_NAME ON TABLE_NAME
```

The most common reason for dropping an index is an attempt to improve performance. Remember that if you drop an index, you can re-create it later. You might need to rebuild an index to reduce fragmentation. It is often necessary to experiment with the use of indexes in a database to determine the route to best performance, which might involve creating an index, dropping it, and eventually re-creating it, with or without modifications.

Summary

In this hour you learned that you can use indexes to improve the overall performance of queries and transactions performed within the database. Database indexes, like an index of a book, enable specific data to be quickly referenced from a table. The most common method for creating indexes is through use of the CREATE INDEX command. Different types of indexes are available among SQL implementations. Unique indexes, single-column indexes, and composite indexes are among those types of indexes. You need to consider many factors when deciding on the index type that best meets the needs of your database. The effective use of indexes often requires some experimentation, a thorough knowledge of table relationships and data, and a little patience—being patient when you create an index can save minutes, hours, or even days of work later.

Q&A

Q. Does an index actually take up space the way a table does?

A. Yes, an index takes up physical space in a database. In fact, an index can become much larger than the table for which the index was created.

Q. If you drop an index so that a batch job can complete faster, how long does it take to re-create the index?

A. Many factors are involved, such as the size of the index being dropped, the CPU usage, and the machine's power.

Q. Should all indexes be unique?

A. No, unique indexes allow no duplicate values. There might be a need for the allowance of duplicate values in a table.

Workshop

The following workshop is composed of a series of quiz questions and practical exercises. The quiz questions are designed to test your overall understanding of the current material. The practical exercises are intended to afford you the opportunity to apply the concepts discussed during the current hour, as well as build upon the knowledge acquired in previous hours of study. Please take time to complete the quiz questions and exercises before continuing. Refer to Appendix C, "Answers to Quizzes and Exercises," for answers.

Quiz

1. What are some major disadvantages of using indexes?

2. Why is the order of columns in a composite index important?

3. Should a column with a large percentage of NULL values be indexed?

4. Is the main purpose of an index to stop duplicate values in a table?

5. True or false: The main reason for a composite index is for aggregate function usage in an index.

6. What does cardinality refer to? What is considered a column of high-cardinality?

Exercises

1. For the following situations, decide whether an index should be used and, if so, what type of index should be used:

    a. Several columns, but a rather small table.

    b. Medium-sized table; no duplicates should be allowed.

    c. Several columns, very large table, several columns used as filters in the WHERE clause.

    d. Large table, many columns, a lot of data manipulation.

2. Write a SQL statement to create an index called EP_POSITION in EMPLOYEES on the POSITION column.

3. Create a statement to alter the index you just created to make it unique. Why doesn't it work?

4. For the FLIGHTS table, choose some columns to make up a unique index for that table. Explain your reasoning behind picking those columns.

5. Study the tables used in this book. List some good candidates for indexed columns based on how a user might search for data.

6. Create a multicolumn index on FLIGHTS. Include the following columns: ROUTEID, AIRCRAFTFLEETID, and STATUSCODE.

7. Create some additional indexes on your tables as wanted.

HOUR 17
Improving Database Performance

What You'll Learn in This Hour:

- ▶ Definition of SQL statement tuning
- ▶ Database tuning versus SQL statement tuning
- ▶ Properly joining tables
- ▶ The problems with full table scans
- ▶ Invoking the use of indexes
- ▶ Avoiding the use of OR and HAVING
- ▶ Avoiding large sort operations

In this hour, you learn how to tune your SQL statement for maximum performance using some simple methods. Although up to this point this book has focused on how to write SQL, it is just as important to learn how to write efficient SQL that can help keep the database running optimally. This hour focuses on simple steps that you can take when working with various queries to ensure that your SQL performs optimally.

What Is SQL Statement Tuning?

SQL statement tuning is the process of optimally building SQL statements to achieve results in the most effective and efficient manner. SQL tuning begins with the basic arrangement of the elements in a query. Simple formatting can play a rather large role in the optimization of a statement.

SQL statement tuning mainly involves tweaking a statement's FROM and WHERE clauses. It is mostly from these two clauses that the database server decides how to evaluate a query. To this point, you have learned the basics of the FROM and WHERE clauses. Now it is time to learn how to fine-tune them for better results and happier users.

Database Tuning Versus SQL Statement Tuning

Before learning about SQL statement tuning, you need to understand the difference between tuning a database and tuning the SQL statements that access the database.

Database tuning is the process of tuning the actual database, which encompasses the allocated memory, disk usage, CPU, I/O, and underlying database processes. Tuning a database also involves the management and manipulation of the database structure, such as the design and layout of tables and indexes. In addition, database tuning often involves the modification of the database architecture to optimize the use of the hardware resources available. You need to consider many other things when tuning a database, but the database administrator (DBA) and system administrator normally accomplish these tasks. The objective of database tuning is to ensure that the database has been designed in a way that best accommodates expected activity within the database.

SQL tuning is the process of tuning the SQL statements that access the database. These SQL statements include database queries and transactional operations, such as inserts, updates, and deletes. The objective of SQL statement tuning is to formulate statements that most effectively access the database in its current state, taking advantage of database and system resources and indexes. The objective is to reduce the operational overhead of executing the query on the database.

NOTE
___

Tuning Is Not One Dimensional

You must perform both database tuning and SQL statement tuning to achieve optimal results when accessing the database. A poorly tuned database might render your efforts in SQL tuning useless, and vice versa. Ideally, it is best to first tune the database, ensure that indexes exist where needed, and then tune the SQL code.

___

Formatting Your SQL Statement

Formatting your SQL statement sounds like an obvious task, but it is worth mentioning. A newcomer to SQL will probably neglect to consider several things when building a SQL statement. The upcoming sections discuss the following considerations: Some are common sense; others are not so obvious:

▶ The format of SQL statements for readability

▶ The order of tables in the FROM clause

▶ The placement of the most restrictive conditions in the WHERE clause

▶ The placement of join conditions in the WHERE clause

Formatting a Statement for Readability

TIP

It's All About the Optimizer

Most relational database implementations have a *SQL optimizer* that evaluates a SQL statement and determines the best method for executing the statement based on the way a SQL statement is written and the availability of indexes in the database. Not all optimizers are the same. Check your implementation or consult the database administrator to learn how the optimizer reads SQL code. You should understand how the optimizer works to effectively tune a SQL statement.

Formatting a SQL statement for readability is fairly obvious, but many SQL statements are not written neatly. Although the neatness of a statement does not affect the actual performance (the database does not care how neat the statement appears), careful formatting is the first step in tuning a statement. When you look at a SQL statement with tuning intentions, making the statement readable is always the first priority. How can you determine whether the statement is well written if it is difficult to read?

Some basic rules for making a statement readable follow:

- ▶ Always begin a new line with each clause in the statement. For example, place the FROM clause on a separate line from the SELECT clause. Then place the WHERE clause on a separate line from the FROM clause, and so on.

- ▶ Use tabs or spaces for indentation when arguments of a clause in the statement exceed one line.

- ▶ Use tabs and spaces consistently.

- ▶ Use table aliases when multiple tables are used in the statement. The use of the full table name to qualify each column in the statement quickly clutters the statement and makes reading it difficult.

- ▶ Use remarks sparingly in SQL statements if they are available within your specific implementation. Remarks are great for documentation, but too many of them clutter a statement.

- ▶ Begin a new line with each column name in the SELECT clause if many columns are selected.

- ▶ Begin a new line with each table name in the FROM clause if many tables are used.

- ▶ Begin a new line with each condition of the WHERE clause. You can easily see all conditions of the statement and the order in which they are used.

Following is an example of a statement that would be hard to decipher:

```
SELECT EMPLOYEES.FIRSTNAME, EMPLOYEES.LASTNAME, AIRPORTS.CITY, AIRPORTS.
AIRPORTNAME, COUNTRIES.COUNTRY
FROM EMPLOYEES INNER JOIN AIRPORTS ON EMPLOYEES.AIRPORTID = AIRPORTS.AIRPORTID
INNER JOIN
COUNTRIES ON AIRPORTS.COUNTRYCODE = COUNTRIES.COUNTRYCODE WHERE EMPLOYEES.
SALARY>70000 AND AIRPORTNAME LIKE 'M%' AND AIRPORTS.City LIKE 'G%';
```

```
FIRSTNAME     LASTNAME      CITY                 AIRPORTNAME    COUNTRY
-----------   -----------   ------------------   ------------   ---------
Violeta       Fawver        Gordonsville         Municipal      United States

(1 row(s) affected)
```

Here the statement has been reformatted for improved readability:

```
SELECT E.FirstName,
       E.LastName,
       A.City,
       A.AirportName,
       C.Country
FROM   Employees AS E INNER JOIN
       Airports AS A ON E.AirportID = A.AirportID INNER JOIN
       Countries AS C ON A.CountryCode = C.CountryCode
WHERE
   (E.Salary > 70000)
   AND (A.AirportName LIKE 'M%')
   AND (A.City LIKE 'G%');
```

```
FIRSTNAME     LASTNAME      CITY                 AIRPORTNAME    COUNTRY
-----------   -----------   ------------------   ------------   ---------
Violeta       Fawver        Gordonsville         Municipal      United States

(1 row(s) affected)
```

Both statements have the same content, but the second statement is much more readable. It has been greatly simplified through the use of table aliases, which have been defined in the query's FROM clause. In addition, the second statement aligns the elements of each clause, making each clause stand out.

Again, making a statement more readable does not directly improve its performance, but it assists you in making modifications and debugging a lengthy and otherwise complex statement. Now you can easily identify the columns selected, the tables used, the table joins performed, and the conditions placed on the query.

NOTE

Always Establish Standards

It is especially important to establish coding standards in a multiuser programming environment. If all code is consistently formatted, shared code and modifications to code are much easier to manage.

Arranging Tables in the FROM Clause

The arrangement or order of tables in the FROM clause might make a difference, depending on how the optimizer reads the SQL statement. For example, it might be more beneficial to list the smaller tables first and the larger tables last. Some users with a lot of experience have found that listing the larger tables last in the FROM clause is more efficient.

Following is an example of the FROM clause:

```
FROM  SMALLEST TABLE,
      LARGEST TABLE
```

NOTE

Check for Performance When Using Multiple Tables

Check your particular implementation for performance tips, if any, when listing multiple tables in the FROM clause.

Ordering Join Conditions

As you learned in Hour 13, "Joining Tables in Queries," most joins use a base table to link tables that have one or more common columns on which to join. The base table is the main table that most or all tables are joined to in a query. The column from the base table is normally placed on the right side of a join operation in the WHERE clause. The tables joined to the base table are normally in order from smallest to largest, similar to the tables listed in the FROM clause.

If a base table doesn't exist, the tables should be listed from smallest to largest, with the largest tables on the right side of the join operation in the WHERE clause. The join conditions should be in the first position(s) of the WHERE clause followed by the filter clause(s), as shown here:

```
FROM TABLE1,                              Smallest table
     TABLE2,                              to
     TABLE3                               Largest table, also base table
WHERE TABLE1.COLUMN = TABLE3.COLUMN       Join condition
  AND TABLE2.COLUMN = TABLE3.COLUMN       Join condition
[ AND CONDITION1 ]                        Filter condition
[ AND CONDITION2 ]                        Filter condition
```

CAUTION

Be Restrictive with Your Joins

Because joins typically return a high percentage of rows of data from the table(s), you should evaluate join conditions after more restrictive conditions.

In this example, TABLE3 is used as the base table. TABLE1 and TABLE2 are joined to TABLE3 for both simplicity and proven efficiency.

The Most Restrictive Condition

The most restrictive condition is typically the driving factor in achieving optimal performance for a SQL query. What is the most restrictive condition? The condition in the WHERE clause of a statement that returns the fewest rows of data. Conversely, the least restrictive condition is the condition in a statement that returns the most rows of data. This hour is concerned with the most restrictive condition simply because it does the most filtering of the data that is to be returned by the query.

It should be your goal for the SQL optimizer to evaluate the most restrictive condition first, because a smaller subset of data is returned by the condition, thus reducing the query's overhead. The effective placement of the most restrictive condition in the query requires knowledge of how the optimizer operates. The optimizers in some cases seem to read from the bottom of the WHERE clause up. Therefore, you want to place the most restrictive condition last in the WHERE clause, which is the condition that the optimizer reads first. The following example shows how to structure the WHERE clause based on the restrictiveness of the conditions and the FROM clause on the size of the tables:

```
FROM TABLE1,                           Smallest table
     TABLE2,                           to
     TABLE3                            Largest table, also base table
WHERE TABLE1.COLUMN = TABLE3.COLUMN    Join condition
  AND TABLE2.COLUMN = TABLE3.COLUMN    Join condition
[ AND CONDITION1 ]                     Least restrictive
[ AND CONDITION2 ]                     Most restrictive
```

CAUTION

Always Test Your WHERE Clauses

If you do not know how your particular implementation's SQL optimizer works, and the DBA does not know, or if you do not have sufficient documentation, you can execute a large query that takes a while to run and then rearrange conditions in the WHERE clause. Be sure to record the time it takes the query to complete each time you make changes. You should have to run only a couple tests to figure out whether the optimizer reads the WHERE clause from the top to bottom or bottom to top. Turn off database caching during the testing for more accurate results.

Following is an example using a phony table:

Table: TEST
Row count: 5,611
Conditions: WHERE LASTNAME = 'SMITH'
                                returns 2,000 rows
                                WHERE STATE = 'IN'
                                returns 30,000 rows
Most restrictive condition: WHERE LASTNAME = 'SMITH'

Following is the first query:

```
SELECT COUNT(*)
FROM TEST
WHERE LASTNAME = 'SMITH'
  AND STATE = 'IN';

  COUNT(*)
----------
     1,024
```

Following is the second query:

```
SELECT COUNT(*)
FROM TEST
WHERE STATE = 'IN'
  AND LASTNAME = 'SMITH';

  COUNT(*)
----------
     1,024
```

Suppose that the first query completed in 20 seconds, whereas the second query completed in 10 seconds. Because the second query returned faster results and the most restrictive condition was listed last in the WHERE clause, it is safe to assume that the optimizer reads the WHERE clause from the bottom up.

NOTE

Try to Use Indexed Columns

It is a good practice to use an indexed column as the most restrictive condition in a query. Indexes generally improve a query's performance.

Full Table Scans

A full table scan occurs when an index is not used by the query engine or there is no index on the table(s) being used. Full table scans usually return data much slower than when an index is used. The larger the table, the slower that data is returned when a full table scan is performed. The query optimizer decides whether to use an index when executing the SQL statement. The index is used if it exists in most cases.

Some implementations have sophisticated query optimizers that can decide whether to use an index. Decisions such as this are based on statistics that are gathered on database objects, such as the size of an object and the estimated number of rows that are returned by a condition with an indexed column. Refer to your implementation documentation for specifics on the decision-making capabilities of your relational database's optimizer.

You should avoid full table scans when reading large tables. For example, a full table scan is performed when a table that does not have an index is read, which usually takes a considerably longer time to return the data. An index should be considered for the majority of larger tables. On small tables, as previously mentioned, the optimizer might choose the full table scan over using the index if the table is indexed. For a small table with an index, you should consider dropping the index and reserving that space for other needy objects in the database.

TIP

There Are Simple Ways to Avoid Table Scans

The easiest and most obvious way to avoid a full table scan—outside of ensuring that indexes exist on the table—is to use conditions in a query's WHERE clause to filter data to be returned.

The following is a reminder of data that should be indexed:

- ▶ Columns used as primary keys
- ▶ Columns used as foreign keys
- ▶ Columns frequently used to join tables
- ▶ Columns frequently used as conditions in a query
- ▶ Columns that have a high percentage of unique values

TIP

Table Scans Are Not Always Bad

Sometimes, full table scans are good. You should perform them on queries against small tables or queries whose conditions return a high percentage of rows. The easiest way to force a full table scan is to avoid creating an index on the table.

Other Performance Considerations

There are other performance considerations when tuning SQL statements. The following concepts are discussed in the next sections:

- ▶ Using the LIKE operator and wildcards
- ▶ Avoiding the OR operator
- ▶ Avoiding the HAVING clause
- ▶ Avoiding large sort operations
- ▶ Using stored procedures
- ▶ Disabling indexes during batch loads

Using the LIKE Operator and Wildcards

The LIKE operator is a useful tool that places conditions on a query in a flexible manner. Using wildcards in a query can eliminate many possibilities of data that should be retrieved. Wildcards are flexible for queries that search for similar data (data that is not equivalent to an exact value specified).

Suppose you want to write a query using EMPLOYEE_TBL selecting the EMP_ID, LAST_NAME, FIRST_NAME, and STATE columns. You need to know the employee identification, name, and state for all the employees with the last name Stevens. Three SQL statement examples with different wildcard placements serve as examples.

The following is Query 1:

```
SELECT EMPLOYEEID, LASTNAME, FIRSTNAME, STATE
FROM EMPLOYEES
WHERE LASTNAME LIKE 'STEVENS';
```

Next is Query 2:

```
SELECT EMPLOYEEID, LASTNAME, FIRSTNAME, STATE
FROM EMPLOYEES
WHERE LASTNAME LIKE '%EVENS%';
```

Here is the last query, Query 3:

```
SELECT EMPLOYEEID, LASTNAME, FIRSTNAME, STATE
FROM EMPLOYEES
WHERE LASTNAME LIKE 'ST%';
```

The SQL statements do not necessarily return the same results. More than likely, Query 1 will return fewer rows than the other two queries and will take advantage of indexing. Query 2 and Query 3 are less specific as to the desired returned data, thus making them slower than Query 1. In addition, Query 3 is probably faster than Query 2 because the first letters of the string for which you are searching are specified. (And the column LASTNAME is likely to be indexed.). So Query 3 could potentially take advantage of an index.

With Query 1, you might retrieve all individuals with the last name Stevens; but can't Stevens be spelled different ways? Query 2 picks up all individuals with the last name Stevens and its various spellings. Query 3 also picks up any last name starting with ST; this is the only way to ensure that you receive all the Stevens (or Stephens).

Avoiding the OR Operator

Rewriting the SQL statement using the IN predicate instead of the OR operator consistently and substantially improves data retrieval speed. Your implementation tells you about tools you can use to time or check the performance between the OR operator and the IN predicate. An example of how to rewrite a SQL statement by taking the OR operator out and replacing the OR operator with the IN predicate follows. Refer to Hour 8, "Using Operators to Categorize Data," for the use of the OR operator and the IN predicate.

Following is a query using the OR operator:

```
SELECT EMPLOYEEID, LASTNAME, FIRSTNAME
FROM EMPLOYEES
WHERE CITY = 'INDIANAPOLIS IN'
   OR CITY = 'KOKOMO'
   OR CITY = 'TERRE HAUTE';
```

Following is the same query using the IN operator:

```
SELECT EMPLOYEEID, LASTNAME, FIRSTNAME
FROM EMPLOYEES
WHERE CITY IN ('INDIANAPOLIS IN', 'KOKOMO',
               'TERRE HAUTE');
```

The SQL statements retrieve the same data; however, through testing and experience, you find that the data retrieval is measurably faster by replacing OR conditions with the IN predicate, as in the second query.

Avoiding the HAVING Clause

The HAVING clause is useful for paring down the result of a GROUP BY clause; however, you can't use it without cost. Using the HAVING clause gives the SQL optimizer extra work, which results in extra time. Not only will the query be concerned with grouping result sets, but it also will be concerned with parsing those result sets down via the restrictions of the HAVING clause. For example, look at the following statement:

```
SELECT A.AIRPORTNAME,
       A.CITY,
       SUM(E.SALARY) AS SALARY_TOTAL,
       SUM(E.PAYRATE*160) AS HOURLY_TOTAL
FROM   Employees AS E INNER JOIN
       Airports AS A ON E.AirportID = A.AirportID INNER JOIN
       Countries AS C ON A.CountryCode = C.CountryCode
WHERE  A.CountryCode='US'
GROUP BY A.AIRPORTNAME,
       A.CITY
HAVING AVG(E.PAYRATE)>18;
```

Here we are trying to determine the total employee cost for airports where the average hourly rate is greater than $18.00/hr. Although this query is fairly simple and our sample database is small, the addition of the HAVING clause introduces some overhead, especially when the HAVING clause has more complex logic and a higher number of groupings to be applied. If possible, you should write SQL statements without using the HAVING clause or design the HAVING clause restrictions so that they are as simple as possible.

Avoiding Large Sort Operations

Large sort operations mean using the ORDER BY, GROUP BY, and HAVING clauses. Subsets of data must be stored in memory or to disk (if there is not enough space in allotted memory) whenever sort operations are performed. You must sort data often. The main point is that these sort operations affect a SQL statement's response time. Because you cannot always avoid large sort operations, it is best to schedule queries with large sorts as periodic batch processes during off-peak database usage so that the performance of most user processes is not affected.

Using Stored Procedures

You should create stored procedures for SQL statements executed on a regular basis—particularly large transactions or queries. Stored procedures are simply SQL statements that are compiled and permanently stored in the database in an executable format.

Normally, when a SQL statement is issued in the database, the database must check the syntax and convert the statement into an executable format within the database (called *parsing*). The statement, after it is parsed, is stored in memory; however, it is not permanent. This means that when other operations need memory, the statement might be ejected from memory. For stored procedures, the SQL statement is always available in an executable format and remains in the database until it is dropped like any other database object. Stored procedures are discussed in more detail in Hour 22, "Advanced SQL Topics."

Disabling Indexes During Batch Loads

When a user submits a transaction to the database (INSERT, UPDATE, or DELETE), an entry is made to both the database table and any indexes associated with the table being modified. This means that if there is an index on the EMPLOYEES table and a user updates the EMPLOYEES table, an update also occurs to the index associated with the EMPLOYEES table. In a transactional environment, having a write to an index occur every time a write to the table occurs is usually not an issue.

During batch loads, however, an index can actually cause serious performance degradation. A batch load might consist of hundreds, thousands, or millions of manipulation statements or transactions. Because of their volume, batch loads take a long time to complete and are normally scheduled during off-peak hours—usually during weekends or evenings. To optimize performance during a batch load that might equate to decreasing the time it takes the batch load to complete from 12 hours to 6 hours, it is recommended that the indexes associated with the table affected during the load are dropped. When you drop the indexes, changes are written to the tables much faster, so the job completes faster. When the batch load is complete, you should rebuild the indexes. During the rebuild, the indexes are populated with all the appropriate data from the tables. Although it might take a while for an index to be created on a large table, the overall time expended if you drop the index and rebuild it is less.

Another advantage to rebuilding an index after a batch load completes is the reduction of fragmentation that is found in the index. When a database grows, records are added, removed, and updated, and fragmentation can occur. For any database that experiences a lot of growth, it is a good idea to periodically drop and rebuild large indexes. When you rebuild an index, the number of physical extents that comprise the index is decreased, there is less disk I/O involved to read the index, the user gets results quicker, and everyone is happy.

Cost-Based Optimization

Often you inherit a database that is in need of SQL statement tuning. These existing systems might have thousands of SQL statements executing at any given time. To optimize the amount of time spent on performance tuning, you need a way to determine what queries are most beneficial. This is where cost-based optimization comes into play. Cost-based optimization attempts to determine which queries are most costly in relation to the overall system resources spent. For instance, say you measure cost by execution duration and you have the following two queries with their corresponding run times:

```
SELECT * FROM EMPLOYEES
WHERE FIRSTNAME LIKE '%LE%'              2 sec

SELECT * FROM EMPLOYEES
WHERE FIRSTNAME LIKE 'G%';               1 sec
```

At first, it might appear that the first statement is the one you need to concentrate your efforts on. However, what if the second statement is executed 1,000 times an hour but the first is performed only 10 times in the same hour? Doesn't this make a huge difference in how you allocate your time?

Cost-based optimization ranks SQL statements in order of total computational cost. Computational cost is easily determined based on some measure of query execution (duration, number of reads, and so on) multiplied by the number of executions over a given period:

> Total Computational Cost = Execution Measure * (number of executions)

This is important because you get the most overall benefit from tuning the queries with the most total computational cost first. Looking at the previous example, if you cut each statement execution time in half, you can easily figure out the total computational savings:

> Statement #1: 1 sec * 10 executions = 10 sec of computational savings
>
> Statement #2: .5 sec * 1000 executions = 500 sec of computational savings

Now it is much easier to understand why your valuable time should be spent on the second statement instead of the first. Not only have you worked to optimize your database, but you've optimized your time as well.

TIP

Performance Tools

Many relational databases have built-in tools that assist in SQL statement database performance tuning. For example, Oracle has a tool called EXPLAIN PLAN that shows the user the execution plan of a SQL statement. Another tool in Oracle that measures the actual elapsed time of a SQL statement is TKPROF. In SQL Server, the Query Analyzer has several options to provide you with an estimated execution plan or statistics from the executed query. Check with your DBA and implementation documentation for more information on available tools.

Summary

In this hour you learned the meaning of tuning SQL statements in a relational database. You learned about two basic types of tuning: database tuning and SQL statement tuning—both of which are vital to the efficient operation of the database and SQL statements within it. Each is equally important and cannot be optimally tuned without the other.

You read about methods for tuning a SQL statement, starting with a statement's actual readability, which does not directly improve performance but aids the programmer in the development and management of statements. One of the main issues in SQL statement performance is the use of indexes. There are times to use indexes and times to avoid using them. For all measures taken to improve SQL statement performance, you need to understand the data itself, the database design and relationships, and the users' needs as far as accessing the database.

Q&A

Q. By following what I have learned about performance, what realistic performance gains, as far as data retrieval time, can I expect to see?

A. Realistically, you could see performance gains from fractions of a second to minutes, hours, or even days.

Q. How can I test my SQL statements for performance?

A. Each implementation should have a tool or system to check performance. Oracle7 was used to test the SQL statements in this book. Oracle has several tools for checking performance. Some of these tools include the EXPLAIN PLAN, TKPROF, and SET commands. Check your particular implementation for tools that are similar to Oracle's.

Workshop

The following workshop is composed of a series of quiz questions and practical exercises. The quiz questions are designed to test your overall understanding of the current material. The practical exercises are intended to afford you the opportunity to apply the concepts discussed during the current hour, as well as build upon the knowledge acquired in previous hours of study. Please take time to complete the quiz questions and exercises before continuing. Refer to Appendix C, "Answers to Quizzes and Exercises," for answers.

Quiz

1. Would the use of a unique index on a small table be of any benefit?

2. What happens when the optimizer chooses not to use an index on a table when a query has been executed?

3. Should the most restrictive clause(s) be placed before the join condition(s) or after the join conditions in the WHERE clause?

4. When is the LIKE operator considered bad in terms of performance?

5. How can you optimize batch load operations in terms of indexes?

6. Which three clauses are the cause of sort operations that harm performance?

Exercises

1. Rewrite the following SQL statements to improve their performance. Use the fictitious EMPLOYEE_TBL and EMPLOYEE_PAY_TBL as described here:

```
EMPLOYEE_TBL
EMP_ID          VARCHAR(9)      NOT NULL      Primary key,
LAST_NAME       VARCHAR(15)     NOT NULL,
FIRST_NAME      VARCHAR(15)     NOT NULL,
MIDDLE_NAME     VARCHAR(15),
ADDRESS         VARCHAR(30)     NOT NULL,
CITY            VARCHAR(15)     NOT NULL,
STATE           VARCHAR(2)      NOT NULL,
ZIP             INTEGER(5)      NOT NULL,
PHONE           VARCHAR(10),
PAGER           VARCHAR(10),
CONSTRAINT EMP_PK PRIMARY KEY (EMP_ID)
EMPLOYEE_PAY_TBL
EMP_ID            VARCHAR(9)        NOT NULL        primary key,
POSITION          VARCHAR(15)       NOT NULL,
DATE_HIRE         DATETIME,
PAY_RATE          DECIMAL(4,2)      NOT NULL,
DATE_LAST_RAISE   DATETIME,
SALARY            DECIMAL(8,2),
BONUS             DECIMAL(8,2),
CONSTRAINT EMP_FK FOREIGN KEY (EMP_ID)
REFERENCES EMPLOYEE_TBL (EMP_ID)
```

    a.
```
SELECT EMP_ID, LAST_NAME, FIRST_NAME,
           PHONE
    FROM EMPLOYEE_TBL
    WHERE SUBSTRING(PHONE, 1, 3) = '317' OR
          SUBSTRING(PHONE, 1, 3) = '812' OR
          SUBSTRING(PHONE, 1, 3) = '765';
```

b. SELECT LAST_NAME, FIRST_NAME
　　FROM EMPLOYEE_TBL
　　WHERE LAST_NAME LIKE '%ALL%';

c. SELECT E.EMP_ID, E.LAST_NAME, E.FIRST_NAME,
　　　　EP.SALARY
　　FROM EMPLOYEE_TBL E,
　　EMPLOYEE_PAY_TBL EP
　　WHERE LAST_NAME LIKE 'S%'
　　　　AND E.EMP_ID = EP.EMP_ID;

2. Add another table called EMPLOYEE_PAYHIST_TBL that contains a large amount of pay history data. Use the following table to write the series of SQL statements to address the following problems. Be sure you take steps to ensure the queries you write perform well.

```
EMPLOYEE_PAYHIST_TBL
PAYHIST_ID          VARCHAR(9)      NOT NULL      primary key,
EMP_ID              VARCHAR(9)      NOT NULL,
START_DATE          DATETIME        NOT NULL,
END_DATE            DATETIME,
PAY_RATE            DECIMAL(4,2)    NOT NULL,
SALARY              DECIMAL(8,2)    NOT NULL,
BONUS               DECIMAL(8,2)    NOT NULL,
CONSTRAINT EMP_FK FOREIGN KEY (EMP_ID)
REFERENCES EMPLOYEE_TBL (EMP_ID)
```

a. Find the SUM of the salaried versus nonsalaried employees by the year in which their pay started.

b. Find the difference in the yearly pay of salaried employees versus nonsalaried employees by the year in which their pay started. Consider the nonsalaried employees to be working full time during the year (PAY_RATE * 52 * 40).

c. Find the difference in what employees make now versus what they made when they started with the company. Again, consider the nonsalaried employees to be full time. Also consider that the employees' current pay is reflected in the EMPLOYEE_PAY_TBL as well as the EMPLOYEE_PAYHIST_TBL. In the pay history table, the current pay is reflected as a row with the END_DATE for pay equal to NULL.

HOUR 18
Managing Database Users

What You'll Learn in This Hour:

- ▶ Types of users
- ▶ User management
- ▶ The user versus the schema
- ▶ The importance of user sessions
- ▶ Altering a user's attributes
- ▶ Dropping users from the database
- ▶ Tools utilized by users

In this hour, you learn about one of the most critical administration functions for any relational database: managing database users. Managing users ensures that your database is available to the required people and application while keeping external entities out. Considering the amount of sensitive commercial and personal data that is stored in databases, this hour is definitely one that you should pay careful attention to.

User Management in the Database

Users are the reason for designing, creating, implementing, and maintaining any database. Their needs are considered when the database is designed, and the final goal in implementing a database is making the database available to users, who in turn utilize the database that you, and possibly many others, have had a hand in developing.

Some believe that if there were no users, nothing bad would ever happen to the database. Although this statement reeks with truth, the database was actually created to hold data so that users could function in their day-to-day jobs.

Although user management is often the database administrator's implicit task, other individuals sometimes take a part in the user management process. User management is vital in the life of a relational database and is ultimately managed through the use of SQL concepts and commands; although they vary from vendor to vendor. The ultimate goal of the database administrator for user management is to strike the proper balance between giving users access to the data they need and maintaining the integrity of the data within the system.

NOTE

Roles Vary Widely

Titles, roles, and duties of users vary widely (and wildly) from workplace to workplace, depending on the size of each organization and each organization's specific data processing needs. One organization's database administrator might be another organization's "computer guru."

Types of Users

There are several types of database users:

▶ Data entry clerks

▶ Programmers

▶ System engineers

▶ Database administrators

▶ System analysts

▶ Developers

▶ Testers

▶ Managers

▶ End users

Each type of user has a unique set of job functions (and problems), all of which are critical to the user's daily survival and job security. Furthermore, each type of user has different levels of authority and a special place in the database.

Who Manages Users?

A company's management staff is responsible for the day-to-day management of users; however, the *database administrator (DBA)* or other assigned individuals are ultimately responsible for the management of users within the database.

The DBA usually handles creating the database user accounts, roles, privileges, and profiles, as well as dropping those user accounts from the database. Because it can become an overwhelming task in a large and active environment, some companies have a security officer who assists the DBA with the user management process.

The *security officer*, if one is assigned, is usually responsible for the paperwork, relaying to the DBA a user's job requirements and letting the DBA know when a user no longer requires access to the database.

The *system analyst*, or system administrator, is usually responsible for the operating system security, which entails creating users and assigning appropriate privileges. The security officer also might assist the system analyst in the same way he does the database administrator.

Maintaining an orderly way in which to assign and remove permissions as well as to document the changes makes the process much easier to maintain. Documentation also enables you to have a paper trail to point to when the security of your system needs to be audited either internally or externally. We expand on the user management system throughout this hour.

The User's Place in the Database

A user should be given the roles and privileges necessary to accomplish her job. No user should have database access that extends beyond the scope of her job duties. Protecting the data is the entire reason for setting up user accounts and security. Data can be damaged or lost, even unintentionally, if the wrong user has access to the wrong data. When the user no longer requires database access, that user's account should be either removed from the database or disabled as quickly as possible.

All users have their place in the database, yet some have more responsibilities and duties than others. Database users are like parts of a human body—all work together in unison to accomplish some goal.

NOTE

Follow a Systematic Approach to User Management

User account management is vital to the protection and success of any database; when not managed systematically, it often fails. User account management is one of the simplest database management tasks, theoretically, but it is often complicated by politics and communication problems.

How Does a User Differ from a Schema?

A database's objects are associated with database user accounts, called schemas. A *schema* is a collection of database objects that a database user owns. This database user is called the *schema owner*. Often schemas logically group like objects in a database and then assign them to a particular schema owner to manage. You could think of it in terms of possibly grouping all the personnel tables under a schema called HR for human resources. The difference between a regular database user and a schema owner is that a schema owner owns objects within the database, whereas most users do not own objects. Most users are given database accounts to access data that is contained in other schemas. Because the schema owner actually owns these objects, he has complete control over them.

Microsoft SQL Server actually goes one step further by having a database owner. The database owner basically owns all objects within the database and has complete control over everything stored within. Within the database are one or more schemas. The default schema is always dbo and is normally the default for the database owner. There may be as many schemas as necessary to logically group the database objects and assign schema owners.

The Management Process

A stable user management system is mandatory for data security in any database system. The user management system starts with the new user's immediate supervisor, who should initiate the access request and then go through the company's approval authorities. If management accepts the request, it is routed to the security officer or database administrator, who takes action. A good notification process is necessary; the supervisor and the user must be notified that the user account has been created and that access to the database has been granted. The user account password should be given only to the user, who should immediately change the password upon initial login to the database.

Creating Users

The creation of database users involves the use of SQL commands within the database. There is no one standard command for creating database users in SQL; each implementation has a method for doing so. The basic concept is the same, regardless of the implementation. There are several *graphical user interface (GUI)* tools on the market that can be used for user management.

When the DBA or assigned security officer receives a user account request, the request should be analyzed for the necessary information. The information should include the company's particular requirements for establishing a user account.

Some items that should be included are Social Security number, full name, address, phone number, office or department name, assigned database, and, sometimes, a suggested user account name.

NOTE

User Creation and Management Varies Between Systems

You must check your particular implementation for the creation of users. Also refer to company policies and procedures when creating and managing users. The following section compares the user creation processes in Oracle, MySQL, and Microsoft SQL Server.

Creating Users in Oracle

Following are the steps for creating a user account in an Oracle database:

1. Create the database user account with default settings.

2. Grant appropriate privileges to the user account.

The following is the syntax for creating a user:

```
CREATE USER USER_ID
IDENTIFIED BY [PASSWORD | EXTERNALLY ]
[ DEFAULT TABLESPACE TABLESPACE_NAME ]
[ TEMPORARY TABLESPACE TABLESPACE_NAME ]
[ QUOTA (INTEGER (K | M) | UNLIMITED) ON TABLESPACE_NAME ]
[ PROFILE PROFILE_TYPE ]
[PASSWORD EXPIRE |ACCOUNT [LOCK | UNLOCK]
```

If you are not using Oracle, do not overly concern yourself with some of the options in this syntax. A *tablespace* is a logical area managed by the DBA that houses database objects, such as tables and indexes. The DEFAULT TABLESPACE is the tablespace in which objects created by the particular user reside. The TEMPORARY TABLESPACE is the tablespace used for sort operations (table joins, ORDER BY, GROUP BY) from queries the user executes. The QUOTA is the space limit placed on a particular tablespace to which the user has access. PROFILE is a particular database profile that has been assigned to the user.

The following is the syntax for granting privileges to the user account:

```
GRANT PRIV1 [ , PRIV2, ... ] TO USERNAME | ROLE [, USERNAME ]
```

NOTE

Implementation Differences for CREATE USER

MySQL does not support the CREATE USER command. Users can be managed using the mysqladmin tool. After a local user account is set up on a Windows computer, a login is not required. However, you should set up a user for each user requiring access to the database in a multiuser environment using mysqladmin.

The GRANT statement can grant one or more privileges to one or more users in the same statement. The privilege(s) can also be granted to a role, which in turn can be granted to a user(s).

In MySQL, the GRANT command can grant users access on the local computer to the current database. For example:

```
GRANT USAGE ON *.* TO USER@LOCALHOST IDENTIFIED BY 'PASSWORD';
```

Additional privileges can be granted to a user as follows:

```
GRANT SELECT ON TABLENAME TO USER@LOCALHOST;
```

For the most part, multiuser setup and access for MySQL is required only in multiuser environments.

Creating Users in Microsoft SQL Server

The steps for creating a user account in a Microsoft SQL Server database follow:

1. Create the login user account for SQL Server, and assign a password and a default database for the user.

2. Add the user to the appropriate database(s) so that a database user account is created.

3. Grant appropriate privileges to the database user account. The discussion of privileges within a relational database is further elaborated on in Hour 19, "Managing Database Security."

Following is the syntax for creating the user account:

```
SP_ADDLOGIN USER_ID , PASSWORD [, DEFAULT_DATABASE ]
```

Following is the syntax for adding the user to a database:

```
SP_ADDUSER USER_ID [, NAME_IN_DB [, GRPNAME ] ]
```

As you can see, SQL Server distinguishes between a login account that is granted access to log in to the SQL Server instance and a database user account that grants access to database objects. You can view this by looking at the security folders in SQL Server Management Studio after you create the login account and then at the database level when you issue the SP_ADDUSER command. This is an important distinction with SQL Server because you can create a login account that does not have access to any of the databases on the instance.

A common error when creating accounts on SQL Server is forgetting to assign them access to their default database. So when you set up accounts, ensure that they have access to at least their default database, or you might be setting up the users to receive an error when logging into your system.

Following is the syntax for granting privileges to the user account:

```
GRANT PRIV1 [ , PRIV2, ... ] TO USER_ID
```

Creating Users in MySQL

The steps for creating a user account in MySQL follow:

1. Create the user account within the database.

2. Grant the appropriate privileges to the user account.

The syntax for creating the user account is similar to the syntax used in Oracle:

```
SELECT USER user [IDENTIFIED BY [PASSWORD] 'password']
```

The syntax for granting the user's privileges is also similar to the Oracle version:

```
GRANT priv_type [(column_list)] [, priv_type [(column_list)]] ...
    ON [object_type]
      {tbl_name | * | *.* | db_name.* | db_name.routine_name}
       TO user
```

Creating Schemas

Schemas are created via the CREATE SCHEMA statement.

The syntax follows:

```
CREATE SCHEMA [ SCHEMA_NAME ] [ USER_ID ]
            [ DEFAULT CHARACTER SET CHARACTER_SET ]
            [PATH SCHEMA NAME [,SCHEMA NAME] ]
            [ SCHEMA_ELEMENT_LIST ]
```

Following is an example:

```
CREATE SCHEMA USER1
CREATE TABLE TBL1
  (COLUMN1    DATATYPE    [NOT NULL],
   COLUMN2    DATATYPE    [NOT NULL]...)
CREATE TABLE TBL2
  (COLUMN1    DATATYPE    [NOT NULL],
   COLUMN2    DATATYPE    [NOT NULL]...)
GRANT SELECT ON TBL1 TO USER2
GRANT SELECT ON TBL2 TO USER2
[ OTHER DDL COMMANDS ... ]
```

Following is the application of the CREATE SCHEMA command in one implementation:

```
CREATE SCHEMA AUTHORIZATION USER1
CREATE TABLE EMP
  (ID       NUMBER        NOT NULL,
   NAME     VARCHAR2(10)  NOT NULL)
```

```
CREATE TABLE CUST
  (ID        NUMBER          NOT NULL,
   NAME      VARCHAR2(10)     NOT NULL)
GRANT SELECT ON TBL1 TO USER2
GRANT SELECT ON TBL2 TO USER2;
Schema created.
```

The AUTHORIZATION keyword is added to the CREATE SCHEMA command. This example was performed in an Oracle database. This shows you (as you have also seen in this book's previous examples) that vendors' syntax for commands often varies in their implementations.

Implementations that do support the creation of schemas often assign a default schema to a user. Most often this is aligned with the user's account. So a user with the account BethA2 normally has a default schema of BethA2. This is important to remember because objects are created in the user's default schema unless otherwise directed by providing a schema name at the time of creation. If you issue the following CREATE TABLE statement using BethA2's account, it is created in the BethA2 schema:

```
CREATE TABLE MYTABLE(
  NAME VARCHAR(50)  NOT NULL );
```

This might not be the wanted location. If this is SQL Server, you might have permissions to the dbo schema and want to create it there. In that case, you need to qualify your object with the schema as shown here:

```
CREATE TABLE DBO.MYTABLE(
  NAME VARCHAR(50) NOT NULL):
```

It is important to remember these caveats when creating users and assigning them permissions so that you can maintain proper order within your database systems without having unintended consequences.

CAUTION

CREATE SCHEMA Is Not Always Supported

Some implementations might not support the CREATE SCHEMA command. However, schemas can be implicitly created when a user creates objects. The CREATE SCHEMA command is simply a method for accomplishing this task in a single step. After a user creates objects, the user can grant privileges that allow access to the user's objects to other users.

MySQL does not support the CREATE SCHEMA command. A schema in MySQL is considered to be a database. So you use the CREATE DATABASE command to essentially create a schema to populate with objects.

Dropping a Schema

You can remove a schema from the database using the DROP SCHEMA statement. You must consider two things when dropping a schema: the RESTRICT option and the CASCADE option. If RESTRICT is specified, an error occurs if objects currently exist in the schema. You must use the CASCADE option if any objects currently exist in the schema. Remember that when you drop a schema, you also drop all database objects associated with that schema.

The syntax follows:

```
DROP SCHEMA SCHEMA_NAME { RESTRICT | CASCADE }
```

NOTE

There Are Different Ways to Remove a Schema

The absence of objects in a schema is possible because objects, such as tables, can be dropped using the DROP TABLE command. Some implementations have a procedure or command that drops a user and can also drop a schema. If the DROP SCHEMA command is not available in your implementation, you can remove a schema by removing the user who owns the schema objects.

Altering Users

An important part of managing users is the ability to alter a user's attributes after user creation. Life for the DBA would be a lot simpler if personnel with user accounts were never promoted, never left the company, or if the addition of new employees were minimized. In the real world, high personnel turnover and changes in users' responsibilities are a reality and a significant factor in user management. Nearly everyone changes jobs or job duties. Therefore, user privileges in a database must be adjusted to fit a user's needs.

Following is an example of altering the current state of a user in Oracle:

```
ALTER USER USER_ID [ IDENTIFIED BY PASSWORD | EXTERNALLY |GLOBALLY AS 'CN=USER']
[ DEFAULT TABLESPACE TABLESPACE_NAME ]
[ TEMPORARY TABLESPACE TABLESPACE_NAME ]
[ QUOTA   INTEGER K|M |UNLIMITED ON TABLESPACE_NAME ]
[ PROFILE PROFILE_NAME ]
[ PASSWORD EXPIRE]
[ ACCOUNT [LOCK |UNLOCK]]
[ DEFAULT ROLE ROLE1 [, ROLE2 ] | ALL
[ EXCEPT ROLE1 [, ROLE2 | NONE ] ]
```

You can alter many of the user's attributes in this syntax. Unfortunately, not all implementations provide a simple command that allows the manipulation of database users.

MySQL, for instance, uses several means to modify the user account. For example, you use the following syntax to reset the user's password in MySQL:

```
UPDATE mysql.user SET Password=PASSWORD('new password')
WHERE user='username';
```

In addition, you might want to change the username for the user. You could accomplish this with the following syntax:

```
RENAME USER old_username TO new_username;
```

Some implementations also provide GUI tools that enable you to create, modify, and remove users.

User Sessions

A user database *session* is the time between when a database user logs in and when the user logs out. During the user session, the user can perform various actions that have been granted, such as queries and transactions.

Upon the establishment of the connection and the initiation of the session, the user can start and perform any number of transactions until the connection is disconnected; at that time, the database user session terminates.

Users can explicitly connect and disconnect from the database, starting and terminating SQL sessions, using commands such as the following:

```
CONNECT TO DEFAULT | STRING1 [ AS STRING2 ] [ USER STRING3 ]
DISCONNECT DEFAULT | CURRENT | ALL | STRING
SET CONNECTION DEFAULT | STRING
```

User sessions can be—and often are—monitored by the DBA or other personnel having interest in user activities. A user session is associated with a particular user account when a user is monitored. A database user session is ultimately represented as a process on the host operating system.

NOTE

Some Databases and Tools Obscure the Underlying Commands

Remember that the syntax varies between implementations. In addition, most database users do not manually issue the commands to connect or disconnect from the database. Most users access the database through a vendor-provided or third-party tool that prompts the user for a username and password, which in turn connects to the database and initiates a database user session.

Removing User Access

You can remove a user from the database or disallow a user's access through a couple of simple commands. Again, however, variations among implementations are numerous, so you must check your particular implementation for the syntax or tools to accomplish user removal or access revocation.

Following are methods for removing user database access:

- ▶ Change the user's password.

- ▶ Drop the user account from the database.

- ▶ Revoke appropriate previously granted privileges from the user.

You can use the DROP command in some implementations to drop a user from the database:

```
DROP USER USER_ID [ CASCADE ]
```

The REVOKE command is the counterpart of the GRANT command in many implementations, allowing privileges that have been granted to a user to be revoked. An example syntax for this command for SQL Server, Oracle, and MySQL follows:

```
REVOKE PRIV1 [ ,PRIV2, ... ] FROM USERNAME
```

Tools Utilized by Database Users

Some people say that you do not need to know SQL to perform database queries. In a sense, they are correct; however, knowing SQL definitely helps when querying a database, even when using GUI tools. Even though GUI tools are good and should be used when available, it is beneficial to understand what happens behind the scenes so that you can maximize the efficiency of utilizing these user-friendly tools.

Many GUI tools that aid the database user automatically generate SQL code by navigating through windows, responding to prompts, and selecting options. Reporting tools generate reports. Forms can be created for users to query, update, insert, or delete data from a database. Tools can convert data into graphs and charts. Certain database administration tools monitor database performance, and others allow remote connectivity to a database. Database vendors provide some of these tools, whereas others are provided as third-party tools from other vendors.

Summary

As you learned in this hour, all databases have users, whether one or thousands. The user is the reason for the database.

There are three necessities for managing users in the database. First, you must create database user accounts for the proper individuals and services. Second, you must grant privileges to the accounts to accommodate the tasks that must be performed within the database. Finally, you must either remove a user account from the database or revoke certain privileges within the database from an account.

Some of the most common tasks of managing users have been touched on; much detail is avoided here because most databases differ in how users are managed. However, it is important to discuss user management due to its relationship with SQL. The American National Standards Institute (ANSI) has not defined or discussed in detail many of the commands to manage users, but the concept remains the same.

Q&A

Q. Is there a SQL standard for adding users to a database?

A. ANSI provides some commands and concepts; although each implementation and each company has its own commands, tools, and rules for creating or adding users to a database.

Q. Can user access be temporarily suspended without removing the user ID completely from the database?

A. Yes, you can temporarily suspend user access by simply changing the user's password or revoking privileges that allow the user to connect to the database. You can reinstate the functionality of the user account by changing and issuing the password to the user or granting privileges to the user that might have been revoked.

Q. Can a user change his own password?

A. Yes, in most major implementations. Upon user creation or addition to the database, a generic password is given to the user, who must change it as quickly as possible to a password of his choice. After the user changes his password, even the DBA does not know the new password.

Workshop

The following workshop is composed of a series of quiz questions and practical exercises. The quiz questions are designed to test your overall understanding of the current material. The practical exercises are intended to afford you the opportunity to apply the concepts discussed during the current hour, as well as build upon the knowledge acquired in previous hours of study. Please take time to complete the quiz questions and exercises before continuing. Refer to Appendix C, "Answers to Quizzes and Exercises," for answers.

Quiz

1. Which command establishes a session?

2. Which option drops a schema that still contains database objects?

3. Which command in MySQL creates a schema?

4. Which statement removes a database privilege?

5. Which command creates a grouping or collection of tables, views, and privileges?

6. What is the difference in SQL Server between a login account and a database user account?

Exercises

1. Describe how you would create a new user 'John' in your CANARYAIRLINES database.

2. Explain the steps you would take to grant access to the EMPLOYEES table to your new user 'John'.

3. Describe how you would assign permissions to all objects within the CANARYAIRLINES database to 'John'.

4. Describe how you would revoke the previous privileges from 'John' and then remove his account.

Managing Database Security

What You'll Learn in This Hour:

- ▶ Definition of database security
- ▶ Security versus user management
- ▶ Database system privileges
- ▶ Database object privileges
- ▶ Granting privileges to users
- ▶ Revoking privileges from users
- ▶ Security features in the database

In this hour, you learn the basics of implementing and managing security within a relational database using SQL and SQL-related commands. Each major implementation differs on syntax with its security commands, but the overall security for the relational database follows the same basic guidelines discussed in the ANSI standard. You must check your particular implementation for syntax and any special guidelines for security.

What Is Database Security?

Database security is simply the process of protecting the data from unauthorized usage. Unauthorized usage includes data access by database users who should have access to part of the database, but not all parts. This protection also includes the act of policing against unauthorized connectivity and distribution of privileges. Many user levels exist in a database, from the database creator to individuals responsible for maintaining the database (such as the database administrator [DBA]) to database programmers to end users. Although end users have the most limited access, they are the users for which the database exists. A user should be granted the fewest number of privileges needed to perform his particular job.

You might be wondering what the difference is between user management and database security. After all, the previous hour discussed user management, which seems to cover security.

Although user management and database security are definitely related, each has its own purpose, and the two work together to achieve a secure database.

A well-planned and maintained user management program goes hand in hand with the overall security of a database. Users are assigned user accounts and passwords that give them general access to the database. The user accounts within the database should be stored with information, such as the user's actual name, the office and department in which the user works, a telephone number or extension, and the database name to which the user has access. Personal user information should be accessible only to the DBA. A DBA or security officer assigns an initial password for the database user; the user should change this password immediately. Remember that the DBA does not need, and should not want to know, the individual's password. This ensures a separation of duties and protects the DBA's integrity should problems with a user's account arise.

If a user no longer requires certain privileges granted to her, those privileges should be revoked. If a user no longer requires access to the database, the user account should be dropped from the database.

Generally, user management is the process of creating user accounts, removing user accounts, and keeping track of users' actions within the database. Database security goes a step further by granting privileges for specific database access, revoking certain privileges from users, and taking measures to protect other parts of the database, such as the underlying database files.

What Are Privileges?

Privileges are authority levels used to access the database, access objects within the database, manipulate data in the database, and perform various administrative functions within the database. Privileges are issued via the GRANT command and are taken away via the REVOKE command.

Just because a user can connect to a database does not mean that the user can access data within a database. Access to data within the database is handled through these privileges. The two types of privileges are system privileges and object privileges.

NOTE

There Are More Aspects to Database Security Than Privileges

Because this is a SQL book, not a database book, it focuses on database privileges. However, you should keep in mind other aspects to database security, such as the protection of underlying database files, which holds equal importance with the distribution of database privileges. High-level database security can become complex and differs immensely among relational database implementations. If you would like to learn more about database security, you can find information on The Center for Internet Security's web page: www.cisecurity.org/.

System Privileges

System privileges are those that allow database users to perform administrative actions within the database, such as creating a database, dropping a database, creating user accounts, dropping users, dropping and altering database objects, altering the state of objects, altering the state of the database, and other actions that could result in serious repercussions if not carefully used.

System privileges vary greatly among the different relational database vendors, so you must check your particular implementation for all the available system privileges and their correct usage.

Following are some common system privileges in SQL Server:

- ▶ CREATE DATABASE—Allows for the creation of a new database
- ▶ CREATE PROCEDURE—Allows for the creation of stored procedures
- ▶ CREATE VIEW—Allows for the creation of views
- ▶ BACKUP DATABASE—Allows the user to control backup of the database system
- ▶ CREATE TABLE—Allows the user to create new tables
- ▶ CREATE TRIGGER—Allows the user to create triggers on tables
- ▶ EXECUTE—Allows the user to execute given stored procedures within the specific database

Following are some common system privileges in Oracle:

- ▶ CREATE TABLE—Allows the user to create new tables in the specified schema
- ▶ CREATE ANY TABLE—Allows the user to create tables in any schema
- ▶ ALTER ANY TABLE—Allows the user to alter table structure in any schema
- ▶ DROP TABLE—Allows the user to drop table objects in the specified schema
- ▶ CREATE USER—Allows the user to create other user accounts
- ▶ DROP USER—Allows the user to drop existing user accounts
- ▶ ALTER USER—Allows the user to make alterations to existing user accounts
- ▶ ALTER DATABASE—Allows the user to alter database properties
- ▶ BACKUP ANY TABLE—Allows the user to backup data from any table in any schema
- ▶ SELECT ANY TABLE—Allows the user to perform a select on any table from any schema

Object Privileges

Object privileges are authority levels on objects, meaning you must have been granted the appropriate privileges to perform certain operations on database objects. For example, to select data from another user's table, the user must first grant you access to do so. Object privileges are granted to users in the database by the object's owner. Remember that this owner is also called the schema owner.

The ANSI standard for privileges includes the following object privileges:

- ▶ USAGE—Authorizes usage of a specific domain

- ▶ SELECT—Allows access to a specific table

- ▶ INSERT(*column_name*)—Allows data insertion to a specific column of a specified table

- ▶ INSERT—Allows insertion of data into all columns of a specific table

- ▶ UPDATE(*column_name*)—Allows a specific column of a specified table to be updated

- ▶ UPDATE—Allows all columns of a specified table to be updated

- ▶ REFERENCES(*column_name*)—Allows a reference to a specified column of a specified table in integrity constraints; this privilege is required for all integrity constraints

- ▶ REFERENCES—Allows references to all columns of a specified table

---

TIP

Some Privileges Are Granted Automatically

The owner of an object has been automatically granted all privileges that relate to the objects owned. These privileges have also been granted with the GRANT OPTION, which is a nice feature available in some SQL implementations. This feature is discussed in the "GRANT OPTION" section later this hour.

Most implementations of SQL adhere to the standard list of object privileges for controlling access to database objects.

You should use these object-level privileges to grant and restrict access to objects in a schema. These privileges can protect objects in one schema from database users who have access to another schema in the same database.

A variety of other object privileges available among different implementations are not listed in this section. The capability to delete data from another user's object is another common object privilege available in many implementations. Be sure to check your implementation documentation for all the available object-level privileges.

Who Grants and Revokes Privileges?

The DBA is usually the one who issues the GRANT and REVOKE commands; although a security administrator, if one exists, might have the authority to do so. The authority on what to grant or revoke would come from management and normally should be carefully tracked to ensure that only authorized individuals are allowed access to these types of permissions.

The owner of an object must grant privileges to other users in the database on the object. Even the DBA cannot grant database users privileges on objects that do not belong to the DBA; although there are ways to work around that.

Controlling User Access

User access is primarily controlled by a user account and password, but that is not enough to access the database in most major implementations. The creation of a user account is only the first step in allowing and controlling access to the database.

After the user account has been created, the database administrator, security officer, or designated individual must assign appropriate system-level privileges to a user for that user to perform actual functions within the database, such as creating tables or selecting from tables. Furthermore, the schema owner usually needs to grant database users access to objects in the schema so that the user can do his job.

Two commands in SQL allow database access control involving the assignment of privileges and the revocation of privileges. The GRANT and REVOKE commands distribute both system and object privileges in a relational database.

The GRANT Command

The GRANT command grants both system-level and object-level privileges to an existing database user account.

The syntax follows:

```
GRANT PRIVILEGE1 [, PRIVILEGE2 ] [ ON OBJECT ]
TO USERNAME [ WITH GRANT OPTION | ADMIN OPTION]
```

Syntax for granting one privilege to a user follows:

```
GRANT SELECT ON EMPLOYEES TO USER1;
Grant succeeded.
```

Syntax for granting multiple privileges to a user follows:

```
GRANT SELECT, INSERT ON EMPLOYEES TO USER1;
Grant succeeded.
```

Notice that when granting multiple privileges to a user in a single statement, each privilege is separated by a comma.

Syntax for granting privileges to multiple users follows:

```
GRANT SELECT, INSERT ON EMPLOYEES TO USER1, USER2;
Grant succeeded.
```

NOTE

Be Sure to Understand the Feedback the System Gives You

Notice the phrase Grant succeeded, denoting the successful completion of each GRANT statement. This is the feedback that you receive when you issue these statements in the implementation used for the book examples (Oracle). Most implementations have some sort of feedback; although the phrase used might vary.

GRANT OPTION

GRANT OPTION is a powerful GRANT command option. When an object's owner grants privileges on an object to another user with GRANT OPTION, the new user can also grant privileges on that object to other users, even though the user does not actually own the object. An example follows:

```
GRANT SELECT ON EMPLOYEES TO USER1 WITH GRANT OPTION;
Grant succeeded.
```

ADMIN OPTION

ADMIN OPTION is similar to GRANT OPTION in that the user who has been granted the privileges also inherits the ability to grant those privileges to another user. GRANT OPTION is used for object-level privileges, whereas ADMIN OPTION is used for system-level privileges. When a user grants system privileges to another user with ADMIN OPTION, the new user can also grant the system-level privileges to any other user. An example follows:

```
GRANT CREATE TABLE TO USER1 WITH ADMIN OPTION;
Grant succeeded.
```

CAUTION

Dropping a User Can Drop Granted Privileges

When a user who has granted privileges using either GRANT OPTION or ADMIN OPTION has been dropped from the database, the privileges that the user granted are disassociated with the users to whom the privileges were granted.

The REVOKE Command

The REVOKE command removes privileges that have been granted to database users. The REVOKE command has two options: RESTRICT and CASCADE. When the RESTRICT option is used, REVOKE succeeds only if the privileges specified explicitly in the REVOKE statement leave no other users with abandoned privileges. The CASCADE option revokes any privileges that would otherwise be left with other users. In other words, if the owner of an object granted USER1 privileges with GRANT OPTION, USER1 granted USER2 privileges with GRANT OPTION, and then the owner revokes USER1's privileges, CASCADE also removes the privileges from USER2.

Abandoned privileges are privileges that are left with a user who was granted privileges with the GRANT OPTION from a user who has been dropped from the database or had her privileges revoked.

The syntax for REVOKE follows:

```
REVOKE PRIVILEGE1 [, PRIVILEGE2 ] [ GRANT OPTION FOR ] ON OBJECT
FROM USER { RESTRICT | CASCADE }
```

Following is an example:

```
REVOKE INSERT ON EMPLOYEES FROM USER1;
Revoke succeeded.
```

Controlling Access on Individual Columns

Instead of granting object privileges (INSERT, UPDATE, or DELETE) on a table as a whole, you can grant privileges on specific columns in the table to restrict user access, as shown in the following example:

```
GRANT UPDATE (NAME) ON EMPLOYEES TO PUBLIC;
Grant succeeded.
```

The PUBLIC Database Account

The PUBLIC database user account is a database account that represents all users in the database. All users are part of the PUBLIC account. If a privilege is granted to the PUBLIC account, all database users have the privilege. Likewise, if a privilege is revoked from the PUBLIC account, the privilege is revoked from all database users, unless that privilege was explicitly granted to a specific user. Following is an example:

```
GRANT SELECT ON EMPLOYEES TO PUBLIC;
Grant succeeded.
```

CAUTION

PUBLIC Privileges Can Grant Unintended Access

Use extreme caution when granting privileges to PUBLIC; all database users acquire the privileges granted. Therefore, by granting permissions to PUBLIC, you might unintentionally give access to data to users who have no business accessing it. For example, giving PUBLIC access to SELECT from the employee salary table would give everyone who has access to the database the rights to see what everyone in the company is paid!

Groups of Privileges

Some implementations have groups of privileges in the database. These groups of permissions are referred to with different names. Having a group of privileges allows simplicity for granting and revoking common privileges to and from users. For example, if a group consists of 10 privileges, the group can be granted to a user instead of individually granting all 10 privileges.

NOTE

Database Privilege Groups Vary Between Systems

Each implementation differs on the use of groups of database privileges. If available, this feature should be used for ease of database security administration.

Oracle has groups of privileges that are called *roles*. Oracle includes the following groups of privileges with its implementations:

▶ CONNECT—Allows a user to connect to the database and perform operations on any database objects to which the user has access.

▶ RESOURCE—Allows a user to create objects, drop objects he owns, grant privileges to objects he owns, and so on.

▶ DBA—Allows a user to perform any function within the database. The user can access any database object and perform any operation with this group.

An example for granting a group of privileges to a user follows:

```
GRANT DBA TO USER1;
Grant succeeded.
```

SQL Server has several groups of permissions at the server level and the database level. Some of the database level permission groups are

▶ DB_DDLADMIN—Allows the user to manipulate any of the objects within the database through any legal data definition language command

▶ DB_DATAREADER—Allows the user to select from any of the tables within the database from which it is assigned

▶ DB_DATAWRITER—Allows the user to perform any data manipulation syntax (INSERT, UPDATE, or DELETE) on any of the tables within the database

Controlling Privileges Through Roles

A *role* is an object created in the database that contains group-like privileges. Roles can reduce security maintenance by not having to grant explicit privileges directly to a user. Group privilege management is much easier to handle with roles. A role's privileges can be changed, and such a change is transparent to the user.

If a user needs SELECT and UPDATE table privileges on a table at a specified time within an application, a role with those privileges can temporarily be assigned until the transaction is complete.

When a role is created, it has no real value other than being a role within a database. It can be granted to users or other roles. Say that a schema named APP01 grants the SELECT table privilege to the RECORDS_CLERK role on the EMPLOYEE_PAY table. Any user or role granted the RECORDS_CLERK role now would have SELECT privileges on the EMPLOYEE_PAY table.

Likewise, if APP01 revoked the SELECT table privilege from the RECORDS_CLERK role on the EMPLOYEE_PAY table, any user or role granted the RECORDS_CLERK role would no longer have SELECT privileges on that table.

When assigning permissions in a database, ensure that you think through what permissions a user needs and if other users need the same sets of permissions. For example, a set of accounting tables might need to be accessed by several members of an accounting team. In this case, unless they each need drastically different permissions to these tables, it is far easier to set up a role, assign the role the appropriate conditions, and then assign the users to the role.

If a new object is created and needs to have permissions granted to the accounting group, you can do it in one location instead of having to update each account. Likewise, if the accounting team brings on a new member or decides someone else needs the same access to its tables, you have to assign the role to only the new user and you are good to go. Roles are an excellent tool to enable the DBA to work smarter and not harder when dealing with complex database security protocols.

NOTE

Roles Are Not Supported in MySQL

MySQL does not support roles. The lack of role usage is a weakness in some implementations of SQL.

The CREATE ROLE Statement

A role is created with the CREATE ROLE statement:

```
CREATE ROLE role_name;
```

Granting privileges to roles is the same as granting privileges to a user, as shown in the following example:

```
CREATE ROLE RECORDS_CLERK;
Role created.
GRANT SELECT, INSERT, UPDATE, DELETE ON EMPLOYEE_PAY TO RECORDS_CLERK;
Grant succeeded.
GRANT RECORDS_CLERK TO USER1;
Grant succeeded.
```

The DROP ROLE Statement

A role is dropped using the DROP_ROLE statement:

```
DROP ROLE role_name;
```

Following is an example:

```
DROP ROLE RECORDS_CLERK;
Role dropped.
```

The SET ROLE Statement

A role can be set for just the user's current SQL session using the SET_ROLE statement:

```
SET ROLE role_name;
```

Following is an example:

```
SET ROLE RECORDS_CLERK;
Role set.
```

You can set more than one role at once:

```
SET ROLE RECORDS_CLERK, ROLE2, ROLE3;
Role set.
```

NOTE

SET ROLE Is Not Always Used

In some implementations, such as Microsoft SQL Server and Oracle, all roles granted to a user are automatically default roles, which means they are set and available to the user as soon as the user logs in to the database. The SET ROLE syntax here is shown so that you can understand the ANSI standard for setting a role.

Summary

This hour showed you the basics on implementing security in a SQL database or a relational database. After a user is created, the user must be assigned certain privileges that allow her access to specific parts of the database. ANSI allows the use of roles as discussed during this hour. Privileges can be granted to users or roles.

The two types of privileges are system and object. System privileges are those that allow the user to perform various tasks within the database, such as actually connecting to the database, creating tables, creating users, and altering the state of the database. Object privileges are those that allow a user access to specific objects within the database, such as the ability to select data or manipulate data in a specific table.

Two commands in SQL allow a user to grant and revoke privileges to and from other users or roles in the database: GRANT and REVOKE. These two commands control the overall administration of privileges in the database. Although there are many other considerations for implementing security in a relational database, this hour discussed the basics that relate to SQL.

Q&A

Q. **If a user forgets her password, what should she do to gain access to the database again?**

A. The user should go to her immediate management or an available help desk. A help desk should reset a user's password. If not, the DBA or security officer can reset the password. The user should change the password to a password of her choosing as soon as the password is reset and she is notified. Sometimes, the DBA can affect this by setting a specific property that forces the user to change her password on the next login. Check your particular implementation's documentation for specifics.

Q. **What can I do if I want to grant CONNECT to a user, but the user does not need all the privileges that are assigned to the CONNECT role?**

A. You would simply not grant CONNECT but only the privileges required. Should you ever grant CONNECT and the user no longer needs all the privileges that go with it, simply revoke CONNECT from the user and grant the specific privileges required.

Q. Why is it so important for the new user to change the password when received from whoever created the new user?

A. An initial password is assigned upon creation of the user ID. No one, not even the DBA or management, should know a user's password. The password should be kept a secret at all times to prevent another user from logging on to the database under another user's account.

Workshop

The following workshop is composed of a series of quiz questions and practical exercises. The quiz questions are designed to test your overall understanding of the current material. The practical exercises are intended to afford you the opportunity to apply the concepts discussed during the current hour, as well as build upon the knowledge acquired in previous hours of study. Please take time to complete the quiz questions and exercises before continuing. Refer to Appendix C, "Answers to Quizzes and Exercises," for answers.

Quiz

1. What option must a user have to grant another user privileges on an object not owned by the user?

2. When privileges are granted to `PUBLIC`, do all database users acquire the privileges or only specified users?

3. What privilege is required to look at data in a specific table?

4. What type of privilege is `SELECT`?

5. What option revokes a user's privilege to an object as well as the other users that they might have granted privileges to by use of the `GRANT` option?

Exercises

1. Log in to your database instance and switch the database instance to use the `CanaryAirlines` database if it is not set as your default.

2. Type the following at the database prompt to get a list of the default tables depending on your implementation:

   ```
   SQL Server:      SELECT NAME FROM SYS.TABLES;
   Oracle:          SELECT * FROM USER_TABLES;
   ```

3. Create a new database user as follows:

   ```
   Username: Steve
   Password: Steve123
   Access: CanaryAirlines database, SELECT on all tables
   ```

4. Get a list of all database users by typing the following depending on your implementation:

```
SQL Server:    SELECT * FROM SYS.DATABASE_PRINCIPALS WHERE TYPE='S';
Oracle:        SELECT * FROM DBA_USERS
```

5. Create a role for your new database user, Steve, from the previous exercise. Call the role `employee_reader` and give the role `SELECT` on just the `EMPLOYEE` table. Assign Steve to this role.

6. Now drop Steve's `SELECT` access to the other tables in the database. Try to select from the `EMPLOYEES`, `AIRPORTS`, and `ROUTES` tables. What happened?

Creating and Using Views and Synonyms

What You'll Learn in This Hour:

▶ What views are and how they are used

▶ Views and security

▶ Storing, creating, and joining views

▶ Data manipulation in a view

▶ Performance of nested views

▶ Managing synonyms

In this hour, you learn about performance, as well as how to create and drop views, how to use views for security, and how to provide simplicity in data retrieval for end users and reports. This hour also includes a discussion on synonyms.

What Is a View?

A view is a virtual table. That is, a view looks like a table and acts like a table as far as a user is concerned, but it doesn't require physical storage. A view is actually a composition of a table in the form of a predefined query, which is stored in the database. For example, you can create a view from EMPLOYEES that contains only the employee's name and city, instead of all columns in EMPLOYEES. A view can contain all rows of a table or select rows from a table. You can create a view from one or many tables.

When you create a view, a SELECT statement is actually run against the database, which defines the view. The SELECT statement that defines the view might simply contain column names from the table, or it can be more explicitly written using various functions and calculations to manipulate or summarize the data that the user sees. Figure 20.1 shows an example view.

FIGURE 20.1
The view

A view is considered a database object, although it is stored in memory only. It takes up no storage space as do other database objects—other than the space required to store the view definition. The view's creator or the schema owner owns the view. The view owner automatically has all applicable privileges on that view and can grant privileges on the view to other users, as with tables. The GRANT command's GRANT OPTION privilege works the same as on a table. See Hour 19, "Managing Database Security," for more information.

A view is used in the same manner that a table is used in the database, meaning that data can be selected from a view as it is from a table. Data can also be manipulated in a view; although, there are some restrictions. The following sections discuss some common uses for views and how they are stored in the database.

CAUTION

Dropping Tables Used by Views

If a table that created a view is dropped, the view becomes inaccessible. You receive an error when trying to query against the view.

Utilizing Views to Simplify Data Access

Sometimes, through the process of normalizing your database or just as a process of database design, the data might be contained in a table format that does not easily lend itself to querying by end users. In this instance, you could create a series of views to make the data simpler for your end users to query. Your users might need to query the employee salary and airport information from the CanaryAirlines database. However, they might not totally understand how to create joins between EMPLOYEES and AIRPORTS. To bridge this gap, you create a view that contains the join and gives the end users the right to select from the view.

Utilizing Views as a Form of Security

Views can be utilized as a form of security in the database. Say you have the EMPLOYEES table. EMPLOYEES includes employee names, addresses, phone numbers, emergency contacts, department, position, and salary or hourly pay. You have some temporary help come in to write a report of employees' names, addresses, and phone numbers. If you give access to EMPLOYEES to the temporary help, they can also see how much each of your employees is paid—you do not want this to happen.

To prevent that, you can create a view containing only the required information: employee name, address, and phone numbers. You can then give the temporary help access to the view to write the report without giving them access to the compensation columns in the table.

TIP

Views Can Restrict Access to Columns

Views can restrict user access to particular columns in a table or to rows in a table that meet specific conditions as defined in the WHERE clause of the view definition.

Utilizing Views to Maintain Summarized Data

If you have a summarized data report in which the data in the table or tables is updated often and the report is created often, a view with summarized data might be an excellent choice.

For example, suppose that you have a table containing information about individuals, such as city of residence, gender, salary, and age. You could create a view based on the table that shows summarized figures for individuals for each city, such as the average age, average salary, total number of males, and total number of females. To retrieve this information from the base table(s) after the view is created, you can simply query the view instead of composing a SELECT statement that might, in some cases, turn out to be complex.

The only difference between the syntax for creating a view with summarized data and creating a view from a single or multiple tables is the use of aggregate functions. Review Hour 9, "Summarizing Data Results from a Query," for the use of aggregate functions.

Creating Views

Views are created using the CREATE VIEW statement. You can create views from a single table, multiple tables, or another view. To create a view, a user must have the appropriate system privilege according to the specific implementation.

The basic CREATE VIEW syntax follows:

```
CREATE [RECURSIVE]VIEW VIEW_NAME
[COLUMN NAME [,COLUMN NAME]]
[OF UDT NAME [UNDER TABLE NAME]
[REF IS COLUMN NAME SYSTEM GENERATED |USER GENERATED | DERIVED]
[COLUMN NAME WITH OPTIONS SCOPE TABLE NAME]]
AS
{SELECT STATEMENT}
[WITH [CASCADED | LOCAL] CHECK OPTION]
```

The following subsections explore different methods for creating views using the CREATE VIEW statement.

TIP

ANSI SQL Has No ALTER VIEW Statement

There is no provision for an ALTER VIEW statement in ANSI SQL; although most database implementations do provide for that capability. For example, in older versions of MySQL, you use REPLACE VIEW to alter a current view. However, the newest versions of MySQL, SQL Server, and Oracle support the ALTER VIEW statement. Check with your specific database implementation's documentation to see what is supported.

Creating a View from a Single Table

You can create a view from a single table. The syntax follows:

```
CREATE VIEW VIEW_NAME AS
SELECT * | COLUMN1 [, COLUMN2 ]
FROM TABLE_NAME
[ WHERE EXPRESSION1 [, EXPRESSION2 ]]
[ WITH CHECK OPTION ]
[ GROUP BY ]
```

The simplest form for creating a view is one based on the entire contents of a single table, as in the following example:

```
CREATE VIEW EMPLOYEES_VIEW AS
SELECT *
FROM EMPLOYEES;
View created.
```

The next example narrows the contents for a view by selecting only specified columns from the base table:

```
CREATE VIEW EMP_VIEW AS
SELECT LASTNAME, FIRSTNAME
FROM EMPLOYEES;
View created.
```

The following is an example of how columns from the base table can be combined or manipulated to form a column in a view. The view column is titled NAMES by using an alias in the SELECT clause.

```
CREATE VIEW NAMES AS
SELECT LASTNAME + ', ' + FIRSTNAME AS DISPLAYNAME
FROM EMPLOYEES;
View created.
```

Now you select the top 10 rows of data from the NAMES view that you created:

```
SELECT TOP 10 *
FROM NAMES;

DISPLAYNAME
-----------------------------
Iner, Erlinda
Denty, Nicolette
Sabbah, Arlen
Loock, Yulanda
Sacks, Tena
Arcoraci, Inocencia
Astin, Christa
Contreraz, Tamara
Capito, Michale
Ellamar, Kimberly

(10 row(s) affected)
```

The following example shows how to create a view with summarized data from one or more underlying tables:

```
CREATE VIEW CITY_PAY AS
SELECT E.CITY, AVG(E.PAYRATE) AVG_PAY
FROM EMPLOYEES E
GROUP BY E.CITY;
View created.
```

Now you can select from your summarized view:

```
SELECT TOP 10 *
FROM CITY_PAY;
```

```
CITY                            AVG_PAY
------------------------------- -------------------------------
AFB MunicipalCharleston SC      NULL
Downtown MemorialSpartanburg    19.320000
Aberdeen                        19.326000
Abilene                         13.065000
Abingdon                        20.763333
Adak Island                     20.545000
Adrian                          21.865000
Afton                           12.680000
Aiken                           16.716666
Ainsworth                       21.960000
Warning: Null value is eliminated by an aggregate or other SET operation.

(10 row(s) affected)
```

By summarizing a view, SELECT statements that might occur in the future are simplified against the underlying table of the view.

Creating a View from Multiple Tables

You can create a view from multiple tables by using a JOIN in the SELECT statement. The syntax follows:

```
CREATE VIEW VIEW_NAME AS
SELECT * | COLUMN1 [, COLUMN2 ]
FROM TABLE_NAME1, TABLE_NAME2 [, TABLE_NAME3 ]
WHERE TABLE_NAME1 = TABLE_NAME2
[ AND TABLE_NAME1 = TABLE_NAME3 ]
[ EXPRESSION1 ] [, EXPRESSION2 ]
[ WITH CHECK OPTION ]
[ GROUP BY ]
```

The following is an example of creating a view from multiple tables:

```
CREATE VIEW EMPLOYEE_SUMMARY AS
SELECT E.EMPLOYEEID, E.LASTNAME, E.POSITION, E.HIREDATE AS DATE_HIRE, A.AIRPORTNAME
FROM EMPLOYEES E,
     AIRPORTS A
WHERE E.AIRPORTID = P.AIRPORTID;
View created.
```

Remember that when selecting data from multiple tables, the tables must be joined by common columns in the WHERE clause. A view is nothing more than a SELECT statement; therefore, tables are joined in a view definition the same as they are in a regular SELECT statement. Recall the use of table aliases to simplify the readability of a multiple-table query.

A view can also be joined with tables and with other views. The same principles apply to joining views with tables and other views that apply to joining tables to other tables. Review Hour 13, "Joining Tables in Queries," for more information.

Creating a View from a View

You can create a view from another view using the following format:

```
CREATE VIEW2 AS
SELECT * FROM VIEW1
```

You can create a view from a view many layers deep (a view of a view of a view, and so on). How deep you can go is implementation-specific. The only problem with creating views based on other views is their manageability. For example, suppose that you create VIEW2 based on VIEW1 and then create VIEW3 based on VIEW2. If VIEW1 is dropped, VIEW2 and VIEW3 are no good. The underlying information that supports these views no longer exists. Therefore, always maintain a good understanding of the views in the database and on which other objects those views rely (see Figure 20.2).

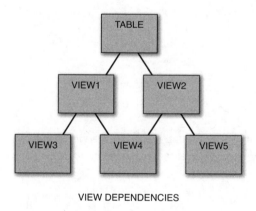

VIEW DEPENDENCIES

FIGURE 20.2
View dependencies

Figure 20.2 shows the relationship of views that are dependent not only on tables, but on other views. VIEW1 and VIEW2 are dependent on the TABLE. VIEW3 is dependent on VIEW1. VIEW4 is dependent on both VIEW1 and VIEW2. VIEW5 is dependent on VIEW2. Based on these relationships, the following can be concluded:

▶ If VIEW1 is dropped, VIEW3 and VIEW4 are invalid.

▶ If VIEW2 is dropped, VIEW4 and VIEW5 are invalid.

▶ If the TABLE is dropped, none of the views is valid.

BY THE WAY

Choose Carefully How You Implement Your Views

If a view is as easy and efficient to create from the base table as from another view, preference should go to the view created from the base table.

WITH CHECK OPTION

WITH CHECK OPTION is a CREATE VIEW statement option. The purpose of WITH CHECK OPTION is to ensure that all UPDATE and INSERT commands satisfy the condition(s) in the view definition. If they do not satisfy the condition(s), the UPDATE or INSERT returns an error. WITH CHECK OPTION actually enforces referential integrity by checking the view's definition to see that it is not violated.

Following is an example of creating a view with WITH CHECK OPTION:

```
CREATE VIEW EMPLOYEE_PHONES AS
SELECT LASTNAME, FIRSTNAME, PHONENUMBER
FROM EMPLOYEES
WHERE PHONENUMBER IS NOT NULL
WITH CHECK OPTION;
View created.
```

WITH CHECK OPTION in this case should deny the entry of any NULL values in the view's PAGER column because the view is defined by data that does not have a NULL value in the PAGER column.

Try to insert a NULL value into the PHONENUMBER column:

```
INSERT INTO EMPLOYEE_PHONES
VALUES ('SMITH','JOHN',NULL);
insert into employee_pagers
            *
ERROR at line 1:
ORA-01400: mandatory (NOT NULL) column is missing or NULL during insert
```

When you choose to use WITH CHECK OPTION during creation of a view from a view, you have two options: CASCADE and LOCAL. CASCADE is the default and is assumed if neither is specified. CASCADED is the ANSI standard for the syntax; however, Microsoft SQL Server and Oracle use the slightly different keyword CASCADE. The CASCADE option checks all underlying views, all integrity constraints during an update for the base table, and against defining conditions in the second view. The LOCAL option checks only integrity constraints against both views and the defining conditions in the second view, not the underlying base table. Therefore, it is safer to create views with the CASCADE option because the base table's referential integrity is preserved.

Creating a Table from a View

You can create a table from a view, just as you can create a table from another table (or a view from another view) in Oracle by using the CREATE TABLE AS SELECT syntax.

The syntax follows:

```
CREATE TABLE TABLE_NAME AS
SELECT {* | COLUMN1 [, COLUMN2 ]
FROM VIEW_NAME
[ WHERE CONDITION1 [, CONDITION2 ]
[ ORDER BY ]
```

BY THE WAY

Subtle Differences Between Tables and Views

Remember that the main difference between a table and a view is that a table contains actual data and consumes physical storage, whereas a view contains no data and requires no storage other than to store the view definition (the query).

First, create a view based on two tables:

```
CREATE VIEW INDIANA_EMPLOYEES AS
SELECT E.*
FROM Employees E,
     Airports A
WHERE E.AirportID = A.AirportID
AND E.State='IN';
View created.
```

Next, create a table based on the previously created view:

```
CREATE TABLE INDIANA_EMPLOYEE_TBL AS
SELECT EmployeeID,LastName,FirstName
FROM INDIANA_EMPLOYEES;
Table created.
```

Finally, select data from the table, the same as any other table:

```
SELECT *
FROM INDIANA_EMPLOYEE_TBL
WHERE ROWNUM <= 10;
```

EmployeeID	LastName	FirstName
21	Joynson	Jacqueline
22	Stream	Modesto
23	Cleamons	Delmar
183	Petito	David
184	Habib	Tanesha
185	Mcglone	Tamica
210	Geppert	Mason
211	Vogle	Daniele
212	Eyler	Jeanine
213	Hagelgans	Cassi

```
10 rows selected.
```

Views and the ORDER BY Clause

You cannot use the ORDER BY clause in the CREATE VIEW statement; however, in Oracle the GROUP BY clause has the same effect as an ORDER BY clause when it's used in the CREATE VIEW statement.

The following is an example of a GROUP BY clause in a CREATE VIEW statement:

```
CREATE VIEW NAMES2 AS
SELECT LASTNAME || ', ' || FIRSTNAME AS NAME
FROM EMPLOYEES
GROUP BY LASTNAME || ', ' || FIRSTNAME;
View created.
```

TIP

Defer the Use of the GROUP BY Clause in Your Views

Using the ORDER BY clause in the SELECT statement that is querying the view is better and simpler than using the GROUP BY clause in the CREATE VIEW statement.

If you select data from the view, the data is in alphabetical order (because you grouped by NAME):

```
SELECT *
FROM NAMES2
WHERE ROWNUM <= 10;
```

```
NAME
-----------------------------
Aarant, Sidney
Abbas, Gail
Abbay, Demetrice
Abbington, Gaynelle
Abdelal, Marcelo
Abdelwahed, Scarlet
Abdou, Clinton
Abendroth, Anastacia
Aberle, Jaunita
Abernatha, Elmira

10 rows selected.
```

Updating Data Through a View

You can update the underlying data of a view under certain conditions:

- The view must not involve joins.

- The view must not contain a GROUP BY clause.

- The view must not contain a UNION statement.

- The view cannot contain a reference to the pseudocolumn ROWNUM.

- The view cannot contain group functions.

- The DISTINCT clause cannot be used.

- The WHERE clause cannot include a nested table expression that includes a reference to the same table as referenced in the FROM clause.

- This means that the view can perform INSERTS, UPDATES, and DELETES as long as they honor these caveats.

Review Hour 14, "Using Subqueries to Define Unknown Data," for the UPDATE command's syntax.

Dropping a View

You use the DROP VIEW command to drop a view from the database. The two options for the DROP VIEW command are RESTRICT and CASCADE. If a view is dropped with the RESTRICT option and other views are referenced in a constraint, the DROP VIEW errs. If the CASCADE option is used and another view or constraint is referenced, the `DROP VIEW` succeeds and the underlying view or constraint is dropped. An example follows:

```
DROP VIEW NAMES2;
View dropped.
```

Performance Impact of Nested Views

Views adhere to the same performance characteristics as tables when they are used in queries. As such, you need to be cognizant that hiding complex logic behind a view does not negate that the data must be parsed and assembled by the system querying the underlying tables. Views must be treated as any other SQL statement for performance tuning. If the query that makes up your view is not preformant, the view itself experiences performance issues.

In addition, some users employ views to break down complex queries into multiple units of views and views that are created on top of other views. Although this might seem to be an excellent idea to break down the logic into simpler steps, it can present some performance degradation. This is because the query engine must break down and translate each sublayer of view to determine what exactly it needs to do for the query request.

The more layers you have, the more the query engine has to work to come up with an execution plan. In fact, most query engines do not guarantee that you get the best overall plan but merely that you get a decent plan in the shortest amount of time. So it is always best practice to keep the levels of code in your query as flat as possible and to test and tune the statements that make up your views.

What Is a Synonym?

A synonym is merely another name for a table or a view. Synonyms are usually created so a user can avoid having to qualify another user's table or view to access the table or view. Synonyms can be created as `PUBLIC` or `PRIVATE`. Any user of the database can use a `PUBLIC` synonym; only the owner of a database and any users that have been granted privileges can use a `PRIVATE` synonym.

Either a database administrator (or another designated individual) or individual users manage synonyms. Because there are two types of synonyms, `PUBLIC` and `PRIVATE`, different system-level privileges might be required to create one or the other. All users can generally create a `PRIVATE` synonym. Typically, only a DBA or privileged database user can create a `PUBLIC` synonym. Refer to your specific implementation for required privileges when creating synonyms.

BY THE WAY

Synonyms Are Not ANSI SQL Standard

Synonyms are not American National Standards Institute (ANSI) SQL standard; however, because several major implementations use synonyms, it is best to discuss them briefly here. You must check your particular implementation for the exact use of synonyms, if available. Note, however, that MySQL does not support synonyms. However, you might implement the same type of functionality using a view instead.

Creating Synonyms

The general syntax to create a synonym follows:

```
CREATE [PUBLIC|PRIVATE] SYNONYM SYNONYM_NAME FOR TABLE|VIEW
```

You create a synonym called EMP, short for Employees table, in the following Oracle example. This frees you from having to spell out the full table name.

```
CREATE SYNONYM EMP FOR Employees;
Synonym created.
SELECT LastName
FROM EMP
WHERE RowNum <= 10;


LastName
------------------------------
Iner
Denty
Sabbah
Loock
Sacks
Arcoraci
Astin
Contreraz
Capito
Ellamar

10 rows selected.
```

It is also common for a table owner to create a synonym for the table to which you have been granted access, so you do not have to qualify the table name by the name of the owner:

```
CREATE SYNONYM FLIGHTS FOR USER1.Flights;
Synonym created.
```

Dropping Synonyms

Dropping synonyms is like dropping almost any other database object. The general syntax to drop a synonym follows:

```
DROP [PUBLIC|PRIVATE] SYNONYM SYNONYM_NAME
```

Following is an example:

```
DROP SYNONYM EMP;
Synonym dropped.
```

Summary

This hour discussed two important features in SQL: views and synonyms. In many cases, these features can aid in the overall functionality of relational database users. Views were defined as virtual table objects that look and act like tables but do not take physical space like tables. Views are actually defined by queries against tables and possible other views in the database. Administrators typically use views to restrict data that a user sees and to simplify and summarize data. You can create views from views, but take care not to embed views too deeply to avoid losing control over their management. There are various options when creating views; some are implementation-specific.

Synonyms are objects in the database that represent other objects. They simplify the name of another object in the database, either by creating a synonym with a short name for an object with a long name or by creating a synonym on an object owned by another user to which you have access. There are two types of synonyms: PUBLIC and PRIVATE. A PUBLIC synonym is one that is accessible to all database users, whereas a PRIVATE synonym is accessible to a single user. A DBA typically creates a PUBLIC synonym, whereas each user normally creates her own PRIVATE synonyms.

Q&A

Q. How can a view contain data but take no storage space?

A. A view does not contain data; it is a virtual table or a stored query. The only space required for a view is for the actual view creation statement, called the view definition.

Q. What happens to the view if a table from which a view were created is dropped?

A. The view is invalid because the underlying data for the view no longer exists.

Q. What are the limits on naming the synonym when creating synonyms?

A. This is implementation-specific. However, the naming convention for synonyms in most major implementations follows the same rules that apply to the tables and other objects in the database.

Workshop

The following workshop is composed of a series of quiz questions and practical exercises. The quiz questions are designed to test your overall understanding of the current material. The practical exercises are intended to afford you the opportunity to apply the concepts discussed during the current hour, as well as build upon the knowledge acquired in previous hours of study. Please take time to complete the quiz questions and exercises before continuing. Refer to Appendix C, "Answers to Quizzes and Exercises," for answers.

Quiz

1. Can you delete a row of data from a view that you created from multiple tables?

2. When creating a table, the owner is automatically granted the appropriate privileges on that table. Is this true when creating a view?

3. Which clause orders data when creating a view?

4. Do Oracle and SQL Server handle the ability to order a view in the same way?

5. Which option can you use when creating a view from a view to check integrity constraints?

6. You try to drop a view and receive an error because of one or more underlying views. What must you do to drop the view?

Exercises

1. Write a statement to create a view based on the total contents of EMPLOYEES table.

2. Write a statement that creates a summarized view containing the average pay rate and average salary for each city in EMPLOYEES table.

3. Create another view for the same summarized data, except use the view you created in Exercise 1 instead of the base EMPLOYEES table. Compare the two results.

4. Use the view in Exercise 2 to create a table called EMPLOYEE_PAY_SUMMARIZED. Verify that the view and the table contain the same data.

5. Write a statement to create a synonym for your new EMPLOYEE_PAY_SUMMARIZED table.

6. Write two queries, one that uses the base EMPLOYEE_PAY_SUMMARIZED table and one that uses your synonym that compares an employee's salary or pay rate with the average salary for the city in which they reside.

7. Write a statement that drops the table, the synonym, and the three views that you created.

Working with the System Catalog

What You'll Learn in This Hour:

▶ Definition of the system catalog

▶ How to create the system catalog

▶ What data the system catalog contains

▶ Examples of system catalog tables

▶ Querying the system catalog

▶ Updating the system catalog

In this hour, you learn about the system catalog, commonly referred to as the data dictionary in some relational database implementations. By the end of this hour, you will understand the purpose and contents of the system catalog and will query it to find information about the database based on commands that you have learned in previous hours. Each major implementation has some form of a system catalog that stores information about the database. This hour shows examples of the elements contained in a few of the different system catalogs for the implementations discussed in this book.

What Is the System Catalog?

The *system catalog* is a collection of tables and views that contain important information about a database. A system catalog is available for each database. Information in the system catalog defines the structure of the database and information on the data contained therein. For example, the Data Definition Language (DDL) for all tables in the database is stored in the system catalog. See Figure 21.1 for an example of the system catalog within the database.

As referenced in Figure 21.1, the system catalog for a database is actually part of the database. Within the database are objects, such as tables, indexes, and views. The system catalog is basically a group of objects that contain information that defines other objects in the database, the structure of the database, and various other significant information.

FIGURE 21.1
The system catalog

The system catalog for your implementation might be divided into logical groups of objects to provide tables that are accessible by the database administrator (DBA) and any other database user. For example, a user might need to view the particular database privileges that she has been granted but doesn't care how this is internally structured in the database. A user typically queries the system catalog to acquire information on the user's own objects and privileges, whereas the DBA needs to inquire about any structure or event within the database. In some implementations, system catalog objects are accessible only to the DBA.

The system catalog is crucial to the DBA or any other database user who needs to know about the database's structure and nature. It is especially important in those instances in which the database user is not presented with a graphical user interface (GUI). The system catalog allows orders to be kept, not only by the DBA and users, but also by the database server.

TIP

Database System Catalogs Vary

Each implementation has its own naming conventions for the system catalog's tables and views. The naming is *not* important; however, learning what the system catalog does *is* important, as is what it contains and how and where to retrieve the information.

How Is the System Catalog Created?

The system catalog is created either automatically with the creation of the database, or by the DBA immediately following the creation of the database. For example, a set of predefined, vendor-provided SQL scripts in Oracle is executed, which builds all the database tables and views in the system catalog that are accessible to a database user.

The system catalog tables and views are system-owned and not specific to any one schema. In Oracle, for example, the system catalog owner is a user account called `SYS`, which has full authority in the database. In Microsoft SQL Server, the system catalog for the SQL server is located in the `master` database. Check your specific vendor documentation to find where the system catalogs are stored.

What Is Contained in the System Catalog?

The system catalog contains a variety of information accessible to many users and is sometimes used for different specific purposes by each of those users.

The system catalog contains information such as the following:

- ▶ User accounts and default settings

- ▶ Privileges and other security information

- ▶ Performance statistics

- ▶ Object sizing

- ▶ Object growth

- ▶ Table structure and storage

- ▶ Index structure and storage

- ▶ Information on other database objects, such as views, synonyms, triggers, and stored procedures

- ▶ Table constraints and referential integrity information

- ▶ User sessions

- ▶ Auditing information

- ▶ Internal database settings

- ▶ Locations of database files

The database server maintains the system catalog. For example, when a table is created, the database server inserts the data into the appropriate system catalog table or view. When a table's structure is modified, appropriate objects in the data dictionary are updated. The following sections describe the types of data that are contained in the system catalog.

User Data

All information about individual users is stored in the system catalog: the system and object privileges a user has been granted, the objects a user owns, and the objects not owned by the user to which the user has access. The user tables or views are accessible to the individual to query for information. See your implementation documentation on the system catalog objects.

Security Information

The system catalog also stores security information, such as user identifications, encrypted passwords, and various privileges and groups of privileges that database users utilize to access the data. Audit tables exist in some implementations for tracking actions that occur within the database, as well as by whom, when, and so on. Database user sessions can be closely monitored through the use of the system catalog in many implementations.

Database Design Information

The system catalog contains information regarding the actual database. That information includes the database's creation date, name, object sizing, size and location of data files, referential integrity information, indexes that exist in the database, and specific column information and column attributes for each table in the database.

Performance Statistics

Performance statistics are typically maintained in the system catalog as well. Performance statistics include information concerning the performance of SQL statements, both elapsed time and the execution method of an SQL statement taken by the optimizer. Other information for performance concerns memory allocation and usage, free space in the database, and information that allows table and index fragmentation to be controlled within the database. You can use this performance information to properly tune the database, rearrange SQL queries, and redesign methods of access to data to achieve better overall performance and SQL query response time.

System Catalog Tables by Implementation

Each implementation has several tables and views that compose the system catalog, some of which are categorized by user level, system level, and DBA level. For your particular implementation, you should query these tables and read your implementation's documentation for more information on system catalog tables. Table 21.1 has examples from the two most popular database implementations, SQL Server and Oracle.

TABLE 21.1 Major Implementation System Catalog Objects

Microsoft SQL Server Table Name	Information On...
SYSUSERS	Database users
SYS.DATABASES	All database segments
SYS.DATABASE_PERMISSIONS	All database permissions
SYS.DATABASE_FILES	All database files
SYSINDEXES	All indexes
SYSCONSTRAINTS	All constraints
SYS.TABLES	All database tables
SYS.VIEWS	All database views
Oracle	
ALL_TABLES	Tables accessible by a user
USER_TABLES	Tables owned by a user
DBA_TABLES	All tables in the database
DBA_SEGMENTS	Segment storage
DBA_INDEXES	All indexes
DBA_USERS	All users of the database
DBA_ROLE_PRIVS	Roles granted
DBA_ROLES	Roles in the database
DBA_SYS_PRIVS	System privileges granted
DBA_FREE_SPACE	Database free space
V$DATABASE	The creation of the database
V$SESSION	Current sessions

These are just a few of the system catalog objects from the main relational database implementations that we cover in the book. Many of the system catalog objects that are similar between implementations are shown here, but this hour strives to provide some variety. Overall, each implementation is specific to the organization of the system catalog's contents.

Querying the System Catalog

The system catalog tables or views are queried as any other table or view in the database using SQL. A user can usually query the user-related tables but might be denied access to various system tables accessible only by privileged database user accounts, such as the DBA.

You create a SQL query to retrieve data from the system catalog just as you create a query to access any other table in the database. For example, the following query returns all rows of data from the Microsoft SQL Server table SYS.TABLES:

```
SELECT * FROM SYS.TABLES;
GO
```

The following query lists all user accounts in the database and is run from the MySQL system database:

```
SELECT NAME
FROM SYS.SYSUSERS

NAME
------------------------------
db_accessadmin
db_backupoperator
db_datareader
db_datawriter
db_ddladmin
db_denydatareader
db_denydatawriter
db_owner
db_securityadmin
dbo
guest
INFORMATION_SCHEMA
public
sys

(14 row(s) affected)
```

NOTE

A Word About the Following Examples

The following examples use the SQL Server system catalog. SQL Server is chosen for no particular reason other than to give you some examples from one of the database implementations talked about in the book.

The following query lists all tables within our CanaryAirlines schema and is run from the INFORMATION_SCHEMA:

```
SELECT TABLE_NAME
FROM INFORMATION_SCHEMA.TABLES WHERE TABLE_CATALOG='CanaryAirlines';
```

```
TABLE_NAME
-------------------------------
Trips
TripItinerary
Countries
Airports
Passengers
Aircraft
AircraftFleet
FlightStatuses
Flights
Routes
vw_FlightNumbersPerDay
vw_FlightInfo
RandomView
Employees
RICH_EMPLOYEES
sysdiagrams

(16 row(s) affected)
```

CAUTION

Manipulating System Catalog Tables Can Be Dangerous

Never directly manipulate tables in the system catalog in any way. (Only the DBA has access to manipulate system catalog tables.) Doing so might compromise the database's integrity. Remember that information concerning the structure of the database, as well as all objects in the database, is maintained in the system catalog. The system catalog is typically isolated from all other data in the database. Some implementations, such as Microsoft SQL Server, do not allow the user to manipulate the system catalog directly to maintain the integrity of the system.

The next query returns all the system privileges that have been granted to the database user BRANDON:

```
SELECT TABLE_NAME, PRIVILEGE_TYPE
FROM INFORMATION_SCHEMA.TABLE_PRIVILEGES
WHERE GRANTEE = 'BRANDON';

TABLE_NAME                         PRIVILEGE_TYPE
-------------------------------    --------------
Countries                          SELECT
Airports                           SELECT
Aircraft                           SELECT
AircraftFleet                      SELECT

(4 row(s) affected)
```

NOTE

These Are Just a Few of the System Catalog Tables Available

The examples shown in this section represent a very small sampling of the information that is available from any system catalog. You might find it extremely helpful to dump data dictionary information using queries to a file that can be printed and used as a reference. Refer to your implementation documentation for specific system catalog tables and columns within those available tables.

Updating System Catalog Objects

The system catalog is used only for query operations—even when the DBA is using it. The database server makes updates to the system catalog automatically. For example, a table is created in the database when a database user issues a CREATE TABLE statement. The database server then places the DDL that created the table in the system catalog under the appropriate system catalog table.

There is never a need to manually update a table in the system catalog even though you might have the power to do so. The database server for each implementation performs these updates according to actions that occur within the database, as shown in Figure 21.2.

FIGURE 21.2
Updates to the system catalog

Summary

In this hour you learned about the system catalog for a relational database. The system catalog is, in a sense, a database within a database. The system catalog is essentially a database that contains all information about the database in which it resides. It is a way of maintaining the database's overall structure, tracking events and changes that occur within the database, and providing the vast pool of information necessary for overall database management. The system catalog is used only for query operations. Database users should not make changes directly to system tables. However, changes are implicitly made each time a change is made to the database structure itself, such as the creation of a table. The database server makes these entries in the system catalog automatically.

Q&A

Q. As a database user, I realize I can find information about my objects. How can I find information about other users' objects?

A. Users can employ sets of tables and views to query in most system catalogs. One set of these tables and views includes information on what objects you have access to. To find out about other users' access, you need to check the system catalogs containing that information. For example, in Oracle you could check the DBA_TABLES and DBA_USERS system catalogs.

Q. If a user forgets his password, is there a table that the DBA can query to get the password?

A. Yes and no. The password is maintained in a system table, but it is typically encrypted so that even the DBA cannot read the password. The password has to be reset if the user forgets it, which the DBA can easily accomplish.

Q. How can I tell which columns are in a system catalog table?

A. You can query the system catalog tables as you query any other table. Simply query the table holding that particular information.

Workshop

The following workshop is composed of a series of quiz questions and practical exercises. The quiz questions are designed to test your overall understanding of the current material. The practical exercises are intended to afford you the opportunity to apply the concepts discussed during the current hour, as well as build upon the knowledge acquired in previous hours of study. Please take time to complete the quiz questions and exercises before continuing. Refer to Appendix C, "Answers to Quizzes and Exercises," for answers.

Quiz

1. In some implementations, what is the system catalog also known as?

2. Can a regular user update the system catalog?

3. Which Microsoft SQL Server system table retrieves information about views that exist in the database?

4. Who owns the system catalog?

5. What is the difference between the Oracle system objects ALL_TABLES and DBA_TABLES?

6. Who makes modifications to the system tables?

Exercises

1. In Hour 19, "Managing Database Security," you looked at the tables in your CanaryAirlines database. Now find some of the system tables that we discussed earlier in this hour. Review them.

2. At the prompt, type in queries to bring up each of the following:

   ▶ Information on all the tables

   ▶ Information on all the views

   ▶ All the usernames in the database

3. Write a query using multiple system tables to retrieve all the users and their associated privileges in your CanaryAirlines database.

Advanced SQL Topics

What You'll Learn in This Hour:

- ▶ Definition of cursors
- ▶ Using stored procedures
- ▶ Definition of triggers
- ▶ Basics of dynamic SQL
- ▶ Using SQL to generate SQL
- ▶ Direct SQL versus embedded SQL
- ▶ Embedding SQL with a call-level interface

In this hour, you are introduced to some advanced SQL topics that extend beyond the basic operations that you have learned so far, such as querying data from the database, building database structures, and manipulating data within the database. By the end of the hour, you should understand the concepts behind cursors, stored procedures, triggers, dynamic SQL, direct versus embedded SQL, and SQL generated from SQL. These advanced features are available in many implementations, all of which provide enhancements to the parts of SQL discussed so far.

NOTE

Some Topics Are Not ANSI SQL-Related

Not all topics covered in this hour are ANSI SQL, so you must check your particular implementation for variations in syntax and rules. A few major vendors' syntax is shown in this hour for comparison.

Cursors

Normally, database operations are commonly referred to as set-based operations. This means that the majority of ANSI SQL commands are geared toward working on a block of data. A *cursor*, however, is typically used to retrieve a subset of data from the database in a row-based operation. Thereby, each row in the cursor can be evaluated by a program, one row at a time.

Cursors are normally used in SQL that is embedded in procedural-type programs. Some cursors are created implicitly by the database server, whereas others are defined by the SQL programmer. Each SQL implementation might define the use of cursors differently.

This section shows syntax examples from the two popular implementations that we have tracked throughout the book: Microsoft SQL Server and Oracle.

The syntax to declare a cursor for Microsoft SQL Server follows:

```
DECLARE CURSOR_NAME CURSOR
FOR SELECT_STATEMENT
[ FOR [READ ONLY | UPDATE {[ COLUMN_LIST ]}]
```

The syntax for Oracle follows:

```
DECLARE CURSOR CURSOR_NAME
IS {SELECT_STATEMENT}
```

The following cursor contains the result subset of all records from EMPLOYEE_TBL:

```
DECLARE CURSOR EMP_CURSOR IS
SELECT * FROM EMPLOYEE_TBL
{ OTHER PROGRAM STATEMENTS }
```

According to the ANSI standard, you use the following operations to access a cursor after it has been defined:

▶ OPEN—Opens a defined cursor

▶ FETCH—Fetches rows from a cursor into a program variable

▶ CLOSE—Closes the cursor when operations against the cursor are complete

Opening a Cursor

You cannot access a cursor until you have opened it. When a cursor is opened, the specified cursor's SELECT statement is executed, and the results of the query are stored in a staging area in memory.

The syntax to open a cursor in Microsoft SQL Server follows:

```
OPEN CURSOR_NAME
```

The syntax in Oracle follows:

```
OPEN CURSOR_NAME [ PARAMETER1 [, PARAMETER2 ]]
```

To open the EMP_CURSOR, use the following statement:

```
OPEN EMP_CURSOR
```

Fetching Data from a Cursor

You can retrieve the contents of the cursor (results from the query) through the FETCH statement after you open the cursor.

The syntax for the FETCH statement in Microsoft SQL Server follows:

```
FETCH NEXT FROM CURSOR_NAME [ INTO FETCH_LIST ]
```

The syntax for Oracle follows:

```
FETCH CURSOR_NAME {INTO : HOST_VARIABLE
[[ INDICATOR ] : INDICATOR_VARIABLE ]
[, : HOST_VARIABLE
[[ INDICATOR ] : INDICATOR_VARIABLE ]]
| USING DESCRIPTOR DESCRIPTOR ] }
```

To fetch the contents of EMP_CURSOR into a variable called EMP_RECORD, your FETCH statement might appear as follows:

```
FETCH NEXT FROM EMP_CURSOR INTO EMP_RECORD
```

When fetching data from a cursor, note that at some time you will come to the end of the cursor. Each implementation has a different way to set up a way to handle this so that you can gracefully close the cursor without receiving an error. Following are pseudocode examples from Microsoft SQL Server and Oracle on how to handle these situations. The syntax is meant to give you a feel for the process of handling cursors.

The syntax for Microsoft SQL Server follows:

```
BEGIN
    DECLARE @custname VARCHAR(30);
    DECLARE namecursor CURSOR FOR SELECT LastName FROM Passengers;
    OPEN namecursor;
    FETCH NEXT FROM namecursor INTO @custname
    WHILE (@@FETCH_STATUS<>-1)
        BEGIN
            IF (@@FETCH_STATUS<>-2)
            BEGIN
                    -- Do something with the variable
            END
    FETCH NEXT FROM namecursor INTO @custname
    END
    CLOSE namecursor
    DEALLOCATE namecursor
END;
```

The syntax for Oracle follows:

```
custname  varchar(30);
CURSOR namecursor
IS
SELECT LastName FROM Passengers;
BEGIN
     OPEN namecursor;
     FETCH namecursor INTO custname;
     IF namecursor%notfound THEN
          -- Do some handling as you are at the end of the cursor
     END IF;
     -- Do something with the variable
     CLOSE namecursor;
END;
```

NOTE

More Variations Exist in Advanced Features

As you can see from the previous examples, variations among the implementations are extensive, especially with advanced features of and extensions to SQL, which are covered in Hour 24, "Extensions to Standard SQL." You must check your particular implementation for the exact usage of a cursor.

Closing a Cursor

You can obviously close a cursor if you can open one. After it's closed, it is no longer available to user programs. Closing a cursor is quite simple.

The Microsoft SQL Server syntax for the closing of a cursor and the deallocation of a cursor follows:

```
CLOSE CURSOR_NAME
DEALLOCATE CURSOR CURSOR_NAME
```

When a cursor is closed in Oracle, the resources and name are released without the DEALLOCATE statement. The syntax for Oracle follows:

```
CLOSE CURSOR_NAME
```

Stored Procedures and Functions

Stored procedures are groupings of related SQL statements—commonly referred to as functions and *subprograms*—that allow ease and flexibility for a programmer. This ease and flexibility are derived from the fact that a stored procedure is often easier to execute than a number of individual SQL statements. Stored procedures can be nested within other stored procedures. That is, a stored procedure can call another stored procedure, which can call another stored procedure, and so on.

Stored procedures allow for procedural programming. The basic SQL DDL (Data Definition Language), DML (Data Manipulation Language), and DQL (Data Query Language) statements (CREATE TABLE, INSERT, UPDATE, SELECT, and so on) allow you the opportunity to tell the database what needs to be done, but not how to do it. By coding stored procedures, you tell the database engine how to go about processing the data.

A stored procedure is a group of one or more SQL statements or functions that are stored in the database, compiled, and ready to be executed by a database user. A *stored function* is the same as a stored procedure, but a function returns a value.

Functions are called by procedures. When a function is called by a procedure, parameters can be passed into a function like a procedure, a value is computed, and then the value is passed back to the calling procedure for further processing.

When a stored procedure is created, the various subprograms and functions that compose the stored procedure are actually stored in the database. These stored procedures are preparsed and are immediately ready to execute when the user invokes them.

The Microsoft SQL Server syntax for creating a stored procedure follows:

```
CREATE PROCEDURE PROCEDURE_NAME
[ [() @PARAMETER_NAME
DATATYPE [(LENGTH) | (PRECISION] [, SCALE ])
[ = DEFAULT ] [ OUTPUT ]]
[, @PARAMETER_NAME
DATATYPE [(LENGTH) | (PRECISION [, SCALE ])
[ = DEFAULT ] [ OUTPUT ]]  [)]]
[ WITH RECOMPILE ]
AS SQL_STATEMENTS
```

The syntax for Oracle follows:

```
CREATE [ OR REPLACE ] PROCEDURE PROCEDURE_NAME
[ (ARGUMENT [{IN | OUT | IN OUT} ] TYPE,
ARGUMENT [{IN | OUT | IN OUT} ] TYPE) ] {IS | AS}
PROCEDURE_BODY
```

An example of a simple stored procedure to insert new rows into the AIRCRAFTFLEET table follows:

```
CREATE PROCEDURE NEW_AIRCRAFTFLEET
(@AIRCRAFTCODE VARCHAR(3), @AIRCRAFTDESIGNATOR VARCHAR(10), @STATUS VARCHAR(50), @
HOMEAIRPORTID INT)
```

```
AS
BEGIN
  INSERT INTO AircraftFleet(AircraftCode,AircraftDesignator,Status,HomeAirportID)
  VALUES (@AIRCRAFTCODE,@AIRCRAFTDESIGNATOR, @STATUS, @HOMEAIRPORTID);
END;
Procedure created.
```

The syntax for executing a stored procedure in Microsoft SQL Server follows:

```
EXECUTE [ @RETURN_STATUS = ]
PROCEDURE_NAME
[[@PARAMETER_NAME = ] VALUE |
[@PARAMETER_NAME = ] @VARIABLE [ OUTPUT ]]
[WITH RECOMPILE]
```

The syntax for Oracle follows:

```
EXECUTE [ @RETURN STATUS =] PROCEDURE NAME
[[ @PARAMETER NAME = ] VALUE | [ @PARAMETER NAME = ] @VARIABLE [ OUTPUT ]]]
[ WITH RECOMPILE ]
```

NOTE

Basic SQL Commands Are Often the Same

You might find distinct differences between the allowed syntax used to code procedures in different implementations of SQL. The basic SQL commands should be the same, but the programming constructs (variables, conditional statements, cursors, and loops) might vary drastically among implementations.

The following example executes the procedure you have created in Oracle:

```
CALL NEW_AIRCRAFTFLEET ('999','ZZZ-1','ACTIVE',3160);
PL/SQL procedure successfully completed.
```

Stored procedures provide several distinct advantages over individual SQL statements executed in the database. Some of these advantages include the following:

▶ The statements are already stored in the database.

▶ The statements are already parsed and in an executable format.

▶ Stored procedures support modular programming.

▶ Stored procedures can call other procedures and functions.

▶ Stored procedures can be called by other types of programs.

▶ Overall response time is typically better with stored procedures.

▶ Stored procedures increase the overall ease of use.

Triggers

A *trigger* is a compiled SQL procedure in the database that performs actions based on other actions occurring within the database. A trigger is a form of a stored procedure that is executed when a specified DML action is performed on a table. The trigger can be executed before or after an INSERT, DELETE, or UPDATE statement. Triggers can also check data integrity before an INSERT, DELETE, or UPDATE statement. Triggers can roll back transactions, and they can modify data in one table and read from another table in another database.

Triggers, for the most part, are good functions to use; they can, however, cause more I/O overhead. Triggers should not be used when a stored procedure or a program can accomplish the same results with less overhead.

The CREATE TRIGGER Statement

You can create a trigger using the CREATE TRIGGER statement.

The ANSI standard syntax is

```
CREATE TRIGGER TRIGGER NAME
[[BEFORE | AFTER] TRIGGER EVENT ON TABLE NAME]
[REFERENCING VALUES ALIAS LIST]
[TRIGGERED ACTION
TRIGGER EVENT::=
INSERT | UPDATE | DELETE [OF TRIGGER COLUMN LIST]
TRIGGER COLUMN LIST ::= COLUMN NAME [, COLUMN NAME]
VALUES ALIAS LIST ::=
VALUES ALIAS LIST ::=
OLD [ROW] ˊ OLD VALUES CORRELATION NAME |
NEW [ROW] ˊ NEW VALUES CORRELATION NAME |
OLD TABLE ˊ OLD VALUES TABLE ALIAS |
NEW TABLE ˊ NEW VALUES TABLE ALIAS
OLD VALUES TABLE ALIAS ::= IDENTIFIER
NEW VALUES TABLE ALIAS ::= IDENTIFIER
TRIGGERED ACTION ::=
[FOR EACH [ROW | STATEMENT] [WHEN SEARCH CONDITION]]
TRIGGERED SQL STATEMENT
TRIGGERED SQL STATEMENT ::=
SQL STATEMENT | BEGIN ATOMIC [SQL STATEMENT;]
END
```

The Microsoft SQL Server syntax to create a trigger follows:

```
CREATE TRIGGER TRIGGER_NAME
ON TABLE_NAME
FOR { INSERT | UPDATE | DELETE [, ..]}
AS
SQL_STATEMENTS
[ RETURN ]
```

The basic syntax for Oracle follows:

```
CREATE [ OR REPLACE ] TRIGGER TRIGGER_NAME
[ BEFORE | AFTER]
[ DELETE | INSERT | UPDATE]
ON [ USER.TABLE_NAME ]
[ FOR EACH ROW ]
[ WHEN CONDITION ]
[ PL/SQL BLOCK ]
```

The following is an example trigger written in the Oracle syntax:

```
CREATE TRIGGER EMP_PAY_TRIG
AFTER UPDATE ON EMPLOYEES
FOR EACH ROW
WHEN ( NEW.PAY_RATE<>OLD.PAY_RATE OR NEW.SALARY<>OLD.SALARY)
BEGIN
  INSERT INTO EMPLOYEE_PAY_HISTORY
  (EMPLOYEEID, PREV_PAY_RATE, PAY_RATE, PREV_SALARY, SALARY, DATE_UPDATED)
  VALUES
  (NEW.EMPLOYEEID, OLD.PAY_RATE, NEW.PAY_RATE,
   OLD.SALARY, NEW.SALARY, SYSDATE);
END;
/
Trigger created.
```

The preceding example shows the creation of a trigger called EMP_PAY_TRIG. This trigger inserts a row into the EMPLOYEE_PAY_HISTORY table, reflecting the changes made every time either the PAY_RATE or the SALARY is updated in EMPLOYEES.

TIP

Triggers Cannot Be Altered

You cannot alter the body of a trigger. You must either replace or re-create the trigger. Some implementations allow a trigger to be replaced (if the trigger with the same name already exists) as part of the CREATE TRIGGER statement.

The DROP TRIGGER Statement

You can drop a trigger using the DROP TRIGGER statement. The syntax for dropping a trigger follows:

```
DROP TRIGGER TRIGGER_NAME
```

Dynamic SQL

Dynamic SQL allows a programmer or end user to create a SQL statement's specifics at runtime and pass the statement to the database. The database then returns data into the program variables, which are bound at SQL runtime.

To comprehend dynamic SQL, you must understand static SQL. Static SQL is what this book has discussed thus far. A *static SQL statement* is written and not meant to be changed. Although static SQL statements can be stored as files ready to be executed later or as stored procedures in the database, static SQL does not quite offer the flexibility that is allowed with dynamic SQL.

The problem with static SQL is that even though numerous queries might be available to the end user, there is a good chance that none of these "canned" queries will satisfy the users' needs on every occasion. Dynamic SQL is often used by ad hoc query tools, which allow a SQL statement to be created on-the-fly by a user to satisfy the particular query requirements for that particular situation. After the statement is customized according to the user's needs, the statement is sent to the database, checked for syntax errors and privileges required to execute the statement, and compiled in the database where the database server carries out the statement. Dynamic SQL can be created by using a call-level interface, which is explained in the next section.

NOTE

Dynamic SQL Is Not Always the Most Performant

Although dynamic SQL provides more flexibility for the end user's query needs, the performance might not compare to that of a stored procedure whose code has already been analyzed by the SQL optimizer.

Call-Level Interface

A *call-level interface (CLI)* embeds SQL code in a host program, such as ANSI C. Application programmers should be familiar with the concept of a CLI. It is one of the methods that allows a programmer to embed SQL in different procedural programming languages. When using a CLI, you simply pass the text of a SQL statement into a variable using the rules of the host programming language. You can execute the SQL statement in the host program through the use of the variable into which you passed the SQL text.

EXEC SQL is a common host programming language command that enables you to call a SQL statement (CLI) from within the program.

The following are examples of programming languages that support CLI:

- ▶ ANSI C

- ▶ C#

- ▶ VB.NET

- ▶ Java

- ▶ Pascal

- ▶ Fortran

NOTE

CLIs Are Platform-Specific

Refer to the syntax of the host programming language with which you are using CLI options. The CLI programming language is always platform-specific; so, an Oracle CLI does not work with a SQL Server CLI.

Using SQL to Generate SQL

Using SQL to generate SQL is a valuable time-budgeting method of writing SQL statements. Assume you have 100 users in the database already. A new role, ENABLE (a user-defined object that is granted privileges), has been created and must be granted to those 100 users. Instead of manually creating 100 GRANT statements, the following SQL statement generates each of those statements for you:

```
SELECT 'GRANT ENABLE TO '|| USERNAME||';'
FROM SYS.DBA_USERS;
```

This example uses Oracle's system catalog view (which contains information for users).

Notice the use of single quotation marks around GRANT ENABLE TO. The use of single quotation marks allows whatever is between the marks (including spaces) to be literal. Remember that literal values can be selected from tables, the same as columns from a table. USERNAME is the column in the system catalog table SYS.DBA_USERS. The double pipe signs (||) concatenate the columns. The use of double pipes followed by ; concatenates the semicolon to the end of the username, thus completing the statement.

The results of the SQL statement look like the following:

```
GRANT ENABLE TO RRPLEW;
GRANT ENABLE TO RKSTEP;
```

You should spool these results to a file, which can be sent to the database. The database, in turn, executes each SQL statement in the file, saving you many keystrokes and much time. The GRANT ENABLE TO USERNAME statement is repeated once for every user in the database.

The next time you write SQL statements and have repeated the same statement several times, allow your imagination to take hold, and let SQL do the work for you.

Direct Versus Embedded SQL

Direct SQL is where a SQL statement is executed from some form of an interactive terminal. The SQL results are returned directly to the terminal that issued the statement. Most of this book has focused on direct SQL. Direct SQL is also referred to as *interactive invocation* or *direct invocation*.

Embedded SQL is SQL code used within other programs, such as Pascal, Fortran, COBOL, and C. SQL code is actually embedded in a host programming language, as discussed previously, with a call-level interface. Embedded SQL statements in host programming language codes are commonly preceded by EXEC SQL and terminated by a semicolon. Other termination characters include END-EXEC and the right parenthesis.

The following is an example of embedded SQL in a host program, such as the ANSI C language:

```
{HOST PROGRAMMING COMMANDS}
EXEC SQL {SQL STATEMENT};
{MORE HOST PROGRAMMING COMMANDS}
```

Windowed Table Functions

Windowed table functions allow calculations to operate over a window of the table and return a value based upon that window. This allows for the calculation of values such as a running sum, ranks, and moving averages. The syntax for the table valued function follows:

ARGUMENT OVER ([PARTITION CLAUSE] [ORDER CLAUSE] [FRAME CLAUSE])

Almost all aggregate functions can act as windowed table functions. They provide five new windowed table functions:

- RANK() OVER

- DENSE_RANK() OVER

- PERCENT_RANK() OVER

- CUME_DIST() OVER

- ROW_NUMBER() OVER

Normally, it would be difficult to calculate something such as an individual's ranking within their location. Windowed table functions would make this calculation a little easier, as shown in the following example for Microsoft SQL Server:

```
SELECT EMPLOYEEID, SALARY, RANK() OVER (PARTITION BY AIRPORTID
ORDER BY SALARY DESC) AS RANK_IN_LOCATION
FROM EMPLOYEES;
```

Not all RDBM implementations currently support windowed table functions, so it is best to check the documentation of your specific implementation.

Working with XML

The ANSI standard presented an XML-related features section in its 2003 version. Since then, most database implementations have tried to support at least part of the released feature set. For example, one part of the ANSI standard is to provide for the output of XML-formatted output from a query. SQL Server provides such a method by using the FOR XML statement, as shown in the following example:

```
SELECT EMP_ID, HIRE_DATE, SALARY FROM
EMPLOYEE_TBL FOR XML AUTO
```

Another important feature of the XML feature set is retrieving information from an XML document or fragment. Oracle provides this functionality through the EXTRACTVALUE function. This function takes two arguments. The first is an XML fragment, and the second is the locator, which returns the first value of the tags matched by the string. The syntax is shown here:

```
ExtractValue([XML Fragment],[locator string])
```

The following is an example of using the function to extract the value in the node a:

```
SELECT EXTRACTVALUE('<a>Red<///a><b>Blue</b>','/a') as ColorValue;
ColorValue
Red
```

It is important to check your individual database's documentation to see exactly what XML support is provided. Some implementations, such as SQL Server and Oracle, have advanced functionality such as specific XML data types. For example, Oracle's XMLTYPE provides a specific API to handle the most used functions with XML data, such as finding and extracting values. Microsoft SQL Server's XML data type allows for the application of templates to ensure that the XML data input into the column is complete.

Summary

Some advanced SQL concepts were discussed in this hour. Although this hour did not go into a lot of detail, it did provide you with a basic understanding of how you can apply the fundamental concepts that you have learned up to this point. You start with cursors, which pass a data set selected by a query into a location in memory. After a cursor is declared in a program, you must open it for accessibility. Then the contents of the cursor are fetched into a variable, at which time the data can be used for program processing. The resultset for the cursor is contained in memory until the cursor is closed and the memory is deallocated.

Stored procedures and triggers were covered next. Stored procedures are basically SQL statements that are stored together in the database. These statements, along with other implementation-specific commands, are compiled in the database and are ready for a database user to execute at any given time. Stored procedures typically provide better performance benefits than individual SQL statements.

This chapter also discussed dynamic SQL, using SQL to generate other SQL statements, and the differences between direct SQL and embedded SQL. Dynamic SQL is SQL code that a user dynamically creates during runtime, unlike static SQL.

Lastly, we discussed windowed table functions and XML. These features may not yet be supported in your database version because they are relatively new but are good to know for future reference. The concepts of some of the advanced topics discussed during this hour illustrate the application of SQL in an enterprise, covered in Hour 23, "Extending SQL to the Enterprise, the Internet, and the Intranet."

Q&A

Q. Can a stored procedure call another stored procedure?

A. Yes, the stored procedure called is referred to as nested.

Q. How do I execute a cursor?

A. Simply use the OPEN CURSOR statement. This sends the results of the cursor to a staging area.

Workshop

The following workshop is composed of a series of quiz questions and practical exercises. The quiz questions are designed to test your overall understanding of the current material. The practical exercises are intended to afford you the opportunity to apply the concepts discussed during the current hour, as well as build upon the knowledge acquired in previous hours of study. Please take time to complete the quiz questions and exercises before continuing. Refer to Appendix C, "Answers to Quizzes and Exercises," for answers.

Quiz

1. Can a trigger be altered?

2. When a cursor is closed, can you reuse the name?

3. Which command retrieves the results after a cursor has been opened?

4. Are triggers executed before or after an INSERT, DELETE, or UPDATE statement?

5. Which MySQL function retrieves information from an XML fragment?

6. Why does Oracle not support the DEALLOCATE syntax for cursors?

7. Why is a cursor not considered a set-based operation?

Exercises

1. Enter a command similar to the one that follows for SQL Server to write out SQL statements to DESCRIBE each table in the database:

   ```
   SELECT CONCAT('DESCRIBE ',TABLE_NAME,';') FROM INFORMATION_SCHEMA.TABLES;
   ```

2. Write a SELECT statement that generates the SQL code to count all rows in each of your tables. (Hint: It is similar to Exercise 1.)

3. Write a series of SQL commands to create a cursor that prints each airport name and the total number of flights originating from the airport for each month. Ensure that the cursor is properly closed and deallocated based on which implementation you use.

Extending SQL to the Enterprise, the Internet, and the Intranet

---

What You'll Learn in This Hour:

▸ SQL and the enterprise

▸ Front-end and back-end applications

▸ Accessing a remote database

▸ SQL and the Internet

▸ SQL and the intranet

The previous hour covered some advanced SQL topics. These topics build on earlier hours in the book and show you practical applications for the SQL you have learned. In this hour, you focus on the concepts behind extending SQL to the enterprise, which involve SQL applications and making data available to all appropriate members of a company for daily use.

SQL and the Enterprise

Many commercial enterprises have specific data available to other enterprises, customers, and vendors. For example, the enterprise might have detailed information on its products available for customers to access in hopes of acquiring more purchases. Enterprise employee needs are included as well. For example, employee-specific data can be made available, such as for timesheet logs, vacation schedules, training schedules, company policies, and so on. A database can be created, and customers and employees can be allowed easy access to an enterprise's important data via SQL and an Internet language.

The Back-End Application

The heart of any application is the *back-end application*. This is where things happen behind the scenes, transparent to the database end user. The back-end application includes the actual database server, the data sources, and the appropriate middleware that connects an application to the Web or a remote database on the local network.

Determining your database implementation is typically the first step in deploying any application, either to the enterprise through a *local area network (LAN)*, to the enterprise's own intranet, or to the Internet. *Deploying* describes the process of implementing an application in an environment that is available for use. The database server should be established by an onsite database administrator (DBA) who understands the company's needs and the application's requirements.

The middleware for the application includes a web server and a tool capable of connecting the web server to the database server. The main objective is to have an application that can communicate with a corporate database.

The Front-End Application

The *front-end application* is the part of an application with which an end user interacts. The front-end application is either a commercial, off-the-shelf software product that a company purchases or an application that is developed in-house using other third-party tools. Commercial software can include applications that utilize a web browser to display content. In the Web environment, web browsers such as Firefox and Internet Explorer (now called Microsoft Edge in new versions) are often used to access database applications. This allows users to have access to the database without having to install special software.

TIP

There Are Many Different Layers to an Application

The front-end application promotes simplicity for the database end user. The underlying database, code, and events that occur within the database are transparent to the user. The front-end application is developed to relieve the end user from guesswork and confusion, which might otherwise be caused by having to be too intuitive to the system. The new technologies allow the applications to be more intuitive, enabling the end users to focus on the true aspects of their particular jobs, thereby increasing overall productivity.

The tools available for developers today are user-friendly and object-oriented by way of icons, wizards, and dragging and dropping with the mouse. Some of the popular tools to port applications to the Web include Borland's C++Builder and IntraBuilder and Microsoft's Visual Studio. Other popular applications used to develop corporate-based applications on a LAN include PowerBuilder by Powersoft, Oracle Forms by Oracle Corporation, and Delphi by Borland.

Figure 23.1 illustrates the back-end and front-end components of a database application. The back-end resides on the host server, where the database resides. Back-end users include developers, programmers, DBAs, system administrators, and system analysts. The front-end application resides on the client machine, which is typically each end user's PC. End users are the vast audience for the front-end component of an application, which can include users such as data entry clerks and accountants. The end user can access the back-end database through a network connection—either a LAN or a *wide area network (WAN)*. Some type of middleware (such as an ODBC driver) provides a connection between the front-end and back-end through the network.

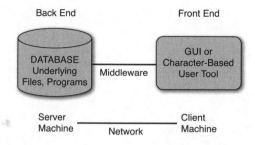

FIGURE 23.1
Back-end and front-end of a database application

Accessing a Remote Database

Sometimes, the database you are accessing is a local one to which you are directly connected. For the most part, you will probably access some form of a remote database. A *remote database* is one that is nonlocal, or located on a server other than the server to which you are currently connected, meaning that you must utilize the network and some network protocol to interface with the database.

You can access a remote database in several ways. From a broad perspective, a remote database is accessed via the network or Internet connection using a middleware product. (Both ODBC and JDBC, standard middleware, are discussed in the next section.) Figure 23.2 shows three scenarios for accessing a remote database.

Figure 23.2 shows access to a remote server from another local database server, a local front-end application, and a local host server. The local database server and local host server are often the same because the database normally resides on a local host server. However, you can usually connect to a remote database from a local server without a current local database connection. For the end user, the front-end application is the most typical method of remote database access. All methods must route their database requests through the network.

ODBC

Open Database Connectivity (ODBC) allows connections to remote databases through a library driver. A front-end application uses an *ODBC driver* to interface with a back-end database. A network driver might also be required for a connection to a remote database. An application calls the ODBC functions, and a driver manager loads the ODBC driver. The ODBC driver processes the call, submits the SQL request, and returns the results from the database.

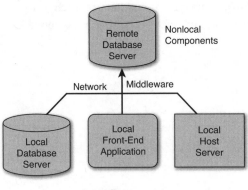

FIGURE 23.2
Scenarios for accessing a remote database

As a part of ODBC, all the relational database management system (RDBMS) vendors have an application programming interface (API) with their database.

JDBC

Like ODBC, *Java Database Connectivity (JDBC)* allows connections to remote databases through a Java library driver. A front-end Java application uses the JDBC driver to interface with a back-end database.

OLE DB

OLE DB is a set of interfaces written using the *Component Object Model (COM)* by Microsoft as a replacement for ODBC. The implementation of OLE DB attempts to extend the feature set of ODBC and address connectivity not only to various database implementations but also to non-database data stored, such as spreadsheets.

Vendor Connectivity Products

In addition to drivers or an API, many vendors have their own products that allow a user to connect to a remote database. Each of these vendor products is specific to the particular vendor implementation and might not be portable to other types of database servers.

Oracle Corporation has a product called Oracle Fusion Middleware that allows connectivity to the Oracle database as well as other applications.

Microsoft produces several products for interacting with its database, such as Microsoft SharePoint Server and SQL Server Reporting Services.

Web Interface

Accessing a remote database through a web interface is similar to accessing one through a local network. The main difference is that all requests to the database from the user are routed through the web server (see Figure 23.3).

FIGURE 23.3
A web interface to a remote database

You can see in Figure 23.3 that an end user accesses a database through a web interface by first invoking a web browser. The web browser connects to a particular URL, determined by the location of the web server. The web server authenticates user access and sends the user request, perhaps a query, to the remote database, which might also verify user authenticity. The database server then returns the results to the web server, which displays the results on the user's web browser. Using a firewall can control unauthorized access to a particular server.

A *firewall* is a security mechanism that ensures against unauthorized connections to and from a server. One or multiple firewalls can be enabled to patrol access to a database or server.

In addition, certain database implementations allow you to restrict access to them via an IP address. This provides another layer of protection because you can limit your traffic that has access to the database to the actual set of web servers that are acting as the application layer.

CAUTION

Be Mindful of Security Concerns with the Internet

Be careful what information you make available on the Web. Always take precautions to properly implement security at all appropriate levels; that might include the web server, the host server, and the remote database. Be especially careful with Privacy Act data, such as individuals' Social Security numbers; protect that data, and don't broadcast it over the Web.

SQL and the Internet

You can embed SQL or use it with programming languages such as C# and Java. You can also embed SQL in Internet programming languages, such as Java and ASP.NET. Text from *Hypertext Markup Language (HTML)*, another Internet language, can be translated into SQL to send a query to a remote database from a Web front-end. After the database resolves the query, the output is translated back into HTML and displayed on the web browser of the individual executing the query. The following sections discuss the use of SQL on the Internet.

Making Data Available to Customers Worldwide

With the advent of the Internet, data became available to customers and vendors worldwide. The data is normally available for read-only access through a front-end tool.

The data that is available to customers can contain general customer information, product information, invoice information, current orders, back orders, and other pertinent information. Private information, such as corporate strategies and employee information, should not be available.

Home web pages on the Internet have become nearly a necessity for companies that want to keep pace with their competition. A web page is a powerful tool that can tell viewers all about a company—its services, products, and other information—with little overhead.

Making Data Available to Employees and Privileged Customers

A database can be made accessible through the Internet or a company's intranet to employees or customers. Using Internet technologies is a valuable communication asset for keeping employees informed about company policies, benefits, training, and so on. However, you must be careful when making information available to Web users. Confidential corporate or individual information should not be accessible on the Web if possible. In addition, only a subset, or copy of a subset of a database, should be accessible online. The main production database(s) should be protected at all costs.

Internet Security Is a Far Less Stable Platform

Database security is much more stable than security on the Internet because database security can be fine-tuned down to the specific levels of the data contained in the system. Although you can implement some security features for data access through the Internet, these are generally limited and not as easily changed as those on the database. Always be sure to use the security features available to you through your database server.

SQL and the Intranet

IBM originally created SQL for use between databases located on mainframe computers and the users on client machines. The users were connected to the mainframes via a LAN. SQL was adopted as the standard language of communication between databases and users. An *intranet* is basically a small Internet. The main difference is that an intranet is for a single organization's use, whereas the Internet is accessible to the general public. The user (client) interface in an intranet remains the same as that in a client/server environment. SQL requests are routed through the web server and languages (such as HTML) before being directed to the database for evaluation. An intranet is primarily used for inner-corporate applications, documents, forms, web pages, and email.

SQL requests made through the Internet must be extremely cognizant of performance. In these scenarios, not only must the data be retrieved from the database, but it also must be presented to the user through her browser. This normally involves transforming the data into some kind of HTML-compliant code to be displayed on the user's browser. The web connection might be slower than a normal intranet connection; therefore, the sending of the data back and forth might be slower as well.

Security should play an important role in a database implementation that is exposed via the Web. A couple considerations must be taken into account to ensure that your data is protected. First, if the data is exposed over public networks, you must try to ensure that the data is protected from outside sources that may try to pick up that traffic. Normally, data is transferred in plain text format so that anyone can read it. You might consider as part of your security implementation using a *Secure Socket Layer (SSL)* to protect the communication. This method uses a certificate to encrypt the data between the client and the application and is typically identified by a website beginning with HTTPS, with the *S* on the end standing for secure.

Another typical consideration is protecting against unintended data entry through data validation. This can be simply from the user or application entering the wrong type of data into the wrong field or something more nefarious such as a SQL injection attack, where a hacker tries to inject his own SQL code onto the database to be run.

The best way to protect against these types of problems is to restrict access for the user accounts accessing the database from the application. A good way to accomplish this is to use stored procedures and functions whenever possible for the calls against the database. This gives you more control over how the data gets out of the system and how the data gets in. In addition, it allows you to perform whatever data validation steps may be necessary from the DBA's point of view to ensure that the data remains consistent.

Summary

Some concepts behind deploying SQL and database applications to the Internet were discussed in this hour. Companies need to remain competitive. To keep up with the rest of the world, it is almost mandatory to obtain a presence on the World Wide Web. In establishing this presence, applications must be developed and even migrated from client/server systems to the Internet on a web server. One of the greatest concerns when publishing any kind or any amount of corporate data on the Web is security. Security must be considered, adhered to, and strictly enforced.

This hour discussed accessing remote databases across local networks as well as over the Internet. Each major method for accessing any type of a remote database requires the use of network and protocol adapters used to translate requests to the database. This has been a broad overview of the application of SQL over local networks, company intranets, and the Internet.

Q&A

Q. Why is it important to know if your data is accessed over a public network via the Internet?

A. The data that is sent between a client and a web application is often just plain text. That means that anyone could intercept the traffic and see exactly what the individual saw, such as sensitive data like Social Security numbers or account numbers. You need to encrypt data whenever possible.

Q. Is a back-end database for a web application any different from a back-end database for a client/server system?

A. The back-end database itself for a web application is not necessarily different from that of a client/server system. However, other requirements must be met to implement a web-based application. For example, a web server accesses the database with a web application. With a web application, end users do not typically connect directly to the database.

Workshop

The following workshop is composed of a series of quiz questions and practical exercises. The quiz questions are designed to test your overall understanding of the current material. The practical exercises are intended to afford you the opportunity to apply the concepts discussed during the current hour, as well as build upon the knowledge acquired in previous hours of study. Please take time to complete the quiz questions and exercises before continuing. Refer to Appendix C, "Answers to Quizzes and Exercises," for answers.

Quiz

1. Can a database on a server be accessed from another server?

2. What can a company use to disseminate information to its own employees?

3. What are products that allow connections to databases called?

4. Can SQL be embedded into Internet programming languages?

5. How is a remote database accessed through a web application?

Exercises

1. Connect to the Internet and look at various companies' home pages. If your own company has a home page, compare it to the competition's home pages. Ask yourself these questions about the pages:

   ▶ Does any of the page content appear to be dynamic?

   ▶ What pages or areas on pages might be data from a back-end database?

   ▶ Do there appear to be security mechanisms on the web page? Can a login be entered to access data that might be stored in a database?

   ▶ Most modern browsers enable you to view the source code of the page returned. Use your web browser to view the source code. Is there any code that would give you a hint as to what the back-end database is?

   ▶ If you uncovered any information in the page's code, such as a server name or a database username, would you consider this a security flaw?

2. Visit the following websites and browse through the content, latest technologies, and companies' use of data on the Web (data that appears to be derived from a database):

   ▶ www.amazon.com

   ▶ www.informit.com

   ▶ www.mysql.com

   ▶ www.oracle.com

   ▶ www.ebay.com

   ▶ www.google.com

Extensions to Standard SQL

What You'll Learn in This Hour:

▶ Various implementations

▶ Differences between implementations

▶ Compliance with ANSI SQL

▶ Interactive SQL statements

▶ Using variables

▶ Using parameters

This hour covers extensions to American National Standards Institute (ANSI)-standard SQL. Although most implementations conform to the standard, many vendors have provided extensions to standard SQL through various enhancements.

Various Implementations

Numerous SQL implementations are released by various vendors. All the relational database vendors could not possibly be mentioned; a few of the leading implementations, however, are discussed. The implementations discussed here are MySQL, Microsoft SQL Server, and Oracle. Other popular vendors providing database products include Sybase, IBM, Informix, Progress, PostgreSQL, and many more.

Differences Between Implementations

Although the implementations discussed in this hour are relational database products, there are specific differences between each. These differences stem from the design of the product and the way data is handled by the database engine; however, this book concentrates on the SQL aspect of the differences. All implementations use SQL as the language for communicating with the database, as directed by ANSI. Many have some sort of extension to SQL that is unique to that particular implementation.

TIP

Vendors Purposely Break with the ANSI Standard

Differences in SQL have been adopted by various vendors to enhance ANSI SQL for performance considerations and ease of use. Vendors also strive to make enhancements that provide them with advantages over other vendors, making their implementation more attractive to the customer.

Now that you know SQL, you should have little problem adjusting to the differences in SQL among the various vendors. In other words, if you can write SQL in a Sybase implementation, you should be able to write SQL in Oracle. Besides, knowing SQL for various vendors improves your résumé.

The following sections compare the SELECT statement's syntax from a few major vendors to the ANSI standard.

Following is the ANSI standard:

```
SELECT [DISTINCT ] [* | COLUMN1 [, COLUMN2 ]
FROM TABLE1 [, TABLE2 ]
[ WHERE SEARCH_ CONDITION ]
GROUP BY [ TABLE_ALIAS | COLUMN1 [, COLUMN2 ]
[ HAVING SEARCH_CONDITION ]]
[ ALL ]
[ CORRESPONDING [ BY (COLUMN1 [, COLUMN2 ]) ]
QUERY_SPEC | SELECT * FROM TABLE | TABLE_CONSTRUCTOR ]
[ORDER BY SORT_LIST ]
```

Following is the syntax for Microsoft SQL Server:

```
[WITH <COMMON_TABLE_EXPRESSION>]
SELECT [DISTINCT][*| COLUMN1 [, COLUMN2, .. ]
[INTO NEW_TABLE]
FROM TABLE1 [, TABLE2 ]
[WHERE SEARCH_CONDITION]
GROUP BY [COLUMN1, COLUMN2,... ]
[HAVING SEARCH_CONDITION]
[ {UNION | INTERSECT | EXCEPT} ][ ALL ]
[ ORDER BY SORT_LIST ]
[ OPTION QUERY_HINT ]
```

Following is the syntax for Oracle:

```
SELECT [ ALL | DISTINCT ] COLUMN1 [, COLUMN2 ]
FROM TABLE1 [, TABLE2 ]
[ WHERE SEARCH_CONDITION ]
[[ START WITH SEARCH_CONDITION ]
```

```
CONNECT BY SEARCH_CONDITION ]
[ GROUP BY COLUMN1 [, COLUMN2 ]
[ HAVING SEARCH_CONDITION ]]
[{UNION [ ALL ] | INTERSECT | MINUS} QUERY_SPEC ]
[ ORDER BY COLUMN1 [, COLUMN2 ]]
[ NOWAIT ]
```

As you can see by comparing the syntax examples, the basics are there. All have the SELECT, FROM, WHERE, GROUP BY, HAVING, UNION, and ORDER BY clauses. Each of these clauses works the same conceptually, but some have additional options that might not be found in other implementations. These options are called *enhancements*.

Compliance with ANSI SQL

Vendors do strive to comply with ANSI SQL; however, none is 100% ANSI SQL-standard. Some vendors have added commands or functions to ANSI SQL, and ANSI SQL has adopted many of these new commands or functions. It is beneficial for a vendor to comply with the standard for many reasons. One obvious benefit to standard compliance is that the vendor's implementation will be easy to learn, and the SQL code used is portable to other implementations. Portability is definitely a factor when a database is migrated from one implementation to another.

For a database to be considered ANSI-compliant, however, it needs to correspond only to a small subset of the functionality of the ANSI standard. The ANSI standard is written by a coalition of database companies. Therefore, most implementations are considered ANSI-compliant even though their SQL implementations might vary widely between one another. Limiting your code to only strict ANSI-compliant statements would improve portability but would most likely severely limit database performance. So, in the end, you need to balance the demands of portability with the performance needs of your users. It is often best to forgo a lot of portability to ensure that your applications are taking advantage of the specific platform you are using to its full extent.

Extensions to SQL

Practically all the major vendors have an extension to SQL. A SQL extension is unique to a particular implementation and is generally not portable between implementations. However, popular standard extensions are reviewed by ANSI and are sometimes implemented as part of the new standard.

PL/SQL, which is a product of Oracle Corporation, and Transact-SQL, which is used by both Sybase and Microsoft SQL Server, are two examples of robust SQL extensions. Both extensions are discussed in relative detail for the examples during this hour.

Example Extensions

Both PL/SQL and Transact-SQL are considered fourth-generation programming languages. Both are procedural languages, whereas SQL is a nonprocedural language. We also briefly discuss MySQL.

The nonprocedural language SQL includes the following statements:

- INSERT

- UPDATE

- DELETE

- SELECT

- COMMIT

- ROLLBACK

A SQL extension considered a procedural language includes all the preceding statements, commands, and functions of standard SQL. In addition, extensions include statements such as

- Variable declarations

- Cursor declarations

- Conditional statements

- Loops

- Error handling

- Variable assignment

- Date conversions

- Wildcard operators

- Triggers

- Stored procedures

These statements allow the programmer to have more control over the way data is handled in a procedural language.

Transact-SQL

Transact-SQL is a procedural language used by Microsoft SQL Server, which means you tell the database how and where to find and manipulate data. SQL is nonprocedural, and the database decides how and where to select and manipulate data. Some highlights of Transact-SQL's capabilities include declaring local and global variables, cursors, error handling, triggers, stored procedures, loops, wildcard operators, date conversions, and summarized reports.

An example Transact-SQL statement follows:

```
IF (SELECT AVG(PAYRATE) FROM EMPLOYEES) > 20
BEGIN
  PRINT 'LOWER ALL PAY BY 10 PERCENT.'
END
ELSE
  PRINT 'PAY IS REASONABLE.'
```

This is a simple Transact-SQL statement. It states that if the average hourly pay rate in EMPLOYEES is greater than 20, the text LOWER ALL PAY BY 10 PERCENT. will be printed. If the average cost is less than or equal to 20, the text PAY IS REASONABLE. will be printed.

Notice the use of the IF...ELSE statement to evaluate conditions of data values. The PRINT command is also a new command. These additional options are a very small sampling of Transact-SQL capabilities.

TIP

SQL Is Not Considered a Procedural Language

Standard SQL is primarily a *nonprocedural language*, which means that you issue statements to the database server. The database server decides how to optimally execute the statement. *Procedural languages* allow the programmer to request the data to be retrieved or manipulated and to tell the database server exactly how to carry out the request.

PL/SQL

PL/SQL is Oracle's extension to SQL. Like Transact-SQL, PL/SQL is a procedural language. PL/SQL is structured in logical blocks of code. A PL/SQL block contains three sections, two of which are optional. The first section is the DECLARE section, which is optional. The DECLARE section contains variables, cursors, and constants. The second section is called the PROCEDURE section and is mandatory. The PROCEDURE section contains the conditional commands and SQL statements. This section is where the block is controlled. The third section is called the EXCEPTION section, and it is optional. The EXCEPTION section defines the way the program should handle errors and user-defined exceptions. Highlights of PL/SQL include the use of variables, constants, cursors, attributes, loops, handling exceptions, displaying output to the programmer, transactional control, stored procedures, triggers, and packages.

An example PL/SQL statement follows:

```
DECLARE
  CURSOR EMP_CURSOR IS SELECT EMPLOYEEID, LASTNAME, FIRSTNAME
                       FROM EMPLOYEES;
  EMP_REC EMP_CURSOR%ROWTYPE;
BEGIN
  OPEN EMP_CURSOR;
  LOOP
    FETCH EMP_CURSOR INTO EMP_REC;
    EXIT WHEN EMP_CURSOR%NOTFOUND;
    IF (EMP_REC.MIDDLENAME IS NULL) THEN
      UPDATE EMPLOYEES
      SET MIDDLENAME = 'X'
      WHERE EMPLOYEEID = EMP_REC.EMPLOYEEID;
      COMMIT;
    END IF;
  END LOOP;
  CLOSE EMP_CURSOR;
END;
```

Two out of the three sections are used in this example: the DECLARE section and the PROCEDURE section. First, a cursor called EMP_CURSOR is defined by a query. Second, a variable called EMP_REC is declared, whose values have the same data type (%ROWTYPE) as each column in the defined cursor. The first step in the PROCEDURE section (after BEGIN) is to open the cursor. After the cursor is opened, you use the LOOP command to scroll through each record of the cursor, which is eventually terminated by END LOOP. Update EMPLOYEES for all rows in the cursor. If the middle initial of an employee is NULL, the update sets the middle initial to 'X'. Changes are committed, and the cursor is eventually closed.

MySQL

MySQL is a multiuser, multithreaded SQL database client/server implementation. It consists of a server daemon, a terminal monitor client program, and several client programs and libraries. The main goals of MySQL are speed, robustness, and ease of use. MySQL was originally designed to provide faster access to large databases.

MySQL is often considered one of the more ANSI-compliant database implementations. From its beginnings, MySQL has been part of a semi-open-source development environment that has deliberately tried to maintain close adherence to the ANSI standards. Since version 5.0, MySQL has been available in both the open-source Community Edition as well as the closed-source Enterprise Edition. In 2009, MySQL was acquired as part of a deal in which Oracle bought Sun Microsystems, which was the original owner of the platform.

Currently, MySQL does not contain major extensions like Oracle or Microsoft SQL Server, but with its recent acquisition, this might change in the near future. To be certain, check your version's documentation for specific extensions that may become available.

Interactive SQL Statements

Interactive SQL statements ask you for a variable, parameter, or some form of data before fully executing. Say you have a SQL statement that is interactive. The statement is used to create users in a database. The SQL statement could prompt you for information such as user ID, name of user, and phone number. The statement could be for one or many users and is executed only once. Otherwise, each user has to be entered individually with the CREATE USER statement. The SQL statement could also prompt you for privileges. Not all vendors have interactive SQL statements; you must check your particular implementation.

Another interesting aspect of using interactive SQL statements is the ability to employ *parameters*. Parameters are variables that are written in SQL and reside within an application. Parameters can be passed into a SQL statement during runtime, allowing more flexibility for the user executing the statement. Many of the major implementations allow use of these parameters. Following are examples of passing parameters for Oracle and SQL Server.

Parameters in Oracle can be passed into an otherwise static SQL statement, as the following code shows:

```
SELECT EMPLOYEEID, LASTNAME, FIRSTNAME
FROM EMPLOYEES
WHERE EMPLOYEEID = '&EMP_ID'
```

The preceding SQL statement returns the EMPLOYEEID, LASTNAME, and FIRSTNAME for whatever EMP_ID you enter at the prompt.

The next statement prompts you for the city and the state. The query returns all data for those employees living in the city and state that you entered.

```
SELECT *
FROM EMPLOYEES
WHERE CITY = '&CITY'
AND STATE = '&STATE'
```

Parameters in Microsoft SQL Server can also be passed into a stored procedure:

```
CREATE PROC EMP_SEARCH
(@EMP_ID)
AS
SELECT LASTNAME, FIRSTNAME
FROM EMPLOYEES
WHERE EMPLOYEEID = @EMP_ID
```

Type the following to execute the stored procedure and pass a parameter:

```
SP_EMP_SEARCH '5593'
```

Summary

This hour discussed extensions to standard SQL among vendors' implementations and their compliance with the ANSI standard. After you learn SQL, you can easily apply your knowledge—and your code—to other implementations of SQL. SQL is portable between vendors; implementations can use most SQL code with a few minor modifications.

The last part of this hour was spent showing two specific extensions used by three implementations. Microsoft SQL Server and Sybase use Transact-SQL, and Oracle uses PL/SQL. You should have seen some similarities between Transact-SQL and PL/SQL. One thing to note is that these two implementations have first sought their compliance with the standard and then added enhancements to their implementations for better overall functionality and efficiency. Also discussed was MySQL, which was designed to increase performance for large database queries. This hour's intent was to make you aware that many SQL extensions do exist and to teach the importance of a vendor's compliance to the ANSI SQL standard.

If you take what you have learned in this book and apply it (build your code, test it, and build upon your knowledge), you are well on your way to mastering SQL. Companies have data and cannot function without databases. Relational databases are everywhere, and because SQL is the standard language with which to communicate and administer a relational database, you have made an excellent decision by learning SQL. Good luck!

Q&A

Q. Why do variations in SQL exist?

A. Variations in SQL exist among the various implementations because of the way data is stored, because of the various vendors' ambition for trying to get an advantage over competition, and because of new ideas that surface.

Q. After learning basic SQL, can I use SQL in different implementations?

A. Yes. However, remember that there are differences and variations between the implementations. The basic framework for SQL is the same among most implementations.

Workshop

The following workshop is composed of a series of quiz questions and practical exercises. The quiz questions are designed to test your overall understanding of the current material. The practical exercises are intended to afford you the opportunity to apply the concepts discussed during the current hour, as well as build upon the knowledge acquired in previous hours of study. Please take time to complete the quiz questions and exercises before continuing. Refer to Appendix C, "Answers to Quizzes and Exercises," for answers.

Quiz

1. Is SQL a procedural or nonprocedural language?

2. What are the three basic operations of a cursor outside of declaring the cursor?

3. Procedural or nonprocedural: With which does the database engine decide how to evaluate and execute SQL statements?

Exercises

1. Research the SQL variations among the various vendors. Go to the following websites and review the implementations of SQL that are available:

   ▶ www.oracle.com

   ▶ www.sybase.com

   ▶ www.microsoft.com

   ▶ www.mysql.com

   ▶ www.informix.com

   ▶ www.pgsql.com

   ▶ www.ibm.com

Common SQL Commands

This appendix details some of the most common SQL commands that you will use. As we have stated throughout the book, check your database documentation because some of the statements vary depending upon your implementation.

SQL Statements

ALTER TABLE

```
ALTER TABLE TABLE_NAME
[MODIFY | ADD | DROP]
  [COLUMN COLUMN_NAME] [DATATYPE|NULL NOT NULL] [RESTRICT|CASCADE]
[ADD | DROP]  CONSTRAINT CONSTRAINT_NAME]
```

Description: Alters a table's columns

COMMIT

```
COMMIT [ TRANSACTION ]
```

Description: Saves a transaction to the database

CREATE INDEX

```
CREATE INDEX INDEX_NAME
ON TABLE_NAME (COLUMN_NAME)
```

Description: Creates an index on a table

CREATE ROLE

```
CREATE ROLE ROLE_NAME
[ WITH ADMIN [CURRENT_USER | CURRENT_ROLE]]
```

Description: Creates a database role to which system and object privileges can be granted

CREATE TABLE

```
CREATE TABLE TABLE_NAME
( COLUMN1      DATA_TYPE      [NULL|NOT NULL],
  COLUMN2      DATA_TYPE      [NULL|NOT NULL])
```

Description: Creates a database table

CREATE TABLE AS

```
CREATE TABLE TABLE_NAME AS
SELECT COLUMN1, COLUMN2,...
FROM TABLE_NAME
[ WHERE CONDITIONS ]
[ GROUP BY COLUMN1, COLUMN2,...]
[ HAVING CONDITIONS ]
```

Description: Creates a database table based on another table

CREATE TYPE

```
CREATE TYPE typename AS OBJECT
( COLUMN1      DATA_TYPE      [NULL|NOT NULL],
  COLUMN2      DATA_TYPE      [NULL|NOT NULL])
```

Description: Creates a user-defined type that can define columns in a table

CREATE USER

```
CREATE USER username IDENTIFIED BY password
```

Description: Creates a user account in the database

CREATE VIEW

```
CREATE VIEW AS
SELECT COLUMN1, COLUMN2,...
FROM TABLE_NAME
[ WHERE CONDITIONS ]
[ GROUP BY COLUMN1, COLUMN2,... ]
[ HAVING CONDITIONS ]
```

Description: Creates a view of a table

DELETE

```
DELETE
FROM TABLE_NAME
[ WHERE CONDITIONS ]
```

Description: Deletes rows of data from a table

DROP INDEX

```
DROP INDEX INDEX_NAME
```

Description: Drops an index on a table

DROP TABLE

```
DROP TABLE TABLE_NAME
```

Description: Drops a table from the database

DROP USER

```
DROP USER user1 [, user2, ...]
```

Description: Drops a user account from the database

DROP VIEW

```
DROP VIEW VIEW_NAME
```

Description: Drops a view of a table

GRANT

```
GRANT PRIVILEGE1, PRIVILEGE2, ... TO USER_NAME
```

Description: Grants privileges to a user

INSERT

```
INSERT INTO TABLE_NAME [ (COLUMN1, COLUMN2,...]
VALUES ('VALUE1','VALUE2',...)
```

Description: Inserts new rows of data into a table

INSERT...SELECT

```
INSERT INTO TABLE_NAME
SELECT COLUMN1, COLUMN2
FROM TABLE_NAME
[ WHERE CONDITIONS ]
```

Description: Inserts new rows of data into a table based on data in another table

REVOKE

```
REVOKE PRIVILEGE1, PRIVILEGE2, ... FROM USER_NAME
```

Description: Revokes privileges from a user

ROLLBACK

```
ROLLBACK [ TO SAVEPOINT_NAME ]
```

Description: Undoes a database transaction

SAVEPOINT

```
SAVEPOINT SAVEPOINT_NAME
```

Description: Creates transaction savepoints in which to roll back if necessary

SELECT

```
SELECT [ DISTINCT ] COLUMN1, COLUMN2,...
FROM TABLE1, TABLE2,...
[ WHERE CONDITIONS ]
[ GROUP BY COLUMN1, COLUMN2,...]
[ HAVING CONDITIONS ]
[ ORDER BY COLUMN1, COLUMN2,...]
```

Description: Returns data from one or more database tables; used to create queries

UPDATE

```
UPDATE TABLE_NAME
SET COLUMN1 = 'VALUE1',
    COLUMN2 = 'VALUE2',...
[ WHERE CONDITIONS ]
```

Description: Updates existing data in a table

SQL Clauses

SELECT

```
SELECT *
SELECT COLUMN1, COLUMN2,...
SELECT DISTINCT (COLUMN1)
SELECT COUNT(*)
```

Description: Defines columns to display as part of query output

FROM

```
FROM TABLE1, TABLE2, TABLE3,...
```

Description: Defines tables from which to retrieve data

WHERE

```
WHERE COLUMN1 = 'VALUE1'
  AND COLUMN2 = 'VALUE2'
. . .
WHERE COLUMN1 = 'VALUE1'
   OR COLUMN2 = 'VALUE2'
. . .
WHERE COLUMN IN ('VALUE1' [, 'VALUE2'] )
```

Description: Defines conditions (criteria) placed on a query for data to be returned

GROUP BY

```
GROUP BY GROUP_COLUMN1, GROUP_COLUMN2,...
```

Description: Divides output into logical groups; a form of sorting operation

HAVING

```
HAVING GROUP_COLUMN1 = 'VALUE1'
   AND GROUP_COLUMN2 = 'VALUE2'
. . .
```

Description: Places conditions on the GROUP BY clause; similar to the WHERE clause

ORDER BY

```
ORDER BY COLUMN1, COLUMN2,...
ORDER BY 1,2,...
```

Description: Sorts a query's results

APPENDIX B
Installing Oracle and Microsoft SQL

The instructions for installing Microsoft SQL Server and Oracle for the Windows operating system have been included in this appendix for your convenience. Oracle is available on other operating systems as well, such as Mac OS and Linux. These instructions are accurate as of the date this book was written. Neither the authors nor Sams Publishing place any warranties on the software or the software support. For any installation problems or to inquire about software support, refer to the particular implementation's documentation or contact customer support for the implementation.

Windows Installation Instructions for Oracle

Use the following instructions to install Oracle on a computer with Microsoft Windows:

1. Go to www.oracle.com and download the appropriate installation package for your machine from the Downloads tab. Use the Oracle 10g Express Edition for the examples in this book because this is the free version of the application.

2. Double-click the installation file to start the installation, and on the first screen, click Next.

3. Click to agree to the license agreement, and click Next.

4. Select the default installation and install location on the screen, as shown in Figure B.1, and click Next.

5. Enter and confirm a password for the SYSTEM (administrator) account, as shown in Figure B.2, and select Next.

6. Click Install on the next screen. The installation process begins.

If your installation is successful, you should see the completion screen shown in Figure B.3.

FIGURE B.1
Oracle installation location

FIGURE B.2
Setting the system password

FIGURE B.3
Oracle installation completion screen

If all the preceding steps were successful, you are ready to use Oracle for exercises in this book.

If you experience problems during the installation, uninstall Oracle and repeat steps 1–6. If you are still unable to obtain or install Oracle, contact Oracle for support, and check the community support forums located on www.oracle.com.

BY THE WAY

Oracle Install Instructions

You might also want to review the current documentation for Oracle for installation instructions. To access the online documentation, go to www.oracle.com and look under Products and Services for the link to the documentation.

Windows Installation Instructions for Microsoft SQL Server

Use the following instructions to install Microsoft SQL Server on a computer with Microsoft Windows:

1. Go to www.microsoft.com/en-us/server-cloud/products/sql-server-editions/sql-server-express. aspx, click the Download button, and choose the appropriate installation package to download for your machine.

2. Double-click the installation file. You should see the initial screen, as shown in Figure B.4.

FIGURE B.4
SQL Server initial installation screen

3. Select the new installation option from the choices in the right pane, as shown in Figure B.5. This begins the installation of some setup and support files that are used during the main installation.

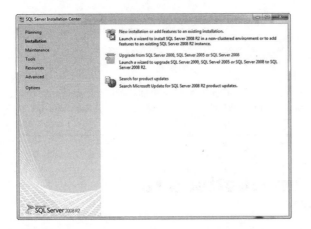

FIGURE B.5
SQL Server installation selection screen

4. Leave the radio button selected for a new installation and click Next.

5. Accept the license terms and click Next.

6. Select all the features and click Next.

7. Select Default instance and click Next.

8. Click Next on the disk space requirements screen.

9. On the Database Engine Configuration screen, click the Add Current User button to add yourself as an administrator of the instance, and then click Next.

10. Click Next on the Error Reporting screen.

11. Click Next on the Installation Configuration Rules page to begin the installation.

If all the preceding steps were successful, you should see a completion screen. You will be ready to use Microsoft SQL Server for exercises in this book.

If you experience problems during the installation, uninstall SQL Server and repeat steps 1–11. If you are still unable to obtain or install Microsoft SQL Server, refer to the Microsoft website at www.microsoft.com.

NOTE

Microsoft SQL Server Install Instructions

You might also want to review the current documentation for Microsoft SQL Server for installation instructions. To get to the online documentation, go to www.microsoft.com/en-us/server-cloud/products/sql-server-editions/sql-server-express.aspx, and look under the Product Information tab for the link to the documentation.

Answers to Quizzes and Exercises

Hour 1, "Welcome to the World of SQL"

Quiz Answers

1. What does the acronym SQL stand for?

    A. SQL stands for Structured Query Language.

2. What are the six main categories of SQL commands?

    A. Data Definition Language (DDL)

       Data Manipulation Language (DML)

       Data Query Language (DQL)

       Data Control Language (DCL)

       Data administration commands (DAC)

       Transactional control commands (TCC)

3. What are the four transactional control commands?

    A. `COMMIT`
       `ROLLBACK`
       `SAVEPOINT`
       `SET TRANSACTIONS`

4. What is the main difference between client/server and web technologies as they relate to database access?

    A. The connection to the database is the main difference. Using the client to connect means you log on to the server directly to access the database. When using the Web, you log on to the Internet to reach the database.

5. If a field is defined as `NULL`, does something have to be entered into that field?

    A. No. If a column is defined as `NULL`, nothing has to be in the column. If a column is defined as `NOT NULL`, something *does* have to be entered.

Exercise Answers

1. Identify the categories in which the following SQL commands fall:

```
CREATE TABLE
DELETE
SELECT
INSERT
ALTER TABLE
UPDATE
```

A. CREATE TABLE—DDL, Data Definition Language

DELETE—DML, Data Manipulation Language

SELECT—DQL, Data Query Language

INSERT—DML, Data Manipulation Language

ALTER TABLE—DDL, Data Definition Language

UPDATE—DML, Data Manipulation Language

2. Study the following tables, and pick out the column that would be a good candidate for the primary key.

EMPLOYEE_TBL	INVENTORY_TBL	EQUIPMENT_TBL
Name	Item	Model
Phone	Description	Year
Start date	Quantity	Serial number
Address	Item number	Equipment number
Employee number	Location assigned to	

A. The primary key for EMPLOYEE_TBL is the employee number. Each employee is assigned a unique employee number. Employees could have the same name, phone, start date, and address.

The primary key for INVENTORY_TBL is the item number. The other columns could be duplicated.

The primary key for EQUIPMENT_TBL is the equipment number. Again, the other columns could be duplicated.

3. No answer required.

Hour 2, "Defining Data Structures"

Quiz Answers

1. True or false: An individual's Social Security number, entered in the format '111111111', can be any of the following data types: constant length character, varying length character, or numeric.

A. True, as long as the precision is the correct length.

2. True or false: The scale of a numeric value is the total length allowed for values.

A. False. The precision is the total length, where the scale represents the number of places reserved to the right of a decimal point.

3. Do all implementations use the same data types?

A. No. Most implementations differ in their use of data types. The data types prescribed by ANSI are adhered to but might differ among implementations according to storage precautions taken by each vendor.

4. What are the precision and scale of the following?
```
DECIMAL(4,2)
DECIMAL(10,2)
DECIMAL(14,1)
```

A. DECIMAL(4,2)—Precision = 4, scale = 2
DECIMAL(10,2)—Precision = 10, scale = 2
DECIMAL(14,1)—Precision = 14, scale = 1

5. Which numbers could be inserted into a column whose data type is DECIMAL(4,1)?

a. 16.2

b. 116.2

c. 16.21

d. 1116.2

e. 1116.21

A. The first three fit; although, 16.21 is rounded off to 16.2. The numbers 1116.2 and 1116.21 exceed the maximum precision, which was set at 4.

6. What is data?

A. Data is a collection of information stored in a database as one of several different data types.

Exercise Answers

1. Take the following column titles, assign them to a data type, decide on the proper length, and give an example of the data you would enter into that column:

   A. `ssn`—Constant-length character; `'111111111'`

   `state`—Varying-length character; `'INDIANA'`

   `city`—Varying-length character; `'INDIANAPOLIS'`

   `phone_number`—Constant-length character; `'(555)555-5555'`

   `zip`—Constant-length character; `'46113'`

   `last_name`—Varying-length character; `'JONES'`

   `first_name`—Varying-length character; `'JACQUELINE'`

   `middle_name`—Varying-length character; `'OLIVIA'`

   `salary`—Numeric data type; `30000`

   `hourly_pay_rate`—Decimal; `35.00`

   `date_hired`—Date; `'01/01/2007'`

2. Take the same column titles and decide if they should be NULL or NOT NULL, realizing that in some cases in which a column would normally be NOT NULL, the column could be NULL or vice versa, depending on the application:

   A. `ssn`—NOT NULL

   `state`—NOT NULL

   `city`—NOT NULL

   `phone_number`—NULL

   `zip`—NOT NULL

   `last_name`—NOT NULL

   `first_name`—NOT NULL

   `middle_name`—NULL

   `salary`—NULL

   `hourly_pay_rate`—NULL

   `date_hired`—NOT NULL

   Some individuals might not have a phone (however rare that might be), and not everyone has a middle name, so these columns should allow NULL values. In addition, not all employees are paid an hourly rate.

3. No answer required.

Hour 3, "Managing Database Objects"

Quiz Answers

1. Does the following CREATE TABLE statement work? If not, what needs to be done to correct the problem(s)? Are there limitations as to what database implementation it works in (MySQL, Oracle, or SQL Server)?

```
CREATE TABLE EMPLOYEE_TABLE AS:
( SSN             NUMBER(9)        NOT NULL,
LAST_NAME         VARCHAR2(20)     NOT NULL,
FIRST_NAME        VARCHAR(20)      NOT NULL,
MIDDLE_NAME       VARCHAR2(20)     NOT NULL,
ST ADDRESS        VARCHAR2(20)     NOT NULL,
CITY              CHAR(20)         NOT NULL,
STATE             CHAR(2)          NOT NULL,
ZIP               NUMBER(4)        NOT NULL,
DATE HIRED        DATE);
```

A. The CREATE TABLE statement does not work because there are several errors in the syntax. The corrected statement follows and is given as an Oracle-specific version. A listing of what was incorrect follows a corrected statement.

```
CREATE TABLE EMPLOYEE_TABLE
( SSN             NUMBER()         NOT NULL,
LAST_NAME         VARCHAR2(20)     NOT NULL,
FIRST_NAME        VARCHAR2(20)     NOT NULL,
MIDDLE_NAME       VARCHAR2(20),
ST_ADDRESS        VARCHAR2(30)     NOT NULL,
CITY              VARCHAR2(20)     NOT NULL,
STATE             CHAR(2)          NOT NULL,
ZIP               NUMBER(5)        NOT NULL,
DATE_HIRED        DATE );
```

The following needs to be done:

1. The AS: should not be in this CREATE TABLE statement.

2. A comma is missing after the NOT NULL for the LAST_NAME column.

3. The MIDDLE_NAME column should be NULL because not everyone has a middle name.

4. The column ST ADDRESS should be ST_ADDRESS. With two words, the database looked at ST as being the column name, which would make the database look for a valid data type, where it would find the word ADDRESS.

5. The CITY column works; although, it would be better to use the VARCHAR2 data type. If all city names were a constant length, CHAR would be okay.

6. The STATE column is missing a left parenthesis.

7. The ZIP column length should be (5), not (4).

8. The DATE HIRED column should be DATE_HIRED with an underscore to make the column name one continuous string.

2. Can you drop a column from a table?

   A. Yes. However, even though it is an ANSI standard, you must check your particular implementation to see if it has been accepted.

3. What statement would you issue to create a primary key constraint on the preceding EMPLOYEE_TABLE?

   A. ALTER TABLE EMPLOYEE_TBL
      ADD CONSTRAINT EMPLOYEE_PK PRIMARY KEY(SSN);

4. What statement would you issue on the preceding EMPLOYEE_TABLE to allow the MIDDLE_NAME column to accept NULL values?

   A. ALTER TABLE EMPOYEE_TBL
      MODIFY MIDDLE_NAME VARCHAR(20), NOT NULL;

5. What statement would you use to restrict the people added into the preceding EMPLOYEE_TABLE to reside only in the state of New York ('NY')?

   A. ALTER TABLE EMPLOYEE_TBL
      ADD CONSTRAINT CHK_STATE CHECK(STATE='NY');

6. What statement would you use to add an auto-incrementing column called 'EMPID' to the preceding EMPLOYEE_TABLE using both the MySQL and SQL Server syntax?

   A. ALTER TABLE EMPLOYEE_TBL
      ADD COLUMN EMPID INT AUTO_INCREMENT;

Exercise Answers

No answer required.

Hour 4, "The Normalization Process"

Quiz Answers

1. True or false: Normalization is the process of grouping data into logical related groups.

   A. True.

2. True or false: Having no duplicate or redundant data in a database and having everything in the database normalized is always the best way to go.

   A. False. Not always; normalization can and does slow performance because more tables must be joined, which results in more I/O and CPU time.

3. True or false: If data is in the third normal form, it is automatically in the first and second normal forms.

   A. True.

4. What is a major advantage of a denormalized database versus a normalized database?

   A. The major advantage is improved performance.

5. What are some major disadvantages of denormalization?

   A. Having redundant and duplicate data takes up valuable space; it is harder to code, and much more data maintenance is required.

6. How do you determine if data needs to be moved to a separate table when normalizing your database?

   A. If the table has redundant groups of data, this data would be a candidate to remove into a separate table.

7. What are the disadvantages of overnormalizing your database design?

   A. Overnormalization can lead to excess CPU and memory utilization, which can put excess strain on the server.

Exercise Answers

1. You are developing a new database for a small company. Take the following data and normalize it. Keep in mind that there would be many more items for a small company than you are given here.

Employees:

Angela Smith, secretary, 317-545-6789, RR 1 Box 73, Greensburg, Indiana, 47890, $9.50 hour, date started January 22, 1996, SSN is 323149669.

Jack Lee Nelson, salesman, 3334 N. Main St., Brownsburg, IN, 45687, 317-852-9901, salary of $35,000.00 year, SSN is 312567342, date started 10/28/95.

Customers:

Robert's Games and Things, 5612 Lafayette Rd., Indianapolis, IN, 46224, 317-291-7888, customer ID is 432A.

Reed's Dairy Bar, 4556 W 10th St., Indianapolis, IN, 46245, 317-271-9823, customer ID is 117A.

Customer Orders:

Customer ID is 117A, date of last order is February 20, 1999, the product ordered was napkins, and the product ID is 661.

A.
Employees	Customers	Orders
SSN	CUSTOMER ID	CUSTOMER ID
SSN	CUSTOMER ID	CUSTOMER ID
NAME	NAME	PRODUCT ID
STREET ADDRESS	STREET ADDRESS	PRODUCT
CITY	CITY	DATE ORDERED
STATE	STATE	
ZIP ZIP	STATE	
PHONE NUMBER	PHONE NUMBER	
SALARY		
HOURLY PAY		
START DATE		
POSITION		

2. No answer required.

Hour 5, "Manipulating Data"

Quiz Answers

1. Use an imaginary PASSENGER_TBL with the following structure:

Column	data type	(not)null
LAST_NAME	varchar2(20)	not null
FIRST_NAME	varchar2(20)	not null
SSN	char(9)	not null
PHONE	number(10)	null

with the following data already in the table:

LAST_NAME	FIRST_NAME	SSN	PHONE
SMITH	JOHN	312456788	3174549923
ROBERTS	LISA	232118857	3175452321
SMITH	SUE	443221989	3178398712
PIERCE	BILLY	310239856	3176763990

What would happen if the following statements were run?

a. INSERT INTO PASSENGER_TBL

    ('JACKSON', 'STEVE', '313546078', '3178523443');

A. The INSERT statement does not run because the keyword VALUES is missing in the syntax.

   b. INSERT INTO PASSENGER_TBL VALUES
      ('JACKSON', 'STEVE', '313546078', '3178523443');

A. One row would be inserted into the PASSENGER_TBL.

   c. INSERT INTO PASSENGER_TBL VALUES
      ('MILLER', 'DANIEL', '230980012', NULL);

A. One row would be inserted into the PASSENGER_TBL, with a NULL value in the PHONE column.

   d. INSERT INTO PASSENGER_TBL VALUES
      ('TAYLOR', NULL, '445761212', '3179221331');

A. The INSERT statement would not process because the FIRST_NAME column is NOT NULL.

   e. DELETE FROM PASSENGER_TBL;

A. All rows in PASSENGER_TBL would be deleted.

   f. DELETE FROM PASSENGER_TBL
     WHERE LAST_NAME = 'SMITH';

A. All passengers with the last name of SMITH would be deleted from PASSENGER_TBL.

   g. DELETE FROM PASSENGER_TBL
     WHERE LAST_NAME = 'SMITH'
     AND FIRST_NAME = 'JOHN';

A. Only JOHN SMITH would be deleted from the PASSENGER_TBL.

   h. UPDATE PASSENGER_TBL
     SET LAST_NAME - 'CONRAD';

A. All last names would be changed to CONRAD.

   i. UPDATE PASSENGER_TBL
     SET LAST_NAME = 'CONRAD'
     WHERE LAST_NAME = 'SMITH';

A. Both JOHN and SUE SMITH would now be JOHN and SUE CONRAD.

   j. UPDATE PASSENGER_TBL
     SET LAST_NAME = 'CONRAD',
     FIRST_NAME = 'LARRY';

A. All passengers are now LARRY CONRAD.

> **k.** UPDATE PASSENGER_TBL
> SET LAST_NAME = 'CONRAD',
> FIRST_NAME = 'LARRY'
> WHERE SSN = '312456788';

A. JOHN SMITH is now LARRY CONRAD.

Exercise Answers

1. Use the AIRCRAFT table for this exercise.

Remove the two aircrafts that were added earlier in the chapter with the AIRCRAFTCODE of 'BBB' and 'CCC'.

> **A.** DELETE FROM AIRCRAFT WHERE AIRCRAFTCODE='BBB';
>
> DELETE FROM AIRCRAFT WHERE AIRCRAFTCODE='CCC';

Add the following aircraft to the aircraft table:

AIRCRAFTCODE	AIRCRAFTTYPE	FREIGHTONLY	SEATING
A11	Lockheed Superliner	0	600
B22	British Aerospace X11	0	350
C33	Boeing Frieghtmaster	1	0

> **A.** INSERT INTO AIRCRAFT(AIRCRAFTCODE, AIRCRAFTTYPE, FREIGHTONLY, SEATING)
> VALUES('A11','Lockheed Superliner',0,600);
>
> INSERT INTO AIRCRAFT(AIRCRAFTCODE, AIRCRAFTTYPE, FREIGHTONLY, SEATING)
> VALUES('B22','British Aerospace X11',0,350);
>
> INSERT INTO AIRCRAFT(AIRCRAFTCODE, AIRCRAFTTYPE, FREIGHTONLY, SEATING)
> VALUES('C33','Boeing Frieghtmaster',1,0);

Write DML to correct the seating associated with the Lockheed Superliner. The correct seating should be 500.

> **A.** UPDATE AIRCRAFT SET SEATING=500 WHERE AIRCRAFTCODE='A11';

An error was made with the C33; this should not have been labeled for FREIGHTONLY and should have a seating capacity of 25. Write the DML to correct this entry.

> **A.** UPDATE AIRCRAFT SET FREIGHTONLY=0, SEATING=25
> WHERE AIRCRAFTCODE='C33';

Now suppose we have decided to cut our supported aircraft line. Remove the three products you just added.

> **A.** DELETE FROM AIRCRAFT WHERE AIRCRAFTCODE IN ('A11','B22','C33');

Before you executed the statements to remove the products you added, what should you have done to ensure that you delete only the desired rows?

A. You should have written a SELECT statement using the same WHERE constraint you used in the DELETE statement so that you can ensure you will be removing the proper rows.

Hour 6, "Managing Database Transactions"

Quiz Answers

1. True or false: If you have committed several transactions, have several more transactions that have not been committed, and issue a ROLLBACK command, all your transactions for the same session are undone.

   A. False. When a transaction is committed, the transaction cannot be rolled back.

2. True or false: A SAVEPOINT command actually saves transactions after a specified number of transactions have executed.

   A. False. A SAVEPOINT is used only as a point for a ROLLBACK to return to.

3. Briefly describe the purpose of each one of the following commands: COMMIT, ROLLBACK, and SAVEPOINT.

   A. COMMIT saves changes made by a transaction. ROLLBACK undoes changes made by a transaction. SAVEPOINT creates logical points in the transaction to which to roll back.

4. What are some differences in the implementation of transactions in Microsoft SQL Server?

   A. SQL Server auto-commits statements unless specifically placed in a transaction and has a different syntax for SAVEPOINT. Also, it does not support the RELEASE SAVEPOINT command.

5. What are some performance implications when using transactions?

   A. Transactions have implications on temporary storage space because the database server has to keep track of all the changes until they are committed in case of a ROLLBACK.

6. When using several SAVEPOINT or SAVE TRANSACTION commands, can you rollback more than one?

   A. No, a ROLLBACK will go back only to the first SAVEPOINT that you ask it to ROLLABACK to.

Exercise Answers

1. Take the following transactions and create a `SAVEPOINT` or a `SAVE TRANSACTION` command after the first three transactions. Then create a `ROLLBACK` statement for your savepoint at the end. Try to determine what the `PASSENGERS` table will look like after you are done.

   A. `INSERT INTO PASSENGERS(FIRSTNAME,LASTNAME,BIRTHDATE,COUNTRYCODE)`
   `VALUES('George','Allwell','1981-03-23','US');`
   `INSERT INTO PASSENGERS(FIRSTNAME,LASTNAME,BIRTHDATE,COUNTRYCODE)`
   `VALUES('Steve','Schuler','1974-09-11','US');`
   `INSERT INTO PASSENGERS(FIRSTNAME,LASTNAME,BIRTHDATE,COUNTRYCODE)`
   `VALUES('Mary','Ellis','1990-11-12','US');`
   `SAVEPOINT;`
   `UPDATE PASSENGERS SET FIRSTNAME='Peter' WHERE LASTNAME='Allwell'`
   `AND BIRTHDATE='1981-03-23';`
   `UPDATE PASSENGERS SET COUNTRYCODE='AU' WHERE FIRSTNAME='Mary'`
   `AND LASTNAME='Ellis';`
   `UPDATE PASSENGERS SET BIRTHDATE='1964-09-11' WHERE LASTNAME='Schuler';`

   `ROLLBACK;`

2. Take the following group of transactions and create a savepoint after the first three transactions.

   Then place a `COMMIT` statement at the end, followed by a `ROLLBACK` statement to your savepoint. What do you think should happen?

   A. `UPDATE PASSENGERS SET BIRTHDATE='Stephen' WHERE LASTNAME='Schuler';`
   `DELETE FROM PASSENGERS WHERE LASTNAME='Allwell' AND BIRTHDATE='1981-03-23';`
   `DELETE FROM PASSENGERS WHERE LASTNAME='Schuler' AND BIRTHDATE='1964-09-11;`
   `SAVEPOINT SAVEPOINT;`
   `DELETE FROM PASSENGERS WHERE  LASTNAME='Ellis' AND BIRTHDATE='1990-11-12';`
   `COMMIT;`
   `ROLLBACK;`

   Because the statement is committed, the `ROLLBACK` statement doesn't have an effect.

Hour 7, "Introduction to the Database Queries"

Quiz Answers

1. Name the required parts for any `SELECT` statement.

   A. The `SELECT` and `FROM` keywords, also called clauses, are required for all `SELECT` statements.

2. In the WHERE clause, are single quotation marks required for all the data?

   A. No. Single quotation marks are required when selecting alphanumeric data types. Number data types do not require single quotation marks.

3. Can multiple conditions be used in the WHERE clause?

   A. Yes. Multiple conditions can be specified in the WHERE clause of SELECT, INSERT, UPDATE, and DELETE statements. Multiple conditions are used with the operators AND and OR, which are thoroughly discussed in Hour 8, "Using Operators to Categorize Data."

4. Is the DISTINCT option applied before or after the WHERE clause?

   A. The DISTINCT option is applied before the WHERE clause.

5. Is the ALL option required?

   A. No. Even though the ALL option can be used, it is not required.

6. How are numeric characters treated when ordering based upon a character field?

   A. They are sorted as ASCII characters. This means that numbers would be ordered like this: 1, 12, 2, 222, 22222, 3, 33.

7. How does Oracle handle its default case-sensitivity differently from MySQL and Microsoft SQL Server?

   A. Oracle by default performs matches as case-sensitive.

8. How is the ordering of the fields in the ORDER BY clause important?

   A. The ordering of the columns in the ORDER BY clause determines the order in which ordering is applied to the statement.

9. How is the ordering determined in the ORDER BY clause when you use numbers instead of column names?

   A. The numbers correspond to the columns defined in the SELECT portion of the query. So the first column is 1, the second is 2, and so on.

Exercise Answers

1. Invoke your RDBMS query editor on your computer. Using your CanaryAirlines database, enter the following SELECT statements. Determine whether the syntax is correct. If the syntax is incorrect, make corrections to the code as necessary. Use the PASSENGERS table for this exercise.

   a.
```
SELECT PASSENGERID, LASTNAME, FIRSTNAME,
FROM PASSENGERS;
```

A. This SELECT statement does not work because there is a comma after the FIRSTNAME column that does not belong there. The correct syntax follows:

```
SELECT PASSENGERID, LASTNAME, FIRSTNAME
FROM PASSENGERS;
```

b.
```
SELECT PASSENGERID, LASTNAME
  ORDER BY PASSENGERS
  FROM PASSENGERS;
```

A. This SELECT statement does not work because the FROM and ORDER BY clauses are in the incorrect order. The correct syntax follows:

```
SELECT PASSENGERID, LASTNAME
FROM PASSENGERS
ORDER BY PASSENGERS;
```

c.
```
SELECT PASSENGERID, LASTNAME, FIRSTNAME
FROM PASSENGERS
WHERE PASSENGERID = '134996'
ORDER BY PASSENGERID;
```

A. The syntax for this SELECT statement is correct.

d.
```
SELECT PASSENGERID BIRTHDATE, LASTNAME
FROM PASSENGERS
WHERE PASSENGERID = '134996'
ORDER BY 1;
```

A. The syntax for this SELECT statement is correct.

e.
```
SELECT PASSENGERID, LASTNAME, FIRSTNAME
FROM PASSENGERS
WHERE PASSENGERID = '134996'
ORDER BY 3, 1, 2;
```

A. The syntax for this SELECT statement is correct. Notice the order of the columns in the ORDER BY. This SELECT statement returns records from the database that are sorted by FIRSTNAME, and then by PASSENGERID, and finally by LASTNAME.

2. Does the following SELECT statement work?

```
SELECT LASTNAME, FIRSTNAME, BIRTHDATE
FROM PASSENGERS
WHERE PASSENGERID = '99999999';
```

A. The syntax is correct and the statement worked, even though no data was returned. No data was returned because there was no row with a PASSENGERID of 333333333.

3. Write a SELECT statement that returns the name and seating capacity of each airplane from the AIRCRAFT table. Which type of plane has the largest capacity? How many planes are freight planes? Where do the freight-only planes show up in your ordered results?

A. `SELECT AIRCRAFTTYPE, SEATING`
`FROM AIRCRAFT ORDER BY SEATING DESC;`

The Boeing 747s are the largest.

Three planes are freight planes.

They end up as the last ones in the list if ordering by `SEATING DESC`.

4. Write a query that generates a list of all passengers who were born after 2015-01-01.

   A. `SELECT * FROM PASSENGERS`
   `WHERE BIRTHDATE>'2015-01-01';`

5. Answers will vary.

Hour 8, "Using Operators to Categorize Data"

Quiz Answers

1. True or false: Both conditions when using the `OR` operator must be `TRUE`.

   A. False. Only one of the conditions must be `TRUE`.

2. True or false: All specified values must match when using the `IN` operator.

   A. False. Only one of the values must match.

3. True or false: The `AND` operator can be used in the `SELECT` and the `WHERE` clauses.

   A. False. The `AND` operator can be used only in the `WHERE` clause.

4. True or false: The `ANY` operator can accept an expression list.

   A. False. The `ANY` operator cannot take an expression list.

5. What is the logical negation of the `IN` operator?

   A. `NOT IN`

6. What is the logical negation of the `ANY` and `ALL` operators?

   A. `<>ANY` and `<>ALL`

7. What, if anything, is wrong with the following `SELECT` statements?

   a. `SELECT AIRCRAFTTYPE`
   `FROM AIRCRAFT`
   `WHERE SEATING BETWEEN 200, 300;`

   A. The `AND` is missing between `200, 300`. The correct syntax is

   `SELECT AIRCRAFTTYPE`
   `FROM AIRCRAFT`
   `WHERE SEATING BETWEEN 200 AND 300;`

b. `SELECT DISTANCE + AIRPLANECODE`
`FROM ROUTES;`

A. The `AIRPLANECODE` column is a `VARCHAR` data type and is in the incorrect format for arithmetic functions.

c. `SELECT FIRSTNAME, LASTNAME`
`FROM PASSENGERS`
`WHERE BIRTHDATE BETWEEN 1980-01-01`
`AND 1990-01-01`
`AND COUNTRYCODE = 'US'`
`OR COUNTRYCODE = 'GB'`
`AND PASSENGERID LIKE '%55%;`

A. The syntax is correct.

Exercise Answers

1. Using the `ROUTES` table, write a `SELECT` statement that returns all routes originating from Indianapolis, with route codes starting with 'IND'. Order your results based on the route name in alphabetical order and then the distance of the route going from largest to smallest.

   A. `SELECT * FROM ROUTES`
   `WHERE ROUTECODE LIKE 'IND%'`
   `ORDER BY ROUTECODE, DISTANCE DESC;`

2. Rewrite the query from Exercise 1 to show only those flights that are between 1000 and 2000 miles long.

   A. `SELECT * FROM ROUTES`
   `WHERE ROUTECODE LIKE 'IND%'`
   `AND DISTANCE BETWEEN 1000 AND 2000`
   `ORDER BY ROUTECODE, DISTANCE DESC;`

3. Assuming that you used the `BETWEEN` operator in Exercise 2, rewrite your SQL statement to achieve the same results using different operators. If you did not use the `BETWEEN` operator, do so now.

   A. `SELECT * FROM ROUTES`
   `WHERE ROUTECODE LIKE 'IND%'`
   `AND DISTANCE >= 1000`
   `AND DISTANCE <= 2000`
   `ORDER BY ROUTECODE, DISTANCE DESC;`

4. Rewrite your query so that instead of showing results where the distance is between 1000 and 2000 miles, you show all distances except that range. Show at least two ways that you could achieve this result.

A. SELECT * FROM ROUTES
WHERE ROUTECODE LIKE 'IND%'
AND (DISTANCE < 1000
OR DISTANCE > 2000)
ORDER BY ROUTECODE, DISTANCE DESC;

SELECT * FROM ROUTES
WHERE ROUTECODE LIKE 'IND%'
AND DISTANCE NOT BETWEEN 1000 AND 2000
ORDER BY ROUTECODE, DISTANCE DESC;

5. Write a SELECT statement that returns the route code, distance, and travel time, and then calculates a cost column by multiplying travel time by the fuel cost per minute value for all routes originating from Indianapolis. Order your results from most expensive routes to least expensive.

A. SELECT ROUTECODE, DISTANCE, TRAVELTIME,
TRAVELTIME * FUELCOSTPERMINUTE AS COST
FROM ROUTES
WHERE ROUTECODE LIKE 'IND%'
ORDER BY 3 DESC;

6. Rewrite your statement from Exercise 5 to include a 10% fuel surcharge added onto the cost.

A. SELECT ROUTECODE, DISTANCE, TRAVELTIME,
(TRAVELTIME * FUELCOSTPERMINUTE)*1.1 AS COST
FROM ROUTES
WHERE ROUTECODE LIKE 'IND%'
ORDER BY 3 DESC;

7. Enhance your statement from Exercise 6 by including those routes with route codes IND-MFK, IND-MYR, and IND-MDA. There are at least two ways to write this constraint.

A. SELECT ROUTECODE, DISTANCE, TRAVELTIME,
(TRAVELTIME * FUELCOSTPERMINUTE)*1.1 AS COST
FROM ROUTES
WHERE ROUTECODE IN ('IND-MFK','IND-MYR','IND-MDA')
ORDER BY 3 DESC;

SELECT ROUTECODE, DISTANCE, TRAVELTIME,
(TRAVELTIME * FUELCOSTPERMINUTE)*1.1 AS COST
FROM ROUTES
WHERE (
ROUTECODE = 'IND-MFK'
OR ROUTECODE = 'IND-MYR'
OR ROUTECODE = 'IND-MDA'
)

8. Now rewrite your statement from Exercise 7, include an additional column called COST_
   PER_MILE, and use the distance column that is in miles to calculate the resulting value.
   Pay special attention to parentheses in your answer.

   A.
   ```
   SELECT ROUTECODE, DISTANCE, TRAVELTIME,
   (TRAVELTIME * FUELCOSTPERMINUTE)*1.1 AS COST,
   ((TRAVELTIME * FUELCOSTPERMINUTE)*1.1)/DISTANCE AS COST_PER_MILE
   FROM ROUTES
   WHERE ROUTECODE IN ('IND-MFK','IND-MYR','IND-MDA')
   ORDER BY 3 DESC;
   ```

Hour 9, "Summarizing Data Results from a Query"

Quiz Answers

1. True or False: The AVG function returns an average of all rows from a SELECT column,
   including any NULL values.

   A. False. The NULL values are not considered.

2. True or False: The SUM function adds column totals.

   A. False. The SUM function returns a total for a group of rows.

3. True or False: The COUNT(*) function counts all rows in a table.

   A. True.

4. True or false: The COUNT([column name]) function counts NULL values.

   A. False.

5. Do the following SELECT statements work? If not, what fixes the statements?

   a.
   ```
   SELECT COUNT *
   FROM EMPLOYEES;
   ```

   A. This statement does not work because the left and right parentheses are missing
   around the asterisk. The correct syntax is

   ```
   SELECT COUNT(*)
     FROM EMPLOYEES;
   ```

   b.
   ```
   SELECT COUNT(EMPLOYEEID), SALARY
   FROM EMPLOYEES;
   ```

   A. Yes, this statement works.

c. `SELECT MIN(PAYRATE), MAX(SALARY)`
`FROM EMPLOYEES`
`WHERE SALARY > 50000;`

A. Yes, this statement works.

d. `SELECT COUNT(DISTINCT EMPLOYEEID) FROM EMPLOYEES;`

A. Yes, this statement works.

e. `SELECT AVG(LASTNAME) FROM EMPLOYEES;`

A. No, because the column value being averaged needs to be numeric.

f. `SELECT AVG(CAST(ZIP AS INT)) FROM EMPLOYEES;`

A. Yes, this statement works because you cast the ZIP column to an integer.

Exercise Answers

1. Use the `EMPLOYEES` table to construct SQL statements to solve the following exercises:

a. What is the average salary?

`SELECT AVG(SALARY) FROM EMPLOYEES;`

b. What is the maximum pay rate for hourly employees?

`SELECT MAX(PAYRATE) FROM EMPLOYEES;`

c. What are the total salaries?

`SELECT SUM(SALARY) FROM EMPLOYEES;`

d. What is the minimum pay rate?

`SELECT MIN(PAYRATE) FROM EMPLOYEES;`

e. How many rows are in the table?

`SELECT COUNT(*)  FROM EMPLOYEES;`

2. Write a query to determine how many employees are in the company whose last names begin with a **G**.

`SELECT COUNT(*)  FROM EMPLOYEES`
`WHERE LASTNAME LIKE 'G';`

3. Write a query to determine the minimum and maximum salary and pay rates per city for employees.

`SELECT CITY, MIN(SALARY) AS MIN_SALARY, MAX(SALARY) AS MAX_SALARY,`
` MIN(PAYRATE) AS MIN_PAYRATE, MAX(PAYRATE) AS MAX_PAYRATE`
`FROM EMPLOYEES`
`GROUP BY CITY;`

4. Write two sets of queries to find the first employee name and last employee name when they are listed in alphabetical order.

```
SELECT TOP 1 FIRSTNAME, LASTNAME FROM EMPLOYEES
ORDER BY LASTNAME, FIRSTNAME;
```

```
SELECT TOP 1 FIRSTNAME, LASTNAME FROM EMPLOYEES
ORDER BY LASTNAME DESC, FIRSTNAME DESC;
```

5. Write a query to perform an AVG function on the employee names. Does the statement work? Determine why it is that you got that result.

```
SELECT AVG(FIRSTNAME) AS AVG_NAME  FROM EMPLOYEES;
```

No; it does not work because the value being averaged needs to be numeric.

6. Write a query to perform an average of the employee's salaries that takes NULL values into account. Hint: You won't be using the AVG function.

```
SELECT SUM(SALARY)/COUNT(*) AS AVG_SALARY  FROM EMPLOYEES;
```

Hour 10, "Sorting and Grouping Data"

Quiz Answers

1. Will the following SQL statements work?

   a.
   ```
   SELECT SUM(SALARY) AS TOTAL_SALARY, EMPLOYEEID
   FROM EMPLOYEES
   GROUP BY 1 and 2;
   ```

   A. No, the AND in the GROUP BY clause needs to be replaced with a comma.

   b.
   ```
   SELECT EMPLOYEEID, MAX(SALARY)
   FROM EMPLOYEES
   GROUP BY SALARY, EMPLOYEEID;
   ```

   A. Yes, the statement will work.

   c.
   ```
   SELECT EMPLOYEEID, COUNT(SALARY)
   FROM EMPLOYEES
   ORDER BY EMPLOYEEID
   GROUP BY SALARY;
   ```

   A. No, the GROUP BY and ORDER BY clauses are out of order.

   d.
   ```
   SELECT YEAR(DATE_HIRE) AS YEAR_HIRED,SUM(SALARY)
   FROM EMPLOYEES
   GROUP BY 1
   HAVING SUM(SALARY)>20000;
   ```

A. No, the 1 in the GROUP BY statement needs to be replaced with YEAR(DATE_HIRE).

2. What is the purpose of the HAVING clause and which other clause is it closest to?

A. The HAVING clause is used to constrain the groups returned by the GROUP BY clause. Therefore, it is closest to the WHERE clause in functionality.

3. True or false: You must also use the GROUP BY clause when using the HAVING clause.

A. False; you do not need the GROUP BY clause unless you have non-aggregated column data in your query.

4. True or false: The following SQL statement returns a total of the salaries by groups:

```
SELECT SUM(SALARY)
FROM EMPLOYEES;
```

A. False, the statement does not contain the column to group by or the GROUP BY clause, so it will display the sum of all salaries.

5. True or false: The columns selected must appear in the GROUP BY clause in the same order.

A. False.

6. True or false: The HAVING clause tells the GROUP BY which groups to include.

A. True.

Exercises

1. No answer required.

2. No answer required.

3. No answer required.

4. Modify the query in Exercise 3 to order the results in descending order, from highest count to lowest.

A.
```
SELECT CITY, COUNT(*) AS CITY_COUNT
FROM EMPLOYEES
GROUP BY CITY
HAVING COUNT(*) > 15
ORDER BY 2 DESC;
```

5. Write a query to list the average pay rate and salary by position from the EMPLOYEES table.

A.
```
SELECT POSITION,
AVG(SALARY) AS AVG_SALARY,
AVG(PAYRATE) AS AVG_PAYRATE,
FROM EMPLOYEES
GROUP BY POSITION;
```

6. Write a query to list the average salary by position from the EMPLOYEES table where the average salary is greater than 40000.

A. SELECT POSITION,
(SALARY) AS AVG_SALARY
FROM EMPLOYEES
GROUP BY POSITION
HAVING AVG(SALARY)>40000;

7. Write the same query you used for Exercise 6, but find the average salary only for those people making more than 40000 grouped by city and position and compare the results. Explain the difference.

A. SELECT CITY,POSITION,
AVG(SALARY) AS AVG_SALARY
FROM EMPLOYEES
WHERE SALARY>40000
GROUP BY CITY,POSITION;

The WHERE clause factors out individual rows, whereas the HAVING clause reduces the number of groups.

Hour 11, "Restructuring the Appearance of Data"

Quiz Answers

1. Match the descriptions with the possible functions.

A.

Description	Function
a. Used to select a portion of a character string	SUBSTR
b. Used to trim characters from either the right or left of a string	LTRIM/RTRIM
c. Used to change all letters to lowercase	LOWER
d. Used to find the length of a string	LENGTH
e. Used to combine strings	||

2. True or false: Using functions in a SELECT statement to restructure the appearance of data in output also affects the way the data is stored in the database.

A. False.

3. True or false: The outermost function is always resolved first when functions are embedded within other functions in a query.

A. False. The innermost function is always resolved first when embedding functions within one another.

Exercise Answers

1. No answer required.

2. No answer required.

3. Write a SQL statement that lists employee email addresses. Email is not a stored column. The email address for each employee should be as follows:

   FIRST.LAST @PERPTECH.COM

   For example, John Smith's email address is JOHN.SMITH@PERPTECH.COM.

   A. `SELECT CONCAT(FIRSTNAME, '.', LASTNAME, '@PERPTECH.COM')`
   `FROM EMPLOYEES;`

4. Write a SQL statement that lists each employee's name and phone number in the following formats:

   a. The name should be displayed as SMITH, JOHN.

   b. The employee ID should be displayed as the first three letters of the last name in uppercase, a dash, and then the employee number. Example: SMI-4203

   c. The phone number should be displayed as (999)999-9999.

   A. `SELECT CONCAT(LASTNAME, ', ', FIRSTNAME),`
   `CONCAT(LEFT(LASTNAME,3), '-',CAST(EMPLOYEEID AS VARCHAR(20))),`
   `CONCAT('(',`
   `SUBSTRING(PHONENUMBER,1,3),')',`
   `UBSTRING(PHONENUMBER,4,3),'-',`
   `SUBSTRING(PHONENUMBER,7,4))`
   `FROM EMPLOYEES;`

Hour 12, "Understanding Dates and Times"

Quiz Answers

1. From where is the system date and time normally derived?

   A. The system date and time are derived from the current date and time of the operating system on the host machine.

2. What are the standard internal elements of a DATETIME value?

   A. YEAR, MONTH, DAY, HOUR, MINUTE, and SECOND

3. What could be a major factor concerning the representation and comparison of date and time values if your company is an international organization?

   A. The awareness of time zones might be a concern.

4. Can a character string date value be compared to a date value defined as a valid DATETIME data type?

    A. A DATETIME data type cannot be accurately compared to a date value defined as a character string. The character string must first be converted to the DATETIME data type.

5. What would you use in SQL Server and Oracle to get the current date and time?

    A. NOW()

Exercise Answers

1. No answer required.

2. No answer required.

3. No answer required.

4. No answer required.

5. Using Exercise 4, determine what day of the week each employee was hired.

    A. Use the following statement to find the answer:

    ```
    SELECT EMPLOYEEID, DAYNAME(HIREDATE)
    FROM EMPLOYEES;
    ```

6. Write a query like Exercise 4 except use a function to show how many days the employee has worked for the company. Could you also estimate years?

    A. Use the following statement to find the answer:

    ```
    SELECT EMPLOYEEID, DATEDIFF(DAY,HIREDATE,GETDATE()) AS DAYS_EMPLOYED
    FROM EMPLOYEES;
    SELECT EMPLOYEEID, DATEDIFF(YEAR,HIREDATE,GETDATE()) AS DAYS_EMPLOYED
    FROM EMPLOYEES;
    ```

7. Write a query to determine today's Julian date (day of year).

    A. Use the following statement to find the answer:

    ```
    SELECT DAYOFYEAR(CURRENT_DATE);
    ```

Hour 13, "Joining Tables in Queries"

Quiz Answers

1. What type of join would you use to return records from one table, regardless of the existence of associated records in the related table?

    A. You would use an outer join.

2. The JOIN conditions are located in what part of the SQL statement?

   A. The JOIN conditions are located in the WHERE clause.

3. What type of JOIN do you use to evaluate equality among rows of related tables?

   A. You would use an equijoin.

4. What happens if you select from two different tables but fail to join the tables?

   A. You receive a Cartesian product by not joining the tables. (This is also called a cross join.)

5. Use the following tables to answer the next questions:

```
ORDERS_TBL
ORD_NUM      VARCHAR2(10)   NOT NULL      primary key
CUST_ID      VARCHAR2(10)   NOT NULL
PROD_ID      VARCHAR2(10)   NOT NULL
QTY          INTEGER        NOT NULL
ORD_DATE     DATE


PRODUCTS_TBL
PROD_ID      VARCHAR2(10)   NOT NULL      primary key
PROD_DESC    VARCHAR2(40)   NOT NULL
COST         DECIMAL(,2)    NOT NULL
```

Is the following syntax correct for using an outer join?

```
SELECT C.CUST_ID, C.CUST_NAME, O.ORD_NUM
FROM CUSTOMER_TBL C, ORDERS_TBL O
WHERE C.CUST_ID(+) = O.CUST_ID(+)
```

   A. No, the syntax is not correct. The (+) operator should follow only the O.CUST_ID column in the WHERE clause. The correct syntax is

```
SELECT C.CUST_ID, C.CUST_NAME, O.ORD_NUM
FROM CUSTOMER_TBL C, ORDERS_TBL O
WHERE C.CUST_ID = O.CUST_ID(+)
```

What would the query look like if you used the verbose JOIN syntax?

   A.
```
SELECT C.CUST_ID, C.CUST_NAME, O.ORD_NUM
FROM CUSTOMER_TBL C LEFT OUTER JOIN ORDERS_TBL O
ON C.CUST_ID = O.CUST_ID
```

Exercise Answers

1. No answer required.

2. No answer required.

3. Rewrite the SQL query from Exercise 2 using the INNER JOIN syntax.

   A. SELECT E.LASTNAME, E.FIRSTNAME, A.AIRPORTNAME
   ```
   FROM EMPLOYEES E
   INNER JOIN AIRPORTS A
   ON E.AIRPORTID=A.AIRPORTID
   AND E.STATE='IN';
   ```

4. Write a SQL statement to return the FLIGHTID, AIRPORTNAME, and CITY columns from AIRPORTS and FLIGHTDURATION and FLIGHTSTART columns from FLIGHTS. Use both types of INNER JOIN techniques. When that's completed, use the queries to determine the average flight duration per city during the month of May, 2013.

   A. SELECT F.FLIGHTID, A.AIRPORTNAME, A.CITY,
   ```
   F.FLIGHTDURATION, F.FLIGHTSTART
   FROM AIRPORTS A
   INNER JOIN ROUTES R ON A.AIRPORTID = R.SOURCEAIRPORTID
   INNER JOIN FLIGHTS F ON R.ROUTEID = F.ROUTEID
   WHERE MONTH(F.FLIGHTSTART)=5 AND YEAR(F.FLIGHTSTART)=2013
   ```

   ```
   SELECT F.FLIGHTID, A.AIRPORTNAME, A.CITY,
   F.FLIGHTDURATION, F.FLIGHTSTART
   FROM AIRPORTS A
   ,ROUTES R
   ,FLIGHTS F
   WHERE MONTH(F.FLIGHTSTART)=5 AND YEAR(F.FLIGHTSTART)=2013
   AND A.AIRPORTID = R.SOURCEAIRPORTID
   AND R.ROUTEID = F.ROUTEID
   ```

5. No answer required.

Hour 14, "Using Subqueries to Define Unknown Data"

Quiz Answers

1. What is the function of a subquery when used with a SELECT statement?

   A. The main function of a subquery when used with a SELECT statement is to return data that the main query can use to resolve the query.

2. Can you update more than one column when using the UPDATE statement with a subquery?

   A. Yes, you can update more than one column using the same UPDATE and subquery statement.

3. Do the following have the correct syntax? If not, what is the correct syntax?

   a. `SELECT PASSENGERID, FIRSTNAME,LASTNAME,COUNTRYCODE`
   ```
   FROM PASSENGERS
   WHERE PASSENGERID IN
   (SELECT PASSENGERID
   FROM TRIPS
   WHERE TRIPID BETWEEN 2390 AND 2400);
   ```

   A. Yes, the syntax is correct.

   b. `SELECT EMPLOYEEID, SALARY`
   ```
   FROM EMPLOYEES
   WHERE SALARY BETWEEN '20000'
   AND (SELECT SALARY
   FROM EMPLOYEES
   WHERE SALARY = '40000');
   ```

   A. It would produce an error because the subquery returns more than one row.

   c. `UPDATE PASSENGERS`
   ```
   SET COUNTRYCODE = 'NZ'
   WHERE PASSENGERID =
   (SELECT PASSENGERID
   FROM TRIPS
   WHERE TRIPID = 2405);
   ```

   A. This would run correctly and update one row.

4. What would happen if you ran the following statement?
   ```
   DELETE FROM EMPLOYEES
   WHERE EMPLOYEEID IN
   (SELECT EMPLOYEEID
   FROM RICH_EMPLOYEES);
   ```

   A. All rows that you retrieved from `RICH_EMPLOYEES` would be deleted from the `EMPLOYEES` table. A `WHERE` clause in the subquery is highly advised.

Exercise Answers

1. No answer required.

2. Using a subquery, write a SQL statement to update the `PASSENGERS` table. Find the passenger with the TripID `3120`, and change the passenger's name to `RYAN STEPHENS`.

   A. `UPDATE PASSENGERS`
   ```
       SET FIRSTNAME='RYAN', LASTNAME='STEPHENS'
       WHERE PASSENGERID =
                   (SELECT PASSENGERID
                    FROM TRIPS
                    WHERE TRIPID = 3120);
   ```

3. Using a subquery, write a query that returns the counts of passengers by country that are leaving on July 4, 2013.

4. Using a subquery, write a query that lists all passenger information for those passengers that are taking trips that are less than 21 days from beginning to end.

Hour 15, "Combining Multiple Queries into One"

Quiz Answers

1. Is the syntax correct for the following compound queries? If not, what would correct the syntax? Use the PASSENGERS and TRIPS tables.

   a.
   ```
   SELECT PASSENGERID, BIRTHDATE, FIRSTNAME
   FROM PASSENGERS
   UNION
   SELECT PASSENGERID, LEAVING, RETURNING
   FROM TRIPS;
   ```

   A. No, the FIRSTNAME column in the first part of the query does not match the datetype of the RETURNING field in the second part of the query.

   b.
   ```
   SELECT PASSENGERID FROM PASSENGERS
   UNION ALL
   SELECT PASSENGERID FROM TRIPS
   ORDER BY PASSENGERID;
   ```

   A. Yes, it works correctly.

   c.
   ```
   SELECT PASSENGERID FROM TRIPS
   INTERSECT
   SELECT PASSENGERID FROM PASSENGERS
   ORDER BY 1;
   ```

   A. Yes, it works correctly.

2. Match the correct operator to the following statements.

Statement	Operator
a. Show duplicates.	UNION ALL
b. Return only rows from the first query that match those in the second query.	INTERSECT
c Return no duplicates.	UNION
d. Return only rows from the first query not returned by the second.	EXCEPT

Exercise Answers

1. Use the PASSENGERS and TRIPS tables to write a compound query to find the passengers who have scheduled a trip.

   A. `SELECT * FROM PASSENGERS`
   `WHERE PASSENGERID IN`
   `      (SELECT PASSENGERID FROM TRIPS)`
   `ORDER BY PASSENGERID;`

2. Write a compound query to find the passengers who have not scheduled a trip.

   A. `SELECT * FROM PASSENGERS`
   `WHERE PASSENGERID NOT IN`
   `      (SELECT PASSENGERID FROM TRIPS)`
   `ORDER BY PASSENGERID;`

3. Write a query that uses EXCEPT to list all the passengers who have taken a trip except those that originated in Albany.

   A. `SELECT * FROM PASSENGERS P`
   `INNER JOIN TRIPS T ON P.PASSENGERID = T.PASSENGERID`
   `WHERE T.SourceFlightID IN`
   `    (`
   `    SELECT FLIGHTID FROM FLIGHTS F`
   `      INNER JOIN ROUTES R ON F.ROUTEID=R.ROUTEID`
   `    WHERE R.SOURCEAIRPORTID`
   `    NOT IN (SELECT AIRPORTID FROM AIRPORTS WHERE CITY='Albany')`
   `    )`
   `ORDER BY P.PASSENGERID;`

Hour 16, "Using Indexes to Improve Performance"

Quiz Answers

1. What are some major disadvantages of using indexes?

   A. Major disadvantages of an index include slowing batch jobs, storage space on the disk, and maintenance upkeep on the index.

2. Why is the order of columns in a composite index important?

   A. Because query performance is improved by putting the column with the most restrictive values first.

3. Should a column with a large percentage of NULL values be indexed?

   A. No. A column with a large percentage of NULL values should not be indexed because the speed of accessing these rows degrades when the value of a large percentage of rows is the same.

4. Is the main purpose of an index to stop duplicate values in a table?

   A. No. The main purpose of an index is to enhance data retrieval speed; although a unique index stops duplicate values in a table.

5. True or false: The main reason for a composite index is for aggregate function usage in an index.

   A. False. The main reason for composite indexes is for two or more columns in the same table to be indexed.

6. What does cardinality refer to? What is considered a column of high-cardinality?

   A. Cardinality refers to the uniqueness of the data within a column. The SSN column is an example of such a column.

Exercise Answers

1. For the following situations, decide whether an index should be used and, if so, what type of index should be used:

   a. Several columns, but a rather small table.

   A. Being a very small table, no index is needed.

   b. Medium-sized table; no duplicates should be allowed.

   A. A unique index could be used.

   c. Several columns, very large table, several columns used as filters in the WHERE clause.

   A. A composite index on the columns used as filters in the WHERE clause should be the choice.

   d. Large table, many columns, a lot of data manipulation

   A. A choice of a single-column or composite index should be considered, depending on filtering, ordering, and grouping. For the large amount of data manipulation, the index could be dropped and re-created after the INSERT, UPDATE, or DELETE jobs were done.

2. No answer required.

3. Create a statement to alter the index you just created to make it unique. Why doesn't it work?

   A. `DROP INDEX EP_POSITON ON EMPLOYEES;`
   ```
                CREATE UNIQUE INDEX EP_POSITION
                ON EMPLOYEES(POSITION);
   ```

   It will not work because there are duplicate values in the column.

4. For the FLIGHTS table, choose some columns to make up a unique index for that table. Explain your reasoning behind picking those columns.

   A. Answers will vary.

5. Study the tables used in this book. List some good candidates for indexed columns based on how a user might search for data.

   A. Answers will vary.

6. Create a multicolumn index on FLIGHTS. Include the following columns: ROUTEID, AIRCRAFTFLEETID, and STATUSCODE.

7. No answer required.

Hour 17, "Improving Database Performance"

Quiz Answers

1. Would the use of a unique index on a small table be of any benefit?

   A. The index might not be of any use for performance issues, but the unique index would keep referential integrity intact. Referential integrity is discussed in Hour 3, "Managing Database Objects."

2. What happens when the optimizer chooses not to use an index on a table when a query has been executed?

   A. A full table scan occurs.

3. Should the most restrictive clause(s) be placed before the join condition(s) or after the join conditions in the WHERE clause?

   A. The most restrictive clause(s) should be evaluated before the join condition(s) because join conditions normally return a large number of rows.

Exercise Answers

1. Rewrite the following SQL statements to improve their performance. Use EMPLOYEE_TBL and EMPLOYEE_PAY_TBL as described here:

```
EMPLOYEE_TBL
EMP_ID          VARCHAR(9)      NOT NULL      Primary key
LAST_NAME       VARCHAR(15)     NOT NULL,
FIRST_NAME      VARCHAR(15)     NOT NULL,
MIDDLE_NAME     VARCHAR(15),
ADDRESS         VARCHAR(30)     NOT NULL,
CITY            VARCHAR(15)     NOT NULL,
STATE           VARCHAR(2)      NOT NULL,
ZIP             INTEGER(5)      NOT NULL,
PHONE           VARCHAR(10),
PAGER           VARCHAR(10),
EMPLOYEE_PAY_TBL
EMP_ID          VARCHAR(9)      NOT NULL    primary key
POSITION        VARCHAR(15)     NOT NULL,
```

```
DATE_HIRE          DATETIME,
PAY_RATE           DECIMAL(4,2)    NOT NULL,
DATE_LAST_RAISE    DATETIME,
SALARY             DECIMAL(8,2),
BONUS              DECIMAL(8,2),
```

a. SELECT EMP_ID, LAST_NAME, FIRST_NAME,
      PHONE
  FROM EMPLOYEE_TBL
    WHERE SUBSTRING(PHONE, 1, 3) = '317' OR
        SUBSTRING(PHONE, 1, 3) = '812' OR
        SUBSTRING(PHONE, 1, 3) = '765';

A. SELECT EMP_ID, LAST_NAME, FIRST_NAME,
      PHONE
  FROM EMPLOYEE_TBL
  WHERE SUBSTRING(PHONE, 1, 3) IN ('317', '812', '765');

Typically, it is better to convert multiple OR conditions to an IN list.

b. SELECT LAST_NAME, FIRST_NAME
  FROM EMPLOYEE_TBL
  WHERE LAST_NAME LIKE '%ALL%';

A. SELECT LAST_NAME, FIRST_NAME
  FROM EMPLOYEE_TBL
  WHERE LAST_NAME LIKE 'WAL%';

You cannot take advantage of an index if you do not include the first character in a condition's value.

c. SELECT E.EMP_ID, E.LAST_NAME, E.FIRST_NAME,
      EP.SALARY
  FROM EMPLOYEE_TBL E,
  EMPLOYEE_PAY_TBL EP
  WHERE LAST_NAME LIKE 'S%'
  AND E.EMP_ID = EP.EMP_ID;

A. SELECT E.EMP_ID, E.LAST_NAME, E.FIRST_NAME,
      EP.SALARY
  FROM EMPLOYEE_TBL E,
  EMPLOYEE_PAY_TBL EP
  WHERE E.EMP_ID = EP.EMP_ID
  AND LAST_NAME LIKE 'S%';

2. Add another table called EMPLOYEE_PAYHIST_TBL that contains a large amount of pay history data. Use the table that follows to write the series of SQL statements to address the following problems. Be sure you take steps to ensure the queries you write perform well.

```
EMPLOYEE_PAYHIST_TBL
PAYHIST_ID         VARCHAR(9)      NOT NULL      primary key,
EMP_ID             VARCHAR(9)      NOT NULL,
START_DATE         DATETIME        NOT NULL,
END_DATE           DATETIME,
PAY_RATE           DECIMAL(4,2)    NOT NULL,
SALARY             DECIMAL(8,2)    NOT NULL,
BONUS              DECIMAL(8,2)    NOT NULL,
CONSTRAINT EMP_FK FOREIGN KEY (EMP_ID)
REFERENCES EMPLOYEE_TBL (EMP_ID)
```

a. Find the SUM of the salaried versus nonsalaried employees by the year in which their pay started.

A.
```
SELECT START_YEAR,SUM(SALARIED) AS SALARIED,SUM(HOURLY) AS
HOURLY
     FROM
     (SELECT YEAR(E.START_DATE) AS START_YEAR,COUNT(E.EMP_ID)     AS
SALARIED,0 AS HOURLY
     FROM EMPLOYEE_PAYHIST_TBL E INNER JOIN
     ( SELECT MIN(START_DATE) START_DATE,EMP_ID
      FROM EMPLOYEE_PAYHIST_TBL
     GROUP BY EMP_ID) F ON E.EMP_ID=F.EMP_ID AND
E.START_DATE=F.START_DATE
     WHERE E.SALARY > 0.00
     GROUP BY YEAR(E.START_DATE)
     UNION
SELECT YEAR(E.START_DATE) AS START_YEAR,0 AS SALARIED,
     COUNT(E.EMP_ID)   AS HOURLY
     FROM EMPLOYEE_PAYHIST_TBL E INNER JOIN
     ( SELECT MIN(START_DATE) START_DATE,EMP_ID
     FROM EMPLOYEE_PAYHIST_TBL
     GROUP BY EMP_ID) F ON E.EMP_ID=F.EMP_ID AND
E.START_DATE=F.START_DATE
     WHERE E.PAY_RATE > 0.00
     GROUP BY YEAR(E.START_DATE)
     ) A
     GROUP BY START_YEAR
     ORDER BY START_YEAR
```

b. Find the difference in the yearly pay of salaried employees versus nonsalaried employees by the year in which their pay started. Consider the nonsalaried employees to be working full time during the year (PAY_RATE * 52 * 40).

A.
```
SELECT START_YEAR,SALARIED AS SALARIED,HOURLY AS HOURLY,
     (SALARIED - HOURLY) AS PAY_DIFFERENCE
     FROM
     (SELECT YEAR(E.START_DATE) AS START_YEAR,AVG(E.SALARY) AS
```

```
SALARIED,
    0 AS HOURLY
    FROM EMPLOYEE_PAYHIST_TBL E INNER JOIN
    ( SELECT MIN(START_DATE) START_DATE,EMP_ID
    FROM EMPLOYEE_PAYHIST_TBL
    GROUP BY EMP_ID) F ON E.EMP_ID=F.EMP_ID AND
E.START_DATE=F.START_DATE
    WHERE E.SALARY > 0.00
    GROUP BY YEAR(E.START_DATE)
    UNION
SELECT YEAR(E.START_DATE) AS START_YEAR,0 AS SALARIED,
    AVG(E.PAY_RATE * 52 * 40 ) AS HOURLY
    FROM EMPLOYEE_PAYHIST_TBL E INNER JOIN
    ( SELECT MIN(START_DATE) START_DATE,EMP_ID
     FROM EMPLOYEE_PAYHIST_TBL
    GROUP BY EMP_ID) F ON E.EMP_ID=F.EMP_ID AND
E.START_DATE=F.START_DATE
    WHERE E.PAY_RATE > 0.00
    GROUP BY YEAR(E.START_DATE)
    ) A
    GROUP BY START_YEAR
    ORDER BY START_YEAR
```

c. Find the difference in what employees make now versus what they made when they started with the company. Again, consider the nonsalaried employees to be full time. Also consider that the employees' current pay is reflected in the EMPLOYEE_PAY_TBL as well as the EMPLOYEE_PAYHIST_TBL. In the pay history table, the current pay is reflected as a row with the END_DATE for pay equal to NULL.

A.
```
SELECT CURRENTPAY.EMP_ID,STARTING_ANNUAL_PAY,CURRENT_
ANNUAL_PAY,
CURRENT_ANNUAL_PAY - STARTING_ANNUAL_PAY AS PAY_DIFFERENCE
FROM
(SELECT EMP_ID,(SALARY + (PAY_RATE * 52 * 40)) AS
CURRENT_ANNUAL_PAY
  FROM EMPLOYEE_PAYHIST_TBL
  WHERE END_DATE IS NULL) CURRENTPAY
INNER JOIN
(SELECT E.EMP_ID,(SALARY + (PAY_RATE * 52 * 40)) AS
STARTING_ANNUAL_PAY
  FROM EMPLOYEE_PAYHIST_TBL E
  ( SELECT MIN(START_DATE) START_DATE,EMP_ID
        FROM EMPLOYEE_PAYHIST_TBL
        GROUP BY EMP_ID) F ON E.EMP_ID=F.EMP_ID AND
E.START_DATE=F.START_DATE
  ) STARTINGPAY ON
  CURRENTPAY.EMP_ID = STARTINGPAY.EMP_ID
```

Hour 18, "Managing Database Users"

Quiz Answers

1. What command establishes a session?

A. The CONNECT TO statement establishes this.

2. Which option drops a schema that still contains database objects?

A. The CASCADE option allows the schema to be dropped if there are still objects under that schema.

3. Which command in SQL Server creates a schema?

A. The CREATE SCHEMA command creates a schema.

4. Which statement removes a database privilege?

A. The REVOKE statement removes database privileges.

5. What command creates a grouping or collection of tables, views, and privileges?

A. The CREATE SCHEMA statement.

6. What is the difference in SQL Server between a login account and a database user account?

A. The login account grants access to the SQL Server instance to log in and access resources. The database user account is what gains access to the database and is assigned rights.

Exercise Answers

1. Describe how you would create a new user 'John' in your CanaryAirlines database.

A. USE CANARYAIRLINES:
   CREATE USER JOHN

2. Explain the steps you would take to grant access to the EMPLOYEE_TBL to your new user 'John'.

A. GRANT SELECT ON TABLE EMPLOYEES TO JOHN;

3. Describe how you would assign permissions to all objects within the CanaryAirlines database to 'John'.

A. GRANT SELECT ON TABLE * TO JOHN;

4. Describe how you would revoke the previous privileges from 'John' and then remove his account.

A. DROP USER JOHN CASCADE;

Hour 19, "Managing Database Security"

Quiz Answers

1. What option must a user have to grant another user privileges to an object not owned by the user?

   A. GRANT OPTION

2. When privileges are granted to PUBLIC, do all database users acquire the privileges or only specified users?

   A. All users of the database are granted the privileges.

3. What privilege is required to look at data in a specific table?

   A. The SELECT privilege.

4. What type of privilege is SELECT?

   A. An object-level privilege.

5. What option revokes a user's privilege to an object as well as the other users that they might have granted privileges to by use of the GRANT option?

   A. The CASCADE option is used with the REVOKE statement to remove other users' access that was granted by the affected user.

Exercise Answers

1. No answer required.

2. No answer required.

3. No answer required.

4. No answer required.

Hour 20, "Creating and Using Views and Synonyms"

Quiz Answers

1. Can you delete a row of data from a view that you created from multiple tables?

   A. No. You can use only the DELETE, INSERT, and UPDATE commands on views you create from a single table.

2. When creating a table, the owner is automatically granted the appropriate privileges on that table. Is this true when creating a view?

   A. Yes. The owner of a view is automatically granted the appropriate privileges on the view.

3. Which clause orders data when creating a view?

> **A.** The GROUP BY clause functions in a view much as the ORDER BY clause (or GROUP BY clause) does in a regular query.

4. Do Oracle and SQL Server handle the ability to order a view in the same way?

> **A.** No. SQL Server does not permit you to order a view inside of the view definition.

5. Which option can you use when creating a view from a view to check integrity constraints?

> **A.** You can use the WITH CHECK OPTION.

6. You try to drop a view and receive an error because of one or more underlying views. What must you do to drop the view?

> **A.** Re-execute your DROP statement with the CASCADE option. This allows the DROP statement to succeed by also dropping all underlying views.

Exercise Answers

1. Write a statement to create a view based on the total contents of EMPLOYEES table.

> **A.**
> ```
> CREATE VIEW EMP_VIEW AS
> SELECT * FROM EMPLOYEES;
> ```

2. Write a statement that creates a summarized view containing the average pay rate and average salary for each city in EMPLOYEES table.

> **A.**
> ```
> CREATE VIEW AVG_PAY_VIEW AS
> SELECT E.CITY, AVG(P.PAYRATE) AS AVG_PAYRATE, AVG(P.SALARY) AS AVG_SALARY
> FROM EMPLOYEES P
> GROUP BY P.CITY;
> ```

3. Create another view for the same summarized data except use the view you created in Exercise 1 instead of the base EMPLOYEES table. Compare the two results.

> **A.**
> ```
> CREATE VIEW AVG_PAY_ALT_VIEW AS
> SELECT E.CITY, AVG_PAY_RATE, AVG_SALARY)
> FROM EMP_VIEW E;
> ```

4. Use the view in Exercise 2 to create a table called EMPLOYEE_PAY_SUMMARIZED. Verify that the view and the table contain the same data.

> **A.** `SELECT * INTO EMPLOYEE_PAY_SUMMARIZED FROM AVG_PAY_VIEW;`

5. Write a statement to create a synonym for your new EMPLOYEE_PAY_SUMMARIZED table.

> **A.** `CREATE SYNONYMN SYN_EMP FOR EMPLOYEE_PAY_SUMMARIZED`

6. Write two queries, one that uses the base EMPLOYEE_PAY_SUMMARIZED table and one that uses your synonym that compares an employee's salary or pay rate with the average salary for the city they are in.

> **A.** Answers will vary.

7. Write a statement that drops the table, the synonym, and the three views that you created.

   A. `DROP TABLE EMPLOYEE_PAY_SUMMARIZED;`
   `DROP VIEW SYN_EMP;`
   `DROP VIEW EMP_VIEW;`
   `DROP VIEW AVG_PAY_VIEW;`
   `DROP VIEW AVG_PAY_ALT_VIEW;`

Hour 21, "Working with the System Catalog"

Quiz Answers

1. In some implementations, what is the system catalog also known as?

   A. The system catalog is also known as the data dictionary.

2. Can a regular user update the system catalog?

   A. Not directly; however, when a user creates an object such as a table, the system catalog is automatically updated.

3. Which Microsoft SQL Server system table retrieves information about views that exist in the database?

   A. `SYSVIEWS` is used.

4. Who owns the system catalog?

   A. The owner of the system catalog is often a privileged database user account called `SYS` or `SYSTEM`. The owner of the database can also own the system catalog, but a particular schema in the database does not ordinarily own it.

5. What is the difference between the Oracle system objects `ALL_TABLES` and `DBA_TABLES`?

   A. `ALL_TABLES` shows all tables that are accessible by a particular user, whereas `DBA_TABLES` shows all tables that exist in the database.

6. Who makes modifications to the system tables?

   A. The database server makes these modifications.

Exercise Answers

1. No answer required.

2. No answer required.

3. No answer required.

Hour 22, "Advanced SQL Topics"

Quiz Answers

1. Can a trigger be altered?

   A. No, the trigger must be replaced or re-created.

2. When a cursor is closed, can you reuse the name?

   A. This is implementation-specific. In some implementations, the closing of the cursor enables you to reuse the name and even free the memory, whereas for other implementations you must use the `DEALLOCATE` statement before you can reuse the name.

3. Which command retrieves the results after a cursor has been opened?

   A. The `FETCH` command does this.

4. Are triggers executed before or after an `INSERT`, `DELETE`, or `UPDATE` statement?

   A. Triggers can be executed before or after an `INSERT`, `DELETE`, or `UPDATE` statement. Many different types of triggers can be created.

5. Which MySQL function retrieves information from an XML fragment?

   A. `EXTRACTVALUE` is used.

6. Why does Oracle not support the `DEALLOCATE` syntax for cursors?

   A. It does not support the statement because they automatically deallocate the cursor resources when the cursor is closed.

7. Why is a cursor not considered a set-based operation?

   A. Cursors are not considered set-based operations because they operate on only one row at a time by fetching a row from memory and performing some action with it.

Exercise Answers

1. No answer required.

2. Write a `SELECT` statement that generates the SQL code to count all rows in each of your tables. (Hint: It is similar to Exercise 1.)

   A. `SELECT CONCAT('SELECT COUNT(*) FROM ',TABLE_NAME,';') FROM TABLES;`

3. Write a series of SQL commands to create a cursor that prints each customer name and the customer's total sales. Ensure that the cursor is properly closed and deallocated based on which implementation you are using.

   A. An example using SQL Server might look similar to this:

```
BEGIN
      DECLARE @custname VARCHAR(30);
      DECLARE @purchases decimal(6,2);
```

```
DECLARE customercursor CURSOR FOR SELECT
C.CUST_NAME,SUM(P.COST*O.QTY) as SALES
FROM CUSTOMER_TBL C
INNER JOIN ORDERS_TBL O ON C.CUST_ID=O.CUST_ID
INNER JOIN PRODUCTS_TBL P ON O.PROD_ID=P.PROD_ID
GROUP BY C.CUST_NAME;
OPEN customercursor;
FETCH NEXT FROM customercursor INTO @custname,@purchases
WHILE (@@FETCH_STATUS<>-1)
        BEGIN
            IF (@@FETCH_STATUS<>-2)
            BEGIN
                PRINT @custname + ': $' + CAST(@purchases AS
VARCHAR(20))
            END
        FETCH NEXT FROM customercursor INTO @custname,@purchases
        END
CLOSE customercursor
DEALLOCATE customercursor
END;
```

Hour 23, "Extending SQL to the Enterprise, the Internet, and the Intranet"

Quiz Answers

1. Can a database on a server be accessed from another server?

    A. Yes, by using a middleware product. This is called accessing a remote database.

2. What can a company use to disseminate information to its own employees?

    A. An intranet.

3. What are products that allow connections to databases called?

    A. Middleware.

4. Can SQL be embedded in Internet programming languages?

    A. Yes. SQL can be embedded in Internet programming languages, such as Java.

5. How is a remote database accessed through a web application?

    A. Via a web server.

Exercise Answers

1. Answers will vary.

2. No answer required.

Hour 24, "Extensions to Standard SQL"

Quiz Answers

1. Is SQL a procedural or nonprocedural language?

   A. SQL is nonprocedural, meaning that the database decides how to execute the SQL statement. The extensions discussed in this hour were procedural.

2. What are the three basic operations of a cursor, outside of declaring the cursor?

   A. OPEN, FETCH, and CLOSE.

3. Procedural or nonprocedural: With which does the database engine decide how to evaluate and execute SQL statements?

   A. Nonprocedural.

Exercise Answers

1. No answer required.

APPENDIX D
Bonus Exercises

The exercises in this appendix are bonus exercises that are specific to SQL Server. This appendix provides an explanation or question and then provides sample Microsoft SQL Server-based SQL code to execute. Remember that the SQL code can vary from implementation to implementation; therefore, some of these statements need to be adjusted depending on the system you work on. Study the question, code, and results carefully to improve your knowledge of SQL.

1. Determine the aircraft that is used the most.

```
SELECT TOP 1 A.AIRCRAFTTYPE, COUNT(*) AS TIMESUSED
FROM AIRCRAFT A
INNER JOIN AIRCRAFTFLEET AF ON A.AIRCRAFTCODE = AF.AIRCRAFTCODE
INNER JOIN FLIGHTS F ON AF.AIRCRAFTFLEETID = F.AIRCRAFTFLEETID
GROUP BY A.AIRCRAFTTYPE
ORDER BY 2 DESC;
```

2. Determine the average length of flight for each type of aircraft.

```
SELECT A.AIRCRAFTTYPE, AVG(F.FLIGHTDURATION) AS AVG_DURATION
FROM AIRCRAFT A
INNER JOIN AIRCRAFTFLEET AF ON A.AIRCRAFTCODE = AF.AIRCRAFTCODE
INNER JOIN FLIGHTS F ON AF.AIRCRAFTFLEETID = F.AIRCRAFTFLEETID
GROUP BY A.AIRCRAFTTYPE;
```

3. Return a list of the top 3 countries in order where passengers are from.

```
SELECT TOP 3 COUNTRYCODE, COUNT(*) AS NUM_PASSENGERS
FROM PASSENGERS
GROUP BY COUNTRYCODE
ORDER BY 2 DESC;
```

4. Determine the 10 longest routes the airline takes. Include the source and destination airports for each of the routes.

```
SELECT TOP 10 R.ROUTECODE, S.AIRPORTNAME AS SOURCE_AIRPORT
, D.AIRPORTNAME AS DEST_AIRPORT, R.DISTANCE
FROM ROUTES R
INNER JOIN AIRPORTS S ON R.SOURCEAIRPORTID = S.AIRPORTID
INNER JOIN AIRPORTS D ON R.DESTINATIONAIRPORTID = D.AIRPORTID
ORDER BY DISTANCE DESC;
```

5. Determine the 10 most expensive routes for the airline based on fuel cost per minute *
number of minutes flown.

```
SELECT TOP 10 R.ROUTECODE, S.AIRPORTNAME AS SOURCE_AIRPORT
, D.AIRPORTNAME AS DEST_AIRPORT, R.TRAVELTIME*R.FUELCOSTPERMINUTE
FROM ROUTES R
INNER JOIN AIRPORTS S ON R.SOURCEAIRPORTID = S.AIRPORTID
INNER JOIN AIRPORTS D ON R.DESTINATIONAIRPORTID = D.AIRPORTID
ORDER BY 4 DESC;
```

6. Determine if any of the 10 routes you found in Exercise 4 are also ones found in
Exercise 5.

```
SELECT A.*
FROM
(
SELECT TOP 10 R.ROUTECODE, S.AIRPORTNAME AS SOURCE_AIRPORT
, D.AIRPORTNAME AS DEST_AIRPORT, R.TRAVELTIME*R.FUELCOSTPERMINUTE AS TOTALCOST
FROM ROUTES R
INNER JOIN AIRPORTS S ON R.SOURCEAIRPORTID = S.AIRPORTID
INNER JOIN AIRPORTS D ON R.DESTINATIONAIRPORTID = D.AIRPORTID
ORDER BY 4 DESC
) A
INNER JOIN (
SELECT TOP 10 R.ROUTECODE, S.AIRPORTNAME AS SOURCE_AIRPORT
, D.AIRPORTNAME AS DEST_AIRPORT, R.DISTANCE
FROM ROUTES R
INNER JOIN AIRPORTS S ON R.SOURCEAIRPORTID = S.AIRPORTID
INNER JOIN AIRPORTS D ON R.DESTINATIONAIRPORTID = D.AIRPORTID
ORDER BY DISTANCE DESC) B ON A.ROUTECODE=B.ROUTECODE;
```

7. Determine the top 10 passengers who have flown the longest number of miles with
the airline.

```
SELECT TOP 10 P.PASSENGERID, P.FIRSTNAME, P.LASTNAME,
P.BIRTHDATE,
SUM( R.DISTANCE + ISNULL(R2.DISTANCE, 0) ) AS TOTAL_DISTANCE
FROM PASSENGERS P
INNER JOIN TRIPS T ON P.PASSENGERID = T.PASSENGERID
INNER JOIN FLIGHTS F ON T.SOURCEFLIGHTID = F.FLIGHTID
LEFT OUTER JOIN FLIGHTS F2 ON T.RETURNFLIGHTID = F2.FLIGHTID
INNER JOIN ROUTES R ON F.ROUTEID = R.ROUTEID
LEFT OUTER JOIN ROUTES R2 ON F2.ROUTEID = R2.ROUTEID
GROUP BY  P.PASSENGERID, P.FIRSTNAME, P.LASTNAME,
P.BIRTHDATE
ORDER BY 5 DESC;
```

8. If frequent flyer miles are given as 1 per every 100 miles, determine what routes the #1 frequent flyer from Exercise 7 might be able to take, if any.

```
SELECT ROUTEID, ROUTECODE
FROM ROUTES
WHERE DISTANCE<=
(
SELECT
SUM( R.DISTANCE + ISNULL(R2.DISTANCE, 0) )/100 AS FLYER_MILES
FROM PASSENGERS P
INNER JOIN TRIPS T ON P.PASSENGERID = T.PASSENGERID
INNER JOIN FLIGHTS F ON T.SOURCEFLIGHTID = F.FLIGHTID
LEFT OUTER JOIN FLIGHTS F2 ON T.RETURNFLIGHTID = F2.FLIGHTID
INNER JOIN ROUTES R ON F.ROUTEID = R.ROUTEID
LEFT OUTER JOIN ROUTES R2 ON F2.ROUTEID = R2.ROUTEID
WHERE P.PASSENGERID=116265
);
```

9. For the #1 frequent flyer, determine the number of miles he logs per month.

```
SELECT A.REPORT_MONTH, SUM(DISTANCE) AS TOTAL_DISTANCE
FROM
(
SELECT
MONTH(LEAVING) AS REPORT_MONTH,
SUM( R.DISTANCE ) AS DISTANCE
FROM PASSENGERS P
INNER JOIN TRIPS T ON P.PASSENGERID = T.PASSENGERID
INNER JOIN FLIGHTS F ON T.SOURCEFLIGHTID = F.FLIGHTID
INNER JOIN ROUTES R ON F.ROUTEID = R.ROUTEID
WHERE P.PASSENGERID=116265
GROUP BY MONTH(LEAVING)
UNION
SELECT
MONTH(RETURNING) AS REPORT_MONTH,
SUM( R.DISTANCE ) AS DISTANCE
FROM PASSENGERS P
INNER JOIN TRIPS T ON P.PASSENGERID = T.PASSENGERID
INNER JOIN FLIGHTS F ON T.RETURNFLIGHTID = F.FLIGHTID
INNER JOIN ROUTES R ON F.ROUTEID = R.ROUTEID
WHERE P.PASSENGERID=116265
GROUP BY MONTH(RETURNING)
) A
GROUP BY REPORT_MONTH;
```

10. Using the query from Exercise 9 as your basis, get the difference between the current month and the previous month for the top 10 frequent flyers.

```
SELECT DISTINCT
A.REPORT_MONTH,
SUM(DISTANCE) OVER (PARTITION BY REPORT_MONTH) AS TOTAL_DISTANCE,
SUM(DISTANCE) OVER (PARTITION BY REPORT_MONTH) -
LAG(DISTANCE,1) OVER (ORDER BY REPORT_MONTH) AS DIFF
FROM
(
SELECT
P.PASSENGERID,
MONTH(LEAVING) AS REPORT_MONTH,
SUM( R.DISTANCE ) AS DISTANCE
FROM PASSENGERS P
INNER JOIN TRIPS T ON P.PASSENGERID = T.PASSENGERID
INNER JOIN FLIGHTS F ON T.SOURCEFLIGHTID = F.FLIGHTID
INNER JOIN ROUTES R ON F.ROUTEID = R.ROUTEID
GROUP BY P.PASSENGERID,MONTH(LEAVING)
UNION
SELECT
P.PASSENGERID,
MONTH(RETURNING) AS REPORT_MONTH,
SUM( R.DISTANCE ) AS DISTANCE
FROM PASSENGERS P
INNER JOIN TRIPS T ON P.PASSENGERID = T.PASSENGERID
INNER JOIN FLIGHTS F ON T.RETURNFLIGHTID = F.FLIGHTID
INNER JOIN ROUTES R ON F.ROUTEID = R.ROUTEID
GROUP BY P.PASSENGERID,MONTH(RETURNING)
) A
INNER JOIN (
SELECT TOP 10 P.PASSENGERID,
SUM( R.DISTANCE + ISNULL(R2.DISTANCE, 0) ) AS TOTAL_DISTANCE
FROM PASSENGERS P
INNER JOIN TRIPS T ON P.PASSENGERID = T.PASSENGERID
INNER JOIN FLIGHTS F ON T.SOURCEFLIGHTID = F.FLIGHTID
LEFT OUTER JOIN FLIGHTS F2 ON T.RETURNFLIGHTID = F2.FLIGHTID
INNER JOIN ROUTES R ON F.ROUTEID = R.ROUTEID
LEFT OUTER JOIN ROUTES R2 ON F2.ROUTEID = R2.ROUTEID
GROUP BY  P.PASSENGERID
ORDER BY 2 DESC
) B
ON A.PASSENGERID = B.PASSENGERID;
```

11. Update your query to rank the months of travel by our frequent flyer by the increase in miles traveled from the previous months.

```
SELECT REPORT_MONTH, TOTAL_DISTANCE, DIFF,
 DENSE_RANK() OVER (ORDER BY DIFF DESC) AS DIFF_RANK
```

```
 FROM
(
SELECT DISTINCT
A.REPORT_MONTH,
SUM(DISTANCE) OVER (PARTITION BY REPORT_MONTH) AS TOTAL_DISTANCE,
SUM(DISTANCE) OVER (PARTITION BY REPORT_MONTH) -
LAG(DISTANCE,1) OVER (ORDER BY REPORT_MONTH) AS DIFF
FROM
(
SELECT
P.PASSENGERID,
MONTH(LEAVING) AS REPORT_MONTH,
SUM( R.DISTANCE ) AS DISTANCE
FROM PASSENGERS P
INNER JOIN TRIPS T ON P.PASSENGERID = T.PASSENGERID
INNER JOIN FLIGHTS F ON T.SOURCEFLIGHTID = F.FLIGHTID
INNER JOIN ROUTES R ON F.ROUTEID = R.ROUTEID
GROUP BY P.PASSENGERID,MONTH(LEAVING)
UNION
SELECT
P.PASSENGERID,
MONTH(RETURNING) AS REPORT_MONTH,
SUM( R.DISTANCE ) AS DISTANCE
FROM PASSENGERS P
INNER JOIN TRIPS T ON P.PASSENGERID = T.PASSENGERID
INNER JOIN FLIGHTS F ON T.RETURNFLIGHTID = F.FLIGHTID
INNER JOIN ROUTES R ON F.ROUTEID = R.ROUTEID
GROUP BY P.PASSENGERID,MONTH(RETURNING)
) A
INNER JOIN (
SELECT TOP 10 P.PASSENGERID,
SUM( R.DISTANCE + ISNULL(R2.DISTANCE, 0) ) AS TOTAL_DISTANCE
FROM PASSENGERS P
INNER JOIN TRIPS T ON P.PASSENGERID = T.PASSENGERID
INNER JOIN FLIGHTS F ON T.SOURCEFLIGHTID = F.FLIGHTID
LEFT OUTER JOIN FLIGHTS F2 ON T.RETURNFLIGHTID = F2.FLIGHTID
INNER JOIN ROUTES R ON F.ROUTEID = R.ROUTEID
LEFT OUTER JOIN ROUTES R2 ON F2.ROUTEID = R2.ROUTEID
GROUP BY  P.PASSENGERID
ORDER BY 2 DESC
) B
ON A.PASSENGERID = B.PASSENGERID
) C
ORDER BY REPORT_MONTH;
```

12. Update your query from Exercise 11 to add a running sum column for the number of miles flown.

```
SELECT REPORT_MONTH, TOTAL_DISTANCE, DIFF,
 DENSE_RANK() OVER (ORDER BY DIFF DESC) AS DIFF_RANK,
 SUM(TOTAL_DISTANCE) OVER (ORDER BY REPORT_MONTH
ROWS BETWEEN UNBOUNDED PRECEDING AND CURRENT ROW) AS RUNNING_TOTAL
 FROM
(
SELECT DISTINCT
A.REPORT_MONTH,
SUM(DISTANCE) OVER (PARTITION BY REPORT_MONTH) AS TOTAL_DISTANCE,
SUM(DISTANCE) OVER (PARTITION BY REPORT_MONTH) -
LAG(DISTANCE,1) OVER (ORDER BY REPORT_MONTH) AS DIFF
FROM
(
SELECT
P.PASSENGERID,
MONTH(LEAVING) AS REPORT_MONTH,
SUM( R.DISTANCE ) AS DISTANCE
FROM PASSENGERS P
INNER JOIN TRIPS T ON P.PASSENGERID = T.PASSENGERID
INNER JOIN FLIGHTS F ON T.SOURCEFLIGHTID = F.FLIGHTID
INNER JOIN ROUTES R ON F.ROUTEID = R.ROUTEID
GROUP BY P.PASSENGERID,MONTH(LEAVING)
UNION
SELECT
P.PASSENGERID,
MONTH(RETURNING) AS REPORT_MONTH,
SUM( R.DISTANCE ) AS DISTANCE
FROM PASSENGERS P
INNER JOIN TRIPS T ON P.PASSENGERID = T.PASSENGERID
INNER JOIN FLIGHTS F ON T.RETURNFLIGHTID = F.FLIGHTID
INNER JOIN ROUTES R ON F.ROUTEID = R.ROUTEID
GROUP BY P.PASSENGERID,MONTH(RETURNING)
) A
INNER JOIN (
SELECT TOP 10 P.PASSENGERID,
SUM( R.DISTANCE + ISNULL(R2.DISTANCE, 0) ) AS TOTAL_DISTANCE
FROM PASSENGERS P
INNER JOIN TRIPS T ON P.PASSENGERID = T.PASSENGERID
INNER JOIN FLIGHTS F ON T.SOURCEFLIGHTID = F.FLIGHTID
LEFT OUTER JOIN FLIGHTS F2 ON T.RETURNFLIGHTID = F2.FLIGHTID
INNER JOIN ROUTES R ON F.ROUTEID = R.ROUTEID
LEFT OUTER JOIN ROUTES R2 ON F2.ROUTEID = R2.ROUTEID
GROUP BY  P.PASSENGERID
ORDER BY 2 DESC
) B
```

```
ON A.PASSENGERID = B.PASSENGERID
) C
ORDER BY REPORT_MONTH;
```

13. Determine which airports the top 10 frequent flyers are most likely to travel from. Get the top airport for each flyer.

```
SELECT DISTINCT A.AIRPORTID, AIR.AIRPORTNAME
FROM
(
SELECT * FROM
    (
        SELECT PASSENGERID,AIRPORTID,
        RANK() OVER (ORDER BY NUM_FLIGHTS DESC) AS AIRPORT_RANK
        FROM
            (
            SELECT T.PASSENGERID,
            R.SOURCEAIRPORTID AS AIRPORTID,
            COUNT(*) AS NUM_FLIGHTS
            FROM TRIPS T
            INNER JOIN FLIGHTS F ON T.SOURCEFLIGHTID = F.FLIGHTID
            INNER JOIN ROUTES R ON F.ROUTEID = R.ROUTEID
            GROUP BY T.PASSENGERID, R.SOURCEAIRPORTID
            ) D
        ) E WHERE AIRPORT_RANK=1
    ) A
INNER JOIN (
SELECT TOP 10 P.PASSENGERID,
SUM( R.DISTANCE + ISNULL(R2.DISTANCE, 0) ) AS TOTAL_DISTANCE
FROM PASSENGERS P
INNER JOIN TRIPS T ON P.PASSENGERID = T.PASSENGERID
INNER JOIN FLIGHTS F ON T.SOURCEFLIGHTID = F.FLIGHTID
LEFT OUTER JOIN FLIGHTS F2 ON T.RETURNFLIGHTID = F2.FLIGHTID
INNER JOIN ROUTES R ON F.ROUTEID = R.ROUTEID
LEFT OUTER JOIN ROUTES R2 ON F2.ROUTEID = R2.ROUTEID
GROUP BY  P.PASSENGERID
ORDER BY 2 DESC
) B
ON A.PASSENGERID = B.PASSENGERID
INNER JOIN AIRPORTS AIR ON A.AIRPORTID = AIR.AIRPORTID;
```

14. Determine which airports are the most likely destinations for the top 10 frequent flyers.

```
SELECT DISTINCT A.AIRPORTID, AIR.AIRPORTNAME
FROM
(
    SELECT * FROM
        (
            SELECT PASSENGERID,AIRPORTID,
```

```
                RANK() OVER (ORDER BY NUM_FLIGHTS DESC) AS AIRPORT_RANK
                FROM
                (
                SELECT T.PASSENGERID,
                R.DESTINATIONAIRPORTID AS AIRPORTID,
                COUNT(*) AS NUM_FLIGHTS
                FROM TRIPS T
                INNER JOIN FLIGHTS F ON T.SOURCEFLIGHTID = F.FLIGHTID
                INNER JOIN ROUTES R ON F.ROUTEID = R.ROUTEID
                GROUP BY T.PASSENGERID, R.DESTINATIONAIRPORTID
            ) D
        ) E WHERE AIRPORT_RANK=1
    ) A
    INNER JOIN (
    SELECT TOP 10 P.PASSENGERID,
    SUM( R.DISTANCE + ISNULL(R2.DISTANCE, 0) ) AS TOTAL_DISTANCE
    FROM PASSENGERS P
    INNER JOIN TRIPS T ON P.PASSENGERID = T.PASSENGERID
    INNER JOIN FLIGHTS F ON T.SOURCEFLIGHTID = F.FLIGHTID
    LEFT OUTER JOIN FLIGHTS F2 ON T.RETURNFLIGHTID = F2.FLIGHTID
    INNER JOIN ROUTES R ON F.ROUTEID = R.ROUTEID
    LEFT OUTER JOIN ROUTES R2 ON F2.ROUTEID = R2.ROUTEID
    GROUP BY  P.PASSENGERID
    ORDER BY 2 DESC
    ) B
    ON A.PASSENGERID = B.PASSENGERID
    INNER JOIN AIRPORTS AIR ON A.AIRPORTID = AIR.AIRPORTID;
```

15. Combine the results from Exercise 13 and Exercise 14 removing duplicates.

```
SELECT DISTINCT A.AIRPORTID, AIR.AIRPORTNAME
FROM
(
    SELECT * FROM
      (
        SELECT PASSENGERID,AIRPORTID,
        RANK() OVER (ORDER BY NUM_FLIGHTS DESC) AS AIRPORT_RANK
        FROM
        (
        SELECT T.PASSENGERID,
        R.SOURCEAIRPORTID AS AIRPORTID,
        COUNT(*) AS NUM_FLIGHTS
        FROM TRIPS T
        INNER JOIN FLIGHTS F ON T.SOURCEFLIGHTID = F.FLIGHTID
        INNER JOIN ROUTES R ON F.ROUTEID = R.ROUTEID
        GROUP BY T.PASSENGERID, R.SOURCEAIRPORTID
      ) D
    ) E WHERE AIRPORT_RANK=1
) A
```

```
INNER JOIN (
SELECT TOP 10 P.PASSENGERID,
SUM( R.DISTANCE + ISNULL(R2.DISTANCE, 0) ) AS TOTAL_DISTANCE
FROM PASSENGERS P
INNER JOIN TRIPS T ON P.PASSENGERID = T.PASSENGERID
INNER JOIN FLIGHTS F ON T.SOURCEFLIGHTID = F.FLIGHTID
LEFT OUTER JOIN FLIGHTS F2 ON T.RETURNFLIGHTID = F2.FLIGHTID
INNER JOIN ROUTES R ON F.ROUTEID = R.ROUTEID
LEFT OUTER JOIN ROUTES R2 ON F2.ROUTEID = R2.ROUTEID
GROUP BY   P.PASSENGERID
ORDER BY 2 DESC
) B
ON A.PASSENGERID = B.PASSENGERID
INNER JOIN AIRPORTS AIR ON A.AIRPORTID = AIR.AIRPORTID
UNION
SELECT DISTINCT A.AIRPORTID, AIR.AIRPORTNAME
FROM
(
   SELECT * FROM
     (
         SELECT PASSENGERID,AIRPORTID,
         RANK() OVER (ORDER BY NUM_FLIGHTS DESC) AS AIRPORT_RANK
         FROM
         (
         SELECT T.PASSENGERID,
         R.DESTINATIONAIRPORTID AS AIRPORTID,
         COUNT(*) AS NUM_FLIGHTS
         FROM TRIPS T
         INNER JOIN FLIGHTS F ON T.SOURCEFLIGHTID = F.FLIGHTID
         INNER JOIN ROUTES R ON F.ROUTEID = R.ROUTEID
         GROUP BY T.PASSENGERID, R.DESTINATIONAIRPORTID
     ) D
  ) E WHERE AIRPORT_RANK=1
) A
INNER JOIN (
SELECT TOP 10 P.PASSENGERID,
SUM( R.DISTANCE + ISNULL(R2.DISTANCE, 0) ) AS TOTAL_DISTANCE
FROM PASSENGERS P
INNER JOIN TRIPS T ON P.PASSENGERID = T.PASSENGERID
INNER JOIN FLIGHTS F ON T.SOURCEFLIGHTID = F.FLIGHTID
LEFT OUTER JOIN FLIGHTS F2 ON T.RETURNFLIGHTID = F2.FLIGHTID
INNER JOIN ROUTES R ON F.ROUTEID = R.ROUTEID
LEFT OUTER JOIN ROUTES R2 ON F2.ROUTEID = R2.ROUTEID
GROUP BY   P.PASSENGERID
ORDER BY 2 DESC
) B
ON A.PASSENGERID = B.PASSENGERID
INNER JOIN AIRPORTS AIR ON A.AIRPORTID = AIR.AIRPORTID;
```

16. Create a view called TOP_AIRPORTS based on the previous query.

```
CREATE VIEW TOP_AIRPORTS AS
SELECT DISTINCT A.AIRPORTID, AIR.AIRPORTNAME
FROM
(
   SELECT * FROM
      (
         SELECT PASSENGERID,AIRPORTID,
         RANK() OVER (ORDER BY NUM_FLIGHTS DESC) AS AIRPORT_RANK
         FROM
         (
         SELECT T.PASSENGERID,
         R.SOURCEAIRPORTID AS AIRPORTID,
         COUNT(*) AS NUM_FLIGHTS
         FROM TRIPS T
         INNER JOIN FLIGHTS F ON T.SOURCEFLIGHTID = F.FLIGHTID
         INNER JOIN ROUTES R ON F.ROUTEID = R.ROUTEID
         GROUP BY T.PASSENGERID, R.SOURCEAIRPORTID
      ) D
   ) E WHERE AIRPORT_RANK=1
) A
INNER JOIN (
SELECT TOP 10 P.PASSENGERID,
SUM( R.DISTANCE + ISNULL(R2.DISTANCE, 0) ) AS TOTAL_DISTANCE
FROM PASSENGERS P
INNER JOIN TRIPS T ON P.PASSENGERID = T.PASSENGERID
INNER JOIN FLIGHTS F ON T.SOURCEFLIGHTID = F.FLIGHTID
LEFT OUTER JOIN FLIGHTS F2 ON T.RETURNFLIGHTID = F2.FLIGHTID
INNER JOIN ROUTES R ON F.ROUTEID = R.ROUTEID
LEFT OUTER JOIN ROUTES R2 ON F2.ROUTEID = R2.ROUTEID
GROUP BY  P.PASSENGERID
ORDER BY 2 DESC
) B
ON A.PASSENGERID = B.PASSENGERID
INNER JOIN AIRPORTS AIR ON A.AIRPORTID = AIR.AIRPORTID
UNION
SELECT DISTINCT A.AIRPORTID, AIR.AIRPORTNAME
FROM
(
   SELECT * FROM
      (
         SELECT PASSENGERID,AIRPORTID,
         RANK() OVER (ORDER BY NUM_FLIGHTS DESC) AS AIRPORT_RANK
         FROM
         (
         SELECT T.PASSENGERID,
         R.DESTINATIONAIRPORTID AS AIRPORTID,
```

```
            COUNT(*) AS NUM_FLIGHTS
            FROM TRIPS T
            INNER JOIN FLIGHTS F ON T.SOURCEFLIGHTID = F.FLIGHTID
            INNER JOIN ROUTES R ON F.ROUTEID = R.ROUTEID
            GROUP BY T.PASSENGERID, R.DESTINATIONAIRPORTID
        ) D
    ) E WHERE AIRPORT_RANK=1
) A
INNER JOIN (
SELECT TOP 10 P.PASSENGERID,
SUM( R.DISTANCE + ISNULL(R2.DISTANCE, 0) ) AS TOTAL_DISTANCE
FROM PASSENGERS P
INNER JOIN TRIPS T ON P.PASSENGERID = T.PASSENGERID
INNER JOIN FLIGHTS F ON T.SOURCEFLIGHTID = F.FLIGHTID
LEFT OUTER JOIN FLIGHTS F2 ON T.RETURNFLIGHTID = F2.FLIGHTID
INNER JOIN ROUTES R ON F.ROUTEID = R.ROUTEID
LEFT OUTER JOIN ROUTES R2 ON F2.ROUTEID = R2.ROUTEID
GROUP BY  P.PASSENGERID
ORDER BY 2 DESC
) B
ON A.PASSENGERID = B.PASSENGERID
INNER JOIN AIRPORTS AIR ON A.AIRPORTID = AIR.AIRPORTID;
```

17. Create a report for a salary increase for these employees that work at these airports. Ticket agents and security officers will receive a 10% pay increase. Baggage handlers and ground operations will receive a 15% increase. Have your query return both the previous salary and hourly wage as well as the new ones.

```
SELECT
E.EMPLOYEEID, E.LASTNAME, E.FIRSTNAME,
E.PAYRATE,
CASE WHEN E.POSITION IN ('Ticket Agent','Security Officer') THEN E.PAYRATE*1.1
    WHEN E.POSITION IN ('Ground Operations','Baggage Handler') THEN
E.PAYRATE*1.15
    ELSE PAYRATE END AS NEW_PAYRATE,
    E.SALARY,
CASE WHEN E.POSITION IN ('Ticket Agent','Security Officer') THEN E.SALARY*1.1
    WHEN E.POSITION IN ('Ground Operations','Baggage Handler') THEN
E.SALARY*1.15
    ELSE SALARY END AS NEW_SALARY
 FROM EMPLOYEES E
INNER JOIN TOP_AIRPORTS TA ON E.AIRPORTID = TA.AIRPORTID;
```

18. Determine if the pay increase figured in Exercise 17 will bring those people to within the top 10% pay range for their respective position company-wide for either salary or hourly amount.

```
SELECT A.EMPLOYEEID, A.LASTNAME, A.FIRSTNAME,
A.PAYRATE, A.NEW_PAYRATE, A.SALARY, A.NEW_SALARY,
CASE WHEN A.NEW_PAYRATE IS NOT NULL AND A.NEW_PAYRATE>=TP.TOP10_PAYRATE THEN
'YES'
```

```
        WHEN A.NEW_SALARY IS NOT NULL AND A.NEW_SALARY>=TP.TOP10_SALARY THEN
        'YES'
        ELSE 'NO'
END AS IS_TOP10PERCENT
FROM
(
SELECT
E.EMPLOYEEID, E.LASTNAME, E.FIRSTNAME,
E.PAYRATE,E.POSITION,
CASE WHEN E.POSITION IN ('Ticket Agent','Security Officer') THEN E.PAYRATE*1.1
    WHEN E.POSITION IN ('Ground Operations','Baggage Handler') THEN
E.PAYRATE*1.15
    ELSE PAYRATE END AS NEW_PAYRATE,
    E.SALARY,
CASE WHEN E.POSITION IN ('Ticket Agent','Security Officer') THEN E.SALARY*1.1
    WHEN E.POSITION IN ('Ground Operations','Baggage Handler') THEN
E.SALARY*1.15
    ELSE SALARY END AS NEW_SALARY
 FROM EMPLOYEES E
INNER JOIN TOP_AIRPORTS TA ON E.AIRPORTID = TA.AIRPORTID
) A
INNER JOIN
(
SELECT MAX(PAYRATE)*.9 AS TOP10_PAYRATE,MAX(SALARY)*.9 AS TOP10_SALARY,
POSITION
FROM EMPLOYEES
GROUP BY POSITION
) TP ON A.POSITION = TP.POSITION;
```

19. Determine the total cost of operating all the flights in the database. Find out the timespan this is valid for.

```
SELECT MIN(F.FLIGHTSTART) AS MIN_START, MAX(F.FLIGHTEND) AS MAX_END,
SUM(R.TRAVELTIME * R.FUELCOSTPERMINUTE) AS TOTAL_COST
FROM FLIGHTS F
INNER JOIN ROUTES R ON F.ROUTEID = R.ROUTEID;
```

20. Determine the yearly employee costs for the entire company. Assume that hourly workers are kept at a 40-hour work week and operations are maintained for 52 weeks a year.

```
SELECT
SUM(PAYRATE*52*40) + SUM(SALARY) AS TOTAL_HRCOST
FROM EMPLOYEES E;
```

21. Determine what the total cost of operations are for the entire company. This would include flight and employee costs. Pay special attention to the time period that you determined for Exercise 19.

```
SELECT A.TOTAL_AIRCRAFTCOST + B.TOTAL_HRCOST AS TOTAL_OPERATINGCOST
FROM
(
SELECT
-- Operating for 4 months. So a year would be *3
SUM(R.TRAVELTIME * R.FUELCOSTPERMINUTE)*3 AS TOTAL_AIRCRAFTCOST
FROM FLIGHTS F
INNER JOIN ROUTES R ON F.ROUTEID = R.ROUTEID
) A,
(
SELECT
SUM(PAYRATE*52*40) + SUM(SALARY) AS TOTAL_HRCOST
FROM EMPLOYEES E
) B
```

APPENDIX E
Glossary

alias   Another name or term for a table or column.

ANSI   American National Standards Institute. This institute is responsible for issuing standards for a variety of topics. This is where the SQL standard is published.

application   A set of menus, forms, reports, and code that performs a business function and typically uses a database.

buffer   An area in memory for editing or execution of SQL.

Cartesian product   The result of not joining tables in the WHERE clause of a SQL statement. When tables in a query are not joined, every row in one table is paired with every row in all other tables.

client   The client is typically a PC, but it can be a server that is dependent on another computer for data, services, or processing. A client application enables a client machine to communicate with a server.

column   A part of a table that has a name and a specific data type.

COMMIT   A clause that makes changes to data permanent.

composite index   An index that is composed of two or more columns.

condition   Search criteria in a query's WHERE clause that evaluates to TRUE or FALSE.

constant   A value that does not change.

constraint   Restrictions on data that are enforced at the data level.

cursor   A work area in memory that uses SQL statements to typically perform row-based operations against a set of data.

data dictionary   Another name for the system catalog. *See* system catalog.

data type   Defines data as a type, such as number, date, or character.

database   A collection of data that is typically organized into sets of tables.

DBA   Database administrator. An individual who manages a database.

DDL   Data Definition Language. The part of the SQL syntax that specifically deals with defining database objects such as tables, views, and functions.

default   A value used when no specification has been made.

distinct   Unique; used in the SELECT clause to return unique values.

DML   Data Manipulation Language. The part of the SQL syntax that specifically deals with manipulating data, such as that used in update statements.

domain   An object that is associated with a data type to which constraints may be attached; similar to a user-defined type.

DQL   Data Query Language. The part of the SQL syntax that specifically deals with querying data using the SELECT statement.

end user   Users whose jobs require them to query or manipulate data in the database. The end user is the individual for which the database exists.

field   Another name for a column in a table. *See* column.

foreign key   One or more columns whose values are based on the primary key column values in another table.

full table scan   The search of a table from a query without the use of an index.

function   An operation that is predefined and can be used in a SQL statement to manipulate data.

GUI   Graphical user interface. This is what an application interface is typically referred to when it provides graphical elements for the user to interact with.

host   The computer on which a database is located.

index   Pointers to table data that make access to a table more efficient.

JDBC   Java Database Connectivity. Software that allows a Java program to communicate with a database to process data.

join   Combines data from different tables by linking columns. Used in the WHERE clause of a SQL statement.

key   A column or columns that identify rows of a table.

normalization   Designing a database to reduce redundancy by breaking large tables into smaller, more manageable ones.

NULL value   A value that is unknown.

objects   Elements in a database, such as triggers, tables, views, and procedures.

ODBC   Open Database Connectivity. Software that allows for standard communication with a database. ODBC is typically used for interdatabase communication between different implementations and for communication between a client application and a database.

operator   A reserved word or symbol that performs an operation, such as addition or subtraction.

optimizer   Internal mechanism of the database (consists of rules and code) that decides how to execute a SQL statement and return an answer.

parameter   A value or range of values to resolve a part of a SQL statement or program.

primary key   A specified table column that uniquely identifies rows of the table.

privilege   Specific permissions that are granted to users to perform a specific action in the database.

procedure   A set of instructions that are saved for repeated calling and execution.

public   A database user account that represents all database users.

query   A SQL statement that retrieves data from a database.

record   Another name for a row in a table. *See* row.

referential integrity   Ensures the existence of every value of a column from a parent that is referenced in another table. This ensures that the data in your database is consistent.

relational database   A database that is organized into tables that consist of rows, which contain the same sets of data items, where tables in the database are related to one another through common keys.

role   A database object that is associated with a group of system or object privileges, used to simplify security management.

ROLLBACK   A command that undoes all transactions since the last COMMIT or SAVEPOINT command was issued.

row   Sets of records in a table.

savepoint   A specified point in a transaction to which you can roll back or undo changes.

schema   A set of related objects in a database owned by a single database user.

security   The process of ensuring that data in a database is fully protected at all times.

spatial reference system   A system that denotes the projection of points onto a map surface.

spatial types   One of the two types of spatial data, geography or geometry.

SQL   Structured Query Language. Designed for use with databases and used to manage the data within those systems.

stored procedure   SQL code that is stored in a database and ready to execute.

subquery   A SELECT statement embedded within another SQL statement.

synonym   Another name given to a table or view.

syntax for SQL   A set of rules that shows mandatory and optional parts of a SQL statement's construction.

system catalog   Collection of tables or views that contain information about the database.

table   The basic logical storage unit for data in a relational database.

transaction   One or more SQL statements that are executed as a single unit.

trigger   A stored procedure that executes upon specified events in a database, such as before or after an update of a table.

user-defined type   A data type that is defined by a user, which defines table columns.

variable   A value that does not remain constant.

view   A database object that is created from one or more tables and can be used the same as a table. A view is a virtual table that has no storage requirements of its own.

Index

X-Y-Z

Learning Labs!

Learn online with videos, live code editing, and quizzes

Learning Labs are interactive, self-paced courses designed to teach learners of all types.

Visit informit.com/learninglabs to see available labs, tryout full samples, and order today.

■ Read the complete text of the book online in your web browser

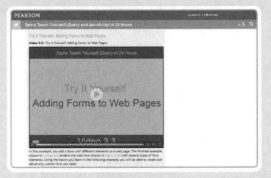

■ Watch an expert instructor show you how to perform tasks in easy-to-follow videos

■ Try your hand at coding in an interactive code-editing sandbox in select products

■ Test yourself with interactive quizzes

Sams **Teach Yourself**

When you only have time
for the answers™

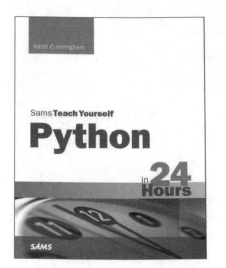

Whatever your need and whatever your time frame, there's a Sams **Teach Yourself** book for you. With a Sams **Teach Yourself** book as your guide, you can quickly get up to speed on just about any new product or technology—in the absolute shortest period of time possible. Guaranteed.

Learning how to do new things with your computer shouldn't be tedious or time-consuming. Sams **Teach Yourself** makes learning anything quick, easy, and even a little bit fun.

Python in 24 Hours

Katie Cunningham
ISBN-13: 978-0-672-33687-4

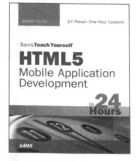

HTML5 Mobile Application Development in 24 Hours

Jennifer Kyrnin
ISBN-13: 978-0-672-33440-5

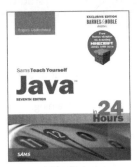

Java in 24 Hours

Rogers Cadenhead
ISBN-13: 978-0-672-33717-8

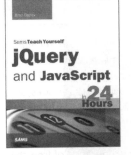

jQuery and JavaScript in 24 Hours

Brad Dayley
ISBN-13: 978-0-672-33734-5

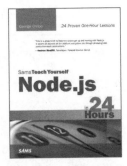

Node.js in 24 Hours

George Ornbo
ISBN-13: 978-0-672-33595-2

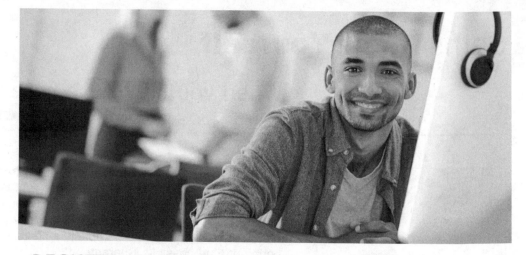

REGISTER YOUR PRODUCT at informit.com/register

Access Additional Benefits and SAVE 35% on Your Next Purchase

- Download available product updates.

- Access bonus material when applicable.

- Receive exclusive offers on new editions and related products.
  (Just check the box to hear from us when setting up your account.)

- Get a coupon for 35% for your next purchase, valid for 30 days. Your code will be available in your InformIT cart. (You will also find it in the Manage Codes section of your account page.)

Registration benefits vary by product. Benefits will be listed on your account page under Registered Products.

InformIT.com—The Truste
InformIT is the online hom   st
education company. At Inf
- Shop our books, e
- Take advantage of
- Sign up for specia
- Read free articles
- Access thousands

Connect with InformIT–V
Learn about InformIT com

informIT.com
the trusted technology learning source

Addison-Wesley · Cisco Press · IBM

ALWAYS LEARNING   RSON